AIDS
on the Agenda

Adapting Development and
Humanitarian Programmes
to Meet the Challenge of
HIV/AIDS

SUE HOLDEN

 act!onaid

 Oxfam

 Save the Children

First published by Oxfam GB in association with ActionAid and Save the Children UK in 2003

© ActionAid, Oxfam GB, and Save the Children UK 2003

ISBN 0 85598 469 4

A catalogue record for this publication is available from the British Library.

Available from Oxfam GB at:

Bournemouth English Book Centre, PO Box 1496, Parkstone, Dorset, BH12 3YD, UK
tel: +44 (0)1202 712933; fax: +44 (0)1202 712930; email: oxfam@bebc.co.u

USA: Stylus Publishing LLC, PO Box 605, Herndon, VA 20172-0605, USA
tel: +1 (0)703 661 1581; fax: +1 (0)703 661 1547; email: styluspub@aol.com

For details of local agents and representatives in other countries, consult the Oxfam website:
www.oxfam.org.uk/publications
or contact Oxfam Publishing, 274 Banbury Road, Oxford OX2 7DZ, UK
tel: +44 (0)1865 311 311; fax: +44 (0)1865 312 600; email: publish@oxfam.org.uk

The Oxfam website has facilities for secure on-line ordering.

Printed by Information Press, Eynsham.

Oxfam GB is a registered charity, no. 202 918, and is a member of Oxfam International.

This publication is the result of research funded by the United Kingdom Department for International Development (DFID), for the benefit of developing countries. The views expressed are not necessarily those of the UK Government, and do not reflect the policy of the Department for International Development.

AIDS
on the Agenda

ActionAid, Oxfam GB, and Save the Children UK

ActionAid is a partnership of people who are fighting for a better world – a world without poverty. As one of the UK's largest development agencies, ActionAid works in over 35 countries in Africa, Asia, Latin America, and the Caribbean, listening to, learning from, and working in partnership with more than nine million of the world's poorest people.

ActionAid, Hamlyn House, Macdonald Road, London N19 5PG, UK

www.actionaid.org

Oxfam GB, founded in 1942, is a development, humanitarian, and campaigning agency dedicated to finding lasting solutions to poverty and suffering around the world. Oxfam believes that every human being is entitled to a life of dignity and opportunity, and it works with others worldwide to make this become a reality. Oxfam GB is a member of Oxfam International, a confederation of 12 agencies of diverse cultures and languages, which share a commitment to working for an end to injustice and poverty – both in long-term development work and at times of crisis.

Oxfam GB, Oxfam House, 274 Banbury Road, Oxford, OX2 6DZ, UK

www.oxfam.org.uk

www.oxfam.org.uk/publications

Save the Children is the UK's leading international children's charity, working to create a better future for children. It is a member of the International Save the Children Alliance, which is active in more than 100 countries worldwide, including the United Kingdom. Drawing on this practical experience, Save the Children also seeks to influence policy and practice to achieve lasting benefits for children within their communities. In all its work, Save the Children endeavours to make children's rights a reality.

Save the Children UK, 17 Grove Lane, London SE5 8RD, UK

www.savethechildren.org.uk

Contents

List of figures

List of tables

Preface

This book is concerned with AIDS (Acquired Immune Deficiency Syndrome), but not with specific responses to it. If you are looking for advice about work that is focused exclusively on the problem of AIDS – home-based care, medical treatment, voluntary counselling and testing, condom promotion, or AIDS education – then you need a different book. But if you are concerned about the devastation that AIDS is causing, and you believe that more needs to be done, and by more people, than can be achieved by AIDS-specific work alone, then read on. You will find ideas based on experiences of adapting mainstream development and humanitarian work to address the problem of AIDS indirectly, along with ways in which organisations can respond from within to protect their employees and their business.

AIDS has changed the world; this book is about the changes needed for effective development and humanitarian work in a world of AIDS.

Research methodology

The idea for the book emerged from a sub-group of the UK NGO AIDS Consortium:[1] four people who were interested both in integrating AIDS-specific work into development and humanitarian programmes, and in 'mainstreaming' AIDS: adapting the everyday activities of such programmes to meet the challenge of the HIV/AIDS pandemic. Jacqueline Bataringaya and Helen Elsey (ActionAid), Mohga Kamal-Smith (Oxfam GB), and Lyn Elliott (Save the Children UK) secured funding for the project from the British government's Department for International Development. The project was co-ordinated by Mohga Kamal-Smith, and Oxfam GB was responsible for editing, designing, and producing the book.

The book draws on three main sources of information. First, websites and published papers, reports, and books. Second, specially commissioned case studies, based on the experiences of staff and partners of ActionAid, Oxfam International, and Save the Children UK. And third, submissions from other agencies in response to the author's call for contributions, circulated via the AIDS Consortium, and through informal networks. The main limitation of the research was that it was all done at a distance, mainly using e-mail. Face-to-face contact between the author and the organisations submitting case studies would have been a more direct and effective means of communication. Only a minority of the organisations followed the suggested format when drafting their case studies, which made comparison between them impossible, and left many issues inadequately explored. However, the methodology did allow coverage of a large number of case studies at low cost, and made it possible to incorporate new data in the closing stages of writing the book.

What this book contains

This book considers the dual challenge for development and humanitarian organisations of 'mainstreaming' HIV and AIDS, which consists (1) of making changes to the internal management of their organisations, with a view to limiting the impacts of AIDS on their employees and their work, and (2) adapting their external work in order to take account of the causes and consequences of AIDS. In arguing that mainstreaming HIV and AIDS is a task for all organisations involved in development and humanitarian work, this book aims to stimulate thinking and debate about ways in which organisations can respond to AIDS without necessarily also doing work specifically focused on AIDS.

The book is organised into three parts, as follows.

Part I: Mainstreaming HIV/AIDS in development and humanitarian programmes: background and rationale

The first part, comprising Chapters 1 to 6, offers a general introduction to the global threat of AIDS and the international community's response to it, and presents the arguments for mainstreaming as an additional strategy. Chapter 2 outlines the salient features of the pandemic, and unravels the complex and mutually reinforcing relationships between HIV/AIDS and under-development. It also examines how various forms of AIDS work and development work can interact and combine to strengthen the overall response to AIDS.

There is currently a great deal of confusion about the terms used to label various strategies for addressing AIDS. Chapter 3 sets out the four main terms and their meanings, as used in this book: *AIDS work, integrated AIDS work, external mainstreaming of AIDS*, and *internal mainstreaming of AIDS*. It identifies some significant (but rarely acknowledged) distinctions, and gives practical examples of what the various terms mean for development and humanitarian organisations.

Chapter 4 presents some case-study material to illustrate direct responses to HIV/AIDS and explores why, so far, this strategy (referred to throughout this book as 'AIDS work') has predominated as the preferred response of development and humanitarian organisations. The chapter also reviews some of the problems which development organisations sometimes face when they embark on AIDS work.

The thinking behind the idea of mainstreaming is presented in Chapter 5, which considers the negative consequences if development and humanitarian organisations fail to take AIDS into account internally in their organisations and externally in their programme work. The chapter also responds to objections to the notion of mainstreaming AIDS. It presents a 'web of causation' for HIV, and argues that different organisations are suited to addressing different levels within the web, according to their 'comparative advantage'. Moreover, the chapter argues that a holistic response to AIDS demands action at all levels of the web. It concludes by considering the implications for development and humanitarian organisations, and recommends that in AIDS-affected countries mainstreaming should be a basic initial strategy. While organisations that have sufficient capacity, skills, and resources should ideally also engage in direct AIDS work, it is proposed that others might form complementary partnerships with other agencies undertaking AIDS work.

Chapter 6 explores in greater detail what mainstreaming AIDS means – or could mean – by describing the features of a hypothetical organisation which has adapted its core programme to meet the challenge of AIDS in an ideal way. It presents short narratives by imaginary staff and community members, in an effort to humanise the issues. Although the scenario is unrealistic, because it is idealised, by exemplifying current thinking on good practice the chapter aims to describe the changes which mainstreaming AIDS might bring about, and a vision of what an organisation which has mainstreamed AIDS might look like.

Part II: Experiences of mainstreaming AIDS

The second part of the book addresses the reality of work on the ground, and the lessons that emerge from the case studies. Chapter 7 is concerned with internal institutional issues: predicting, reducing, and coping with the impacts of AIDS on an organisation, including the need for specific AIDS work to support employees.

Experiences of mainstreaming AIDS externally in development and humanitarian work are covered in Chapters 8 and 9 respectively. Chapter 10 reflects on lessons to be learned from the attempts of non-government organisations to mainstream gender-related issues in their work.

Part III: Ideas for mainstreaming AIDS

The last part of the main text presents practical ideas for agencies seeking to mainstream HIV/AIDS into their work. Chapter 11 provides some generic strategies for initiating and sustaining mainstreaming, and proposes some guiding principles. Chapter 12 offers ideas for internal mainstreaming of AIDS, and Chapter 13 offers suggestions for external mainstreaming in both development and humanitarian programmes. Chapter 14 presents an overview of the issues and challenges involved in promoting and adopting the strategy of mainstreaming. The book's arguments are summarised in the concluding chapter.

Resources

The Resources section at the back of the book provides further practical ideas for mainstreaming AIDS, in the form of a series of ten user-friendly Units, designed to stimulate readers to think how they might introduce mainstreaming into their own organisations.

Bibliography

An extensive bibliography lists the case studies on which the main text is based; provides details of all the secondary sources cited in the text; and points the reader to practical resources such as fact sheets, guidelines, checklists, and training packages, most of them available free of charge via the Internet.

Feedback from readers

The agencies that collaborated on this project are keen to assess its impact and promote further discussion. Readers are invited to send their feedback on the book, and contributions to the debate on mainstreaming HIV/AIDS in development and humanitarian work, using the questionnaire printed on the last page, which follows the index.

Acknowledgements

I am grateful to the many people who have contributed to this book in a variety of ways, ranging from sharing information with me, to writing a case study, commenting on the draft text, and editing and designing the book. They include the following, in alphabetical order:

John Abuya, Santos Alfredo, Patience Alidri, Susan Amoaten, Craig Ash, Ellen Bajenja, Jacqueline Bataringaya, Roxanne Bazergan, Alison Beaumont, Abeba Bekele, Vera Bensmann, Renuka Bery, Saida Bogere, Tania Boler, Samuel Braimah, Sr Carol Breslin, Ned Breslin, Audace Buderi, Rogers Bulsuwa, Kate Butcher, Dawn Cavanagh, Sifiso Chikandi, Joe Collins, Louise Davis, Chris Desmond, Jill Donahue, Michael Drinkwater, Janet Duffield, Lyn Elliott, Helen Elsey, Tabitha Elwes, Andrew Fitzgibbon, Josef Gardiner, Afonsina Gonzaga, Angela Hadjipateras, Jim Henry, Alexander Heroys, Fortunate Hofisi, Ulli Huber, Liz Hughes, Elaine Ireland, Rick James, Phoebe Kajubi, Kristin Kalla, Mohga Kamal-Smith, Juma Kariburyo, Dinah Kasangaki, Lawrence Khonyongwa, Kate Kilpatrick, Akua Kwateng-Addo, Sarah Lee, Rachel MacCarthy, Ryann Manning, David Mawejje, Rosemarie McNairn, John Mkwere, Duduzile Moyo, Dan Mullins, Carmen Murguia, Hussein Mursal, Tom Muzoora, Kondwani Mwangulube, Dennis Nduhura, Stella Neema, Jack van Niftrick, Josephine Niyonkuru, Nellie Nyang'wa, Grace Odolot, Akua Ofori-Asumadu, Joseph Okello, Alfred Okema, Nick Osborne, Sam Page, Bill Rau, Jenny Rawden, Linnea Renton, Catherine Robinson, Jose Sluijs, Rose Smart, Anne Smith, Hilary Standing, Woldemedhin Tekletsadik, Bridgette Thorold, Daphne Topouzis, Dolar Vasani, Rachel Waterhouse, Douglas Webb, Jo White, and Alan Whiteside.

The bibliography lists the organisations that have contributed case studies, and the authors of the case studies.

On a personal note, I thank my partner Dave Horton for his loving support throughout the long gestation of this project.

Sue Holden
Lancaster, June 2003
sueholden@ntlworld.com

Acronyms and abbreviations

ACORD	Agency for Cooperation and Research in Development
AfFOResT	African Farmers' Organic Research and Training
AIDS	Acquired Immune Deficiency Syndrome
ART	antiretroviral therapy
ASO	AIDS support organisation
BERDO	Bwanje Valley Environmental Rural Development Organisation
CAFOD	Catholic Agency for Overseas Development
CBO	community-based organisation
COMPASS	Community Partnerships for Sustainable Resource Management
FAO	Food and Agriculture Organization of the United Nations
FIDA	International Federation of Women Lawyers
GB	Great Britain
GIPA	Greater Involvement of People with AIDS
IASC	Inter-Agency Standing Committee
ILO	International Labour Organization
HEARD	Health Economics and HIV/AIDS Research Division (at the University of Natal)
HIV	Human Immunodeficiency Virus
KAP	knowledge, atitudes, and practice
MoA	Ministry of Agriculture
NGO	non-government organisation
NIAID	National Institute for Allergy and Infectious Disease
PWA	people with AIDS
SC UK	Save the Children UK
SHSLP	Shire Highlands Sustainable Livelihoods Programme
STI	sexually transmitted infection
SWAp	sector-wide approach
TB	tuberculosis

UK	United Kingdom
UNAIDS	The Joint United Nations Programme on HIV/AIDS
UNDP	United Nations Development Programme
UNHCR	United Nations High Commissioner for Refugees
UNRISD	United Nations Research Institute for Social Development
USA	United States of America
VDC	village development committee
WFP	World Food Programme
WHO	World Health Organization

Glossary

AIDS support organisations	Organisations dedicated to, or working with a primary focus on, AIDS work, including prevention, care, and treatment.
asymptomatic phase	The years between infection with HIV and the development of opportunistic infections which lead to AIDS. In developing countries, the phase generally lasts for about four to seven years, during which time the person feels healthy, but can infect others with HIV.
dependency ratio	The number of people under 15 years of age, or over 64 years old (the dependent population), divided by the number of people between those ages (the productive population).
endemic	(disease) Continuously prevalent in a particular geographic location, community, or population.
epidemic	A widespread outbreak of a disease within a population.
food security	Physical and economic access to sufficient, safe, and nutritious food to meet dietary needs and food preferences for an active and healthy life.
gender	Refers to socially constructed differences between men's and women's roles, behaviours, and opportunities, rather than biological differences between the two sexes.
HIV-positive	When HIV enters someone's blood, it multiplies and stimulates the development of antibodies; hence a person who is infected with HIV is said to be HIV (antibody) positive (HIV-positive or HIV+). HIV gradually destroys the immune system, leaving the person susceptible to other infections.
HIV prevalence	The proportion of people in a population who are HIV-positive at a given time – usually measured as the percentage of infected adults aged 15–49.

iatrogenic infection	The inadvertent spread of HIV infection through unsafe medical procedures such as the use of contaminated instruments (needles, syringes, scalpels, etc., that are re-used without being adequately disinfected or sterilised), or transfusion with contaminated blood, or exposure of open wounds to infected blood.
mode of HIV transmission	The spread of HIV in one of three ways: during unprotected vaginal, anal, and (rarely) oral sex; or by blood contaminated with HIV entering the bloodstream – during a blood transfusion, through sharing unsterile needles, or during other unsterile procedures involving blood; or from mother to child during pregnancy, childbirth, and breastfeeding.
opportunistic infections	Parasitic, bacterial, viral, and fungal infections which take hold when someone's immune system is weakened. Common infections include tuberculosis, thrush, shingles, meningitis, and pneumonia. They may resist treatment, and have a high rate of relapse. People with HIV are also prone to developing cancers, including those caused by viruses and cancers of the immune system.
palliative care	Relief and treatment of symptoms of sickness (for example, the alleviation of pain), rather than the application of a cure for the causes.
pandemic	A widespread disease outbreak affecting the population of an extensive area of the world.
positive living	A concept developed by people living with HIV infection. It entails acknowledging that they have HIV; eating a well-balanced diet; exercising, while also getting rest and avoiding stress; abstaining from sexual activity, or practising safer sex; getting treatment for opportunistic infections; attending to their mental and spiritual health. Positive living may also include preparing for death, such as making a will, and making prior arrangements for dependants.
safer sex	Sexual activities which reduce or eliminate the exchange of body fluids that can transmit HIV

	(blood, semen, pre-ejaculatory fluid, vaginal or cervical fluid), by using barriers such as condoms, or engaging in sexual practices in which those fluids are not exchanged.
sector-wide approaches	A new approach to aid, whereby a recipient/government takes the lead in developing a coherent policy and expenditure programme for a particular sector. Donors work in partnership with government to fund the entire sectoral programme, rather than supporting separate projects.
sexual and gender-based violence	Includes physical, sexual, and psychological abuse, such as non-consenting sexual acts, sex with a minor, rape, female genital mutilation, forced marriage, domestic abuse, involuntary prostitution, and sexual harassment.
susceptibility to HIV infection	Refers to the likelihood of individuals becoming infected with HIV, but can also be applied to groups of people, for example to the probability of an organisation experiencing HIV infection among its employees, or the likelihood of a society experiencing an HIV epidemic. Susceptibility is determined by the economic and social character of a society, relationships between groups, livelihood strategies, culture, and balance of power (particularly with regard to gender).
syndromic STI management	Entails diagnosis of sexually transmitted infections on the basis of evident groups of symptoms, rather than the results of laboratory tests, followed by treatment according to standard guidelines. As it is cheap and immediate, syndromic STI management is recommended by WHO and UNAIDS in all resource-poor settings.
universal precautions	A standard set of procedures for health workers to minimise the risk of transmission of blood-borne viruses, including HIV, in health-care settings. Universal precautions consist of hand-washing; use of protective clothing such as gloves; safe handling of sharp instruments; safe disposal of medical waste, including sharps; and decontamination and sterilisation of instruments and equipment.

vulnerability to the impacts of AIDS | Refers to the likelihood of suffering adverse consequences from the effects of excess morbidity and mortality caused by AIDS. Can be applied to individuals, or groups of people such as households, organisations, or societies. Vulnerability is determined by poverty, fragmented social and family structures, and gender inequality.

window period | The period between infection with HIV and the detectable presence of antibodies to HIV. It lasts from several weeks to several months, during which the person is very infectious. The window period often includes an episode of illness resembling influenza.

Part 1: Mainstreaming AIDS in development and humanitarian programmes: background and rationale

1 Introduction

Two out of three women in the world presently suffer from the most debilitating disease known to humanity. Common symptoms of this fast-spreading ailment include chronic anaemia, malnutrition, and severe fatigue. Sufferers exhibit an increased susceptibility to infections of the respiratory and reproductive tracts. And premature death is a frequent outcome. In the absence of direct intervention, the disease is often communicated from mother to child, with markedly higher transmission rates among females than males. Yet, while studies confirm the efficacy of numerous prevention and treatment strategies, to date few have been vigorously pursued. The disease is poverty.
(Jacobson 1992:3)

The starting point for this book is an acknowledgement of the inequality and poverty which currently pervade the world; the extreme differences in opportunities and quality of life which exist within and between countries and in the respective life experiences of men and women; and the devastating effects of conflict and environmental disasters. Development and humanitarian agencies are dedicated to challenging these conditions, but their work is subject to all kinds of changing circumstances, such as new governments, relative levels of peace and conflict, climate change, cultural shifts, and economic trends. Twenty years ago, a new and highly potent element – HIV/AIDS – emerged, with the potential to undermine everything that such agencies aspire to achieve. This book is concerned with the challenge of adapting development and humanitarian work in a time of AIDS; and with the task of tackling inequality and poverty when AIDS relentlessly compounds and deepens those problems.

The book is written for people engaged in managing, funding, or doing development and humanitarian work. Although the language and analysis are intended to be accessible rather than academic, the book is likely to be of most use and interest to managers and policy makers. It focuses on the experiences of non-government and community-based organisations (NGOs and CBOs), but its core ideas are applicable also to others engaged in development work, such as government agencies, faith-based groups, and donors funding the work of others. Organisations already responding to HIV and AIDS will, it is hoped, find the book relevant, but it is primarily aimed at the wider development community, working in sectors such as agriculture, water and sanitation, micro-finance, health care, and education. Most of the data in the book are from the region hardest hit by AIDS, sub-Saharan Africa, but the arguments apply to any place where HIV and AIDS are likely to affect, and be affected by, development and humanitarian work.

Basic information about HIV and AIDS

This section provides basic information about HIV and AIDS in non-technical language. Sources of more detailed explanations about HIV transmission, accounts of how HIV leads to AIDS, and detailed information about treatment, are listed in the bibliography.

Transmission of HIV

HIV is an acronym for Human Immunodeficiency Virus, the virus which causes AIDS, the Acquired Immune Deficiency Syndrome. HIV is transmitted from one person to another in blood, semen, vaginal fluids, and breast milk. It is not found in sufficient quantities to be transmitted via other body fluids, such as sweat, tears, saliva, urine, faeces, and vomit. As a result, HIV is not transmitted through casual contact such as sharing food utensils, towels, or toilets. Nor is HIV spread by the bite of insects such as mosquitoes or bedbugs.

One route of transmission is sexual intercourse, when HIV in the semen or vaginal fluids of an infected person is transferred to his or her sexual partner through the lining of the vagina, vulva, penis, rectum, or mouth. Transmission of HIV is more likely to happen if either person already has another sexually transmitted infection, and particularly an ulcerous infection, or abrasions and fissures resulting from sexual activity, particularly anal sex or violent sex. This form of HIV transmission can be prevented through consistent and correct use of condoms.

Another way in which HIV can be transmitted is through medical procedures, particularly blood transfusions and injections, where HIV from a blood donor or patient is inadvertently introduced into the body of another patient. This kind of transmission can be minimised through careful recruitment of blood donors, screening of donated blood, and adherence to protocols to ensure that all equipment is sterilised. HIV may also be passed though invasive procedures, using shared equipment during non-medical practices such as female and male circumcision, and scarification of the skin. Similarly, injecting drug users who share needles and syringes may become infected via the presence of small amounts of blood containing HIV in their shared equipment.

HIV can also be transmitted from a woman who has HIV to her baby, before or during birth, or afterwards through breastfeeding. Without intervention, HIV is passed to the babies of infected mothers in a substantial proportion of cases: between one quarter and one third. By taking certain drugs the rate can be halved, and in the USA a combination of drugs, obstetric delivery by caesarean section, and formula feeding of infants has been found to reduce the rate very significantly (NIAID 2000).

It is important to note that the likelihood of HIV transmission in any particular context varies according to circumstances. For example, individuals are more susceptible to a range of infections, including HIV, if they are malnourished, have parasitic infections, or are generally in poor health (Stillwaggon 2002:1). This means that different people engaging in the same type of sexual behaviour may have very different chances of becoming infected with HIV, according to their individual health status. The likelihood of HIV being transmitted varies also according to the type of HIV, with some sub-types being more easily acquired than others.

Individuals are more susceptible to HIV if they are malnourished, have parasitic infections, or are generally in poor health.

Progress from HIV infection to AIDS

Progression from HIV infection to AIDS is commonly thought of in terms of four stages, as summarised in Table 1.1. In the first stage, when someone is infected with HIV, the body produces antibodies to fight the infection. After a 'window period' lasting from three weeks to three months (depending on the test used), the presence of these antibodies to HIV can be detected by a test which, if positive, indicates that the person has HIV. Hence, people who are infected with HIV are often referred to as being 'HIV-positive'. Following HIV infection, there is a second stage: an 'asymptomatic' period, with no visible signs of the presence of HIV. However, as soon as HIV is in someone's body, it is attacking and weakening the immune system. In time, HIV's damage to the immune system opens the door to what are known as 'opportunistic infections', because they exploit the opportunity presented by a weak immune system. This is the third, symptomatic, stage of HIV infection. Many of the opportunistic infections are rarely seen in people with normal immune systems; if they do occur, they do not cause much harm. For someone with HIV, however, they may be severe. They include parasitic, bacterial, viral, and fungal infections and malignancies, and commonly result in diseases such as tuberculosis, thrush, shingles, meningitis, and pneumonia. People with HIV are also prone to developing certain cancers, especially those caused by viruses, such as Kaposi's sarcoma and cervical cancer, and cancers of the immune system. Other symptoms of HIV infection include lack of energy, weight loss, and loss of short-term memory.

Opportunistic infections may initially be treatable, though resistant to treatment and likely to reoccur. Periods of ill health may be interspersed with periods of comparative health. But when the 'symptomatic period' of HIV infection is severe, the person is said to have AIDS, and has reached the fourth stage of infection. This stage can be determined by a blood test which assesses the condition of the immune system, and by the presence of one or more of 26 clinical conditions which may affect people at this stage. AIDS may also be determined clinically, if laboratory tests are not available. The World Health Organization's definition is that AIDS is suspected if someone has two out of three major symptoms (chronic diarrhoea, persistent fever, and weight loss), and one minor sign (skin infections, enlarged glands, persistent cough, shingles, herpes simplex infection, and a history of herpes zoster infection) (Grant and de Cock 2001).[1] The fourth stage ends with death, which is caused not by HIV itself, but by any or several of the diseases collectively known as AIDS.

Table 1.1 Stages of HIV infection: a summary

Stage 1: The initial 'window period', by the end of which an HIV test can detect HIV antibodies. Individuals are particularly infectious during this stage, and often have an illness resembling influenza.

Stage 2: The asymptomatic stage, when individuals have no symptoms of HIV infection, except perhaps swollen glands, although they are infectious.

Stage 3: The phase of symptomatic HIV infection, characterised by the onset of opportunistic infections and cancers that the immune system would normally prevent.

Stage 4: Progression to AIDS, which may be diagnosed by blood tests, or clinically.

The time taken to move from Stage 1 to Stage 4 depends on factors specific to the individual, and the context in which he or she lives. People who are overworked, poorly nourished, and who have parasitic diseases already have weakened immune systems, and so they progress more quickly than those who are well fed and in good health (Stillwaggon 2002:4). Progression through the stages is also accelerated by an environment where opportunistic diseases are rife, and treatments for them are poor or entirely absent. As a result, the average time between HIV infection and the onset of AIDS is much shorter in developing countries than in richer nations. On average, in developing nations some four to eight years are thought to elapse between HIV infection and death from AIDS

(Mutangadura et al. 1999a: 4; Jackson et al. 1999: 8). In developed nations, the period is closer to eleven years and is now lengthening substantially, due to the widespread use of antiretroviral therapies (ARTs). These drugs do not destroy HIV or cure AIDS, but they can delay or reverse the onset of AIDS, thereby improving the quality of life, and extending life expectancy.

What is different about HIV/AIDS?

HIV and AIDS are extraordinary, in fact unique, among the problems that jeopardise development initiatives. This might seem an exaggerated claim, given that there are many other diseases, such as malaria and tuberculosis, which debilitate and kill millions of people each year. However, there are two ways in which HIV and AIDS are different from all other diseases.

First, there are factors linked to the biological functioning of HIV. Globally, a significant proportion of men and women with HIV (and probably the majority of them) are thought to have become infected through sexual activity. This mode of transmission raises a range of uncomfortable issues, including the buying and selling of sexual services; sexual infidelity; sex before marriage; under-age sex; men having sex with men; cultural practices involving sex; and sexual abuse. As with other sexually transmitted infections (STIs), the sexual mode of transmission means that HIV is highly stigmatised by taboos, moral judgements, misinformation, and blame. However, unlike other STIs, HIV is widely known to lead to AIDS, and AIDS is widely known to be fatal. Although antiretroviral treatment can extend the lives of people who are infected with HIV, it is not available to the vast majority of people living in the developing world. So a diagnosis of HIV infection is commonly understood as a death sentence.

However, the long asymptomatic period of HIV infection means that, unlike other epidemics, which become visible relatively quickly, large-scale HIV epidemics remain invisible for years. This lengthy asymptomatic stage encourages denial at individual, community, national, and international levels. Such denial, when added to the stigma resulting from HIV's association with the sexual behaviours listed above, and its association with death, frustrates effective prevention work. Unlike other common illnesses, many women and men deny that they are at risk of HIV infection, do not want to be tested for HIV infection, and resist a diagnosis of AIDS even when the symptoms have become evident. At the level of government, officials may be slow to take action, believing that the population is protected by its religious beliefs or moral values, or that people with AIDS have behaved badly and so should be left to their fate.

Second, HIV infection and AIDS are intimately linked with inequality between men and women, with poverty, and with the failures of development. (The next chapter explores this claim in more detail.) In itself, the relationship between HIV and underdevelopment is not extraordinary. Many forms of ill-health are closely linked to gender inequality and poverty, with people who are more powerful and wealthy being better able to protect themselves from preventable diseases, and better able to cope with the impact of illness. However, unlike illnesses which mainly affect the young and the old, HIV spreads, invisibly, among the most sexually active people, who are also the economically productive age-groups, on whom the young and old depend. This means that AIDS has deeper and more sustained impacts than other illnesses, with repercussions extending across generations, and through communities, regions, and nations. The impacts of AIDS are compounded by the scale on which HIV has infected some populations, with as many as one in three adults infected in Botswana, the country with the highest rate of HIV prevalence in the world. In assessments of the most common causes of death, AIDS is fourth in global terms (after ischaemic heart disease, cerebrovascular disease, and lower respiratory infections), and top of the list for sub-Saharan Africa (WHO 2002:186).

In assessments of the most common causes of death, AIDS is fourth in global terms, and top of the list for sub-Saharan Africa.

The extraordinary nature of AIDS has demanded specialised responses. For example, people living with HIV and AIDS have fought to challenge stigma, to get access to treatment, and to tackle the discrimination which affects their lives, such as the constraints on their employment prospects. Campaigns to change people's behaviour have attempted not only to inform and educate the public, but also to tackle the denial of AIDS. Focused action such as this is essential in order to respond to the special challenges of HIV. However, AIDS can simultaneously be seen in a quite different light – not only as an extraordinary issue to be addressed by activists and specialists, but also as an everyday development issue, to be tackled by all development workers through their usual work. The premise of this book is that non-specialist staff can respond to AIDS indirectly, by perceiving it as a mainstream development issue which they can help to address through development and humanitarian work. The process by which non-specialist staff and non-specialist organisations can achieve this is the subject of this book: a process labelled 'mainstreaming'.

2 AIDS as a development issue

The AIDS pandemic is destroying the lives and livelihoods of millions of people around the world ... The situation is worst in regions and countries where poverty is extensive, gender inequality is pervasive, and public services are weak. In fact, the spread of HIV/AIDS at the turn of the twenty-first century is a sign of maldevelopment – an indicator of the failure to create more equitable and prosperous societies over large parts of the world.
(Collins and Rau 2000:6)

This disease has not spared any one or any area of our District. It has taken a holistic approach.
(Community Development Worker, Oxfam GB Malawi Case Study 2001:18)

Introduction

This chapter begins by outlining the key features of the AIDS pandemic (or global epidemic), in terms of levels of HIV infection by region, and among different groups of people. It then discusses how AIDS became defined as a development problem, and explores the complex and reinforcing relationships between HIV/AIDS and under-development. It also looks at the relationship between AIDS work and development work, and shows how direct and indirect responses to AIDS can strengthen each other and the overall response to HIV and AIDS.

Susceptibility and vulnerability

Before considering HIV prevalence levels and trends, it is important to explain how the terms 'susceptibility' and 'vulnerability' are used in this book, because they are key to the analysis. Although the two terms are often used interchangeably in literature about HIV/AIDS, here they denote quite distinct concepts.

In this book, *susceptibility* always refers to the likelihood of HIV infection. This susceptibility may be biological: malnourished people who have parasitic infections are more likely to become infected with HIV, if exposed to it, than those who are well nourished and in better health. Susceptibility to HIV infection is also determined by much wider influences, such as culture, livelihood strategies, and the balance of power between men and women. For example, a woman living in a society where it is not acceptable for her to propose using a condom is, all other things being equal, more susceptible to HIV infection than a woman who lives in a society where women commonly carry and use condoms. Note that the idea of susceptibility can apply to an individual or to groups of people. For example, one can consider if a particular organisation is likely, via its employees, to be more or less susceptible to HIV infections, or one can consider the probability of a society experiencing a severe HIV epidemic.

In this book the term *vulnerability* refers to the likely impacts of HIV and AIDS, once HIV transmission has taken place. Like susceptibility, vulnerability is determined by a wide range of influences. For example, someone who is HIV-positive and has few assets and little support from family or friends, and lives in a society which lacks welfare support, is more vulnerable to the impacts of AIDS than someone with more wealth, supportive social structures, and access to assistance from the State. Again, the concept can be used on different scales, from the vulnerability of an individual or household, to the vulnerability of organisations or societies.

Prevalence levels and relevant trends

This section explains how levels of HIV prevalence vary by region and among different kinds of people. At the outset, it is important to note that the measure of HIV prevalence used by UNAIDS and other authorities is based on the proportion of people aged 15 to 49 who are thought to have HIV. This means that prevalence rates, unless otherwise stated, exclude HIV infection among people who are younger than 15 or older than 49.

HIV epidemics are commonly viewed as belonging to one of three types. In *nascent* epidemics, adult HIV prevalence is less than five per cent among all groups whose specific behaviours make them highly susceptible to HIV infection: for example, people who inject illegal drugs, or who sell sexual services commercially. If that rate exceeds five per cent, but the rate among pregnant women attending ante-natal clinics (the proxy for sexually active adults) is less than one per cent, then the epidemic is said to be *concentrated*. When the rate among pregnant women rises above one per cent, the epidemic is described as *generalised* (Barnett and Whiteside 2000:17).

Some words of caution

Measuring and tracking changes in HIV prevalence is not an exact science: it depends on estimates and extrapolations, using the best models available. This is because expense and ethical and logistical problems preclude the only accurate way of ascertaining precise levels of HIV prevalence, which is to test every person in a population. In countries where the epidemic is nascent, blood testing may focus on the specific groups who show some level of HIV infection. However, because the behaviours which make these groups susceptible to HIV infection are stigmatised and often illegal – buying and selling sex, male/male sexual activity, and injecting prohibited drugs – these surveys may not be very reliable.

In order to ascertain whether HIV is 'crossing over' to the general population, authorities do HIV tests on the blood that is routinely taken from pregnant women attending antenatal clinics. This information is gathered at selected clinics in both rural and urban areas, and may be supplemented with data obtained by testing the blood of donors, and the blood of groups with high-risk behaviours, such as people attending STI clinics. While the resulting estimates for HIV prevalence among the population aged 15 to 49 are thought to be reasonably accurate (Monitoring the AIDS Pandemic 2000:17), this may not be the case where the system of surveillance is poorly developed. Moreover, in situations of armed conflict, the system usually does not function at all. For example, the collection of antenatal data in Sierra Leone was confined to one urban site between 1989 and 1996, and has not taken place at all since then (UNAIDS 2002a), so the progress of HIV there, and in other conflict-affected countries such as Liberia and the Democratic Republic of Congo, is largely unknown (Smith 2002:4).

The World Health Organization estimates that five to ten per cent of global HIV infections are caused by the use of unsafe blood and blood products.

Another complicating factor is the difficulty of being certain about the relative contribution made by the various modes of transmission to rates of HIV infection. There is disagreement about the significance of iatrogenic infection: that is, where HIV is inadvertently transmitted through medical procedures such as blood transfusions and injections. While it is generally agreed that the main mode of HIV transmission in sub-Saharan Africa is sexual activity between men and women, a recent piece of research questions that assumption. Having reviewed all the available data, including anomalies such as HIV-positive infants who have HIV-negative mothers, Gisselquist et al. (2002:666) concluded: 'our observations raise the serious possibility that an important portion of HIV transmission in Africa may occur through unsafe injections and other unsterile medical procedures'. The World Health Organization estimates that five to ten per cent of global HIV infections are caused by the use of unsafe blood and blood products,[1] while, at least in 1997, UNAIDS acknowledged that globally up to 4 million blood donations a year were not tested for HIV or Hepatitis B, and that '*in many countries, regulations on* blood donations, screening and transfusions exist, but are not adhered to' (UNAIDS 1997:2). Thus, in addition to the modes listed in Table 2.1, the possibility of iatrogenic infection should also be borne in mind. This is likely to be particularly pertinent in countries where the health service is severely under-funded, and in situations where armed conflict disrupts the procedures designed to prevent HIV transmission during medical intervention.

Regional levels of HIV infection

AIDS was first identified by doctors and scientists at the beginning of the 1980s, among small groups of men in a few urban centres of North America. Since then HIV has become a global phenomenon, with reported cases in every country of the world (Barnett and Whiteside 2002:9). Table 2.1 summarises UNAIDS' global HIV statistics for the end of 2002, by region. As the numbers illustrate, HIV infection is not evenly spread. Sub-Saharan Africa is thought to be home to 70 per cent of the total number of people of all ages infected with HIV, while the less developed nations together account for more than 90 per cent of the world's 42 million HIV-positive people. Deaths from AIDS are even more concentrated in the poorer nations, with the less developed nations thought to account for 98 per cent of the world's AIDS deaths in 2002 (UNAIDS 2002b:36). And, as UNAIDS reports, without enormous and effective prevention efforts, an extra 45 million people are expected to become infected with HIV in the less developed countries by 2010 (UNAIDS 2002b:5).

Without enormous and effective prevention efforts, an extra 45 million people are expected to become infected with HIV in the less developed countries by 2010.

In 2002, the average HIV prevalence among adults for **sub-Saharan Africa** as a whole was almost nine per cent (UNAIDS 2002b:6), with young women and men aged 15 to 24 accounting for a third of the total of 29.4 million people living with HIV in the region. Within sub-Saharan Africa HIV initially flourished in East Africa, but rates there have since been exceeded by those in Southern Africa. Botswana has the highest adult HIV prevalence in the world, at almost 39 per cent, and in Lesotho, Swaziland, and Zimbabwe the HIV-infection rate is at or approaching one in three adults. West Africa has, so far, had much lower rates of HIV infection. However, by the end of 2002, eight West African nations were thought to have prevalence rates in excess of five per cent, with the rate in two of those – the Central African Republic and Cameroon – exceeding ten per cent (UNAIDS 2002b:16-17).

The situation in **North Africa and the Middle East** is far from clear, as the surveillance systems are poor; however, prevalence rates are generally

Table 2.1 HIV/AIDS statistics by region, for the end of 2002

Region	Adult prevalence rate*	Number of adults & children who are HIV-positive	% of HIV-positive adults who are women	Main modes of transmission for HIV-positive adults#
Sub-Saharan Africa	8.8%	29,400,000	58%	Heterosexual
North Africa & Middle East	0.3%	550,000	55%	Heterosexual, IDU
South & South-East Asia	0.6%	6,000,000	36%	Heterosexual, IDU
East Asia & Pacific	0.1%	1,200,000	24%	IDU, heterosexual, MSM
Latin America	0.6%	1,500,000	30%	MSM, IDU, heterosexual
Caribbean	2.4%	440,000	50%	Heterosexual, MSM
Eastern Europe & Central Asia	0.6%	1,200,000	27%	IDU
Western Europe	0.3%	570,000	25%	MSM, IDU
North America	0.6%	980,000	20%	MSM, IDU, heterosexual
Australia & New Zealand	0.1%	15,000	7%	MSM
Total	**1.2%**	**42,000,000**	**50%**	

*   estimated proportion of all adults aged 15 to 49 who are HIV-positive

\#   heterosexual = sexual transmission among men and women

IDU = transmission through injecting drug use

MSM = sexual transmission among men who have sex with men

Source: UNAIDS (2002c:6)

considered to be low but rising. In about half of the nations in the region, HIV infection seems to be associated with injecting drug use (UNAIDS 2002b:22).

In **Asia and the Pacific**, there are only three countries – Cambodia, Myanmar, and Thailand – with generalised HIV epidemics, although the rates of infection among adults there are still low. However, the comparatively low national rates of HIV infection in the region disguise the actual numbers of people living with HIV in the highly populated countries: almost four million in India, and another million in China. At present within the region, HIV infection is still mainly localised, and concentrated in marginalised groups: women and men who sell sex, injecting drug users, and men who have sex with men. Rates among marginal groups are sometimes very high, and there are well-founded fears that HIV infection could cross over into the wider population and so become generalised. While in 2002 the region accounted for around 20 per cent of all new HIV infections globally, by 2010 it is expected to be the site of some 40 per cent of new infections (UNAIDS 2002b:5).

In **Latin America and the Caribbean**, experience of HIV so far is very varied. The Andean nations, including Bolivia and Ecuador, have very low prevalence rates. National adult rates are highest in the Caribbean and parts of Central America, with Haiti being the worst-affected country outside sub-Saharan Africa: its national adult HIV prevalence exceeds six per cent. Eleven other nations in the Caribbean and Central America are thought to have generalised HIV epidemics. In the other countries of Central America and South America, HIV epidemics are generally concentrated among injecting drug users and men who have sex with men. However, the proportion of women among those acquiring HIV is rising, because men who have sex with men commonly also have sex with women, while women also inject drugs, or are sexual partners of men who inject drugs (UNAIDS 2002b:19-20).

The region with the fastest-growing HIV epidemic in the world is **Eastern Europe and Central Asia**, largely due to the injection of illegal drugs. Throughout the region this behaviour is increasing, particularly among young people, such that authorities estimate that one per cent of the adult population now injects drugs (Monitoring the AIDS Pandemic 2001:10). Given that these young people share equipment, that they are sexually active, and that there are high and rising levels of STIs among the general population, analysts believe that generalised HIV epidemics may be imminent in the region. Ukraine is the worst-affected country, with a national prevalence rate among adults of just above one per cent, and there and in Belarus the proportion of new HIV infections due to heterosexual activity is rising. In contrast, in Central Europe, rates of new HIV infections and HIV prevalence remain low (UNAIDS 2002b:12-15).

In the high-income countries of **North America, Western Europe, Australia, and New Zealand,** HIV prevalence rates among the general population are low. However, surveillance in certain cities shows that rates among men who have sex with men, which had declined, are now rising once more. For example, in Vancouver, Canada, the rate of HIV infection among gay men rose from an average of less than one per cent in the late 1990s to approaching four per cent in the year 2000 (UNAIDS 2001:20). Injecting drugs also features in the high-income nations' epidemics. For example, it accounted for the majority of new HIV cases in Spain in 2002, where some 20 to 30 per cent of injecting drug users are thought to be HIV-positive (UNAIDS 2002b:23). Many countries are also seeing more new infections occurring through sex between men and women. Another important trend among the high-income nations is a rise in the numbers of people living with HIV and AIDS – around 13 per cent every year since 1996 in England and Wales – due to the life-extending effects of antiretroviral (ART) drugs (Monitoring the AIDS Pandemic 2000:22).

Axes of difference

Behind the contrasting regional and national statistics of HIV prevalence, there lie further differences in infection rates according to a range of factors, which include age, gender, ethnicity, wealth, and occupation.

Although the specific trends by age vary between the regions, HIV infection is generally concentrated among the most sexually active age groups, which also tend to be those age groups with the highest rates of injecting drug use. A universal pattern is that children and young people between the ages of 5 and 14 have low levels of infection. This is because the majority of babies who are infected via their mothers die before reaching the age of five (although the age of death is higher in high-income countries), and infection through sexual activity or injecting drug use does not generally occur before the teenage years.

Gender is another axis, with differing ratios between infected men and women resulting from the different patterns by which HIV is being transmitted. As Table 2.1 shows, in sub-Saharan Africa and the Caribbean, where sex between men and women is thought to be the main mode of transmission, the number of women who are infected equals or exceeds the number of infected men. In all other parts of the world, HIV-positive men outnumber HIV-positive women. In Australia and New Zealand, where sex between men is the main mode of HIV transmission, there are nine HIV-positive men for every one HIV-positive woman. In other regions, where drug-injection and sexual relations between men and women also play a role, the ratio is lower: for example, around two men to each woman in Latin America (UNAIDS 2002b:20). Moreover, these patterns change over time. In the Russian Federation most infection is related to the injection of illegal drugs by young men, so men outnumber women by four to one. However, among new cases of HIV there is one woman for every two men, which suggests that young women are now also injecting drugs, and/or that they are being infected through sexual activity (UNAIDS 2001:11).

Some patterns of prevalence are determined by ethnicity. In England and Wales, black Africans form less than one per cent of the population, but account for more than half of the HIV infections which are due to sex between men and women (Monitoring the AIDS Pandemic 2000:22). In the USA, where the HIV epidemic is growing most rapidly among minority ethnic groups (NIAID 2000:1), African Americans form 12 per cent of the population, but more than 33 per cent of all reported cases of HIV/AIDS (Collins and Rau 2000:32).

Finally, there is the factor of wealth and opportunity. Generally, while richer and more educated people are more likely to be infected in the early stages of a local epidemic, over time – and for reasons which will become clear – HIV tends to become concentrated among poorer people. And with regard to work, HIV rates tend to be higher among women and men working in certain occupations which make them more susceptible to HIV infection. These include commercial sex work and jobs involving working away from home for long periods, such as mining, lorry driving, and service in the armed forces.

In sub-Saharan Africa the mean age of death among HIV-positive women is around 25 years, whereas for men the average is 35 years.

Of course, these axes of difference do not exist in isolation. For example, analysis by gender and ethnicity shows that in the USA rates of HIV/AIDS are more than twenty times higher for black women than for white women (Monitoring the AIDS Pandemic 2000:22). And in sub-Saharan Africa, analysis by gender and age reveals that the mean age of death among HIV-positive women is around 25 years, whereas for men the average is 35 years.

However, although analysis by these axes illuminates some important patterns in HIV infection, it does not shed light on why those patterns exist. The next two sections take a closer look at the complex relationships between gender, poverty, and other factors related to both AIDS and development.

How AIDS became a development issue

This section describes how perceptions of the problem of AIDS have evolved during the past two decades, and illustrates how the proposed solutions have changed as the framing of the problem has developed.

AIDS was first recognised in 1981, when doctors in the USA found cases of unusual immune-system failures among men who had sex with men. Seeing the phenomenon as being a problem of gay men, they labelled the new syndrome GRID, standing for 'Gay Related Immune Deficiency Syndrome'. Within the year, however, cases among heterosexual men, women, and children emerged, and the modes of HIV transmission were identified. The GRID label was clearly wrong, and in 1982 the syndrome was duly renamed AIDS. The 'A' for 'Acquired' signals that HIV infection results from an action – someone doing something, or having something done to them – rather than from casual contact (Barnett and Whiteside 2002:28).

AIDS was then predominantly framed as being a medical problem, and the world's interest focused on biomedical aspects of HIV and AIDS, and on finding a cure for AIDS or a vaccine for HIV, in order to 'win the fight against AIDS'. Although this was an accurate perception, it was also a narrow one. Seeing HIV as something to be examined through microscopes, and dealt with by medical scientists, precluded perception and investigation of the bigger picture, and the sharing of resources and responsibility with other professionals. Moreover, by first focusing research on the virus itself, rather than on how HIV interacts with the host (the infected person), scientists were slow to attend to the social and economic dimensions of biological susceptibility to HIV, such as the role of malnutrition and parasitic infection (Stillwaggon 2002:3).

Alongside the notion of AIDS as a medical problem was its common association with 'deviant' behaviour. Attention was focused on groups of people engaging in risky behaviours, including gay men, sex workers, injecting drug users, and the sexually promiscuous. This framing of the problem led to efforts to change the behaviour of members of 'risk groups', mainly through information and education campaigns, but sometimes also through legislation and harassment. The idea of warning and informing those people whose behaviours put them most at risk of HIV infection made good sense, and the logic of focusing efforts on groups exhibiting higher levels of infection, before HIV crosses from them to the general population, is still defensible. However, the framing of AIDS as being due to deviant behaviours had three major flaws. Firstly, the assumption that individuals can change their behaviour if they have the right information was too simplistic, and often proved to be wrong. Education for behaviour change works best with people who take individual responsibility for their health and their future, and who are sufficiently empowered to be able to change their behaviours. These conditions rarely applied to members of the groups at risk. Secondly, the focus on certain groups of marginalised people led to their being blamed and stigmatised by the rest of society, which made it harder to support them, and to care for those who were infected with HIV. Thirdly, people who did not belong to any of the risk groups were inadvertently encouraged to assume that they were not at risk. They were also prone to reject the available protective measures – especially condoms – which they saw as labels of social deviance.

The focus on reducing risky behaviours among gay men in North America and Western Europe did achieve positive results. Here the stigmatised group had some coherence through the existence of gay community networks, and important resources in the form of relatively skilled, educated, and affluent members. It also had a history of fighting for rights, and drew on all these things to demand funding and treatment, and to create its own education campaigns and support services. The gay community experienced many deaths, which were known and recognised as being caused by AIDS. All of these factors led to changes in behaviour, particularly reductions in the numbers of sexual partners and increases in condom use. (Recent rises in HIV infection among gay men suggest that new campaigns are needed for a new generation, who may be less worried about AIDS now that life-extending antiretroviral treatment is available to them.)

However, in sub-Saharan Africa, success was harder to achieve, and levels of HIV infection rose rapidly among members of the risk groups and the general population. The role of biological susceptibility caused by malnutrition and endemic parasitic infections was largely ignored by public-health authorities; instead, the assumption was made that high rates of HIV infection could be mainly explained by sexual behaviour. The resulting education campaigns could show results in informing people about HIV and AIDS, and about safer sex practices, but they could rarely demonstrate significant and sustained behaviour change. Over time, the perception of AIDS as a behavioural problem to be solved by individuals acting on information has become harder to sustain. Detailed social research has revealed the complex factors which affect women's and men's behaviour, and which extend far beyond their influence. To this day many organisations still emphasise that 'education is the key to stopping AIDS', but among others this stance has gradually been modified, as AIDS has begun to be defined in a variety of other ways, reflecting the interacting constraints which hinder behaviour change.

For example, AIDS is now seen as a question of **human rights**, because many of the impediments to behaviour change are linked to the denial of people's basic rights, such as access to food security, health care, and education. Moreover, much of the discrimination faced by people who are HIV-positive is due to violations of their rights to move freely, to work, and to obtain access to treatment. AIDS is now understood also as a problem of **poverty**, because – among many reasons – poorer people and especially young women are generally less able to afford health care, including STI treatment and condoms; are more likely to be poorly nourished and to have weakened immune systems; and are more likely to provide sexual services – either commercially or through regular relationships – as a way of obtaining cash, goods, or favours. Equally, AIDS is recognised as a problem of **gender**, because gender-linked cultural and economic factors mean that men and women have different degrees of control over their lives, including decisions about sexual relations. Because environmental disasters and conflict are associated with increased HIV transmission and reduced standards of care and treatment, AIDS can be understood as a **humanitarian issue**. And, given the way in which AIDS has most affected poor and heavily indebted countries, AIDS is also becoming defined as a problem of **globalisation** and the uneven spread of resources in the world (Barnett and Whiteside 2002).

There are many other ways of perceiving the AIDS problem – economic, moral, historical, cultural – but among them the most salient to emerge is the catch-all notion of AIDS as a problem of development – or, more accurately, of **under-development**. As the previous section outlined, AIDS has not affected all nations or all types of people equally. HIV flourishes where conditions of underdevelopment – of poverty, disempowerment, and gender inequality – enable it to spread, and undermine efforts to prevent its transmission.

HIV flourishes where conditions of under-development – of poverty, disempowerment, and gender inequality – enable it to spread, and undermine efforts to prevent its transmission.

This book adopts the broad view of AIDS as a development issue, a general definition which implicitly encompasses many of the other ways of seeing AIDS. AIDS is, however, still mainly perceived, researched, and responded to as a medical and behavioural problem. As two prominent and experienced analysts note:

> *Until very recently the main focus of UNAIDS and all national and regional programmes to do with HIV/AIDS has been on the clinical-medical and behavioural levels. Little attention has been paid...to the broader factors which contribute to the development of social and economic environments – what we describe as risk environments – in which infectious disease can expand and develop rapidly into an epidemic.*
> (Barnett and Whiteside 2002:73)

A problem with no obvious solution?

The framing of something as a problem suggests that a solution exists, or can be found. But the 'war on AIDS' is more than two decades old, and in that time HIV has spread across the globe, reaching prevalence levels in Southern Africa which were once not thought to be possible. In the absence of a spectacular scaling-up of the response to AIDS, substantial increases in the numbers of people infected with HIV are predicted, particularly in less developed countries. However, although no solution has yet been found to the problem of AIDS, progress has been made in terms of dealing with AIDS as both a medical and behavioural problem.

Progress through medical interventions

Research has led to major advances in terms of understanding how HIV works, and in particular in developing antiretroviral therapy, or ART. These advances are having two major impacts, and there is potential for their further development and use in the future.

First, ART can reduce the likelihood of HIV being transmitted from HIV-positive women to their babies. In the developed nations, a combination of ART, delivery by caesarean section, and formula feeding has reduced the proportion of babies born to HIV-positive women from around 20 per cent to less than five per cent. In developing countries, the rate of mother-to-child transmission is ordinarily higher, at around 30 per cent, due to high rates of breastfeeding. Trials in developing countries of shorter and cheaper courses of ART have shown that the transmission rate can be reduced to around ten per cent if babies are not breastfed, or 15 to 20 per cent if the infants are breastfed for up to 12 months (UNAIDS 2000b:1). Many developing countries, including the most impoverished ones such as Mozambique, are beginning to offer the treatment, predominantly (to begin with) to urban women.

Second, ART can hinder the way in which HIV replicates itself and attacks the body's immune system; it thereby extends the lives of HIV-positive people and improves their quality of life and their productivity. In developed nations, where around half a million people were taking antiretrovirals at the end of 2001, the drugs have greatly improved the prognosis for people living with HIV and AIDS, and have dramatically reduced HIV/AIDS-related mortality (UNAIDS 2002b:23). In developing countries, however, where more than 90 per cent of people with HIV live, fewer than four per cent of those in need of antiretroviral drugs were receiving them at the end of 2001. The figure for sub-Saharan Africa was about one per cent, or around 35,000 people. Substantial progress has been made, however, in reducing the price of ART in poorer nations. In Uganda, for example, importing generic drugs from India and Brazil, rather than patented drugs from the USA and Europe, has reduced the price from around $600 a month per person to $30 per month. As a result of this and its extensive voluntary counselling and testing services, Uganda had around 10,000 people paying to be on ART at the end of 2002 (IRIN News 2003). Meanwhile, relatively prosperous Botswana has become the first African country to undertake to make antiretrovirals available to all citizens who need them, although only about 2,000 people were benefiting from that commitment at the end of 2002 (UNAIDS 2002b:18). Large businesses, agencies such as the UN, and NGOs are also increasingly making ART available to their employees. Some governments, such as Malawi's, hope to secure external funding to make ART freely available to their citizens, although the scale of such schemes is, at least to begin with, likely to be small, due mainly to insufficient funding.

Aside from the cost of ART, there are, however, other challenges to efforts to extend access to ART in developing nations, and particularly in rural areas and to poor women and men. One prerequisite is that if significant numbers of HIV-positive people are to benefit from ART, voluntary and confidential counselling and testing services need to be widely available and acceptable, in order that people can know and accept their HIV status. Such counselling is also essential to encourage ART users to take the drugs correctly, because failure to follow dosing regimens encourages the development of drug-resistant strains of HIV. In the UK, around one fifth of newly HIV-positive people have acquired drug-resistant strains (Barnett and Whiteside 2002:32). And it must be acknowledged that antiretroviral drugs do not work for all people, and can cause serious side effects (amfAR 2002:7). Another constraining factor is that many developing nations would need to invest heavily in their health-care infrastructure in order to develop the capacity to deliver ART effectively and widely. For example, globally some 40 per cent of women lack access to antenatal and postnatal care, which is essential in order to implement a minimum package of care for HIV-positive women and their infants. Another problem is that reductions in mother-to-child transmission are optimised when babies are fed on formula milk, but replacing breastmilk with formula milk is often not affordable, nor safe for the baby; and in cultures where breastfeeding is the norm, the use of formula milk makes it impossible for a woman to keep her HIV status secret (UNAIDS 1999).

If significant numbers of HIV-positive people are to benefit from ART, voluntary and confidential counselling and testing services need to be widely available.

Despite these challenges, however, the use of ART, both to reduce mother-to-child transmission and to treat people infected with HIV, is considered to be a practical and plausible intervention which, in circumstances with sufficient infrastructure and investment, can substantially reduce the impacts of HIV. A combination of advocacy, investment in developing appropriate systems, and growing experience in administering ART in developing nations is sure to foster an expansion in access to ART in the future.

Progress through behaviour-change interventions
On the behavioural side, prevention work with marginalised groups has, in some instances, proved very effective. For example, needle-exchange

programmes can dramatically reduce the transmission of HIV between injecting drug users, by providing them with sterile equipment and reducing the need to share equipment. Focused and empowering work with commercial sex workers can achieve dramatic improvements in their sexual health through use of condoms and STI treatment, and so reduce their susceptibility to HIV infection. And efforts to counter the discrimination faced by men who have sex with men, and to encourage them to adopt safer sex practices, have also led to significant behavioural change in some contexts.

Moreover, experience from a few countries shows that prevention work can have an impact on behaviour among the wider population, and so reduce HIV prevalence. Thailand and Cambodia successfully lowered their national HIV prevalence rates among adults, through prompt preventative action focused on commercial sex workers and their clients, as well as the general public. Uganda has achieved more dramatic reductions in HIV prevalence, with UNAIDS stating that the nation *presents proof that the epidemic does yield to human intervention'* (UNAIDS 2002b:17). In Uganda, the proportion of pregnant women testing HIV-positive has fallen for eight consecutive years, from a high of almost 30 per cent in 1992 to just over 11 per cent in 2000 (UNAIDS 2001:17). The reasons for this reduction are thought to include decisions by young people to delay becoming sexually active by about two years; people choosing to have fewer non-regular sexual partners; reduced buying and selling of sexual services; and increased condom use (Kaleeba et al. 2000:5, UNAIDS 2002b:17). However, Uganda's reduction in HIV rates has come after a million Ugandans have died of AIDS, probably including many of those who were most at risk of HIV infection. And with a (keenly debated) adult prevalence rate of at least five per cent, Uganda will continue to have significant levels of HIV infection and AIDS in the future.

Combining medical and behavioural approaches

We really do want antiretrovirals...we know that they won't cure the illness, but it will give some hope to the patients ...there is no hope after the HIV test. If the ART drugs are there, people will come. If we have a good treatment facility here and people know their HIV status, then there will be behavioural change. These things are inter-related.
(District Health Officer, Kasungu Hospital, Malawi[2])

A lesson which was learned early in the global epidemic was that medical and behaviour-change approaches are linked; that prevention, care, and treatment generally reinforce each other. In Brazil, for example, a combination of public education, focused prevention work with men who have sex with men, and with injecting drug users, efforts to counter stigma, and large-scale provision of care and treatment, including ART, have all helped to stabilise the nation's HIV epidemic. And in the Mbeya region of Tanzania, a comprehensive programme of AIDS control – including prevention, palliative care, and treatment of STIs and opportunistic diseases – has led to some important achievements. These include a reduction in HIV infection rates among pregnant women attending antenatal clinics, from 20 per cent in 1994 to 15 per cent in 1999; higher condom use than in other parts of Tanzania; less discrimination against people living with HIV and AIDS; and almost two thirds of people with AIDS enabled to obtain access to home-based care (Jordan-Harder et al. 2000:81).

Searching for a solution

The important advances made so far have certainly reduced the scale of the misery associated with AIDS in some countries, and particularly in the developed world. However, none of them individually or together represents an actual solution to the problem of HIV and AIDS. Even if access to ART could be radically and quickly extended across the developing nations, preventing mother-to-child transmission is much less desirable than preventing HIV infection in women in the first place. And prolonging the lives of HIV-positive people is not the same as preventing their infection, or being able to cure it. Moreover, changes in behaviour might not be sustained; as experience with rising HIV rates among gay men in high-income countries shows, downward slopes on the graphs of HIV prevalence are not necessarily maintained. And the behaviour-change success stories, particularly among general populations, are comparatively few and limited. In the Tanzanian example above, the reduction in infection rates among pregnant women was the result of ten years of significant and focused investment, yet 15 per cent of this group were still infected. The report documenting the work was entitled 'Hope for Tanzania', but one might argue that the results do not give much cause for optimism.

There is hope for the on-going medical efforts to stop AIDS through the development of drugs to disarm HIV, or to restore damaged immune systems; microbicides which, when applied before sexual intercourse, can block or reduce the transmission of HIV; a vaccine providing protection against HIV; or a cure for AIDS. Any of these could have a massive impact on the AIDS pandemic. However, some people doubt that such medical advances would lead to HIV being eradicated, or reduced to low rates in poor nations, because extreme global differences in life chances and quality of living are already tolerated. For example, at present, fewer than ten per cent of people with HIV/AIDS have access to palliative care or treatment for opportunistic infections (UNAIDS 2002b:4), despite the fact that the necessary drugs are cheap, have been available for a long time, and are easily administered. Moreover, people in developing nations continue to suffer from treatable and therefore 'unnecessary' diseases such as malaria, cholera, and TB, along with other curable problems such as malnutrition. As a former director of UNDP's HIV and Development Programme once stated, even if a supply of pure drinking water was the cure for AIDS, it would be unavailable to large numbers of people (Klouda 1995:478[3]).

Even if a supply of pure drinking water was the cure for AIDS, it would be unavailable to large numbers of people.

Of course, this point of view does not suggest that there is no need for medical advances against HIV and AIDS; rather it reinforces the case of those who demand that such benefits should be made available to people in the developing nations. However, it does propose that medicine alone will not solve the AIDS problem. It also seems improbable that behaviour change can rid the world of AIDS, or at least reduce HIV prevalence to very low levels, given the current scale of the pandemic. For that to happen, the 42 million people now infected would need to live and die without passing HIV to anyone else. It is estimated that 90 per cent of them are unaware that they are infected (UNAIDS 2000a:11). Every day another 15,000 people unknowingly become infected.

Rather than holding on to the hope of 'stopping AIDS' with medicine and behaviour change, this book takes the pragmatic position that HIV and AIDS are here to stay, particularly in the under-developed regions of the world. HIV should not be expected to peak and fall away in the manner of, say, a measles epidemic; it has become *endemic*, an on-going and entrenched problem. Although viewing HIV and AIDS as a problem with no obvious solution may be demotivating, the situation is not, as the previous sections have argued, without hope. Moreover, seeing AIDS as a long-term problem brings it into the purview of development agencies, and may motivate them to expand their response to AIDS. Rather than leaving the immediate tasks of preventing HIV transmission and providing AIDS care to the health sector and AIDS organisations, development agencies must confront the long-term challenges of containing and coping with HIV infection and the impacts of AIDS, within their broader agenda of working for a more equitable world.

Causes and consequences

The causes and consequences of the HIV epidemic are closely associated with wider challenges to development, such as poverty, food and livelihood insecurity, gender inequality. HIV/AIDS tends to exacerbate existing development problems through its catalytic effects and systemic impact.
(Topouzis 1998:3)

This section looks in more detail at the two-way relationship between under-development and AIDS. It presents a model of **causes and consequences**, and then describes some of the main components of the model. It includes some imaginary 'voices', in an attempt to convey the complexity of the issues, and the ways in which they may be experienced. Each fictional speaker has been created by the author, but the testimonies are based on case studies of real people's experiences.

The notion of reinforcing causes and consequences which have made HIV endemic is illustrated in Figure 2.1. On the **causes** side are the main factors which, singly or cumulatively, make individuals, groups, and whole populations more susceptible to HIV infection. Other factors include labour migration, globalisation, and environmental damage. On the **consequences** side are some of the impacts of HIV infection and AIDS, as they affect households, communities, and nations. The important dynamic in the model is that the two sides reinforce each other: high susceptibility leads to higher levels of infection, which leads to AIDS, the consequences of which cause increased susceptibility, and so on.

Causes of susceptibility to HIV infection

Looking first at the **causes** side of the model, **poverty** can cause susceptibility to HIV infection in many different ways. In terms of biology, poverty is linked to a greater likelihood of acquiring HIV due to the synergistic effects on the immune system of malnourishment and parasitic and other infections. There may also be a link between vitamin A deficiency, which is most common among poor communities in the tropics, and susceptibility to STIs, including HIV, because vitamin A plays an important role in preventing infection through keeping the skin and mucus membranes healthy. This may partly explain why ulcerous STIs – which increase the efficiency with which HIV is transmitted – are much more common in developing nations (Stillwaggon 2002:9-11).

In addition to enhanced biological susceptibility, poverty has a funda-mental psychological effect: it tends to displace long-term concerns such as the possibility of developing AIDS in the future. As Collins and Rau

Figure 2.1: Causes and consequences of AIDS: social, economic, and political

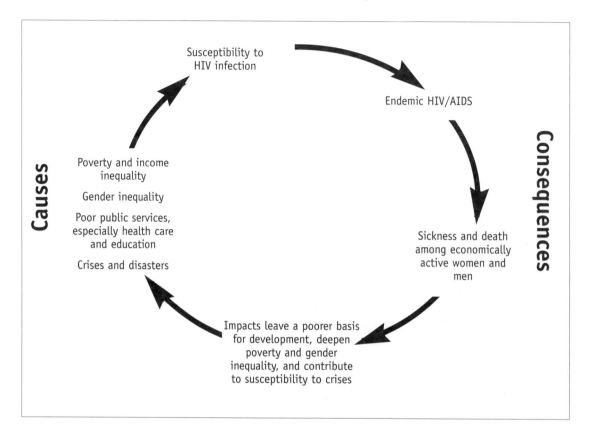

(2000:29) have noted, *'to take the long view in sexual or other behaviours is antithetical to the condition of being poor. For the poor it is the here and now that matters.'* Disempowerment and belief in fate or 'the will of God' also undermine poor people's motivation to protect themselves against HIV infection. Impoverished people's responses to livelihood insecurity and a lack of employment opportunities, often connected to a lack of education, can also heighten susceptibility to HIV infection. Sex is a key resource used by the poor, and particularly girls and women, to obtain cash, goods, protection, and favours. This might be via commercial sex work, or through informal sexual exchange with varying degrees of commitment. When migrating to find work, young women may typically find themselves in employment which increases their susceptibility to HIV infection, such as working as house maids or bar girls. And men who migrate to find work often face long separations from home and family, which are associated with having higher numbers of sexual partners. Poor work conditions and living conditions can make things worse, as this voice, echoing experiences of migrant miners working in South Africa (and locked into conventional 'male' roles), makes clear:

> *Today at the hostel compound we saw a play about AIDS. Really, we know AIDS is terrible, but they think we are children, not men! Every day we go down the mine, knowing we may emerge injured or dead. We return not to our families, but to the filthy dormitory. Beer and women are our only pleasures. They tell us to have fewer partners, but as we say, 'a man is like a dog', he is never satisfied, his body has that desire. And condoms are wasting my time, they cost money and spoil the pleasure. I can always get some treatment for those problems which come up from time to time. Sometimes I worry about AIDS, but more likely I will be killed by a rock fall, or by TB. I hate this work, but my family depend on me, and since my sister died I'm responsible for her children too. If I had an education, I could get a better job. Instead there's nothing I can do but accept what happens.*
> (Written by the author, based on quotes from several miners in Campbell 1997)

Gender inequality is another factor which increases susceptibility to HIV infection. Compared with boys and men, girls and women are economically disadvantaged and have less control over their lives. Inequality is reproduced across generations by cultural biases which favour men: for example, the notion that it is more important to educate boys than girls. Inequality may be compounded by formal and informal discrimination against women in, for example, the failure to respect their rights to divorce and inheritance. This imaginary girl's prospects would have been better if her mother had been able to keep her property, once widowed:

Sex is a key resource used by the poor, and particularly girls and women, to obtain cash, goods, protection, and favours.

> *When I was quite young, my father died, and his family blamed my mother. We had been living in a nice house – I remember the cassette recorder – but they took it all away and sent us to my mother's village, where Uncle took us in. Later, when mother fell sick, I helped Auntie look after her, but she died anyway. I work hard now, looking after the little ones and working in the garden, but I'm always hungry and lacking basic things. Some of the local boys say they love me, but they can't help me in my situation. When I play sex with my uncle he gives me things, and I feel cared for. Auntie says I must leave soon and get married. Perhaps I will follow the other girls who have gone to the city. They have managed to get good clothes.*
> (Written by the author, based on quotes from orphans, in ActionAid 2002a and Ayieko 1997)

Another barrier to behaviour change is that **social norms** may sanction violence against women if, for example, they attempt to refuse sex with a regular partner, or propose using condoms. And women's social susceptibility to HIV infection multiplies during times of crises such as conflict or environmental disaster. While the whole of the affected population may suffer heightened susceptibility as a result of impoverishment, displacement, loss of assets, and disruption to social support networks, women tend to suffer disproportionately. Moreover, they are more likely than men to be subject to **rape and sexual violence**, and to resort to their one portable asset – their bodies – in order that they and their dependants may survive. Listen to this imaginary woman's voice, based on the experiences of refugee women in East and West Africa:

I believe I am lucky to be alive – so many were killed when the rebels came – but my life is not much now. I don't know where my husband is, I have no belongings, and no way to make a living. There's food and sheeting in this camp, but it's sometimes hard for us single women to get our fair share without giving in to the monitors' demands. They know we have only our bodies to trade. And I feel so scared. Leaving the camp to collect firewood fills me with dread: others have been raped.

I try to forget what happened to me, it is too shameful, but at night I wake up in fear, overcome with memories of the brutal soldiers. If I had the courage, perhaps the doctor could help, could stop the pain and bleeding, but I can't face him. Instead I trust in God to heal me and to give me a future by having a child.
(Written by the author, based on reports and quotes in Marshall 1995, Kinnah 1997, Human Rights Watch 2000)

Finally, **poor public services** can cause susceptibility to HIV infection. This may happen very directly, as is the case where poorly funded health services fail to ensure the safety of blood and blood products, and of invasive medical procedures. The level of HIV infections caused inadvertently through medical intervention is unknown, but it is far more likely to occur in impoverished settings where health-care providers lack sterile equipment, where blood-screening procedures are not adhered to, and where staff are not trained in preventing iatrogenic HIV infection. This form of susceptibility is compounded by ill health among poor people, because conditions such as chronic anaemia, which is commonly caused by malaria or malnutrition, make it more likely that they will need a blood transfusion, and so risk being infected through contaminated blood (UNAIDS 1997:7). Poor public services can also indirectly increase susceptibility to HIV infection. For example, where education services are inadequate and literacy rates, particularly among girls and women, are low, prevention efforts are generally less effective.

Consequences of HIV infection

Within the limited available research into the **consequences** of HIV and
AIDS (Barnett and Whiteside 2002:165), the impacts of AIDS are best
understood at the level of the individual and household. Indeed, analysts
have been able to identify broad sequences of reactions among AIDS-
affected households in various settings (Mutangadura et al. 1999b:18).
Table 2.2 illustrates a sequence of three stages.

As with impact of AIDS at regional and national levels, the severity of the
impacts on households depends on the level of vulnerability. Key factors
include access to resources, household size and composition, access to
resources of extended families, and the ability of the community to
provide support (Mutangadura et al. 1999b:19). A household with
sufficient resources in the form of labour, savings, and other assets will
certainly feel the impact of a death from AIDS, but may be able to rely on
strategies from the first stage of Table 2.2, and so recover from the shock
(Shah et al. 2002). Poor households with fewer resources and fewer
options are more vulnerable, and may reach the third stage of permanent

Table 2.2 Household strategies in response to HIV/AIDS

Stages	Strategies
First Reversible mechanisms involving protective assets	Seeking wage labour or migrating temporarily to find paid work
	Switching to producing low-maintenance subsistence food crops (which are usually less nutritious)
	Liquidating savings accounts or stores of value such as jewellery or livestock (excluding draught animals)
	Tapping obligations from extended family or community members
	Soliciting family or marriage remittances
	Borrowing from formal or informal sources of credit
	Reducing consumption
	Reducing spending on education, non-urgent health care, or other human-capital investments
Second Disposal of productive assets	Selling land, equipment, or tools
	Borrowing at exorbitant interest rates
	Further reducing consumption and expenditure on education or health care
	Reducing amount of land farmed and types of crops produced
Third Destitution	Depending on charity
	Breaking up household
	Distress migration

(Source: Donahue (1998), adapted from M.A. Chen and E. Dunn (1996): Household Economic Portfolios, AIMS Paper, Harvard University and University of Missouri-Columbia – reprinted with the permission of the author.)

impoverishment. This is more likely where there is denial about the terminal nature of AIDS, and a determination to prolong life, as this voice, based on a case study from East Africa, recounts:

Before my husband fell sick, he earned a good amount as a carpenter, while I grew crops and cared for our four children and seven heads of cattle. When he first got rashes and diarrhoea, he went to a private clinic for a week. He recovered quickly, but was soon back there again. After three visits, all his savings were gone. Then I found myself pregnant and very weak. The doctor told me to do only very light work. My mother-in-law helped a lot, and my eldest daughter dropped out of school. When my husband fell sick again, he wanted to go back to the clinic, so he sold a big tree on his land for timber, and his cousin paid the traditional healer. He got better and said that it was not AIDS. He worked hard to earn some money, but fell down again. This time he paid the medical bills by selling a calf and his bicycle; the following time he sold a bull and a cow.

I gave birth to a girl, but she was sick, and I could only rest for a week because the garden was overgrown, as was my mother-in-law's. We both became short of food, and borrowed small amounts from friends. We cared for my husband at home, and followed his instructions to sell another cow to pay for traditional healers and special liquid foods. He died four weeks later. The garden was so overgrown that we had to slash a space for his grave. Other women helped me to plant some beans, but our situation is desperate. The baby is always ill, and the children are hungry and out of school. I am tired and sick, but I must carry on. If I accept my illness, then where and what will my children eat?

(Written by the author, based on a case study in Rugalema 1999)

As Chapter 5 will explain, the consequences of AIDS are also felt cumulatively at the level of each sector. Suffice to note here that AIDS puts particular pressure on the health service, and so undermines its quality, and that the delivery of all State services may be affected by the consequences of sickness and death among staff. The repercussions of AIDS may also damage future development efforts, as the imaginary voice of this head teacher demonstrates:

Managing this school has never been easy, but with AIDS it is getting so much harder. Two of my teachers have been sick on and off sick for months, and I have yet to find a replacement for the one who died last year. We are back to having far too many kids in each class, and the attendance of many is increasingly sporadic, because they are needed at home. Perhaps they are not very impressed by what we can offer them. Those that are orphaned often

drop out, or move away. God help those who end up on the streets, wandering in gangs like stray dogs. When I look to the Ministry for support, I find it in confusion – certainly there is no funding for bursaries, and there are rumours that the school feeding programme must stop. Education is so important to the future of our children and our nation, and yet we seem to be going backwards.
(Written by the author, based on information in JTK Associates 1999 and ActionAid 2002a)

The impacts of AIDS at the nation-state level are still poorly understood, and have been modelled but not yet measured (Barnett and Whiteside 2002:162). In general, it is thought that AIDS causes economies to grow more slowly – around a half to one per cent more slowly than if AIDS did not exist – but not to contract (Barnett and Whiteside 2002:289). One area of great concern is the potential consequences of AIDS for social cohesion and national stability. In 2000, AIDS became the first health-related issue ever to be addressed by the United Nations Security Council, which has since adopted a resolution which emphasises the pandemic's potential threat to international security, especially in conflict and peacekeeping situations (UNAIDS 2002c:1). A review of the mechanisms by which this might happen (Manning 2001) predicts that crime may rise in response to deepening poverty; disaffected orphans may be easily attracted to gangs and militia; civil society may be undercut by deaths among economically active age groups; and State legitimacy may be threatened where key functions such as the judicial system or electoral administration fail. The assessment of the USA's Central Intelligence Agency in 2000 was that the burden of persistent infectious disease, and in particular HIV/AIDS, is likely to *'aggravate and, in some cases, may even provoke, economic decay, social fragmentation, and political destabilisation in the hardest hit countries in the developing and former communist worlds'*. It concluded that *'the relationship between disease and political instability is indirect but real'* (CIA 2000:4).

Two points are worth noting about the model of causes and consequences. First, the factors on the causes side are neither novel nor special; poverty, gender inequality, poor public services, and crises created by armed conflict and environmental disaster are familiar and pervasive development issues which were around long before HIV emerged. Any society with such problems is susceptible to HIV. Second, and in direct contrast, the consequences are both new and exceptional: AIDS hits economically productive people, and has unprecedented cumulative impacts. For each adult infected, there are typically around two years of recurrent illness, including a year being bedridden (Rugalema 1999:42), with knock-on effects within the household and beyond. The aggregate impacts are sufficient to slash life expectancy – the average for sub-Saharan Africa has dropped from 62 years to only 47 (UNAIDS 2001:12) – and to reverse decades of development gains. Chapter 5 considers these impacts and their implications for development in more detail.

Deepening gender inequality

If the idea that AIDS compounds poverty is easily accepted, the fact that it deepens gender inequality is perhaps less evident. This section outlines the ways in which AIDS has differential consequences for men and women.

Consider a pair of twins, a sister and a brother who are both heterosexual. Even in a totally egalitarian society, she is more vulnerable to HIV infection than he, due to differences in their genitals and sexual fluids: a woman's genitals have a greater surface area of mucous membrane through which HIV can enter, and a young woman's risks are heightened because of her immature cervix and thinner mucous membranes. Women's genitals 'hold' men's larger quantities of sexual fluids after intercourse, and the semen of HIV-positive men contains higher concentrations of the virus than the vaginal fluids of HIV-positive women. This is partly why, where HIV is predominantly transmitted through heterosexual sexual activity, more women are infected than men.

If both the twins were to contract a sexually transmitted infection, it would increase the likelihood of HIV transmission to (and from) each of them, but the girl's STI is more likely to go untreated, because it is not so visible. In addition, she may be less likely to seek treatment, because there is stronger social disapproval directed towards her for having contracted a sexually transmitted infection. Her brother's behaviour is more likely to be excused, or even approved of. On maturity, the girl twin is also more likely than her brother to acquire HIV through a blood transfusion, because pregnancy and childbirth are associated with anaemia and haemorrhage, which lead to women having more transfusions (Grant and de Cock 2001).

If someone in the twins' household becomes ill with AIDS, the girl is more likely to be taken out of school before her brother – or not enrolled in the first place – in order to work at home. Any pre-existing inequalities between the twins, including their working hours, access to education and health services, and nourishment levels, are likely to be accentuated if the household is under stress.

Next, consider the twins' sexual partners. A pragmatic Nigerian adage says, *'no romance without finance'* (Barnett and Whiteside 2002:85). Because sex is often connected to some form of exchange, it is probable that the girl's sexual partner will be older than her, perhaps considerably so. Older men are more able than younger men to provide things for exchange: things such as money, practical goods, gifts such as material or beauty products, and social status. However, the age gap compounds the gendered imbalance of power within the relationship, making it very difficult for the girl to influence sexual decision making, such as whether to use a condom or other form of contraception. Her older partner is also more likely to be infected with HIV than men of her own age, because he has been sexually active for longer.

In contrast to his twin sister, who is likely to find a sexual partner or partners easily and to get married before him, the boy may struggle to find a sexual partner or partners, because he lacks the attractions and resources of an older man. When he does have sex, however, he is in a position of greater power than his sister, regardless of the age of his partner or the nature of the relationship. He may well hold many prejudices against using a condom; but if he is determined to protect himself, then he is able to do so.

Furthermore, if either twin is subjected to sexual abuse, forced sex or rape, it is far more likely to be the girl than the boy. While boys and men are sexually abused and raped in many parts of the world, especially in prisons and the armed forces, the bulk of abuse occurs against girls and women. This is true for the extreme circumstances of conflict, and the more ordinary sexual and gender-based violence which occurs within households and communities each day. Violent sexual practices are more likely to cause injuries which increase the likelihood of HIV transmission.

If both twins were to become infected with HIV, it is probable that the sister would be infected first. If they lived in Botswana, for example, she would be twice as likely to be infected before the age of 14, and three times more likely to be infected than her brother in the years from 15 to 30 (UNDP 2000:3). She would also, therefore, probably develop AIDS first. Her progression from being asymptomatic to having AIDS might also be faster, because she is more prone to being undernourished, and having an immune system weakened by other health problems and the bodily demands of pregnancy and childbirth. However, while she would probably die before her brother – she in her twenties, he in his thirties – her sexual partner, being older, might well fall ill and die before her.

A Kenyan study, for example, found that in seven out of ten cases, orphans' fathers had died before their mothers (Ayieko 1997:10). She may have little say in the management of household resources, and find that their savings and capital are depleted in her partner's search for a cure and effective treatment, leaving little for her and her children's future. And, unlike her brother, she is likely to devote a lot of time to caring for her partner or other relatives when they are sick, because that is seen in her culture as women's work.

Finally, if each of the twins' partners die first, the impacts on them as widow and widower will also be unequal. Although details vary according to local custom, in general, the widowed brother would retain his property and maintain more control over his life – for example, deciding whether to take a new partner, and who should care for his children. His sister is more likely to be dispossessed, to be sent back to her parental home, to be remarried by arrangement, and to have to care for the children without support from her partner's relatives. She may receive support from her brother, but she might also have to look after his children.

These are some of the ways in which the consequences of AIDS deepen gender-determined inequality, to the detriment of girls and women. The situation is different, however, if the brother is having sex with other boys or men, and being penetrated by them. In that case he will be more biologically vulnerable than his sister, because HIV is transmitted through the anal passage more effectively than through the vagina (Panos 1998:3). His social situation may be similar to hers if he is adopting a female gender role – being the subordinate partner with less control – and/or having sex with older men in exchange for money or favours. However, his relationship with another man might be a more equal one, and he is likely to revert to male gender roles, adopting a position of relative power, if he has sexual relationships with women.

Synergies between development work and AIDS work

There are no easy answers or simple technical and scientific solutions to dealing with the epidemic's spread and impact. The most effective response, or the best international 'vaccine' against this disease is sustained, equitable development.
(Loewenson and Whiteside 2001:24)

AIDS depends for its success on the failures of development. If the world was a more equitable place, if opportunities and outcomes for men and women were more fair, if everyone were well nourished, good public services were the norm, and conflict was a rarity, then the HIV virus would not have spread to its current extent, nor would the impacts of AIDS be as great as those which are now emerging. The close links between AIDS and development are the reason for this book's call for a renewed focus on core development issues as an additional way of addressing AIDS. This is not to argue that medical interventions and behaviour-change work should be abandoned; as has been stated, if HIV is a symptom of development gone wrong, then we need to tackle the diseased development as we also deal with the symptom of HIV (Collins and Rau 2000:39). Instead, we advocate that the field of vision should be widened, not only to include the core medical issues and strategies, and then the behavioural issues, but also to bring into focus the significance of wider development problems, including poverty, gender inequality, poor public services, and political and environmental crises. Chapter 5 presents a more detailed consideration of these elements of the response to AIDS, and the kinds of organisation best suited to working at each level.

AIDS depends for its success on the failures of development.

Addressing AIDS through development and humanitarian work is an additional strategy, which should interact with existing AIDS-focused work to form a virtuous circle, countering the vicious circle spun by AIDS and underdevelopment. Figure 2.2 depicts the positive dynamics existing between the three strategies of development work, HIV prevention, and AIDS care and treatment.

It has long been known, and argued, that efforts to prevent infection and care for HIV-positive people are mutually reinforcing. For example, education about HIV helps to reduce the numbers of people needing AIDS care and support, and also helps to challenge stigma against HIV-positive people, including the belief that they do not deserve, or cannot benefit from, treatment. For its part, care and support for people with HIV/AIDS helps to prevent HIV infection by encouraging the practice of safer sex by people who know they are HIV-positive, and by countering public denial through making the existence of AIDS more visible. The existence of treatment, and particularly of antiretroviral treatment, can also encourage more people to take an HIV test in the first place, again helping prevention efforts by reducing denial and promoting positive living. (There are, however, some concerns that where effective antiretroviral treatment is widely available, it may actually undermine prevention efforts, because people may assume that AIDS is curable.)

However, Figure 2.2 also shows how both forms of AIDS work and development and humanitarian work are mutually reinforcing. Successful

Figure 2.2 Synergies between development work and AIDS work

HIV Prevention

- Education about: modes of HIV transmission; means of preventing, or reducing the likelihood of, HIV infection; how HIV differs from AIDS
- Condom promotion and distribution
- STI treatment

Reduces susceptibility to infection, and increases effectiveness of prevention work:

- Better nutrition and health status ➡ lower biological susceptibility
- Less poverty and livelihoods insecurity ➡ less need to sell sex for survival
- Better health services ➡ greater access to STI treatment and condoms and less iatrogenic infection
- Greater gender equality ➡ women and men more able to act on prevention messages

Reduces numbers of people infected, therefore reduces all impacts of AIDS on development

Delayed sexual initiation and use of condoms also affect non-AIDS problems, such as unwanted pregnancies and associated school drop-outs, and STIs

Reduces numbers of people infected with HIV, and therefore numbers needing care

Education counteracts stigma by challenging misinformation about how HIV is transmitted

Promotes counselling, HIV testing, positive living, and seeking treatment. Involvement of HIV+ people may provide role models for this

Care and support to HIV+ people makes AIDS more visible, which counters denial in the general population

Voluntary counselling and testing enables people to discover their HIV status and encourages safer sex practices

Care and support helps HIV+ people to accept their condition and to live positively, including practising safer sex

Development

- Poverty alleviation
- Food and livelihoods security
- Health, water, and sanitation
- Education
- Humanitarian work following environmental crisis and conflict

AIDS Care

- Voluntary counselling and HIV testing
- Support for positive living, including material and spiritual support
- Treatment of opportunistic infections
- Anti-retroviral treatments
- Care when AIDS develops, at home or in a medical setting

Better health services ➡ strengthened systems for provision of counselling, testing, treatment, and care for people with AIDS

Less poverty and improved nutrition, water supply, and sanitation promote health of HIV+ people

Care and support reduce the impact of illness and death:

- Treatments enable HIV+ people to live and work longer
- Positive living reduces unproductive spending on 'cures', and encourages planning for death, e.g. making a will and arrangements for dependants

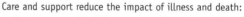

AIDS-prevention programmes reduce the numbers of people who are HIV-infected, and so reduce the impacts of AIDS on development. Care, treatment, and support for people with AIDS can help to reduce the impacts of AIDS on individuals and their families, through extending lives, reducing unproductive expenditure on 'cures', improving their productivity, and helping people to plan for their dependants' futures. In this way AIDS care and support can also help to reduce the numbers of households that slide irrevocably into destitution as a result of AIDS.

Of course, the three work strategies shown in Figure 2.2 and the causes and consequences model in Figure 2.1 are related. Prevention work addresses some of the causes of vulnerability to HIV infection, while care work is focused on reducing some of the consequences of AIDS. Development work, in all its variety, ought to tackle both sides of the model. On the one hand, addressing core development problems such as poverty and gender inequality should undermine the factors which cause susceptibility to HIV infection. On the other, the benefits of development should help to reduce vulnerability to the impacts of AIDS, so helping households and communities to cope better with the consequences of AIDS when they become affected. This book and the notion of mainstreaming AIDS by addressing it through development and humanitarian work are grounded in the challenge of realising and maximising the positive effects of that work on efforts to reduce both the causes of susceptibility to HIV infection and the consequences of AIDS.

Summary

This chapter has shown how the perception of AIDS has evolved from relatively simple biological and behavioural understandings to complex interpretations embracing a wide range of influences. It has argued that the AIDS pandemic has flourished because of various factors of underdevelopment, including poverty, gender inequality, failing public services, and crises created by armed conflict or natural disasters. The model of causes and consequences shown in Figure 2.1 depicts how AIDS and factors of underdevelopment reinforce each other in a vicious circle.

The chapter has argued that, despite significant advances, medical and behaviour-change approaches cannot overcome AIDS alone. As such, it has proposed that the pragmatic position is to accept AIDS as an endemic problem which is here for the long term. However, by describing AIDS as a problem with no obvious solution, the chapter has suggested not that the situation is hopeless, but that understanding AIDS as an entrenched problem which is intimately linked to issues of development means that development work should make a greater contribution to addressing AIDS. Figure 2.2 illustrates how development and humanitarian can work positively with AIDS-focused work of prevention and care, to enhance and strengthen the overall response to AIDS.

Following this presentation of the background to, and dynamics of, AIDS as a development issue, the next chapter takes a closer look at various types of response to HIV and AIDS.

3 Terms, meanings, and examples

Introduction

It soon became apparent in the early stages of planning this book that development and humanitarian workers do not share a common vocabulary to describe and refer to the various strategies for addressing AIDS. For example, the same term may be used to mean a variety of differing activities and approaches, and it is clear from the literature that such ambiguities are widespread. This chapter is devoted to setting out the terms and meanings used in this book, along with some examples, so that readers will know, rather than assume, what is meant here.

There is another motive for investing in explanations of terms and meanings. This is the belief that the quality of the response to AIDS is influenced by the clarity of the analysis and strategic thinking behind it. Organisations are able to act more decisively, and with greater impact, when staff are clear about the terms and meanings used, because such clarity enables them to develop shared visions, to conduct more thorough analysis, and to plan with greater precision. Confusion and uncertainty about key terms will adversely affect the impact of their work. A group of people cannot, for example, plan and implement effectively if they have differing views about what their stated aims actually mean.

The research for this book found that the terms *'expanded response'*, *'multi-sectoral'*, *'integrated'*, and *'mainstreamed'* are used in a variety of ways, sometimes interchangeably, and sometimes denoting very different work strategies. Often the terms are used without any explanation of their meaning. *'Expanded response'* and *'multi-sectoral'* are generally understood to imply that professionals and organisations outside the health sector should engage with AIDS. Calls for AIDS to be integrated or main-streamed are commonly understood in the same way, but they often also have different ideas ascribed to them.

Of course, there is no arbiter to pronounce that a certain definition is the correct one, nor to enforce consistent use of development terminology. Multiple interpretations persist for most technical terms. However, none of the existing meanings given to *'mainstreaming'* covers the ideas which are at the core of this book. So the book's terms and novel meanings, and the distinctions between them, are explicitly spelled out here, with definitions and examples.

The terms in brief

- *'AIDS work'* is used in this book to denote work directly focused on AIDS prevention, or care, treatment, or support for those infected – work which is distinct, and implemented separately, from other existing development and humanitarian work. For example, efforts to change behaviour, and home-based care programmes.

- *'Integrated AIDS work'* is used to mean AIDS work which is implemented along with, or as part of, development and humanitarian work. The focus is still on direct prevention, care, treatment, or support, but with the difference that the work is conducted in conjunction with, and linked to, other projects, or within wider programmes. For example, HIV prevention as part of broader health-promotion programmes, or treatment as part of wider health services.

- *'Mainstreaming AIDS externally'* refers to adapting development and humanitarian programme work in order to take into account susceptibility to HIV transmission and vulnerability to the impacts of AIDS. The focus is on core programme work in the changing context created by AIDS. For example, an agricultural project which is adjusted to the needs of vulnerable households in an AIDS-affected community.

- *'Mainstreaming AIDS internally'* is about changing organisational policy and practice in order to reduce the organisation's susceptibility to HIV infection and its vulnerability to the impacts of AIDS. The focus is on AIDS and the organisation. It has two elements: AIDS work with staff, such as HIV prevention and treatment, and modifying the ways in which the organisation functions; for example, in terms of workforce planning and budgeting.

- *'Complementary partnerships'* involves organisations focusing on their strengths, while linking actively with other organisations that can address other aspects of the AIDS pandemic. For example, an agricultural project forms a partnership with an AIDS Support Organisation which is providing home-based care to people with HIV/AIDS. When agricultural extension workers are asked about AIDS by community members, or encounter people needing home-based care, they are able to refer them to the ASO. Meanwhile, the agricultural project holds a training session with the ASO's volunteers about the long-term impacts on livelihoods when AIDS-affected households liquidate productive agricultural assets. As a result, the volunteers become more willing to discuss this with people living with HIV/AIDS, with a view to reducing the impacts of AIDS on the household.

The ASO also refers vulnerable households among its clients to the agricultural project, which is able to provide support to those households which is relevant to their current and future needs.

Similarities and differences

The first two terms – **AIDS work** and **integrated AIDS work** – are the most similar, as they both refer to work which directly addresses AIDS through prevention and care. The precise line between AIDS work and integrated AIDS work may be difficult to locate, but the general types are easily recognised. Many AIDS projects, and much of the work of AIDS Support Organisations, are stand-alone interventions, while AIDS work undertaken within wider health and education programmes is comparatively integrated.

Mainstreaming AIDS externally is not about initiating AIDS work.

Internal mainstreaming includes **AIDS work**, because an organisation's susceptibility to HIV infection and vulnerability to AIDS is largely determined by the level of HIV infection among its employees, and by how they cope with AIDS. However, internal mainstreaming entails more than this, because the way in which the organisation functions also affects its susceptibility and vulnerability. By modifying how it operates with regard to internal issues such as recruitment, workforce planning, and budgeting strategies, an organisation can improve or protect the way in which it functions in a time of AIDS. This broader way of taking AIDS into account is shared with the strategy of **external mainstreaming**; rather than concentrating directly on AIDS, both forms of mainstreaming require a wider perspective of development work in a time of AIDS. Internal mainstreaming aims to ensure that organisations can continue to operate effectively, despite AIDS, while external mainstreaming is about ensuring that development and humanitarian work is relevant to the challenges brought by AIDS, so furthering the virtuous circle depicted earlier in Figure 2.2 on page 36.

The biggest contrast among the terms is between **AIDS work**, whether stand-alone or integrated, and **external mainstreaming** of AIDS. While AIDS work has at its heart goals related to AIDS, such as preventing HIV transmission, or improving care for people with AIDS, the focus of a project which has mainstreamed AIDS remains the original goal, for example improving food security, or raising literacy rates. Mainstreaming AIDS externally, as it is understood here, is not about initiating AIDS work.

Finally, the term **complementary partnerships** emphasises the synergies between AIDS work and development work which are illustrated in

Figure 2.2. The notion behind complementary partnerships is that different types of organisation are better suited to undertaking different aspects of the response to AIDS. Where possible, it is likely to be effective for those organisations to link and benefit from each other's expertise, rather than for each organisation to attempt to undertake all types of response.

Mainstreaming is not...

Mainstreaming is not concerned with completely changing an organisation's or sector's core functions and responsibilities, but with viewing them from a different perspective.

In addition to the definitions above, and the examples which follow, it may be useful to indicate a few ways of responding to AIDS which this book does not categorise as mainstreaming. For example, mainstreaming does not mean that other sectors simply support the health sector, nor take over its functions. Also it is not concerned with completely changing an organisation's or sector's core functions and responsibilities, but with viewing them from a different perspective, and making alterations as appropriate. Connected to this, mainstreaming is not about orientating all work to serve only AIDS-affected people, nor necessarily ensuring that all projects are accessible to all people affected by AIDS.

How to implement a mainstreaming policy? It is not a one-off event, but a process. And internal mainstreaming involves more than doing AIDS work with staff, although that is important. Finally, mainstreaming is not about 'business as usual'; although some changes may be small, the process should result in changes which make the organisation better able to function in a context of AIDS, and make its work more relevant to that context.

Examples

The following examples aim to bring the terms to life, by outlining the core function of five organisations in five different development sectors, and what each might do if it were to adopt each of the five strategies. The examples are hypothetical, but are based on actual experiences of AIDS work and integration, and ideas about how mainstreaming could be implemented.

Agricultural extension

Imagine that a CBO providing agricultural extension decides to respond to AIDS. Its core business is to help community members to improve their access to food and income. If the CBO were to begin a new AIDS project, recruiting and training Community AIDS Volunteers to promote and sell condoms, then it would be engaging in **AIDS work**. If instead it were to train its agricultural extension workers to promote and sell condoms to farmers, then the new AIDS work would be **integrated** with its existing work.

The CBO could, however, respond to AIDS without doing any AIDS-focused work, by **mainstreaming AIDS externally**. Imagine that it does some research with households affected by AIDS and finds that it is excluding them: women are too busy caring for the sick to travel to farmer-training sessions, and adolescents (including orphans now in charge of their households) are not eligible to participate. The CBO responds by seeking out affected households that are keen to take part in the extension work, and offers to hold training days on their land, so that they can attend and benefit from the labour input of the other trainees. The organisation also broadens its livestock programme to include rabbits and chickens, which are preferred by vulnerable families because they give quick returns and, as assets, are more divisible than cattle and goats.

The CBO is unsure how to work with young people, so seeks advice from a youth-focused NGO operating in a nearby town. The two organisations realise that they can support each other, and form a **complementary partnership**. The NGO provides training to the agricultural extension workers, challenging their prejudices against working with young people, and enabling their work to become more youth-friendly. The CBO provides agricultural expertise to the NGO, by running sessions about farming for the NGO's youth group.

As for **internal mainstreaming**, the CBO already has a policy on terminal diseases and provides medical and funeral benefits for staff members who are HIV-positive, but no one has considered how AIDS may affect the organisation in the future. A small team is formed and charged with predicting the likely impacts of AIDS on the organisation's finances and human resources, with a view to minimising those impacts. The team's work is hampered by a lack of data, but its estimates suggest that within five years the costs will rise substantially, perhaps beyond the organisation's ability to pay. They establish management systems in order to gather accurate information on absenteeism, medical costs, and other benefits paid, and so set in motion the process of reviewing the terminal-diseases policy. The strategy aims to ensure that the organisation can survive the financial impacts of AIDS.

Health promotion

A health-promotion agency sees its core business as increasing awareness and use of preventative and curative health measures, which it mainly does through performance of community theatre. If it wanted to begin **AIDS work**, it might conduct AIDS education through a new programme of drama performances and video shows. If it preferred to do **integrated AIDS work**, it could fit messages about AIDS, sexual health, and safer sex into some of its other plays. But suppose the agency opts to **mainstream AIDS externally**. It begins by reflecting on its work. It finds that its drama performances are popular because they create an entertaining community event, but that this, with the presence of alcohol vendors, provides an environment for unsafe sexual activity. Following consultation, the agency continues the drama work, but often with women, men, and young people as separate audiences. At evening performances for the whole community, the agency **integrates AIDS work** to reduce the likelihood of unsafe sex, by making sure that condoms and non-alcoholic drinks are made available. The organisation also develops a new sketch about alcohol use and unsafe sex, and uses it as a starting point for discussions with the audience. This leads to requests from community members for more information and personal support related to AIDS and HIV prevention. As there are no local organisations offering counselling with whom the agency could form a **complementary partnership**, the managers decide to apply for funds to begin such a service.

The agency also embarks on **internal mainstreaming of AIDS**, and decides to tackle the long-tolerated problem that some of the staff who perform the dramas are engaging in unsafe sex with community members. It runs some problem-solving sessions on sexual health with male and female staff members in separate groups. Consultations with staff result in two new policies: no alcohol consumption while working, and the facility for staff to have field expenses paid into their bank accounts, rather than in cash on departure. The agency also provides condoms to its employees; and, where possible, evening performances finish in time for the staff to return to their homes. Having begun discussing AIDS and their own potential for contracting and spreading infection, a few staff members press for a policy to address staff awareness and health care.

Micro-finance

Now take the case of an NGO providing micro-finance services through community groups. The staff see their core business as the provision of savings and credit schemes in order to support financially viable and productive activities. The NGO heeds government calls for all sectors to respond to AIDS, and considers initiating a separate project of **AIDS work**, giving loans to people with AIDS, with terms and conditions different from those available in its core programme. However, by talking with other micro-finance institutions they learn that because repayment rates are likely to be low, the approach could undermine the sustainability of the institution. In any case, due to stigma and low rates of HIV testing, it is unlikely that many people would apply for the loans. Instead, the NGO opts to **integrate AIDS work** with its existing work, by distributing leaflets about HIV prevention and AIDS to all the members of its micro-finance groups.

Later on, the NGO learns of **external mainstreaming**, and reviews its micro-finance work in the light of how AIDS affects its clients and their participation in the micro-finance groups. It discovers several ways of modifying its approach in order to meet the needs of its clients when their households are affected by AIDS, without compromising the sustainability of the micro-finance groups or the NGO itself. These include allowing clients to miss meetings without penalties, and allowing them a 'rest' from the savings and credit cycle. The NGO also changes its rules so that other household members can take over payment of loans, and take on new loans, should the original member become sick or die.

Although the NGO decides not to target loans to people with AIDS, it is able to form a **complementary partnership** with an AIDS Support Organisation which wants to begin an income-generating project with a group of HIV-positive people. The NGO is able to give advice on establishing appropriate rules and guidelines, and proposes two realistic aims for the project: that it should help the group members to avoid destitution, and encourage them to give each other moral support through working together. Meanwhile, the NGO provides funding to the ASO to visit each of its micro-finance groups to discuss HIV prevention and living with AIDS.

In the course of **internal mainstreaming**, the NGO discovers that it is over-reliant on two micro-finance specialists; if either or both became sick, the organisation's ability to do its work would be badly affected. It begins training and involving other staff in those functions, and standardising documentation systems so that everyone's work is more accessible and comprehensible to their colleagues. It also engages in discussions with its donors to sensitise them to the potential future impacts on its capacity, should such key staff fall ill or die. One donor agrees to the NGO's proposal to add in extra budget lines for temporary staff cover, and to plan for increased expenditure on recruitment and staff development.

Education

A Ministry of Education sees its core business as providing good-quality basic education for primary-school students. Engaging in **AIDS work** might involve supporting schools to set up anti-AIDS clubs, providing them with guidelines and basic materials. **Integrated AIDS work** might consist of introducing topics of sexual health and HIV transmission into the school curriculum, or training school nurses in HIV prevention and basic counselling skills.

Mainstreaming AIDS externally would require research into the ministry's work, and into how AIDS affects the demand for, and the quality and relevance of, education. For example, research with AIDS-affected households might reveal a variety of reasons why many girls and boys, including AIDS orphans, do not attend school, or do not attend regularly. The ministry might respond by supporting expanded in-school feeding programmes and bursaries, or by reducing school fees for children in need, including orphans. It could relax rules on compulsory school uniforms, or allow schools to open for more flexible hours, in order to extend some education to those children who have to work. Or it might put more emphasis on life-skills education, to equip pupils with skills which are relevant to their practical needs. In this regard, a **complementary partnership** might involve linking with the Ministry of Agriculture, to provide pupils with training in basic farming skills.

Internal mainstreaming would aim to reveal and deal with the threats posed by AIDS to the education system and its ability to provide relevant services. If research shows that the supply of new teachers is dwarfed by the growing number lost to illness and death, the ministry might decide to invest in treatment for staff, so that those who are HIV-positive are able to work for longer. It might also aim to increase the number of newly trained teachers. However, it learns that potential teachers, particularly women, find it difficult to attend the year-long residential teacher-training course. The ministry might respond to this constraint by introducing long-distance learning and in-service training. In the short term it could offer incentives to qualified teachers who have left the profession, to encourage them to return to teaching. The ministry might also begin an analysis of long-term workforce implications, not only for teachers, but also for members of the management, administration, and support functions.

Water and sanitation

Finally, imagine a refugee camp where an NGO is responsible for water supply and sanitation. The core business is seen as ensuring that everyone has access to potable water, washing facilities, and latrines, so reducing illness caused by poor hygiene. The NGO is being encouraged by its main funder to respond to AIDS. It considers doing **AIDS work** through establishing a separate AIDS project, writing and distributing leaflets about AIDS, and promoting and distributing free condoms. However, it opts for an **integrated** approach, by starting to include AIDS and sexual-health education alongside its existing hygiene-education work.

The idea of **mainstreaming AIDS externally** is initially dismissed by staff, because they do not see any connection between AIDS and their water and sanitation work. However, a curious project officer begins to explore the possibility with users, and discovers two ways in which the NGO's work is linked to HIV and AIDS. First, many women are afraid to collect water, particularly after dark. Unbeknown to the NGO staff, there have been instances where women have been threatened and abused, including two rapes. The women would welcome the installation of lighting to improve the social surveillance of the tap-stands, and the removal of some taps to locations which they believe are safer. These measures would reduce their susceptibility to HIV infection, and improve their access to water. Second, the project officer's conversations with women reveal the out-of-sight needs of the bedridden people within the camp, including those with AIDS. These people need a lot of water for washing, because of the fevers, vomiting, and diarrhoea from which they suffer. Carers are unable both to look after them and to collect adequate amounts of water; as a result, hygiene standards and infection control are both compromised. Carers would welcome having tap-stands close at hand, assistance in collecting water, or special deliveries of water to bedridden people. The NGO discusses the problem with the agency responsible for health care in the camp, and they form a **complementary partnership** aimed at supporting carers in a variety of practical ways.

The NGO also embarks on **internal mainstreaming**, by examining its own functioning with regard to HIV transmission. It recognises that many of its staff are young, away from home, and relatively wealthy and powerful, compared with the communities with whom they are working. The NGO fears that some staff use their influence, or the organisation's resources, to buy sexual favours or to coerce refugees into supplying them. It takes action by training all staff in the avoidance of HIV transmission, and emphasises their responsibilities to the community members. The training also covers the disciplinary measures to be taken in cases of corruption and abuse, and a subsequent incident provides the opportunity to demonstrate management commitment to implementing the policies.

Summary

This chapter has defined and given examples of five strategies for responding to AIDS, which are summarised in Table 3.1. It is worth noting, however, that some activities may be hard to categorise, and that differences of opinion over what types of work belong to which approach are likely. For example, at a workshop which used these definitions, participants were asked to categorise various types of project; they put a lot of the projects on the border-line between two terms, because they could not agree on one or the other category.[1] As an example, some saw HIV-prevention work with school pupils as AIDS work, while others argued that it should be classified as external mainstreaming, because it concerns modifying the schools' core work of educating children. However, even though this chapter cannot eliminate all ambiguity about terms and meanings, it is hoped that it will assist readers to understand what the author means, and may facilitate discussions about various types of response to AIDS.

Internal mainstreaming involves much more than organising AIDS seminars for staff and ensuring supplies of condoms in the toilets.

The examples in this chapter show that there is a lot of difference between AIDS work – be it separate or integrated – and mainstreaming AIDS externally. For the former, the starting point is the problem of AIDS, and AIDS projects are developed in response. For the latter, the starting point is organisations' existing development work, with processes modified as appropriate to take account of susceptibility to HIV transmission and vulnerability to the impacts of AIDS.

Whereas the term 'mainstreaming' is often used to refer to everyone doing AIDS work, or to AIDS work being implemented across budget lines, this chapter has shown the distinct meaning given to the term in this book. In each of the above cases, the outcome of external mainstreaming is to adapt existing work in response to AIDS. In the cases of the health-promotion dramas and the sexual abuse linked to water collection, the adaptations aim to reduce susceptibility to HIV transmission. In the other examples, the modifications are concerned with reducing vulnerability to the impacts of AIDS. Each of those changes makes the existing work more relevant to those affected by AIDS, be they families needing agricultural advice, orphans wishing to attend school, members of micro-finance groups, or people bedridden by AIDS.

This chapter has also shown that internal mainstreaming involves much more than organising AIDS seminars for staff and ensuring supplies of condoms in the toilets. For the organisations engaged in health promotion and water and sanitation, mainstreaming brings up the largely

Table 3.1 Summary of terms, meanings, and examples

Term	Meaning	Focus	Examples
AIDS work	Interventions directly focused on HIV prevention and AIDS care	AIDS prevention, care, treatment, or support	Stand-alone behaviour change, treatment, or home-based care programmes
Integrated AIDS work	Interventions directly focused on HIV prevention and AIDS care	AIDS prevention, care, treatment, or support	Behaviour change, treatment, or home-based care programmes which are linked to, or part of, other work
Mainstreaming AIDS externally	Adapting development and humanitarian programme work to take into account susceptibility to HIV transmission and vulnerability to the impacts of AIDS	Core programme work in the context of changes related to AIDS	An agricultural project which is tuned to the needs of vulnerable households in an AIDS-affected community
Mainstreaming AIDS internally	Adapting organisational policy and practice in order to reduce the organisation's susceptibility to HIV infection and its vulnerability to the impacts of AIDS	AIDS and the organisation, now and in the future	AIDS work with staff, such as HIV prevention and treatment; and modifying how the organisation functions, for example, in terms of workforce planning, budgeting, and ways of working
Complementary partnerships	Organisations focusing on their strengths, and linking actively with other organisations that can address different aspects of the AIDS pandemic	Collaborating with those more able to address needs beyond the organisation's expertise	An agricultural project and an AIDS Support Organisation linking to share their relative strengths and expertise

unacknowledged issue of unsafe sex and sexual bargaining between staff and community members. The micro-finance NGO and the Ministry of Education are both faced with human-resource issues which threaten the effectiveness of their work. And the agricultural CBO faces the task of balancing the rights and needs of staff infected with HIV against the organisation's prospects of survival.

Four of the examples include ways in which complementary partnerships might enable an organisation which is mainstreaming AIDS to link beneficially with others. However, it may often be the case, as with the example of the health-promotion agency, that there is no suitable organisation with which to link. In such instances, managers are faced with a choice between not responding to the need for direct AIDS work, and deciding to begin AIDS work, even if it lies outside the area of the organisation's expertise. As Chapter 5 will argue more thoroughly, this book advocates that in the first instance development and humanitarian organisations should prioritise mainstreaming, and then form complementary partnerships to meet AIDS-specific needs. Organisations with sufficient capacity might also respond to the need for AIDS work by initiating or funding new AIDS-focused projects, particularly where it is not possible for them to form a satisfactory complementary partnership. However, those organisations without the capacity to begin work beyond their core expertise may risk harming their core work if they try to act similarly, and their AIDS work may also be of poor quality.

Before going on to analyse reasons for mainstreaming AIDS in Chapter 5, we shall now consider some examples of AIDS work, both stand-alone and integrated.

4 AIDS work: the direct response

Introduction

Chapter 3 described three approaches to working on AIDS in programmes: stand-alone AIDS work, integrated AIDS work, and mainstreaming AIDS within development and humanitarian work. The first two approaches are direct, as they focus on AIDS itself through HIV prevention and care, treatment, and support for people who are HIV-positive. In contrast, the approach of mainstreaming AIDS externally is indirect, as the focus is on modifying existing programme work while retaining its core objectives, in order to make it more relevant to individuals and communities affected by AIDS.

Chapter 2 described how AIDS has come to be seen as a development issue. In policy and programming terms, this idea has led to general consensus among governments, donors, and agencies of all sizes that the task of responding to AIDS extends beyond the health sector. This realisation is behind calls for 'intensified action', an 'expanded response', 'multi-sectoral' and 'integrated' strategies, and 'mainstreaming' of AIDS. What all these approaches have in common is that they demand the involvement of diverse sectors. What differentiates them is whether the course of action entails direct AIDS work (be it stand-alone or integrated), or external mainstreaming by adapting existing work in the light of AIDS – or, indeed, a combination of approaches. The predominant rhetoric favours the strategy of all sectors undertaking AIDS work, but in practice this strategy has not been widely adopted. UNAIDS research published in 2000 showed that among African governments, only around 40 per cent of Ministries of Education had HIV/AIDS policies (not to mention activities!), a figure which fell to just ten per cent for Ministries of Agriculture (Mullins 2001:8). The World Bank has noted that despite State efforts to spread involvement beyond health ministries, in practice, action against AIDS is far from being multi-sectoral (World Bank 1999:49). A UNDP overview concurred with this assessment: *'It is now commonplace to argue that policy and programming responses to the HIV epidemic need to be multisectoral and multidimensional. But what has happened on the ground has generally been a far cry from this'* (Cohen 1999:1). On the whole, the most common activity across sectors is raising awareness of HIV prevention and AIDS. The most conspicuous evidence of the integration of AIDS work and a multi-sectoral response is in the incorporation of AIDS prevention and life skills in school curricula.

This book is concerned with the challenge of mainstreaming AIDS as a first step for development and humanitarian agencies which may or may not be able also to do direct AIDS work. However, before considering the arguments for, and examples of, mainstreaming, this chapter discusses the direct response to AIDS through AIDS work, both stand-alone and integrated. The chapter first describes some examples taken from case studies of NGO implementation of AIDS work. It then explores the reasons why, to date, the direct response of AIDS work (whether integrated or not) dominates as *the* response to AIDS, and it considers some of the implications of this predominance. It concludes with an overview of some of the problems faced by development and humanitarian agencies that undertake AIDS work.

Examples of AIDS work

The following examples are taken from case studies commissioned for this book; they are listed at the beginning of the Bibliography. While some relate to interventions that are clearly stand-alone initiatives, in general the case studies are not detailed enough to make it possible to judge the degree to which the AIDS work is integrated with, or distinct from, other development work. The case studies also lack information on the impacts of the work. Nevertheless, the examples described here provide some useful examples of how development NGOs have undertaken AIDS work alongside a variety of other programmes.

Stand-alone AIDS work

The most evident form of stand-alone AIDS work in the case studies is seen where agencies support the work of AIDS Support Organisations. For example, **ActionAid-Mozambique** has an HIV/AIDS programme which supports partners, including **MONASO**, which is the national network for ASOs, and **Kindlimuka**, the first support group for HIV-positive people in Mozambique. NGOs may also support education work, such as **ActionAid-Burundi**'s production of a video and brochure about AIDS, and its support to the organisation *Etoile Filante* to broadcast a popular TV show about AIDS. Then there are practical services to provide counselling, HIV testing, and home-based care. The **Ruyigi Health Province**, a partner of ActionAid-Burundi, provides treatment for opportunistic diseases, and HIV testing and counselling. ActionAid-Burundi helped it to set up and fund a mobile counselling and HIV testing service, which led to a rapid rise in the numbers of local people seeking testing. Another strategy is to support institutional structures, such as ActionAid-Burundi's mobilising of an informal local network of parties interested in AIDS, which has developed into a functioning provincial AIDS committee. And at national and international levels, NGOs have been active in advocacy related to AIDS, on topics such as funding, and access to basic and antiretroviral drugs. These very brief examples give some flavour of the variety of ways in which development NGOs can specifically initiate or support direct AIDS work.

AIDS work and reproductive health

The Ghana programme of **Save the Children UK** (SC UK) began its **Family Reproductive Health Programme** in 1995 (SC UK Ghana Case Study). It operates through three national NGOs, each of which manages and undertakes capacity building with the local NGOs who implement the work. Surprisingly, at the outset, the project did not seek to collaborate with NGOs already engaged in health work, but purposely sought out developmental NGOs from sectors such as rural water supply and sanitation, agro-forestry, and the environment. The intention was to work with partners which had both a broad development perspective and pre-existing strong relationships with the communities. The disadvantages of this strategy were that the NGOs, understandably, had weak capacity on reproductive-health issues. As a result, Ministry of Health officials were initially reluctant to collaborate with them.

The project is concerned with overall reproductive health, but the local NGOs have aimed to focus first on the health needs of greatest concern to community members. In the case of one NGO, **Zuuri Organic Vegetable Farmer's Association**, women in the community prioritised achieving an end to female genital mutilation. The NGO's careful awareness raising and facilitation encouraged community members to discuss the topic openly, and reportedly this has led to a decline in the practice of female genital mutilation. Another NGO, **Tiyumtaba Integrated Development Association**, responded to the community's priority of improving poor nutrition through provision of a grinding mill. Part of the purchase-scheme deal with the mill's owner was that women could have free access to grind 'weanimix', a nutritious baby-weaning food made of local grains. In both these cases the NGOs believe that their subsequent reproductive-health activities were easier to implement because they had built up trust and communication with the community members through the initial intervention.

However, community members' expressed problems did not include HIV and AIDS, so only one of the programme's 20 participating local NGOs was addressing AIDS directly. In 1998, SC UK organised a workshop for all the project partners, aimed at strengthening and integrating the HIV/AIDS components of their work. One of the issues that arose, given the link between STIs and HIV, was the need to train all the nurses attached to the NGOs' projects in the syndromic management of STIs (i.e. undertaking diagnosis and treatment by observing symptoms, rather than by laboratory tests). Until then, the National AIDS Control Programme had targeted only more senior medical staff for training in syndromic STI management. With training, however, the nurses have proved their ability to identify and treat STIs, and so to extend STI services from formal clinics into the community.

In 1999, the Save the Children UK programme in Ghana adopted HIV/AIDS as a cross-cutting issue. As part of this initiative, it created the new position of HIV/AIDS Programme Officer, whose task with the Family Reproductive Health Programme was to strengthen both the youth and HIV/AIDS elements of the programme's work. Subsequent reviews found that the programme had a weak peer-education component, mainly because there was no standard training package for peer education, nor reliable methods of monitoring and evaluation. Fortunately, another NGO, the **Planned Parenthood Association of Ghana**, had invested heavily in developing a sexual-health workshop programme for adolescents, and, in partnership with them, SC UK began to retrain all the programme's peer educators. As a result, the work of the local NGOs such as the Zuuri Organic Vegetable Farmer's Association now includes extensive peer-education work, and condom distribution.

Certainly, SC UK and the three national NGOs have made concerted efforts to ensure that HIV and AIDS issues are integrated into the local NGOs' project activities. Looking back, the project management conclude in their case study that *'integration of HIV/AIDS activities has been a gradual, sometimes laborious process'*. They also acknowledge that there is still work to be done: *'HIV/AIDS messages need to be improved, better social monitoring of interventions and subsequent changes need to be captured, and capacity in many different areas and at every level needs to be continuously developed.'* This project demonstrates, however, that where expressed needs from communities do not include HIV and AIDS, investment and support 'from above' can effectively stimulate the response of AIDS work among project partners.

Another organisation which has exploited the connections between HIV and reproductive health is **IES** (*Instituto de Educacion y Salud*, or Institute for Education and Health), a Peruvian NGO and partner of **Save the Children UK** (SC UK Peru Case Study). IES aims to enable young people to develop the capacity to make decisions which allow them to enjoy sexual health. Although the prevention of HIV and AIDS is at the heart of its mission, its work embraces the more pressing sexual-health issues which it has found to be of greatest concern to young people, particularly how to avoid unwanted pregnancy, and STIs. IES trains around 300 'peer educators' each year, who provide guidance to their schoolmates on matters of sexual health. The organisation also trains teachers to provide guidance on sexual health to pupils; works with health institutions to make their services more adolescent-friendly; and organises mass events to reach parents and the wider community. All of this work fits within a much broader programme of empowering young people to influence their communities, to understand their individual rights and responsibilities, to overcome gender inequities, and to improve their access to employment, and to education and health services. The case of IES demonstrates how direct AIDS work can be integrated with other work addressing both the community's felt needs concerning sexual health, and much wider issues.

AIDS work and public health

While the overlaps between HIV and reproductive health are clear, the links between HIV and the water and sanitation sector are less obvious to many people. **The Kawempe Programme** is an urban initiative funded by the Uganda programme of **Save the Children UK**. It focuses on promoting child health by reducing common childhood diseases, by increasing access to safe drinking water, and by improving sanitation standards. In participatory appraisals, communities did raise AIDS as an issue of concern to them, so the project took advantage of funding and technical support provided by SC UK and embarked upon AIDS work. It began by including HIV/AIDS in the topics for training community members. The project then expanded the AIDS work to include training peer educators, supporting drama groups, establishing child-to-child clubs in schools, and creating a youth information centre. When the increased workload and technical demands proved too onerous for the existing staff, the programme recruited a youth worker with responsibility for HIV and AIDS.

Although the HIV/AIDS work forms a separate project from the public-health elements of the Kawempe Programme, there are a number of ways in which the two overlap. For example, when the AIDS youth worker visits peer educators in a particular neighbourhood, he also checks up on the taps and latrines there, and reports back to his colleagues. They, in turn, include HIV and AIDS in their awareness-raising work. Furthermore, the theatre groups that the project supports present dramas which include messages both on AIDS and on water and sanitation issues. Aside from the greater efficiency of integrating in these ways, the staff report benefits to both projects. First, the AIDS work has been easier to implement because the project already had good relationships with community members and institutions as a result of its existing work. Second, the relationships built with the schools through the child-to-child clubs have opened the door for improving water and sanitation facilities in the schools. This programme, then, demonstrates some of the benefits of linking AIDS work to other work. The activities described here are labelled 'AIDS work', rather than mainstreaming, because the HIV-prevention work has been added to the water and sanitation activities, rather than adapting existing core work to better address the particular needs of people affected by, or susceptible to, HIV and AIDS. However, in addition to this direct AIDS work, the Kawempe Programme has undertaken elements of external mainstreaming of AIDS, which are outlined in Chapter 8.

Disabled people may be more susceptible to HIV infection because they may be subject to sexual abuse, and are generally less able to obtain access to education, including information about AIDS.

AIDS work and disability

In her case study for this book, **ActionAid-Ethiopia**'s HIV/AIDS Officer defined mainstreaming as '*not designing a vertical HIV/AIDS programme on its own, but to bring in, initiate, institute anti-AIDS work within the existing development work, whenever possible using the existing intervention system*'. Hence, when the focus of ActionAid-Ethiopia shifted from general community-based health care to HIV/AIDS, it encouraged its existing partners to integrate AIDS. One partner which responded to this encouragement was **Voluntary Council for the Handicapped** (VCH), a local CBO engaged in community-based rehabilitation and disability-prevention projects. VCH was able to see the links between HIV and disability, particularly in terms of stigma, denial, and discrimination. It also recognised that disabled people may be more susceptible to HIV infection because they may be subject to sexual abuse, and are generally less able to obtain access to education, including information about AIDS.

Although staff from VCH initially feared that they lacked the skills to tackle AIDS, they have been able to embark on a programme of AIDS-awareness raising, focusing on the same groups targeted by their disability-awareness programme, including school children, youth, and women. VCH has also included its groups of disabled young people in the AIDS work through AIDS-awareness training. And, as with community-based rehabilitation, VCH has trained volunteers in caring for people with AIDS. A possibility for the future is to extend home visits not only to people with disabilities, but also to people with AIDS. Although the AIDS programme is still in its initial phases, this case illustrates how an organisation can adapt to doing AIDS work, using its established ways of working, and building on its established strengths and links with the community.

AIDS work and adult literacy

Within its REFLECT adult literacy programme, **ActionAid-Burundi** has trained all the facilitators in the basics of HIV and AIDS. Equipped with accurate information about HIV transmission, testing, and care for people with AIDS, the facilitators are better able to lead discussions about AIDS as they arise in the REFLECT learning circles. **ActionAid-Mozambique** also runs REFLECT adult literacy programmes, and has integrated learning units on reproductive health and AIDS into the curriculum. This strategy is referred to here as integrating AIDS work, rather than mainstreaming, because it concerns slotting in information on HIV prevention and AIDS care, rather than modifying the REFLECT project to (for example) enable older orphans to take part. However, some might categorise it as mainstreaming, because the core function (education) is being modified in the light of AIDS, by adding in information about HIV and AIDS.

AIDS work and gender

As is often the case where AIDS is highly stigmatised, **ActionAid-Mozambique** found that AIDS was rarely raised as a concern during community needs assessments. In Maputo Province, staff learned a good deal about AIDS by not mentioning AIDS directly, but raising related issues such as social relations, polygamy, and attitudes towards sexual behaviour. One of the places which community members identified as a locus of risk was Bobole market place, which functions as a truck stop and sustains trade in sexual services. ActionAid-Mozambique formed a partnership with the national NGO *Muleide* (Women, Law and Development), which worked with women in the market to form the Bobole Market Women's Group. The approach was not focused on AIDS; as one member, Adela, recalls, '*when Muleide first came, they said they wanted to help us form a group of friends, and they began to give lessons on how women can get on well with each other and with their relatives, and how we can solve* *conflicts by talking things through... I thought: "I should stay with this group so I can learn to solve my problems and advise others"'* (ActionAid-Mozambique Case Study 2001:8).

Among the domestic problems discussed by the group, AIDS did emerge as a major concern. The group received AIDS education and got access to condoms, but the women remained susceptible to HIV infection,because of their need to earn money, and their clients' and regular partners' dislike of condoms. ActionAid arranged for four members of the group to join another ActionAid-supported women's group to learn batik fabric-printing techniques, as an alternative source of income generation for the group. Unfortunately the training for just a few members of the group caused divisions which led the group to split. Through their contact with ActionAid programmes, however, several women from the Bobole group began attending REFLECT literacy classes. One implication of ActionAid-Mozambique's experience is that work to address gender inequality and susceptibility to HIV infection ideally needs to involve both men and women. This is the approach taken by ActionAid's Stepping Stones communications training package (Welbourn 1995), which **ActionAid-Mozambique** has used. Stepping Stones is a process of guided discussion and skills building for community members on issues related to HIV, gender, and sexual health. The programme has integrated HIV prevention and AIDS care with work on the wider issues of gender and sexual health, and as such it may be viewed as an unusually sophisticated, participatory, and broad-based approach to AIDS work.

Work to address gender inequality and susceptibility to HIV infection ideally needs to involve both men and women.

From its use of Stepping Stones, ActionAid-Mozambique has found that reported use of condoms increased among participants of the programme. While this outcome relates directly to AIDS, many of the other changes reported to have been brought about by Stepping Stones do not. For example, in one review, participants cited ways in which gender relations have shifted, including a greater willingness on the part of men to help their wives with cleaning and child rearing, to the extent of one washing his baby's nappies. Men also talked about sharing their wages with their wives and jointly planning monthly expenditure, while some women reported much better relations in the home, with a shift from arguing to discussing things with their partners. Given the broad scope of Stepping Stones, and the wide nature of the changes that it promotes, it is not surprising that several ActionAid programmes see the training package as a valuable tool for tackling AIDS in an integrated way, alongside issues of gender and reproductive health.

AIDS work in a variety of settings

Voluntary Service Overseas (VSO) works through funding and placing skilled volunteers with government and non-government organisations. In 2000 it launched its Regional AIDS Initiative for Southern Africa (RAISA),[1] which aims to strengthen the response across all sectors to HIV and AIDS in the region. In part this is being achieved directly, by increasing the number of VSO volunteers placed with AIDS Support Organisations and in health-sector projects involving AIDS work. However, RAISA is also investing in encouraging *all* the other VSO volunteers in the region to make their contribution, however small, to responding to AIDS. Before starting work on their placements, volunteers are given an induction pack which acquaints them with basic facts and issues. Once in place, they participate in training workshops, have access to a small grant fund, and can communicate with other volunteers through an e-mail discussion group. Although VSO refers to the project as mainstreaming AIDS, by this book's definitions the agency is supporting its volunteers to initiate direct AIDS work, rather than trying to instigate any modifications to the core business of the institutions with which they work.

A review of the first two years of the project found that around 70 per cent of the 250 volunteers in the region had initiated some HIV/AIDS-related activities in their placement or community (VSO 2002:7). VSO has documented nine especially interesting cases in a publication about the RAISA project (Wilkins and Vasani 2002). These examples of AIDS work include instigating a Voluntary Counselling and Testing facility within a rural hospital; establishing an AIDS programme within a government directorate; introducing AIDS themes into training courses for English-language teachers; training AIDS educators from farmers' groups; training community members in home-based care; persuading a university to adopt an HIV/AIDS policy; and adapting the Stepping Stones training package for use in secondary schools. These examples, and the RAISA project in general, show how people who are not AIDS specialists can get involved in tackling AIDS through AIDS work.

AIDS work in camps for displaced people and refugees

When flooding led to large-scale displacement in 2000, **ActionAid-Mozambique** decided to include AIDS work as part of its response in camps (ActionAid-Mozambique Case Study 2001). The team first did some basic work with women and men to assess their knowledge of STIs and HIV/AIDS, and their use of condoms. They also assessed displaced women's sexual and reproductive-health needs, through focus groups involving more than 150 women. This gave the team a better understanding of life in the camps, enabling them to respond to three specific issues of importance to the women. First, ActionAid distributed more sanitary cloths, because the constant rain was making it difficult for women to dry the few cloths that they owned. Second, the team publicised the dates and times when food was to be distributed, as some women who did not know when the distribution was due were afraid to leave the camp to attend the clinic with their children. Third, they distributed more cooking pans and cups, because women were having to borrow from each other, which was time-consuming and inconvenient.

One part of ActionAid-Mozambique's programme of AIDS work – on-site counselling and STI treatment – was not implemented, because these services were available at health posts within reach of the camps. The rest of the programme went ahead, largely implemented by ActionAid's pre-emergency partners of ASOs and groups of HIV-positive people. They began with raising AIDS awareness through drama, initially using theatre groups from Maputo. Later, they offered training in theatre-for-development techniques to camp residents, who performed plays which engaged the attention of community members by reflecting real and authentic experiences. Members of the groups of HIV-positive people were involved in training community leaders to analyse their situation, and to propose practical activities for which they were responsible, such as distributing condoms and leaflets. Community educators from other partner organisations worked with women and with young people, discussing sexual health and ways of supporting each other, especially in cases of violence.

ActionAid-Mozambique found that working with existing partners was an effective strategy, building on the agency's good relationships with skilled people, who were well accepted in the camps. Furthermore, the strategy allowed for post-emergency continuity. For example, one CBO followed up its work with women in the camps once the women were resettled. As resettlement began, ActionAid trained community educators in the *Stepping Stones* methodology, recognising that resettlement is a time of flux, when communities may more fruitfully be encouraged to reflect on gender-related issues, and to change power dynamics.

A well-documented case of AIDS work with refugees was carried out by a group of NGOs (**AMREF, CARE, AIDSCAP, JSI, and PSI**) in Tanzania in 1994, in two large camps housing nearly 350,000 Rwandan refugees. Epidemiological data pointed to the high potential for the HIV epidemic to spread, with refugees from urban Rwanda thought to have infection rates of 35 per cent, compared with rates of only five to seven per cent among the rural refugees and Tanzanians living close to the camps. The project began with a rapid clinical STI assessment and a survey of men's and women's knowledge, attitudes, beliefs, and practices with regard to sex and sexual health. The survey found high levels of STIs, low reported condom use, and sexual norms which enhanced susceptibility to HIV infection. The AIDS-prevention programme comprised elements of awareness raising, peer education, condom distribution, syndromic STI diagnosis, STI case management, and antenatal screening for syphilis.

The programme had two significant impacts: demand for condoms rose substantially, and STI rates stayed constant, although they usually rise in such situations. However, sexual behaviour did not appear to change. The project also acknowledged the problem of rising levels of sexual violence, but lacked any strategy to address sexual violence as a factor which prevents safer sex and heightens women's and children's susceptibility to HIV (Smith 2002:20-21).

Both of these initiatives suffered from the fact that the AIDS work began some time after the onset of the emergency. In Tanzania, the NGOs' project started four months after the start of the crisis, and key components of peer education, condom distribution, and STI treatment began much later. One lesson learned from the experience was that the programme should have been set up more rapidly (Smith 2002:20). ActionAid-Mozambique's HIV/AIDS Coordinator reflected that their AIDS work was

> ...less integrated than intended, because it was an afterthought. When the planning team in the first weeks identified their key issues and developed the plans, they left AIDS to the AIDS team, and we didn't get to the field to do our analysis until after the main plan had been developed. AIDS therefore became a sub-clause in the main plan.[2]

ActionAid-Mozambique also found that, having hired someone to coordinate its emergency AIDS programme, it was 'very difficult after that to integrate AIDS in the planning and reporting of each district team, as each of them left it all to the HIV/AIDS Coordinator.'[3] These problems, however, relate partly to the NGOs' focus on AIDS work, rather than on mainstreaming HIV and AIDS in the core functions of the humanitarian response. As Chapter 13 will explore, if AIDS were mainstreamed, then, at least theoretically, attention to it and to related issues of gender and sexual health would begin to be paid at the outset, as part of the initial needs assessments and plans.

Summary

The examples above illustrate a variety of ways in which direct AIDS work can be implemented alongside, or integrated within, development and humanitarian work. As such they provide a flavour of the ways in which NGOs have responded to AIDS so far. Unfortunately, it is not possible from the information in the case studies to comment on the effectiveness or sustainability of the initiatives, nor on how the NGOs coped with getting involved with, or supporting, AIDS work. These limitations, however, are not specific to these case studies, because it is rare for literature about AIDS work (and, more widely, development work) to include measures of impact and cost-effectiveness.[4]

The notion has endured that we must – and we can – stop AIDS, and the emphasis on health-related interventions continues to predominate.

The imperative of AIDS work

This book promotes the strategy of responding to AIDS indirectly, by making core development and humanitarian work relevant to the changes wrought by AIDS – without necessarily doing AIDS work. However, it is clear from the literature that to date AIDS work (in the form of prevention, care, and treatment activities) dominates the global response. This was also true for the case studies gathered for this book: while there was a surplus of data about stand-alone and integrated AIDS work, much less emerged with regard to the external mainstreaming of AIDS.

This section proposes three reasons for the current primacy of AIDS work, explaining why the strategy of adapting development and humanitarian programmes to meet the challenge of the pandemic remains largely ignored so far.

'We must stop AIDS'

In the early years of the pandemic, AIDS was commonly depicted as a war to be won, an evil to be eliminated, or a crisis to overcome. At the 1994 Paris AIDS Summit, which set the agenda for the newly formed UNAIDS, the declaration stated that the work to be undertaken by UNAIDS '...*can halt the pandemic and lead to a world free of AIDS*'. Since then, however, rates of HIV infection have soared to unforeseen heights in parts of sub-Saharan Africa, and the virus has entered the population of every country in the world. As a result, there has been some movement from perceiving HIV/AIDS as an epidemic which is expected to peak and wane, to seeing it as an endemic, or entrenched and on-going, global problem. The shift in thinking has been only partial, however. Despite the numbers of people now infected with HIV, the notion has endured that we must – and we can – stop AIDS, and the emphasis on health-related interventions continues to predominate.

Rhetoric urging the need for action to halt – rather than cope with or contain – AIDS persists partly because the pandemic is dynamic and changing. One dynamic is a spatial one. At present most countries in the world have low rates of HIV infection, so agencies such as UNAIDS, appealing for action to 'stop AIDS' in those countries, base their advocacy on the hope of containing the spread of local epidemics. This is not unreasonable, because where HIV infection is still highly concentrated among population sub-groups, there is a very real opportunity to prevent it from becoming generalised, and so contain it, as Brazil, for example, is doing. The pandemic also has a temporal dynamic: even in highly affected countries, AIDS is portrayed as stoppable if the next generation can be protected from HIV infection. This optimistic view is supported by localised evidence of behaviour change among young people; for example, in South Africa, although HIV prevalence among all pregnant women has been rising throughout the last decade, the level of infection among pregnant teenagers fell by 25 per cent in the years 1998 to 2001 (UNAIDS 2002b:17).

The persistence of the notion of 'stopping AIDS', however, probably owes less to logic and more to human psychology. At least among people drawn to development work, there is a strong preference in favour of thinking – or at least saying – that AIDS can somehow be stopped (Holden 1995:64). And in terms of advocacy and fundraising, it is far more powerful and motivating to speak simply of stopping AIDS than to use more realistic, but 'defeatist' language, such as reducing the rate of increase in HIV infections, or adapting to AIDS as an on-going and complex problem. For example, ActionAid, Oxfam GB, and Save the Children UK are among 15 British agencies behind the 'Stop AIDS Campaign'. The campaign website[5] states: *'HIV/AIDS is a global emergency claiming the lives of 8,000 people every day in some of the poorest countries of the world. The Stop AIDS Campaign is working to end this.'* Similar messages exist in advocacy among agencies. For example, a recent World Bank press release argues that *'education offers a window of hope unlike any other for countries, communities, and families to escape the deadly grip of HIV/AIDS'*. It also talks of using the 'education vaccine' to overcome HIV/AIDS, and confidently claims that *'...the fight against HIV/AIDS can only be won with multi-sectoral efforts'* (World Bank 2002).

These generalised calls to eliminate AIDS are sometimes made more specific, as in the case of UNDP's Botswana Human Development Report for 2000 (UNDP 2000), which aims for an *'AIDS-free generation'* by the year 2016, a time when *'...the spread of HIV will have stopped so that there* will be no new infections by the virus that year' (UNDP 2000:1). Although Botswana has the highest rates of HIV infection in the world, 80 per cent of the whole population (rather than the age groups assumed to be sexually active) are still uninfected, and more than half of them are under 15 years old. The notion that an AIDS-free generation is attainable by 2016 is based on the belief that it would be possible to protect every child born from 2000 onwards from HIV.

When British NGOs speak of 'freeing the world from AIDS', they do not say what they mean, how they will achieve it, nor within what time-frame.

Much of the discourse of the campaign to stop AIDS is vague. When British NGOs speak of 'freeing the world from AIDS', they do not say what they mean, how they will achieve it, nor within what time-frame. When the World Bank talks of 'winning the fight against AIDS', it does not spell out what 'winning' entails. Has Uganda, for example, won its battle? It is rightly regarded as a success story, because its HIV-prevalence rates have fallen dramatically, yet at least five per cent of its adult population are infected with HIV, and rates could remain at that level, or rise once more, in the future. And when, as in the case of Botswana, the objective is more explicit, the viability of the strategy does not stand up to scrutiny. Although UNDP's work describes how poverty and other factors constrain behaviour change in Botswana, no solution is offered for those problems. Instead, UNDP's strategy is based on faith in the ability to impose moral discipline, to eliminate intergenerational sexual activity, and to guarantee that all sexual liaisons are 'safe' ones between members of the same age group. But this radical shift in behaviour is to be achieved by using the same 'weapons' as have always been used against AIDS: *'There is no cure for AIDS. Therefore, comprehensively mobilising society to consistently observe the ABC of safe sex* [Abstain! Be faithful! Use Condoms!] *is still the best response to the epidemic'* (UNDP 2000:4).

It is striking how few people have challenged the claims that AIDS is stoppable. While there has been major controversy over whether HIV causes AIDS, and vigorous activism to challenge drug patents and improve access to antiretroviral treatments, there have been few challenges to the conventional notion of HIV as something which can be eliminated. One dissenting voice is that of development specialist Tony Klouda, who has stated, *'It is as impossible to envisage the total elimination of HIV as it is to envisage the elimination of syphilis, poverty or conflict'* (Klouda 1995:483). For other serious STIs, such as syphilis, there are effective treatments, but they persist even in wealthy nations with good health-care infrastructures. In the author's opinion, the scale of HIV infection – most of it unseen, and unknown to those who are infected – makes the goal of eliminating HIV unrealistic. However, this is not something that people want to hear, or to accept. The idea – or perhaps the prayer – that AIDS can be stopped lives on. It is an idea which could deter agencies from adopting the strategy of mainstreaming, because, as the next section explains, it presents the fight against AIDS as a direct one.

The main benefit of the narrative of 'stopping AIDS' is psychological: it provides hope, and a motivating force which encourages people to donate funds, to advocate for an expanded response, including treatment for people living with HIV and AIDS, and to get involved in – and stay committed to – AIDS work. The alternative of accepting that AIDS and its impacts are here to stay in the long term might have the opposite effect of encouraging defeatism. However, campaigns to 'stop AIDS' risk fostering hope in short-term projects and simplistic 'solutions', most prominently the idea that increased awareness of AIDS automatically leads to sufficient and sustained behaviour change to reduce the rate of HIV infection. The emphasis on 'stopping AIDS' also distracts attention from the long-term impacts of HIV and AIDS which need to be addressed; even if an anti-HIV vaccine were universally and effectively administered free of charge today, the impacts on already-affected families would continue for years. And the notion of halting AIDS draws attention to the roles of health and AIDS specialists, and away from the contributions that are needed from development and humanitarian agencies. In this sense, the idea of 'stopping AIDS' may be an impediment to such agencies adopting the strategy of mainstreaming AIDS, and an encouragement to them to engage only in AIDS work.

Campaigns to 'stop AIDS' risk fostering hope in short-term projects and simplistic 'solutions'.

AIDS is the problem, AIDS work is the solution

It is important to note that it is AIDS which is seen to be the problem, rather than the more general failure of development efforts which has allowed AIDS (and conflict, and malnutrition, and human trafficking, and so on) to flourish. Epidemiologists recognise that there are many reasons for disease epidemics, as encapsulated by the metaphor of the 'web of causation' (Holden 1995:15). Figure 4.1 shows HIV at the centre of a spider's web, with the factors that encourage the spread of HIV and compound the impacts of AIDS extending outwards. Nearest to the centre of the web are the bio-medical factors which influence the efficiency of HIV transmission, such as different types of HIV, and the susceptibility of the individual according to his or her state of health, including the presence of sexually transmitted infections. Beyond those medical factors lie the behavioural ones, such as the number of sexual partners, the age gap between them, and use of condoms. The web then stretches further out to the micro-environment in which people live, including social, cultural, and economic influences which affect their decision making and sexual behaviour, such as gender relations, poverty, and migration. The outside edges of the web concern the macro-environment of regional, and finally global, factors, including national wealth, income distribution, and the effects of conflict.

Figure 4.1 HIV/AIDS: the web of causation

From the perspective of controlling HIV and AIDS, it is widely assumed that if strands can be cut close to the centre of the web – by developing a vaccine, or through behaviour change – then there is no need to act upon the wider issues contributing to the pandemic. These wider issues, such as poverty and gender inequality, seem far more intractable than the medical and lifestyle problems near to the centre of the web. So although the role of inequity and under-development in influencing HIV transmission has become widely recognised, in terms of the response to AIDS the focus remains on the centre of the web. As Collins and Rau note, '...*while poverty is often cited in relation to HIV/AIDS, it has become something of a throwaway explanation. We can't do anything about poverty, we are told, so it makes more sense to concentrate on what we know best: individual behaviour change'* (Collins and Rau 2000:22). And as Eileen Stillwaggon observes:

> *The use of condoms can directly prevent cases of HIV transmission. Consequently, the most immediate short-term programme for AIDS prevention is provision of condoms. Given the expense of any prevention programme, the complexities of dealing with host governments with differing political agendas, and the seeming enormity of resolving the more fundamental causes of AIDS, prevention essentially stops there. AIDS, like other infectious diseases, is the result of all the complex and interrelated factors that exist in poor countries. Leaving prevention essentially to condom provision (and treatment of STIs) reinforces the notion that HIV transmission is narrowly the result of levels of sexual activity and fails to address other HIV determinants, such as general health, the effects of poverty, and gender relations.*
> (Stillwaggon 2000:990)

This book argues that effective responses to AIDS demand action in all parts of the web, through AIDS work (both medical and behavioural) *and* mainstreaming AIDS. This is particularly the case in countries with generalised HIV epidemics, where the opportunity to stop HIV from crossing over from population sub-groups to the wider population has been missed.

Interestingly, health problems are not necessarily solved by medicine alone; much of the decline in infectious diseases in the West, for example, was achieved by environmental changes such as improved sanitation, clean water supplies, and better nutrition and housing standards (Holden 1995:10). As Klouda notes, '*Health is primarily modulated by the social environment, and small further modulations are provided by services and information. Programmes which aim merely to provide the latter are unlikely to have (and so far have not had) much influence on health in general. It is like trying to put in the windows in a house before the walls are built'* (Klouda 1995:470). To use Klouda's metaphor, 'windows' such as the ABC of HIV prevention (A̲bstain! B̲e faithful! Use C̲ondoms!) are most useful to those people who have the 'walls' of education, economic independence, and relative control over their lives, but they are of little use – and potentially disempowering – to those who do not. However, in the absence of the means to provide the walls quickly, and in the context of narratives of urgency and the need to stop AIDS, AIDS-work 'windows' are seen as the appropriate response. The World Bank, for example, advocates that AIDS work can be bolted on by 'retrofitting' existing projects with AIDS components (World Bank 1999:37).

The default of embarking on AIDS work, regardless of the existing remit of the organisation, is most evident in the way in which HIV education is added on to other development initiatives. As a programme officer from ActionAid-Mozambique stated:

> *We have to recognise that this is the 'illness of the century', as they say. There can never be enough opportunities to try and spread the messages about prevention and care, so we have to use any chance that comes up. For example, if we are working in food security, we have to include messages not only on agricultural extension, but also on AIDS – because this eventually affects all our work.*
> (ActionAid-Mozambique Case Study 2001:4)

In some cases, adding AIDS-prevention work to existing work may be very straightforward. For example, in Malawi, the Ministry of Agriculture has sometimes included leaflets about AIDS inside packets of seeds (Oxfam GB 2001b:1) This is a low-cost means of disseminating basic AIDS information, though probably not very effective if done in isolation from other efforts. A more expensive strategy, which is promoted by the World Bank (World Bank 1999:56), is to invest in training agricultural extension workers to conduct AIDS education. In Zambia, extension staff have been trained in participatory information-sharing, facilitation, and basic counselling, and are said to have achieved *'some successes in passing on information'* (UNAIDS/GTZ 2002:14). The FAO reports, however, that in one of its projects, despite training, few extension workers discuss AIDS or hand out condoms, finding the issue of AIDS too awkward, and believing that it is a task for health workers (Topouzis and du Guerny 1999:55). In Malawi, the assessment of the Ministry of Agriculture was that the extension staff were not sufficiently trained to be specialists in HIV, and that there was little evidence of their efforts affecting behaviour.

(This is not surprising, given that even when it is undertaken by AIDS specialists, there is no guarantee that imparting information about AIDS will lead to behaviour change.) At the same time, the extension workers spent less time doing their much-needed agricultural development work, which was not adapted to meet the changing needs of AIDS-affected households and communities.[6]

In Uganda, recent research by the Ministry of Agriculture and FAO among farming households in four hard-hit parts of the country found that 77 per cent of the households were growing less food than ten years ago, and that 60 per cent had land which they were not using, for lack of labour. The research found high levels of knowledge about HIV transmission and the signs of AIDS, and four-fifths of the respondents said they had been exposed to AIDS education messages in the past three months. However, with regard to behaviour, two-thirds of respondents who were married or with a regular partner said that they had had sex with someone else in the past twelve months, and only fifteen per cent of all the respondents reported ever having used a condom. The report's recommendations recognise that extension workers need to pass on information which links HIV/AIDS and agricultural production, but greater emphasis is placed on needing to equip them with the skills to do AIDS education. The rationale is that *'the issue is not lack of knowledge, but rather behaviour change...the messages to be incorporated into agricultural extension should be able to empower the farmers and fishing folk to change risky behaviours...'* (MAAIF and FAO 2002:10). The analysis fails to acknowledge the improbability that such messages can empower people, and, although it notes how few extension agents there are, and how their work has suffered due to AIDS, it makes no provisions for how they will take on the extra burden of AIDS work.

There is no guarantee that imparting information about AIDS will lead to behaviour change.

The impulse to respond with AIDS education – to tell people about HIV so that they can (theoretically) protect themselves – seems constant across sectors. In Uganda, the aforementioned Kawempe Programme reports that *'...at the moment every NGO/CBO in the division has HIV/AIDS awareness as one of its programmes. The players are now many. There is a need to identify the unmet needs especially on care and rights of the infected and orphaned'* (SC UK Uganda Case Study 2001:5). In Vietnam, the NGO CARE came to the conclusion *'...HIV/AIDS should be part of every CARE project regardless of what "sector" has initiated it...to maximise the results of any programme, HIV/AIDS education must be part of it'* (CARE Vietnam 2001:1). A survey of 22 African micro-finance institutions found that the most common response to AIDS was to introduce AIDS education; only a few organisations had taken the mainstreaming route of changing the way in which they worked in order to serve their clients better in a time of AIDS (Development Alternatives Incorporated 2000:28). In general, the idea of a multi-sectoral response to AIDS is understood as introducing AIDS focal points and HIV-prevention activities in various ministries, and adding HIV/AIDS-specific initiatives to existing programmes (Topouzis 2001:32). From an individual's perspective, consider the thoughts of this development worker, from a CBO partner of Oxfam in Malawi which promotes dairy farming:

> *In the last two years, five out of the 150 farmers that we worked with have died. In all cases, the business has failed – either before their death or after it. We raise AIDS in our meetings, but we feel out of our depth – because people know about it, but don't change behaviour. We need serious input from others to encourage people to take action.*
> (Oxfam Malawi Case Study 2001:37)

The final sentence of this quotation provides an important clue to the drive for AIDS education. Whenever the response to AIDS focuses on AIDS education, then the change which is being sought is among the community members. In other words, if AIDS is the problem, then it is a problem of *their* behaviour, and *they* need to change if AIDS is to be stopped. This is in stark contrast to the mainstreaming approach, which starts with the premise that *organisations* may need to change the way in which they work, because AIDS is changing the very context of development work, and will continue to do so in the long term. However, such mainstreaming ideas appear, so far, to have been ignored, perhaps because they have been crowded out by the emphasis on AIDS work.

What else can we do?

A third reason for the predominance of AIDS work, and the relative obscurity of mainstreaming, is that there is a substantial body of experience in the former, and a lack of experience in the latter. The first responses to AIDS were direct, and since then it has been the approaches of prevention, care, and treatment which have been further developed, refined, and replicated. AIDS work is also the focus of most of the literature on AIDS, and of media attention to the issue. As a result, when an organisation considers what it can do, it is most likely to emulate existing AIDS-work approaches, and particularly the elements which appear to be comparatively straightforward: awareness raising and condom distribution. As few organisations have made the connections between their core business and its relevance to HIV transmission and the impacts of AIDS, and even fewer have documented their work, the notion of mainstreaming AIDS remains largely untested and unknown. One of the motivations behind this book is to promote thinking about mainstreaming, and raise its profile, in order that more development and humanitarian organisations might consider it as an option, alongside that of doing AIDS work.

Problems of integrating AIDS work into core programmes

This section does not review all the challenges that development and humanitarian organisations face when integrating AIDS, because many of those are faced also when mainstreaming, and will therefore be covered in Chapters 7 to 11. Instead, it outlines three main challenges specific to integrating AIDS work, and describes how they relate to the agenda for mainstreaming AIDS.

AIDS work may not be the community's priority

Some weeks ago I was in Malawi and I met with a group of women living with HIV. As I always do when I meet people living with AIDS and other community groups, I asked them what is their highest priority. Their answer was clear and unanimous: food. Not care, not drugs for treatment, not stigma, but food.
(Peter Piot, Executive Director of UNAIDS (Piot 2001))

ActionAid's Global HIV/AIDS Co-ordinator lists several obstacles to integrating AIDS work, among them the stark issue of *'overwhelming poverty; it is difficult to address HIV/AIDS and sexual and reproductive health issues if basic needs are not met'* (Bataringaya 2000b:2). This is a recurrent problem for agencies implementing AIDS work: poverty and other issues are the priority for community members, rather than AIDS. While this may be partly due to stigma and lack of awareness, and to the preference for 'hard benefits' such as schools (Bataringaya 2000b:2), it is always linked to the primacy of other problems. In the earlier example from SC UK in Ghana, only one of the 20 NGOs implementing the Family Health Reproductive Programme was responding to AIDS, because the communities' felt needs did not include HIV and AIDS, which is not surprising, given the comparatively low level of HIV infection in Ghana at the time.

One tactic, already illustrated by some of the case studies, is to meet people's priority needs first. To give another example, in India the NGO **Gram Bharati Samiti** found that the principal factor behind HIV transmission in Rajasthan was the unsafe behaviour of rural sex workers and their clients. However, the sex workers' priorities were not condoms and AIDS, but safe drinking water, general health care, and education for their children. Correspondingly, the NGO drilled a bore-hole, arranged primary health-care outreach, and started a primary school, before going on to do direct AIDS work (UK NGO AIDS Consortium 1996:56, 125). Cases such as this are rare, however. Although several have been outlined here, that is testimony to the fact that 'good practice' is more readily documented than the absence of good practice (Webb 2001:3). In most cases, organisations intending to do AIDS work are unable to respond first to such diverse higher-priority needs, lacking the time, funding, remit, and skills to do so. Instead, they proceed with their AIDS agenda. For example, a review by the NGO CAFOD and four of its partners engaged in AIDS work found that, despite high HIV prevalence in all the fieldwork locations, AIDS was never identified as the communities' main problem. In Malawi, the main problems listed by young men and young women included other stigmatised issues such as sexual violence, and alcohol and drugs, along with lack of employment, shortage of money, and unequal access to education. Very few of their priority issues were being addressed by development agencies, or any other institutions. In Zimbabwe, the disjunction between one local NGO's work and community needs was expressed vividly by the local Chief: '*You come to us with your AIDS programme, while we have a bigger problem of elephants destroying our fields. Why don't you ask the National Park to kill the elephants?*' (Smith and Howson 2000:94).

'You come to us with your AIDS programme, while we have a bigger problem of elephants destroying our fields. Why don't you ask the National Park to kill the elephants?'

Of course, in some cases, such as SC UK's Kawempe Programme in Uganda, the community does identify AIDS as a major problem, and NGOs can then respond and enjoy the support and participation of community members. But where target groups do not prioritise AIDS, NGOs intent on responding to AIDS face a difficult situation. The most effective strategy is to address AIDS through responding to related felt needs, as in the case of the Peruvian NGO IES described above, which integrated AIDS within a broader agenda of rights and sexual and reproductive health. However, the links between AIDS and other issues – safe drinking water, or indeed, elephants – do not lend themselves so easily to integration. An organisation may decide that AIDS work is a priority, even if the community does not realise this, but it is unlikely thereby to engage the community and so maximise the impact of its work.

With mainstreaming, however, the dilemma of whether AIDS is a community priority does not apply, because the aim is not to implement direct AIDS work, but to modify existing work as necessary. The focus of the work remains as before, with the extent and types of adaptation dependent upon the kind of project, the transmission of HIV, and the local impacts of AIDS. Mainstreaming, then, avoids the danger of imposing AIDS work, because it is about addressing AIDS indirectly, through development and humanitarian work which – ideally – does meet communities' priorities.

AIDS work is not the responsibility of every profession

As this chapter has already noted, the idea of an expanded or multi-sectoral response to AIDS is often understood as requiring all sectors, and all development workers, to take on responsibility for responding directly to HIV and AIDS. The question of whether they have the capacity to do this, and the possible opportunity costs in terms of being diverted from their core work, are rarely mentioned. This idea of other sectors getting involved in AIDS work is most commonly expressed, and implemented, through non-health field workers taking on the role of AIDS educators. One of the main problems faced by those promoting AIDS work in all sectors is that the sectors and individuals in them fail to embrace and act upon the idea. As ActionAid-Ethiopia's HIV/AIDS Officer states:

> *Many development workers are still not convinced of taking AIDS work as their responsibility. For many, AIDS is still a health issue. While many people agree that AIDS affects all sectors of development and everyone can contribute something to curb its spread, in practice taking AIDS as one's responsibility has still not been internalised.*
> (ActionAid-Ethiopia Case Study, 2001:6)

Another constraint, identified by ActionAid-Uganda and ActionAid-Mozambique, is lack of time for the addition of AIDS work: *'the problem of too much workload in doing development work at the same time as sensitising people about HIV/AIDS'* (ActionAid-Uganda Case Study 2001:16). Lack of time points to two likely repercussions: that the AIDS work may not be of good quality, and that squeezing it in may have negative impacts on the quality of core development work. Furthermore, overloading development workers can affect morale and cause resentment. Within one bilateral development organisation, staff were very concerned that plans to integrate HIV/AIDS would increase their already heavy workload. One senior manager commented that *'integrated rural development projects are not a vendor's tray to be loaded with each and every topic'* (Hemrich and Toupouzis 2000:88). In a similar vein, a review of micro-finance institutions found that many professionals were wary of getting involved with HIV and AIDS issues. Their common refrain was *'we cannot get embroiled in the social problems of our clients. We can't solve all their problems for them'* (Donahue et al. 2001:29).

SafAIDS – the Southern Africa AIDS Information Dissemination Service – has identified five main reasons why development NGOs have largely failed to embark on AIDS work (Jackson et al. 1999:34). Two have already been mentioned: that communities do not name AIDS as a key issue; and that the organisations are already over-stretched with other issues. The other factors are that NGOs see ASOs as the experts, who are more capable of doing AIDS work; that NGOs are deterred by the specialist language which has developed around AIDS work; and that many NGOs see AIDS as a health problem, so if they do not have a health programme they see AIDS as outside their mandate.

Overall, these problems stem from the notion that doing direct AIDS work is something that every sector, and every development worker, should do. A key weakness of the direct response to AIDS, then, is that it entails the initiation and incorporation of new and unfamiliar AIDS work. Moreover, often agencies attempt to do this without adequate resources, both human and financial. And generally, there are risks attached to the decision to diversify, when undertaken without sufficient planning and resources, as organisational development specialist Rick James attests:

> There are many cases among development organisations, as well as from the private sector, that demonstrate the dangers of organisations drifting from their core business, without careful consideration of the consequences. In general, investment and attention is diverted to the new programmes and so the quality of the core work suffers, plus the organisation may not have the necessary expertise to undertake the new work properly.[7]

The direct response to AIDS is very different from external mainstreaming of AIDS, which aims to modify – rather than add to – existing work. Although mainstreaming still requires time and energy, it does not demand that all development workers must internalise their responsibility for AIDS work, but instead that they bring AIDS into focus as another important influence on the lives and prospects of the people with whom they work. They do not need to take on the extra burden of AIDS work, but to consider if they need to make any changes to the way they work in the light of the changes wrought by AIDS. And while development NGOs may call on the specialist help of ASOs – particularly with regard to internal mainstreaming – in external mainstreaming they remain the experts, because the focus remains on their core work. Moreover, because mainstreaming does not require AIDS work, agencies do not need to learn the jargon of AIDS work. Finally, while direct AIDS work may be beyond the mandate of some NGOs, the concept of mainstreaming proposes that no development organisation is excused from responding indirectly to AIDS. In this sense, mainstreaming broadens the response to AIDS, and provides a strategy which may prove more palatable across all sectors than undertaking AIDS work.

AIDS work is only part of the response

This chapter has already challenged the idea of AIDS work being *the* solution to AIDS, arguing that there is no obvious solution, and that as such AIDS is here to stay. However, even when AIDS work is not seen to be the solution as such, it is still largely perceived as the only possible response to AIDS. In other words, any organisation seeking to address AIDS must select from the menu of existing AIDS-work initiatives, including education, condom promotion, STI treatment, voluntary counselling and testing, treatment and care, support to HIV-positive people, and orphan support. It is these activities which currently count as 'responding to AIDS'; the alternative or additional strategy of doing wider development and humanitarian work, but with AIDS mainstreamed in it, is not on the menu, and is barely considered. This is partly because the idea of mainstreaming is underdeveloped, and there is little experience so far for agencies to learn from and emulate.

The concept of mainstreaming proposes that no development organisation is excused from responding indirectly to AIDS.

ActionAid-Uganda's case study for this book reported: *'ActionAid-Uganda has taken HIV/AIDS as an issue deterring development of the area in terms of agriculture and is working with partners who are more on the ground in the fight against AIDS. They have embarked on sensitisation, and have carried out a number of seminars, video shows that focus on HIV/AIDS matters relating to prevention and morals, and provision of condoms.'* The sense conveyed by this case study, like others, is that the organisation has responded to AIDS. While none claims to have addressed AIDS exhaustively, they can at least be satisfied that they are doing, or funding, AIDS work. Thus, on an imaginary checklist of development problems, many organisations are able to tick the box marked 'HIV/AIDS'. With the category ticked, there is little need to think about further, less direct, and less explicit responses to AIDS. To take one of the examples described at the beginning of this chapter, the Zuuri Organic Vegetable Farmer's Association responded first to the priority issue of female genital mutilation, before embarking on AIDS work. However, the task of mainstreaming AIDS in its core work was left undone. A decision to mainstream AIDS would have involved its area of expertise – organic farming – and the farmers with whom it already had a trusting relationship; for example, aiming to help farmers to build up their assets so that they are less vulnerable to the impacts of AIDS. Instead, embarking on AIDS work entailed an entirely new work area – sexual health – and the need to build new relationships within the community and with institutions such as the Ministry of Health. However effective the resulting AIDS work might be, the risk is that the organisation's core work remains blind to AIDS. And, as the next chapter will explore more fully, that core work might be unwittingly enhancing susceptibility to HIV infection, or making households more vulnerable to the impacts of AIDS, when it could be contributing to the response to AIDS by reducing susceptibility and helping people to cope with AIDS.

Of course, not all organisations do AIDS work. Some realise that they do not have the expertise or capacity to embark on any of the activities currently on the AIDS-work menu. Having decided to concentrate on their own work and leave AIDS work to others, they mark their imaginary checklist with a cross by 'HIV/AIDS'. Again, these organisations fail to consider the basic strategy of responding indirectly through mainstreaming, because that option does not appear on the current menu. As earlier chapters have argued, direct AIDS work is very important and much needed. However, this book proposes that AIDS work needs to be complemented by mainstreaming by all development and humanitarian organisations, if the response to the AIDS pandemic is truly to be expanded.

Summary

This chapter has described a range of cases of stand-alone AIDS work, and cases where direct responses to AIDS have been integrated with other development work. It has proposed that these examples are broadly representative of the kinds of response to AIDS which development agencies have, to date, initiated. The chapter has also attempted to unravel some of the reasons behind the dominance of AIDS work as the only response to AIDS. It has suggested three key factors: the short-term ideal of stopping AIDS rather than coping with it; the focus on the problem of AIDS and its nearest determinants, rather than the wider influences and shortcomings of the development process; and the limited alternative provided by mainstreaming, as a currently under-developed and little practised strategy.

The final section of the chapter outlined three problems with the strategy of integration: that AIDS work may not be a priority for community members; that AIDS work is not the responsibility of every sector and every profession; and that AIDS work is only part of the response to AIDS. The section proposed that the strategy of mainstreaming AIDS does not face the first two problems, and that the menu of appropriate responses to AIDS should be expanded to include mainstreaming AIDS in development and humanitarian work. The next chapter will explore in more detail the argument for mainstreaming, and the proposal that development and humanitarian organisations should mainstream AIDS as a basic initial strategy in their response, while also undertaking AIDS work where they have sufficient capacity.

5 Why mainstream AIDS?

Introduction

There is a bewildering array of new and not-so-new concepts in the development world, as fashions in approaches to development come and go. Mainstreaming is currently a popular prescription, advocated as being the way for all sectors to get involved in fighting AIDS. This chapter explores the arguments for mainstreaming, as it is understood in this book. It goes on to respond to some of the possible objections to mainstreaming, and concludes by discussing the implications in terms of how development and humanitarian organisations respond to HIV and AIDS. Owing to the limited experience of mainstreaming AIDS to date among development agencies, much of the argument is theoretical rather than derived from evidence.

Mainstreaming AIDS externally

Given that many problems arising from the epidemic are not specific to HIV/AIDS, policy and programme responses need not be HIV/AIDS-specific but must address the root causes and consequences of the wider challenges to rural development. In other words, a developmental rather than an AIDS-specific focus is critical to tackling the multi-sectoral complexity of the epidemic and its systemic impact and to ensuring the sustainability of both HIV/AIDS responses and rural development efforts.
(Topouzis 1998:17)

In Chapter 2, Figure 2.2 (page 36) illustrated how development work can contribute to a virtuous circle, interacting positively with HIV prevention and AIDS care to reduce susceptibility to HIV infection, and vulnerability to the impacts of AIDS. That chapter also argued that development work, in all its variety, ought to tackle both sides of the causes and consequences model shown in Figure 2.1 (page 26). In an ideal world, these positive dynamics between development and AIDS work would occur without special effort; the development work would be totally participatory, and always attuned to the variable needs, abilities, vulnerabilities, and options of different sections of the community. In the real world this is not the case. Development work may fail to exploit opportunities for reducing susceptibility to HIV infection, and for helping people to become less vulnerable to the impacts of AIDS.

Significantly, development work may even have negative effects, unintentionally increasing susceptibility and vulnerability. The idea that development work could be working with, rather than against, AIDS – making things worse rather than better – seems unlikely, but there are several potential risks, which this section considers under three headings. It is important to note that the negative effects listed here are things which can and do happen, but this is not to say that development and humanitarian work always has these unwanted effects, nor to detract from its opposite and positive impacts.

Development and humanitarian work can increase susceptibility to HIV infection

Effective development work undermines the causes of susceptibility to HIV infection, by empowering poor comunities, alleviating poverty, raising the status of women, and improving public services. However, as ActionAid's HIV/AIDS Co-ordinator recognises, *'our development work may unwittingly have created conditions that have facilitated the spread of HIV'* (Bataringaya 2000a:1). This is a rare and important admission, and a possibility which few agencies have acknowledged. One problem that she identifies is that

> *the presence of development workers in communities has created a new 'social caste' that has disposable income available throughout the year – in contrast to community members who may depend on harvest seasons. Separation of ActionAid staff from their spouses, and the cash they can offer sexual partners in the community, may lead to behaviour that increases vulnerability to HIV.*
> (Bataringaya 2000a:1).

Or, in the words of an ActionAid-Uganda employee, *'ActionAid staff are looked at as economic heavy weights, so local women are drawn to them'* (ActionAid-Uganda 1998:20). In such situations, heightened suscept-ibility to HIV infection is experienced by both development workers and community members, and this may sometimes be exacerbated by an organisation's actions. For example, the Ministry of Education in Ghana has noted that its teachers often

> *fall either in the category of those with high financial liquidity or the poorly resourced, as a result of the late reimbursement or payment of salaries. In the latter case the female teacher is at the mercy of those who can provide funds,*

*and in the former especially the males become much 'sought after' and have
more bargaining power for sexual negotiations.*
(Ghana Ministry of Education 2002:x)

Unsafe sex between development workers and community members may
not always be consensual; while the scale of the problem is unknown, it is
clear that individuals may use their position and control over resources to
exploit others. This may be particularly the case in emergency situations.
One Oxfam GB worker believes that *'abuse isn't just linked to stress – more
often to simply taking advantage of the opportunity to enforce one's will on
others. Those involved run the spectrum from drivers, warehousemen, project
officers and so on; many are actually members of the host community, and are
dealing with people who may be displaced from other areas, perhaps speaking
different languages, members of different religions, and who will probably leave
later. So it's easy to take advantage. Kosovo, Timor, Mozambique – it can
happen anywhere.*[1] His view is supported by a recent investigation by UNHCR
and Save the Children UK in West African refugee camps, which found
evidence of a *'chronic and entrenched pattern'* of abuse against girls, mostly
involving locally employed workers for international NGOs. More than 40
organisations – including some of the most respected – and 67
individuals were implicated in allegations that aid was withheld unless
paid for by sexual favours. The report states that *'girl children have found
that they have to use their bodies to provide food, clothing, and at times
educational support, for themselves, their parents and their siblings....
Unfortunately, humanitarian agencies have created a conducive environment
in which sexual exploitation has thrived'* (Gillan 2002).

The unwelcome notion that the benefits of development may sometimes
be used as leverage for sexual abuse, or for trading sexual services, also
extends to those community members who are given control over
development resources. During an ActionAid-Uganda seminar, development staff realised that the appointed caretakers in water projects are
usually older men, while the water collectors are generally young women
and girls. They did not know if abuse occurred, but recognised the risks
inherent in ActionAid giving the responsibility – and so the power – to the
men (ActionAid-Uganda 1998). As Chapter 3 noted, it is also the case that
people can acquire power through seizing control of development
resources. In refugee camps, for example, self-appointed water monitors
have used their control over scarce water supplies to coerce women into
providing sexual favours (UK NGO AIDS Consortium 1997:6).

In setting up and running camps for refugees or displaced people, humanitarian agencies make many decisions which indirectly relate to HIV transmission. Some of the layout features known to foster sexual violence are communal latrines, tap-stands located far away from dwellings, and inadequate lighting. Rapes are more likely to take place if girls and women have to leave the camp to gather firewood or water, and if unaccompanied girls and women are sheltered unsuitably, for instance on the edge of the camp (UK NGO AIDS Consortium 1997:9). Distribution systems also have implications for HIV transmission. In addition to the potential for abuse by staff and community members who are involved in the distribution, if some people do not get their fair share they may have to trade sexual favours in order to gain access to food, clothing, and other essential items (ibid.:9, Marshall 1995:1). Distribution via male heads of households makes it more likely that women who head households, and unaccompanied girls and boys, will not obtain rations. As a worker in the humanitarian relief programme in northern Iraq in 1991 recalls,

> *When a few refugees took over food distribution after days of utter confusion, we thought we'd achieved a lot. Later however, UNHCR staff realised that food was not going to families headed by women. Only then did they notice that all the distributors they had appointed were men. The result: malnutrition, exploitation, suffering.*
> (WHO 2000:30)

Successful development projects may also, paradoxically, increase the likelihood of HIV transmission. For example, effective income-generating projects increase the amount of cash in households, which, it is assumed, is beneficial because the money will be spent on food, health care, and education. However, the additional money may also be spent on alcohol and sex, be it through buying sexual services commercially or through maintaining other relationships. This is less likely to happen where women have control over the additional income. Similarly, improving access to markets allows farmers and other producers to get a better price for their products, but the result is that male farmers are away from home with an unusually large amount of money (Mullins 2000:3). Such situations relate directly to HIV susceptibility, because they tend to result in increased numbers of sexual partners, and a greater likelihood of unsafe sex. They also link indirectly to heightened susceptibility to HIV infection, through the friction caused in households, and the resulting increases in extra-marital relationships and divorce. During research by CARE in Malawi, women said that when a man has money in his hand, his extra-marital sexual partners benefit more than his wife, so there is the temptation for wives to seek other partners. The women also felt that many women have more sexual partners when they find that their husband has been unfaithful, *'to get even with their husbands'* (Shah et al. 2002:75). These repercussions are far from what NGOs envisage when they set out to raise household incomes.

Income-generating projects aimed at women may also bring unanticipated problems. For example, businesses such as selling tea at night, brewing beer, or travelling to trade fish are all, in the opinion of ActionAid-Uganda staff, potentially linked to higher risks of unsafe sex for the women involved (ActionAid-Uganda 1998:18). In northern Uganda, the NGO ACORD discourages women in its income-generating programme from establishing beer-brewing businesses, due to its links to violence and unsafe sex (ACORD Case Study 2002:4). Moreover, empowering women – through literacy programmes, or supporting them to reject violence, or to refuse unsafe sex – may have unpredictable outcomes. A woman who escapes from an exploitative relationship but lacks economic independence is likely to turn to another man, or a series of men, for support.

Projects to increase household incomes may also intensify inequalities between men and women; for example, the promotion of cash crops may mean that women's food crops are displaced by the cultivation of male-controlled varieties. The women lose the production that was in their charge, but still have to feed their families; they contribute their labour to the cash crops, but the money from the sale of the harvest is in the men's hands (Wallace 1996:6). Women are left with less power, and both men and women are inadvertently rendered more susceptible to HIV infection.

Finally, large-scale infrastructure projects have many unplanned effects on local people's lives, including their sexual health. The intrusion of moneyed and unaccompanied construction workers into an area is associated with rising STI rates, as has been documented in Malawi with regard to road construction, and in Lesotho following the Highland Water Project (Thompson and Whiteside 1999:8). Local women are more likely to offer sexual services to construction workers if the infrastructure project displaces them from their land, as occurred in the well-known case of the Akosombo River Dam in Ghana. Thirty years after its construction, and via an unforeseen chain of events, the rural district adjoining the dam had HIV-infection rates some five to ten times higher than the national average (Topouzis and du Guerny 1999:24). On a smaller scale, ActionAid-Uganda staff have observed greater mobility in a project area where the NGO had improved the roads, and posited that more travel for trading could be linked to HIV transmission (ActionAid-Uganda 1998:13). Significant improvements in transport infrastructure are also known to stimulate labour migration, leading to more families being separated for long periods of time, and an associated rise in numbers of sexual partners.

Of course, the implication of the problems outlined in this sub-section is not that development activities must stop, in order to avoid undesirable repercussions. Rather, the point is to call attention to the potentially negative implications of development and humanitarian efforts, which, through mainstreaming AIDS, agencies and communities may be able to avoid or at least reduce.

Development and humanitarian work may increase vulnerability to the impacts of AIDS

If development and humanitarian agencies always knew, and responded effectively to, the changing needs of individuals and families in the communities whom they served, their work would, by default, help households to cope with the consequences of AIDS. Development projects would benefit families who already had a member living with AIDS, and not-yet-affected households which might, in the future, face similar problems. However, where agencies are not in tune with the changes brought by AIDS, their work may inadvertently make households more vulnerable to the impacts of AIDS, and so compound its negative consequences.

In general, this may happen when the mode of development is poorly suited to the situation faced by those badly affected by AIDS. For example, a development organisation may promote activities, such as agricultural practices, which require a lot of labour. Or it may encourage new methods which are dependent on cash outlay, such as encouraging farmers to buy seeds which are thought to be more productive, rather than to save their own seeds. New methods of cultivation, harvesting, or processing may also be dependent on cash expenditure, whether for inputs such as pesticides, or for the hire or purchase of equipment. In some cases, agencies' ideas may entail higher inputs of labour and cash, such as labour-intensive cash crops requiring chemical dressing, or new methods of irrigation requiring high maintenance of channels and expenditure on pumps.

Without AIDS the innovations may be very successful: with sufficient labour and investment, the cash crops are profitable, and the irrigation leads to much higher yields. Even in communities with high HIV prevalence, the majority of people are not infected, and there are some families who are not badly affected. Development programmes might work with those less affected individuals and households, who may participate and benefit from the innovations for some time. However, when AIDS strikes, there is the risk that what was beneficial becomes burdensome. The extra demands on labour are debilitating, and medical and funeral costs compete with the cash needs of the new practices. The effects of AIDS may mean that households which were initially suited to the new practices can no longer cope with them. If they have turned land for food crops over to cash crops, or fallen into debt, households may be less able to cope with the impacts of AIDS than if they had not taken up the innovations.

It is important to note that the single label 'AIDS-affected' covers a wide range of circumstances. It is difficult to generalise about the impacts of AIDS, given that households have differing starting points in terms of their composition and resources, and that they react differently when they are affected directly or indirectly by AIDS. However, some analysts have presented general schemes identifying degrees of impacts, according to different circumstances. An example based on work in sub-Saharan Africa is given in Table 5.1, focusing on how AIDS increases poverty and increases labour constraints. Clearly, the situation is dynamic. A household might begin as moderately affected, with two adults caring for a relative's orphans, then become severely affected if the

Table 5.1: Impacts of AIDS on households in terms of increasing poverty and labour constraints

Moderate	Two adults caring for orphans
	Two adults nursing a sick relative
Severe	Widow caring for orphans
	One adult nursing a sick relative
	Grandmother caring for orphans
	Main bread-winner suffering from AIDS-related infections
Very severe	HIV+ widow caring for orphans
	HIV+ wife nursing her sick husband/relative
	Children nursing a sick parent/relative
	Orphans fending for themselves

(Source: Page 2002:28 – reprinted with the permission of the author)

bread-winner falls ill, and then very severely affected if, in time, the task of caring for the sick parents fall to the children.

The limitation of the phrase 'AIDS-affected' is that it masks differing levels of impacts of AIDS among community members, and differing levels of vulnerability to those impacts, both between and within households. As this chapter will explore later, mainstreaming AIDS entails development and humanitarian workers having a better under-standing of, and ability to respond to, these differences.

Development and humanitarian work may exclude households affected by AIDS

The HIV/AIDS epidemic and strategies for mitigating its impact are often not given specific attention by rural development workers. Projects operating in high-prevalence areas inadvertently bypass the households struck by the epidemic, as those households have neither time nor resources to participate in, and benefit from, project activities. This frequently leads to further marginalisation and destitution of affected households.
(FAO 2001: point 34)

If development work is not tuned to the consequences of AIDS and the needs of affected households, then it will often exclude them, albeit unintentionally, from the development process and its benefits. In the example above, any household already directly experiencing AIDS would be unlikely to take up cultivation of cash crops, or new irrigation methods. The inability to participate might be due not only to the lack of sufficient labour or capital: other potential barriers are social stigma – whether perceived or real – and the time needed to participate in the project. Exclusion may occur even if the project's target group implicitly includes households affected by AIDS. For example, a Zambian programme designed to serve food-insecure households – which would include many families directly affected by AIDS – found that it was not reaching them; the reason was believed to be the investment of time required by participation (Topouzis and du Guerny 1999:42).

In general, members of AIDS-affected households, and particularly girls and women, are less likely to take advantage of development opportunities, such as literacy programmes and capacity-building exercises, or awareness-raising events. A detailed Tanzanian study of how one woman cared for her sick husband found that she halved the time that she spent on village activities and on agriculture, in order to look after him. Moreover, she was unable to participate in community activities regularly, or with any predictability, because her availability depended on his state of health, which, as is typical of AIDS, was very variable. The same study found that children from affected households were doing much more work than is culturally expected in childhood (Rugalema 1999:43). Not surprisingly, orphans are less likely to attend school; 1998 data from rural Zambia showed that they are almost twice as likely to be out of school as their peers with parents (Kelly 1999:4), and a Guatemalan study found that more than a third of children orphaned by AIDS drop out of school (Loewenson and Whiteside 2001:9). While unaffordable investments of time and cash are the usual reasons for such forms of exclusion, in some cases people may actually be ejected from projects. In particular, micro-finance groups often require members' regular attendance at meetings, and consistent adherence to savings and loan repayment schedules. These rules – which keep the groups together and impose monetary discipline – may mean that AIDS-affected members are excluded from the groups (Donahue et al. 2001:3). In the following case, the exclusion prevented the client from rebuilding her business and so recovering from the consequences of AIDS.

Mary was a micro-finance client in rural Uganda who spared no expense in trying to help her two adult children to regain their health ... she sold her own assets and took time away from her business to attend to them... when the first child died, the grandchildren became Mary's responsibility. She sold some of her land to pay hospital bills, and by the time her second child died, her business was dead too. More orphans came to live with her. Throughout all this she did not default on her loan, but sent someone to the micro-finance group meetings to make her repayments. But when she went back to her group, they had pushed her out because of poor attendance. They allowed her to continue saving with them, but refused to accept her as a lending member. She says 'I scratch around, but I can't start anything big because I don't have enough cash to restart my business. I cannot get that sum of cash by my own personal means. Caring for my children drained all my resources, but I still know how to run a business, I still have my skills.'
(Abridged with permission from Donahue et al. 2001:7)

Another form of exclusion stems from the failure of development agencies to update their targeting strategies as household structures change. A focus on working with men as heads of households automatically excludes the increasing numbers of novel, and highly vulnerable, households in AIDS-affected communities: those comprising grandparents and orphans, orphans living without adults, and female-headed households. Although the proportion of these novel households may be significant – back in 1997 seven per cent of Zambian households were thought to be headed by a child under the age of fourteen (Kelly 1999:2) – standard development work may simply pass them by. In 1988, a FAO survey found that globally only seven per cent of agricultural extension resources were directed at young farmers – not to mention children – and just five per cent were focused on female farmers (Baier 1997:11).

Exclusion is also likely to result where development staff have judgemental attitudes towards people affected by AIDS. This is a poorly researched topic, but it is clear that some staff feel that some people with AIDS are paying the price for their 'promiscuous' behaviour. In situations where demand exceeds supply, workers might ration project benefits in favour of certain people (such as 'innocent' AIDS widows and orphans), while discriminating against those thought to be responsible for their infection (such as sex workers and men with multiple partners). Although such discrimination is not documented, it is known that the attitudes of health staff lead to discrimination: for example, in the treatment of young unmarried people who have STIs or who are pregnant.[2]

Where development agencies do not notice, or confront, stigmatisation from within the community, they implicitly condone discrimination against people with HIV and AIDS.

Another likely form of exclusion stems from assumptions about the worth of people with AIDS. If they are seen to be 'as good as dead', there will be a bias against including people with AIDS in project activities, even during periods of improved health. This discrimination may extend to the spouses of people with AIDS, if people judge that those spouses are likely also to develop AIDS. A third element of potential discrimination arises out of development workers' denial of, and distaste for, AIDS. It seems safe to assume that individuals who are trying to convince themselves that they are not at risk of HIV, or who wish to avoid meeting people who are visibly affected by AIDS, will be biased against interacting with affected community members. In addition, where development agencies do not notice, or confront, stigmatisation from within the community, they implicitly condone discrimination against people with HIV and AIDS. This also applies to attitudes and behaviours within organisations where, for example, someone suspected of being HIV-positive may be discriminated against in terms of training and promotion opportunities, and more generally stigmatised.

Finally, and significantly, AIDS-affected households are likely to be under-represented in consultations about community needs, and in community forums. Their members are also less likely to take on responsibilities through development structures such as village development committees. The failure to include them at the needs- assessment stage of the project cycle makes their exclusion at subsequent stages even more probable.

AIDS undermines development work

In the past, one could travel up-country and be dropped off, and ask 'where is the funeral?'; people now reply 'which funeral?', and the wailing from many funerals in the same locality can be heard.
(Human-resource manager, working in Kenya (Save the Children UK 2001:14))

The previous three sections have shown how development work may, unwittingly, increase people's susceptibility to HIV transmission and vulnerability to the impacts of AIDS. This is not to criticise the way in which development work changes things – by making people more mobile, or raising expectations of greater gender equity – but to note the potential for such work to produce unintended negative repercussions with regards to HIV and AIDS. The rationale behind external mainstreaming of AIDS is that some of those adverse effects of programme work could be avoided, and that organisations could proactively exploit opportunities to address susceptibility to HIV transmission and the vulnerability to the impacts of AIDS, indirectly through development work. There is, however, another stark argument for external mainstreaming: ignoring AIDS leads to failed development work. Even if that work does not have any of the negative effects outlined above, in countries which are hard hit by AIDS, continuing with 'business as usual' means ineffective, or less effective, development work.

International development goals

A clear illustration of the problem of the 'business as usual' approach is seen when projects are planned, and objectives formed, without regard for the projected impacts of HIV and AIDS. For example, in 1997, the Development Assistance Committee of the Organisation for Economic Cooperation and Development produced a list of bilateral development priorities and goals. These included having equal numbers of boys and girls in school by 2005, ensuring universal primary education in all countries by 2015, and halving the proportion of people living in extreme poverty by 2015. None of the goals took AIDS into account, and, partly because of AIDS (in addition to other factors such as insufficient political and financial commitment), it is arguable that none of them is achievable within the stated timeframes (Badcock-Walters and Whiteside 2000:1). In 2000, 150 world leaders agreed an updated set of targets, called the Millennium Development Goals. One of the seven goals is to combat HIV/AIDS, malaria, and other diseases, with the AIDS-specific target of halting and reversing the spread of HIV by 2015. While it is commendable that the leaders singled out HIV/AIDS, so highlighting the significance of AIDS for development, the problem remains that, at least in sub-Saharan Africa, the goals are unrealistic. A review by ActionAid of progress towards the Millennium Development Goals states:

> *Over and over again African countries appear at the bottom of the human development indicators. Child death rates and maternal mortality are increasing; one in three children is malnourished; one in five people is affected by conflict; almost half the population of the continent is living on less than $1 a day; and life expectancy is falling. On current trends sub-Saharan Africa will become even poorer in the next 15 years and fail to meet all of the goals.*

(ActionAid Alliance 2002:9)

More recently, African leaders have created the New Partnership for Africa's Development (NEPAD), whose goals include accelerated economic growth and the eradication of poverty. In a 60-page document, however, AIDS is referred to only four times, in the context of a range of communicable diseases which require action. The plan states in passing that *'unless these epidemics [of communicable diseases, in particular HIV/AIDS, tuberculosis and malaria] are brought under control, real gains in human development will remain a pipe dream'* (NEPAD 2001: point 128). However, the proposed actions are limited to the health sector, and the plan lacks any recognition of the need for action across all sectors in order to address AIDS. As such, the leaders do not seem to have accounted for the way in which HIV and AIDS may contribute to making NEPAD's aims rather improbable (Akukwe 2002). Each of these cases illustrates how, despite more sophisticated understandings of AIDS as a complex development issue, it may be over-simplified and perceived as merely related to health care, rather than being mainstreamed within policy development.

Capacity building and participation

If development objectives are to be realised in the context of the AIDS pandemic, development agencies need to understand the ways in which AIDS undermines their efforts. Capacity building is a popular development strategy which is directly affected by AIDS. Where levels of HIV infection are high, it is inevitable that some of the trainees will develop AIDS, and their skills will be lost. In Malawi, for example, an FAO 'training of trainers' programme was threatened by the deaths of one in four of the trainers (Topouzis and du Guerny 1999:55). In situations where the skills base is being eroded by AIDS, it may be more pragmatic to plan training programmes aimed at capacity *maintenance*, rather than capacity building.

At the general level, as already argued, AIDS inhibits the participation of affected households, because labour is diverted to care for the sick and to the increased burden of everyday tasks as the dependency ratio rises. If agencies do not assess the needs of AIDS-affected households, and those households do not participate in the project activities, then the development process will certainly fail them. However, AIDS can also interfere with community-wide participation if frequent funerals and mourning periods disrupt work. In Zimbabwe, the effects on one development initiative – animal-dip tanks – have been evident in the closure of the tanks on funeral days, and the fact that fewer farmers can find the time to dip their livestock. Tick-borne diseases were on the increase (Munyombwe et al. 1999:27). In Southern Africa, the FAO found that on average farmers miss one in six of its pest-management training sessions because they are attending funerals and visiting the sick (Topouzis and du Guerny 1999:54). Moreover, in Zimbabwe and Namibia, researchers found that agricultural extension staff have been spending at least ten per cent of their time attending funerals (Engh et al. 2000:5, Ncube 1999:17). Of course, funeral customs can and do change, but these examples illustrate how AIDS may affect community participation in, and hence the success of, development activities.

The FAO estimates that Uganda had, by the year 2000, already lost twelve per cent of its agricultural labour force to AIDS.

Agriculture

In agriculture, the impacts of AIDS stem from a combination of reductions in the quality and quantity of labour, loss of skills and experience, and sales or confiscation of productive assets.

Part of the loss of labour is due to women spending less time on farming while they are caring for someone with AIDS; in an Ethiopian study, AIDS-affected households were found to be spending only two-fifths of the time that non-affected families were devoting to agriculture (Loewenson and Whiteside 2001:10). Productive labour time may be lost through attendance at funerals and observing mourning customs. In the worst-affected parts of Namibia, research in 2000 found that farmers were sometimes losing more than a quarter of the time available for critical production tasks such as sowing and weeding (Engh et al. 2000:5). Where farming systems need certain tasks to be done at certain times, production may be particularly vulnerable to the effects of AIDS.

The bulk of labour loss, however, is due to deaths from AIDS. The FAO estimates that Uganda had, by the year 2000, already lost twelve per cent of its agricultural labour force to AIDS. By 2020, Namibia is forecast to lose a quarter of the people working in the agricultural sector (FAO 2001: Table 2). In East Africa, labour shortages have already produced many documented effects at the household level, including less land cultivated; delayed activities such as planting and weeding; more pests; loss of soil fertility; fewer crops per household; decline in livestock production; and lower yields. There have also been shifts from cash crops to subsistence crops, and from labour-intensive crops, such as bananas and beans, to less demanding – and often less nutritious – foods such as cassava and sweet potato (Baier 1997:5, Topouzis 2001:4). A study found similar shifts in crops in Thailand, along with a reduction in the area under rice cultivation (Barnett and Whiteside 2002:231). In Zimbabwe, over five years, agricultural output in one communal area declined by almost 50 per cent among households affected by AIDS, compared with those not directly affected (Topouzis 2001:3). Reduced yields and fewer crops are directly linked to deepening poverty and poorer nutrition. Furthermore, deaths among farmers are weakening the agricultural skills base, with many unable to pass their knowledge on to their children before AIDS intervenes through illness and death.

Deaths among farmers are weakening the agricultural skills base, with many unable to pass their knowledge on to their children before AIDS intervenes through illness and death.

The harsh consequences of AIDS for subsistence farming are also caused by diversion of cash to the treatment and burial of household members. Livelihood security is further undermined when household resources are depleted, by using up savings, and selling equipment, land, or livestock, in order to raise money for health care, funeral costs, or basic needs. A study in Thailand found that two-fifths of affected households disposed of land after the death of an adult (Loewenson and Whiteside 2001:10). Some households have enough resources to withstand the depletion, and to maintain production by hiring in labour. However, for others the loss of labour and of productive assets causes a rapid and permanent fall in their standard of living (Richards 1999:105, Shah et al. 2002:60). All of these impacts on agriculture make for a very difficult context for agricultural extension work, but it is clear that for projects to be successful, they need to take the impacts of AIDS into account. Where AIDS has a strong hold, projects aiming to increase overall production may be unachievable, and established working strategies may be irrelevant. For example, in sub-Saharan Africa, agricultural policies are generally based on the now questionable assumption that there is a plentiful supply of labour (Topouzis 2001:xii). As the FAO has noted with regard to State interventions, *'the pertinence of certain MoA policies and strategies may be called into question, given the conditions created by the HIV epidemic'* (Topouzis 2001:viii).

The far-reaching repercussions of AIDS on agriculture became evident in the 2002–2003 food crisis in Southern Africa, where the impacts of AIDS are generally acknowledged to have been a significant influence, among a range of other factors. For example, an FAO/WFP study in Malawi in 2002 identified a number of links between AIDS and the onset of household food insecurity. These included the loss of able-bodied labour in households, the loss of remittances from working family members, the additional challenge of caring for orphans, the limited capacity of child-headed families, and increased expenditures on health care and funerals. Another study in the same year found that about 70 per cent of households in Central Malawi had suffered labour losses due to sickness, and that more than half of poor households affected by chronic illnesses had delayed their own farming – and so reduced their food production – in order to try to earn cash incomes elsewhere. UNAIDS concludes that *'Malawi's longstanding and severe HIV/AIDS epidemic is a powerful contributing factor to the food crisis in this country'* (UNAIDS 2002b:27). While AIDS is by no means the only factor behind the food crisis in Southern Africa, evidence of the influence of AIDS on a situation where, at the end of 2002, some 14.4 million people were at risk of famine demonstrates powerfully that AIDS is much more than a matter of health. Chapter 9 describes some ways in which consideration of AIDS is being mainstreamed into the humanitarian response to the crisis.

Without AIDS, Zimbabwe was expected to have had a life expectancy of about 70 years by 2001; instead, with AIDS, it was estimated to be 38 years.

Health

With regard to health, the impacts of AIDS can be so great as to reverse the gains which had been made in key indicators, such as life expectancy at birth. At the turn of the twenty-first century, life expectancy in Haiti was 49 years, whereas before AIDS it had been predicted to be 57 years. In the Bahamas in 2000, life expectancy was estimated at 71 years, instead of the predicted 80 years; and in Thailand and Cambodia it was around three years lower than was expected (Barnett and Whiteside 2002:23). However, it is in the highly affected nations of sub-Saharan Africa that the impacts of AIDS on life expectancy are most stark. Without AIDS, Zimbabwe was expected to have had a life expectancy of about 70 years by 2001; instead, with AIDS, it was estimated to be 38 years (Barnett and Whiteside 2002:22, 278). And predictions suggest that, in the absence of widespread and effective access to antiretroviral therapies, life-expectancy rates will continue to fall. A model by USAID predicts that life expectancy at birth will drop to approximately 30 years by 2010 in 11 sub-Saharan countries. The same model predicts that by 2010 Botswana, Mozambique, Lesotho, Swaziland, and South Africa will experience negative population growth (Boseley 2002).

AIDS is also affecting another key indicator: the under-five child-mortality rate. To take Zimbabwe as an example, in 2000 the child-mortality rate was three times higher than would have been expected without AIDS. About 70 per cent of deaths among children under the age of five are due to AIDS. By 2010 the gap between the likely rate and the 'without AIDS rate' is expected to have widened further. Whereas it might have been around 30 children per 1,000, it is predicted to be around 150 children per 1,000 (Barnett and Whiteside 2002:23, 279).

A different way of looking at the impact of HIV/AIDS on health and the prospects for development is to assess lifetime risk of dying from AIDS. A UNAIDS model from 2000 predicts that if the risk of being infected with HIV remains unchanged, then around two-thirds of today's 15-year-old boys in countries such as Zimbabwe will, at some stage in their lives, die from AIDS. Even if effective prevention efforts were to halve the risk of being infected by HIV, around half of today's 15-year-old boys would still be expected to die from AIDS (UN 2001:2, Barnett and Whiteside 2002:22).

Having HIV makes the development of active TB ten times more likely.

It is obvious that AIDS has major impacts on health through its effects on people who are HIV-positive. In addition, however, AIDS also has various impacts on the health of the remaining population, the people who are not infected with HIV. One way is via the general impoverishment that AIDS brings to households and communities, leading to more work, poorer nutrition, and less access to health care. Another route is via other infectious diseases, primarily TB, which opportunistically infect HIV-positive people. Having HIV makes the development of active TB ten times more likely. If left untreated, each person with active TB infects, on average, ten to fifteen others, whether HIV-positive or not; as a result, the numbers of TB cases trebled in some African countries during the 1990s (Blinkhoff et al. 1999:5).

AIDS can also undermine general standards of health care, as institutions try to respond to the tide of people needing treatment and care due to AIDS. There are some indications that public-health spending on AIDS and its related diseases could displace other types of expenditure on health care and social welfare. One forecast estimates that treatment costs may account for half of Kenya's health spending by 2005 (CIA 2000:21). Another projection, using a 'best-case scenario' and excluding the costs and benefits of antiretroviral treatments, suggests that South Africa's public-health spending would need to increase by more than double by 2010 if 1995 levels of care were to be maintained (LoveLife 2000:20). Without large increases in health funding, deteriorating standards and rationing are inevitable. In Botswana, hospital admissions doubled in only six years, with at least half of all patients having an HIV-related condition. Overcrowding is leading to cross-infection, particularly where there is insufficient space to isolate people with TB. Staffing is being affected not only by illness and death among health workers, but by health professionals escaping the stress by taking jobs in private practice, or in other countries (UNDP 2000:22). Clearly, this is a challenging situation, with AIDS directly threatening the health of the HIV-infected, indirectly affecting much of the rest of the population, and weakening service delivery. As with agriculture, the present and future impacts of AIDS may, without substantial increases in investment, make attempts to improve health standards improbable.

Education

Education is generally regarded as a critical sector for the future development of a nation. This is all the more so in an era of AIDS, as education is charged with protecting the 'window of hope' – the uninfected children who are the next generation of workers and parents. Schools provide the opportunity to impart HIV-prevention messages; but more significantly, education in general enhances the potential for young people to make discerning use of information and to plan for the future, and it accelerates a range of socio-economic changes which reduce susceptibility to HIV infection.

Many of the impacts of AIDS on the education sector have already been mentioned: sickness and death among teachers and other professionals; low rates of participation among children from affected households and orphans; a widening gender gap between male and female enrolment. Although all regions of the world are making progress towards the Millennium Development Goal of ensuring that by 2015 all children will complete their primary education, in 2001 in sub-Saharan Africa around 40 per cent of children did not enrol in primary education, and 80 million places would need to be created if they were all to enrol.[3] Globally, of those who do enter school, one in four drops out before attaining literacy (World Bank 2002). Furthermore, quality is rarely addressed, and little distinction is made between education and mere attendance at school.

The World Bank describes the impacts of AIDS on education as 'turbulent', because they swirl in different directions. For example, the growing shortage of teachers will to some extent be countered by reductions in the numbers of school-age children, caused by deaths among women of child-bearing age (UNAIDS 2000c). Forecasts for highly affected countries, however, predict an environment in which maintaining standards, let alone improving them, will prove challenging. A detailed study for Swaziland's Ministry of Education, for example, found that it needs to train more than twice as many teachers annually if it is to maintain the service levels of 1997. Without significant increases in teacher training, the ratio of pupils to each teacher is expected to deteriorate to fifty to one, reversing all gains made since Independence. The study concludes that the AIDS epidemic will make it increasingly difficult, if not impossible, for the Ministry to fulfil its mandate as effectively as it has in the past (JTK Associates 1999:4).

AIDS is certainly affecting the numbers of children who enrol and stay in school, but differences in national levels of enrolment are not explained by AIDS alone (Ainsworth et al. 2002). For example, among the sub-Saharan countries considered to be likely to achieve the Millennium Development Goal of universal primary-school completion by 2015 are some of those most badly affected by AIDS: Namibia, Botswana, and Zimbabwe.[4] In Tanzania, where some 40 per cent of children between the ages of seven and thirteen were not attending school in 2001, researchers found that orphanhood was associated with not going to school, but only to the same extent as children from 'disjointed households': children who have two living parents but reside with only one or neither of them, many living in impoverished female-headed households. The study also analysed orphans' reasons for not attending school, and found them to be similar to those of non-orphans who do not go to school: either a lack of money and the need to do paid work, or problems inherent in the schools system (Huber and Gould, 2002). Such findings suggest that in countries where there are many poor children who are not in school, orphanhood is an unsuitable criterion for targeting assistance, and that efforts to raise enrolment levels need to focus on vulnerable children in general, as well as improving the services offered by the education system. However, the situation varies from country to country, and in some places such as Brazil and Zimbabwe, where enrolment rates are high among the poor and lower among orphans, it may be beneficial to focus assistance on out-of-school orphans (Ainsworth and Filmer 2002:32).

A study for Swaziland's Ministry of Education found that it needs to train more than twice as many teachers annually if it is to maintain the service levels of 1997.

In general, the current and predicted impacts of AIDS on the education sector raise questions about how governments and NGOs train educators, how they deliver education, the appropriate content and purpose of education, and the means of reaching the vast numbers of children, and especially girls, who are currently excluded from school. As in the cases of agriculture and health, the way in which AIDS undermines development efforts in the field of education, and alters the context in which agencies are working, demands that AIDS is factored into external programming through mainstreaming, if the sector is to respond fully to the pandemic.

Mainstreaming AIDS internally

As Chapter 3 outlined, internal mainstreaming is concerned with reducing the effects of AIDS on the ways in which organisations function, in an effort to maintain effectiveness. In essence, the argument for mainstreaming is akin to that for taking out insurance: that organisations need to invest in the process in order to avoid or reduce inevitable future problems. The prospects for those organisations which do nothing are potentially very damaging.

Unfortunately, because few development organisations or government ministries monitor the indicators which AIDS affects, there is less documentation on the actual extent of the internal impacts of AIDS to date than one might expect. Some impressions are filtering through, however. Zambia's Ministry of Agriculture has revealed that increased morbidity and mortality among senior staff has *'definitely affected'* its planning and administrative capacity, while in Uganda, the MoA has reported that sickness among focal-point officers has rendered the *'implementation of certain key activities impossible'* (Topouzis 2001:15). Businesses have been more active in assessing the impact on their profits. As an example, in 1996, a tea estate in Malawi found that employee deaths had risen by six times in a period of five years, with an annual cost to the firm of six per cent of profits (Government of Malawi and World Bank 1998:8). A Kenyan agro-estate found that its medical costs soared by 600 per cent over six years (Rau 2002:25). In South Africa, the insurance industry experienced a four-fold increase in disability claims in just eighteen months, with the proportion of insured employees unable to work due to HIV/AIDS rising from four to sixteen per cent (Lifeworks 2002).

While the impacts of AIDS on development organisations have not been precisely measured, the types of cost are similar to those incurred by businesses. Table 5.2 presents them under headings of **direct**, **indirect**, and **systemic** costs. Within any organisation, the cascade of effects begins with HIV infection among staff members and among their families. The general process thereafter is broadly predictable. When HIV infection leads to AIDS-related illnesses, the organisation suffers from the periodic absence of the affected staff member, either because the employee is ill, or because the employee is caring for a sick relative. When an HIV-positive staff member becomes unable to work any more, the organisation loses skills, and the investments made in that person. On death, work stops so that colleagues can attend the funeral; several of the organisation's vehicles may be used to transport the coffin and mourners. Where there are medical and death-benefit schemes, which may also cover employees' family members, there are the monetary costs of treatment, terminal benefits, and burial costs. Then there is the expense of advertising for, recruiting, and training a replacement member of staff. All of these impacts multiply as more people are affected. Cumulatively, the absenteeism and accelerated turnover of staff lead to lower productivity levels, and recruitment of suitably qualified replacements may become difficult. The unpredictable nature of absenteeism and death may lead to stressed systems and crisis management, while this and the experience of losing colleagues can undermine staff morale and motivation. Finally, the costs of treatments and benefits, and of recruitment, may undermine investment in the organisation, or its work. In the extreme, they might threaten the financial viability of the organisation.

Internal mainstreaming cannot shield an organisation from all of these impacts – some are inevitable if a staff member develops AIDS – but it can reduce their severity. Internal mainstreaming aims to reduce susceptibility to HIV infection among staff members, and to help HIV-positive employees to manage their status through positive living. It also

Table 5.2: Workplace impacts of HIV and AIDS

DIRECT COSTS	INDIRECT COSTS	SYSTEMIC COSTS
Benefits package	**Absenteeism**	**Loss of workplace cohesion**
• Health care	• Sick leave	• Reduction in morale and motivation
• Health insurance	• Other leave taken by sick employees	• Disruption of schedules and work teams
• Disability insurance	(formal and informal)	• Breakdown of workplace discipline
• Pension fund	• Compassionate leave	(unauthorised absences, theft)
• Death benefit	• Attending funerals	
• Funeral expenses	• Leave to care for dependants with AIDS	
Recruitment	**Sickness**	**Employee attributes**
• Costs of advertising and interviewing	Reduced performance of individuals, due to HIV/AIDS sickness while working	Reduction in average levels of skill, performance, institutional memory, and experience of employees
• Costs to productivity of vacant posts		
Training	**Management resources**	**Quality of employment**
• Induction	Managers' time and effort responding to workplace impacts	Cumulative costs reduce the quality of the workplace environment and reputation of the organisation
• In-service and on-the-job training costs		

(Source: adapted from Barnett and Whiteside (2002:256), and reproduced with the permission of Palgrave Macmillan, the publisher)

aims to modify organisational policies and systems to reduce the organisation's susceptibility and its vulnerability to the impacts of AIDS through absenteeism and higher levels of staff turnover. Finally, internal mainstreaming entails proactive research and impact assessment to preempt possible financial problems caused by AIDS. These strategies are considered in more detail in Chapters 6, 7, and 11.

As well as the direct benefits to organisations which mainstream AIDS internally, it seems reasonable to hypothesise that there may also be comparative advantages for organisations which mainstream when others do not. An agency which has solid and supportive HIV policies and is not embroiled in crisis management is likely to be a more attractive place to work, and better able to recruit and retain qualified staff. And if its work is relatively effective despite AIDS, compared with organisations struggling with absenteeism, vacant posts, and low morale, the agency may be better able to attract funding and use it to good effect. Significantly, the organisation which has successfully mainstreamed internally is likely also to have a greater ability to respond to AIDS in its programme work, whether through external mainstreaming or AIDS work, because its staff should better accept and understand AIDS in all its complexity, and because they and the organisation will be more likely to practise what they preach.

An agency which has solid and supportive HIV policies and is not embroiled in crisis management is likely to be a more attractive place to work, and better able to recruit and retain qualified staff.

While it is argued here that internal mainstreaming of AIDS makes sense for all organisations, particularly in highly affected countries, it is likely to be more challenging for small organisations, due to a combination of two factors. First, for an organisation with a small number of employees, it is hard to predict if and when AIDS may have an impact. Even where HIV prevalence is high, such an organisation might enjoy many years without any employees falling ill. Conversely, as in the case of one NGO with only a handful of staff, it might lose half its workforce in a single year (Page 2002:36). Second, small organisations typically have fewer resources on which to draw, and so are more vulnerable to the impacts of AIDS: '...*organisational costs [of AIDS] are likely felt to be most acutely by organisations with 11–20 staff – the size of many local NGOs in sub-Saharan Africa....[they can] little afford to lose workers to absenteeism or to bear the brunt of increased funeral or health costs*' (James and Mullins 2002:3). The situation for many small organisations appears to be directly analogous to that of poor households: those with meagre resources are most vulnerable to, and most likely to be badly affected by, AIDS.

Arguments against mainstreaming AIDS

Having reviewed the rationale for mainstreaming, this section addresses some possible objections to the idea. The arguments are speculative, in that they are not evident in development literature, but are partly based on barriers to mainstreaming found during research for this book. Equally, it should be noted, the arguments for mainstreaming, and in particular external mainstreaming, are theoretical, because there has been too little experience to date for evidence to emerge to substantiate the case for mainstreaming.

Mainstreaming is a distraction

Most agencies respond to AIDS directly through AIDS work, with efforts to prevent HIV transmission and to address some of the problems faced by people with HIV and AIDS, by providing care and treatment. Mainstreaming may be seen as a threat to the familiar call that 'we must all act now to fight AIDS', because it proposes a strategy which might divert resources away from doing direct AIDS work. Where there is a need for more agencies to get involved in AIDS work – for example, where a population lacks basic information about HIV and AIDS, or where HIV-testing facilities are not available – then the notion of mainstreaming may seem like a distraction, or a low priority. Mainstreaming also seems to ignore what appear to be the obvious issues requiring attention: HIV transmission, illness, and death. However, the notion that all agencies should prioritise getting involved in AIDS work is problematic for two main reasons.

First, development organisations are not all equally suited to embarking on AIDS work. Some have a comparative advantage in doing AIDS work, by virtue of their capacity, experience, relationships with particular groups within the community, and involvement of people directly affected by AIDS. Others are in a comparatively weak position: for example, they are small in size, they have no experience in sexual-health issues, they work in unrelated fields, favour top-down and didactic methodologies, or lack the capacity to take on new and unfamiliar work. They are probably better placed to mainstream AIDS in their existing work. It is important to recognise that poor-quality AIDS work can be ineffective and thus wasteful of limited funds, or even damaging, for instance if it unintentionally stigmatises 'high-risk' people, or people with AIDS, or impoverishes the beneficiaries of non-viable income-generating activities (Page 2002:14). Common mistakes in AIDS work may also undermine other agencies' efforts, for example, through well-meant but unsustainable hand-outs, or loans with little expectation of repayment. The additional workload imposed by taking on AIDS work can also harm an organisation's core work. In particular, where the decision to respond to AIDS is funding-led, an organisation's former projects and target groups may easily become neglected.

Second, the many problems of under-development persist, and, as Chapter 2 argued, they are allowing the AIDS pandemic to flourish. Hence, core development work is needed more than ever. If AIDS is mainstreamed in it, that development work can also tackle the causes of HIV susceptibility, and help to reduce the impact of AIDS. By mainstreaming AIDS, all organisations can contribute to the virtuous circle shown in Figure 2.2. But failing to mainstream can lead to the various problems outlined at the beginning of this chapter – making people more susceptible, or more vulnerable, excluding people from development, and making development organisations ineffectual – all of which lead to ineffective development work If that analysis is true, then mainstreaming AIDS is crucial for responding to AIDS, and for ensuring that development work and AIDS work are mutually enhancing. In this sense, mainstreaming is not a distraction but a critical, additional strategy. And, as the final section of this chapter will explore, agencies do not necessarily face the choice of *either* mainstreaming *or* doing AIDS work: those with sufficient capacity may be able to do both.

Agencies do not necessarily face the choice of either mainstreaming or doing AIDS work: those with sufficient capacity may be able to do both.

Mainstreaming is an excuse to do nothing

One of the concerns about mainstreaming gender, which also applies to AIDS, is that the process renders the issue – gender or AIDS – invisible. Whereas it is very obvious if an organisation has special women's projects, or focused AIDS work, it is not immediately apparent whether concerns about gender or AIDS are being dealt with within general development and humanitarian programmes. This leads to the suspicion that an organisation can use mainstreaming as an excuse for not acting directly, and can claim to have addressed the issue without having done very much.

It is a question of credibility and honesty. Organisations prone to exaggerating their achievements can do so if undertaking direct AIDS work – for example, claiming to have comprehensive prevention programmes, but actually doing little more than delivering lectures and distributing leaflets. It would not be fair to reject the idea of mainstreaming on the basis that it may be used cynically: any development strategy is open to misuse, particularly if it can attract funding.

Cynicism aside, mainstreaming AIDS is not an easy option. As later chapters will show, it is a fairly complex and on-going process which requires the involvement and commitment of people throughout an organisation. Far from being an excuse to do nothing, mainstreaming means reflecting, assessing, making connections, and acting on both internal and external issues. Long-established ways of working may have to change, so mainstreaming is not 'an easy way out'. To prevent AIDS becoming invisible or forgotten, systems for institutionalising and monitoring the process can ensure that AIDS is not mainstreamed into non-existence, but is rather a permanent concern which permeates all development and humanitarian work.

Mainstreaming is unnecessary

Development practitioners who are already listening to the concerns of community members, for example through participatory appraisals, may feel that they do not need a special mainstreaming strategy for AIDS. They would expect AIDS-related issues to arise from their needs assessments, and to be dealt with through the normal project cycle. Someone who read a draft copy of this book wrote in the margin: *'Is this very different from what we should be doing anyway?'* In many ways she is right. However, there are several reasons why the work of development and humanitarian agencies may fall short of the outcomes that mainstreaming proposes.

Many of the constraints stem from staff skills and attitudes. Workers who refuse to believe in AIDS, who understand it as a product of witchcraft, or punishment for promiscuity or for men having sex with men, or who are fearful of people with AIDS, will not be able to tackle AIDS constructively at community level. Internal mainstreaming is partly about helping staff members to address their own fears, prejudices, and denial, so that they can better face up to AIDS as it affects them and others. Staff are also likely to need training in order to assess needs among various groups within the community, because issues relating to AIDS – including death, sex, sexual health, and sexual violence – are sensitive topics which are unlikely to emerge unless staff ask the right questions in the right way. Furthermore, without training to understand the complexity of AIDS, development workers may miss the relevance of apparently unconnected issues, such as the significance of who in the household gets the profits of income-generating activities. Untrained staff are also likely to be unaware of the possibility that their work might need to be modified, for example, if it is excluding some households or groups of people.

Another problem is that the issues faced by AIDS-affected households may not emerge during appraisals. In general, when development agencies seek to know 'the community's priorities', they risk ignoring the diversity of needs and vulnerabilities within the population, and their project designs often unintentionally privilege the ideas of those with greater influence, health, and ability. This problem, which leads to some people, and in particular poorer women and young people, being marginalised, is all the more harmful in a time of AIDS. Participants who are directly affected by AIDS may not speak up, fearing the stigma that revealing themselves may bring. And, as this chapter has already stated, those individuals who are most vulnerable and susceptible may be unable to spare the time to take part in assessment exercises. While huge numbers of organisations use participatory appraisal techniques, such techniques, unless used thoroughly, may not lead to rigorous analysis of vulnerability, or differentiation within communities and within households, or social inclusion. External mainstreaming involves deliberately seeking the input of affected households, just as participatory appraisals should always obtain the views of the poorest, the 'non-participants', and people of different ages and both sexes. Moreover, 'affected households' are not homogeneous: development workers need to learn about the different needs of people in different situations, such as those who are ill, recovered, widowed, orphaned, or newly heading a household. One researcher hints that development workers may be unaware of the needs of AIDS-affected households, reporting that *'project staff who accompanied us on our survey of HIV/AIDS-affected households were genuinely shocked at the extent of the poverty and starvation in their area'* (Page 2002:25).

If job descriptions do not routinely include AIDS, then staff and consultants can forget or deny their responsibility for taking AIDS into account.

Other constraints, which could be dealt with through internal main-streaming, stem from organisational systems. If an organisation plans only a few years ahead, it may lack the long-term perspective needed to consider, and act upon, the future impacts of AIDS. If funding is closely tied to specific sectors, and AIDS is seen as a health issue, then for 'unrelated' activities, such as agriculture, it may be difficult to obtain funds for AIDS-related expenditure. If job descriptions and terms of reference do not routinely include AIDS, alongside gender and other cross-cutting issues, then staff and consultants can forget or deny their responsibility for taking AIDS into account. And if an organisation's personnel procedures lack confidentiality and do not support HIV-positive staff, a culture of denial and discrimination may prevail, leaving it poorly placed to consider and respond to AIDS internally or externally. Thus, not only is external mainstreaming necessary to ensure that AIDS and the needs of AIDS-affected households are taken into account in programme work, but internal mainstreaming is needed to enable organisations to respond indirectly but fully to HIV and AIDS.

Mainstreaming is not feasible in an emergency

The idea of mainstreaming AIDS may be resisted by those working in humanitarian programmes, who may consider the additional demands to be unrealistic and unnecessary. However, although some aspects of mainstreaming AIDS involve additional work, many of the relevant measures already form part of the good practice to which humanitarian organisations aspire. To a large extent, then, if such good practice is realistic – through better preparedness, training, funding, planning, and implementation – then so too is the aspiration to mainstream AIDS. For example, in refugee camps it is routinely accepted that agencies should listen to and involve residents, and particularly women and young people, in planning the layout and key functions of the camp. The same listening and involvement are crucial mechanisms for mainstreaming AIDS. Positioning toilets, tap-stands, and lighting in ways that discourage sexual violence is a basic aspect of protection in refugee camps, and these precautions also reduce susceptibility to HIV transmission associated with forced sex and rape. Treating STIs is part of the recommended health package once an emergency situation has stabilised, and it also helps to reduce the efficacy of HIV transmission. And in food-aid distributions, agencies aim to ensure that the most vulnerable people receive their rations, which should include those affected by chronic illness, including AIDS. Chapters 9 and 11 consider in more detail experiences of, and ideas for, mainstreaming AIDS in humanitarian work.

The Rwandan genocide in 1994 saw extensive use of rape as a weapon of war, with lasting effects for the nation; in one survey, 17 per cent of the women who had been raped were found to be HIV-positive, compared with 11 per cent who had not been raped.

Moreover, while responding to AIDS indirectly may appear to be unnecessary, emergency situations, and particularly those involving conflict, create virtually all the conditions likely to increase susceptibility to and transmission of HIV. The downstream effects of not responding are higher levels of HIV infection, and the many interconnected ways in which AIDS undermines reconstruction and development. Failing to mainstream AIDS in emergency programmes could have damaging effects during the crisis – for example, through sexual violence – and for generations afterwards through the impacts of HIV infection. The Rwandan genocide in 1994 saw extensive use of rape as a weapon of war, with lasting effects for the nation; in one survey, 17 per cent of the women who had been raped were found to be HIV-positive, compared with 11 per cent who had not been raped (Christian Aid 2002:11).

Mainstreaming is irrelevant where HIV rates are low

... the current HIV prevalence forewarns an AIDS epidemic that is only beginning in many countries. The scale and scope of this epidemic over the next decade can be broadly predicted, planned for and mitigated. However, like people living on the riverbanks, we seem unable or unwilling to take action on the flood until we are knee-deep in water.
(Loewenson and Whiteside 2001:3)

It is understandable, and common, that organisations are reluctant to be proactive in advance of what appears to be a distant or unlikely threat. There seem to be three possible strategies to adopt with regard to mainstreaming in situations where an HIV epidemic is nascent or concentrated, or where the impacts of a generalised epidemic are not yet evident. The first is to do nothing. The second is to encourage mainstreaming of AIDS nonetheless, albeit at a lower level of intensity than in a high-prevalence setting. This strategy involves engaging in the same processes of mainstreaming AIDS externally and internally, with the advantage that organisations would be well prepared when, or if, HIV rates begin to rise. The drawback, as reported by officials engaged in the government of Ghana's commendably early response to AIDS, is that it is very hard to mobilise people to act on an unseen problem whose impacts, in a low HIV-prevalence setting, are as yet generally invisible.[5]

It is very hard to mobilise people to act on an unseen problem whose impacts, in a low HIV-prevalence setting, are as yet generally invisible.

The third strategy, given the many immediate pressures on development organisations, is to accept that it is not plausible to expect those working in regions with low rates of HIV infection to mainstream AIDS. In this case, it may be more relevant to think of mainstreaming gender or sexual-health issues. Gender inequality and sexual ill-health are important development problems, regardless of HIV. In programme work, external main-streaming of gender and sexual health might lead to adaptations to empower women, to reduce sexual violence, unwanted pregnancies, and STIs, and to modify work in order to help impoverished female-headed households to become more food-secure and less vulnerable to external shocks. In The Gambia, where HIV prevalence is low but STI rates are high, ActionAid and the Medical Research Council have orientated their Stepping Stones workshops to address issues relating to gender inequality, conception, STIs, and infertility, rather than HIV (Shaw and Jawo 2000:74). Such efforts can tackle immediate problems, while also addressing factors linked to HIV susceptibility and vulnerability to the impacts of AIDS. Meanwhile, internal mainstreaming of gender and sexual health would help staff members to understand and act upon the links between their work and problems of gender and sexual health, and would reduce gender-based discrimination within organisations. Internal mainstreaming could also involve globally relevant measures such as developing a policy on chronic illness (to include AIDS), putting in place policies to prevent discrimination in employment (including discrimination by HIV status), and improving systems such as ways of covering for staff absences.

The third strategy of mainstreaming gender and sexual health does not, however, mean that mainstreaming AIDS would be unnecessary if HIV rates subsequently rose. Although mainstreaming AIDS would probably be facilitated by the earlier work on gender and sexual health, work to understand the impacts of AIDS at the household level and to learn from AIDS-affected households would still be needed. Much of the process of internal mainstreaming of AIDS would also need to be addressed. Chapter 11 provides more ideas about how organisations in countries with low HIV prevalence might respond to the agenda of mainstreaming AIDS.

Of course, as this book argues throughout, in the overall response to the problem, the strategy of mainstreaming is additional to that of direct AIDS work. In situations where HIV infection has yet to be generalised, development agencies with suitable experience and capacity may well focus on undertaking AIDS work with the sub-groups of the population among whom HIV is concentrated, for example injecting drug users or commercial sex workers, both to support them personally and to help to prevent HIV from crossing over into the general population.

Implications for development and humanitarian agencies

This chapter has, so far, presented the thinking behind the strategy of mainstreaming AIDS. However, as Chapter 4 reported, there is little mainstreaming – internal or external – happening among development and humanitarian agencies. The dominant response to AIDS is direct AIDS work, whether stand-alone or integrated. This is clear from the examples of the various terms and their meanings in Chapter 3; the illustrations of AIDS work are easily related to actual projects, while those of mainstreaming are unfamiliar, and far from being common practice.

As Chapter 4 argued, the generic response of doing AIDS work, rather than mainstreaming (with or without additional AIDS work), seems to have some limitations. On the one hand, organisations unsuited to undertaking AIDS work nevertheless try to do so. Their efforts may not be very effective, or might even be damaging, and the additional workload may be detrimental to their core work. On the other hand, organisations which find that they are not well placed to do AIDS work, or which see AIDS as the responsibility of others, may conclude that they do not need to do anything. In either case, regardless of whether or not the organisations take on AIDS work, they do not mainstream AIDS externally in their core business, and may take only limited action on internal issues. As a result, their programme work may inadvertently enhance susceptibility to HIV transmission and vulnerability to the impacts of AIDS; they are also likely to be missing opportunities to act positively but indirectly on the causes and consequences of AIDS, so boosting the overall response to AIDS. More generally, the assumption that AIDS work is the proper response to AIDS means that the strategies of mainstreaming internally and externally are largely ignored. As a result, the concept of mainstreaming remains underdeveloped theoretically, little tried, and poorly documented. It is significant that this book – exploring ideas and experiences of mainstreaming AIDS, though not best practice – has relevance some twenty years since the start of the AIDS pandemic.

Chapter 4 also introduced the idea, from epidemiology, of HIV's 'web of causation', where influences on HIV transmission and the impacts of AIDS spread outwards from bio-medicine at the centre, to behavioural factors, then the micro-context and finally the macro-environment. This was illustrated in Figure 4.1 on page 66. Table 5.3 re-presents the same categories, along with a list (not exhaustive) of the determinants of HIV infection and relevant programme responses. It is clear from the column of responses that each level is suited to particular professions and types of organisation. Organisations must decide at which level they can best make their contribution to the overall response to AIDS.

The first level, **bio-medicine,** is plainly the domain of medical scientists, health professionals, and traditional healers. This is where many organisations which deliver health services, including NGOs, ASOs, and faith-based agencies, are most likely to operate, offering or arguing for direct AIDS work through treatment and care. The second level, relating to **behaviour,** is probably best served by local individuals and indigenous CBOs, such as community leaders, ASOs, and faith-based organisations, offering AIDS work in the form of HIV-prevention programmes and counselling. The third level, that of the **micro-environment**, is mainly the realm of local government and development and humanitarian NGOs, undertaking indirect AIDS work through acting on the local development-related causes and consequences of AIDS. And finally, the fourth level, the

Table 5.3: Determinants of, and programme responses to, HIV infection

Level	Determinants of HIV infection	Programme responses
1 Bio-medical *Focus on the body*	Virus sub-types Stage of infection and viral load Presence of STIs Physiology – women more susceptible Circumcision Iatrogenic infection Immune-system status	Research into vaccine and cure Treatment of opportunistic infections Antiretroviral treatment STI treatment Condoms Blood screening, sterilising equipment
2 Behavioural *Focus on what men, women, boys, and girls do, or have done to them*	Number of sexual partners Rate of partner change Concurrent partners Age gap between partners Sexual practices Condom use Violent sex Rape Alcohol use Intravenous drug use	Provide information and education Seek sexual-behaviour change: • fewer partners • using condoms • delay beginning of sexual activity • same-age partners • get STIs treated Promote and distribute condoms Voluntary counselling and testing Needle-exchange programmes
3 Micro-environment *Focus on the local context in which men, women, boys, and girls live*	Poverty Women's rights and status Health status and access to health care Literacy Mobility and migration Levels of violence Gender norms, cultural practices and traditions	Poverty reduction Empowerment Nutrition programmes Health care Education Livelihoods security Promotion of human rights Legal reform
4 Macro-environment *Focus on national and global contexts*	National wealth Income distribution Governance International trade Natural disasters and climate change Conflict	Economic policy Taxation Redistributive social policy Good governance Terms of trade Debt relief Promotion of human rights

(Source: adapted from Barnett and Whiteside (2002:78), and reproduced with the permission of Palgrave Macmillan)

macro-environment, is the mandate of the State and international agencies such as the United Nations and World Trade Organization, and the organisations which aim to influence them through advocacy, acting indirectly on the global issues that help to fuel the pandemic.

In addition to the above analysis, the following implications are based on two premises. First, if, as this book has argued, AIDS is a development issue, then action at all four levels of the spider's web is needed, in order to ensure a holistic response to AIDS involving all sectors and comprising both direct and indirect approaches. Second, the combined effect of the work of organisations across sectors in responding to AIDS is likely to be greatest if each agency begins by focusing on its area of comparative advantage: in other words, if each organisation (at least initially) concentrates on what it does best.

These two premises carry the following implications:

- **Internal issues:** all organisations have staff who may be or may become HIV-positive. As such, all organisations are vulnerable, to some extent, to the impacts of AIDS. This implies that they all need to engage with the strategy of mainstreaming AIDS internally, if they are to function effectively into the future. This applies to organisations operating at all levels of the spider's web, from small ASOs to international NGOs and government ministries. In settings of low HIV prevalence, certain elements of internal mainstreaming are likely to be fruitful, as Chapter 14 will argue.

- **Programme issues:** for organisations engaged in medical and behavioural AIDS work at levels 1 and 2 of the web, external main-streaming may be useful. However, because those organisations should already be orientated to and directly engaged with the issues raised by AIDS, mainstreaming is likely to be less relevant to them. After all, the meaning given to mainstreaming in this book is the modification of development and humanitarian work, in order to take AIDS into account and to act indirectly upon AIDS.

Development and humanitarian organisations generally engage in work at the third level of the spider's web, and they all work with people who are susceptible, to some extent, to HIV infection. To ensure that their existing programme work is indirectly working *against* rather than *with* AIDS – that it is helping to minimise susceptibility to HIV transmission and vulnerability to the impacts of AIDS, rather than exacerbating them – all those organisations need to mainstream AIDS externally. Similarly, those agencies operating on the macro-issues at the fourth level of the web need to ensure that they mainstream AIDS, so that their policies take account of HIV transmission and the impacts of AIDS. As was argued earlier in this chapter, in low-prevalence situations it may make sense to engage in a scaled-down process of external mainstreaming, or a similar process focused on related and immediate issues such as gender and sexual health.

This book, then, proposes that internal mainstreaming of AIDS is essential for all organisations, and that external mainstreaming of AIDS is a basic strategy for all humanitarian and development organisations. However, AIDS also demands specialised AIDS work, and, as Chapter 4 outlined, there is a strong impetus towards doing such work, rather than mainstreaming. Suppose that a development agency undertakes community research as part of mainstreaming AIDS in an agriculture project, and discovers three things: that AIDS-affected households are being excluded from the project; that there are low levels of knowledge about AIDS among young people; and that carers for bedridden people with AIDS are desperately in need of support. If the agency were to adhere to the mainstreaming agenda, it would respond to the first need, and try to make links to, or draw in, specialist organisations who are better placed to address the remaining two needs. A complementary partnership with a specialist agency would mean that each organisation could focus on its strengths, while linking with the other to address different aspects of AIDS, and different levels of the web. This might involve sharing services and expertise, mutual supporting, or funding.

However, in practice this may not be very feasible. Specialist organisations are likely to be running already at full capacity, and there may be a great shortage of them, or even a total absence. Managers of the agriculture project have four choices. First, they can prioritise their existing core work and ignore the needs for AIDS education and care, along with the many other non-agricultural needs that the project does not attempt to address. Second, management could decide to continue with the core agriculture work, but begin to advocate for AIDS work in the area, proactively approaching potential partners, and perhaps offering incentives for organisations to expand their AIDS work to cover the area. Third, managers could decide to add limited low-cost elements of AIDS work to the core work, such as distributing leaflets about HIV transmission, and booklets about how to care for someone with AIDS at home. Fourth, they could fully embark on AIDS work, opting to undertake HIV education, and to support home-based care, either as separate projects, or integrated with the agricultural work. Each of these options has advantages and disadvantages for the organisation and for different people within the community. Organisations which are mainstreaming AIDS in situations where specialist support services do not exist are likely to face some difficult decisions.

As an aside, it is interesting to note that, while many development organisations want to respond directly to AIDS, many AIDS organisations want to respond to the development-related needs of their clients, including income generation, micro-finance, and food security. This may be equally, or even more challenging; in the view of Noerine Kaleeba, when she headed TASO, The AIDS Support Organisation,

> *ActionAid is in a more privileged position than TASO...you are starting with development and slotting in AIDS. But for us it is more difficult to try to fit development aspects into AIDS – development is very wide, and we are trying to fit it into this small drawer! If we try to do too much, the rest of our work will suffer.*
> (Holden 1995:63)

ASOs which get involved in development work often face problems similar to those of development agencies embarking on AIDS work, in terms of taking on work outside their area of expertise without sufficient resources, capacity, and technical skills. They also face the same dilemma if there is no suitable organisation with which to form a complementary partnership.

Summary

This chapter has described three ways in which development and humanitarian work may, unwittingly work with, rather than against, AIDS, indirectly hindering the efforts of organisations engaged in AIDS work by increasing susceptibility to HIV infection, increasing vulnerability to the impacts of AIDS, and excluding those affected by AIDS from the development process. This chapter has also reviewed the ways in which AIDS can cause development work to fail, and how it can undermine the very functioning and sustainability of development organisations and other institutions. It has also proposed and responded to five arguments against mainstreaming AIDS, and, overall, has aimed to put forward the rationale behind the idea of mainstreaming.

The final section of the chapter presented an overview of HIV's 'web of causation', derived from a view of AIDS as a development issue, which comprises four levels of determinants and related programme responses.

The section argued that while the web presents the whole picture, and so the whole response to AIDS, at present the global response to AIDS, including that of development and humanitarian organisations, is biased towards the bio-medical and behavioural levels. The section proposed that organisations are variously suited to act at different levels, and that development and humanitarian organisations should adopt main-streaming of AIDS as their basic strategy. By doing so they can both operate within their area of comparative advantage and provide coverage to an area of the web which has been, to date, largely ignored.

The chapter has argued that, particularly in areas with existing and increasing HIV epidemics, 'business as usual' is a short-sighted strategy which holds many dangers. By failing to mainstream, development agencies can cause negatively reinforcing repercussions which are at odds with development goals and the fight against AIDS. Significantly, by not mainstreaming, agencies also miss the opportunity to be proactive in addressing AIDS indirectly, both inside and outside the organisation. At present, many development organisations, with and without AIDS projects, continue the bulk of their development work, and the way they run their business, as if AIDS did not exist. In a sense, by mainstreaming AIDS, all of them could continue to do what they do, but do it better.

At present, many development organisations, with and without AIDS projects, continue the bulk of their development work, and the way they run their business, as if AIDS did not exist.

Development and humanitarian agencies can ideally make mutually useful links to specialist organisations engaged in AIDS work. However, where this is not possible, a development organisation with the capacity and resources both to mainstream and undertake AIDS work might do both. As Figure 2.2 depicted, the two strategies of direct and indirect approaches to AIDS are not mutually exclusive, but complementary aspects of the overall response to AIDS. For other organisations, for whom taking on AIDS work might compromise their core work, responding directly to AIDS may not be the best way of making their contribution to fighting poverty and inequality. Table 5.4 (overleaf) summarises this chapter's implications for development and humanitarian organisations' response to HIV and AIDS, while the next chapter explores what the idea of mainstreaming would mean if it were implemented in full.

Table 5.4: Summary of implications for development and humanitarian agencies' response to HIV and AIDS

Internal mainstreaming of AIDS	Necessary for all organisations in affected countries; some aspects of the process relevant to all organisations in countries with low HIV prevalence.
External mainstreaming of AIDS	The basic initial strategy for all development and humanitarian agencies in affected countries. The process could be modified – either scaled down, or focused on related issues such as gender equity and sexual health – in settings with low HIV prevalence.
AIDS work (stand-alone and integrated)	An important complementary strategy for those development and humanitarian agencies with sufficient capacity to undertake both mainstreaming of AIDS and AIDS work. Those without such capacity should, where possible, form partnerships with others engaged in AIDS work.

6 Mainstreaming AIDS in an idealised world

Introduction

Chapter 5 presented the case for mainstreaming AIDS, and the next three chapters consider actual experiences of mainstreaming. First, however, this chapter explores in more detail what mainstreaming AIDS means – or could mean – by describing the features of a hypothetical organisation which has mainstreamed AIDS in an ideal way. The imaginary organisation is an NGO in a highly affected country, which both implements projects itself, and supports the work of its CBO partners. The chapter presents short narratives from seven of the NGO's staff, from one of its partners, and from two community members, in an effort to bring the idea of mainstreaming to life. Each of these imaginary narratives is followed by a summary of key points or strategies for mainstreaming.

The hypothetical scenario presented here will not be realised by any single organisation, because it is idealised. However, by exemplifying current thinking on good practice, this chapter aims to provide a sense of some of the changes that mainstreaming AIDS might bring about, and a vision of what an organisation which has mainstreamed AIDS could look like. As such, it aims to expand on and give life to the definitions already provided in Chapter 3, and to add substance to the (as yet under-developed) notion of mainstreaming AIDS.

Internal mainstreaming

Internal mainstreaming of AIDS entails changing organisational policy and practice in order to reduce the organisation's susceptibility to HIV infection and vulnerability to the impacts of AIDS. The overall process requires high-level support within an organisation, and sufficient resources to turn commitment into action which, over time, institutionalises responses to HIV and AIDS. Here, one of the staff members acting as a focal point for mainstreaming describes the important contextual features from his own perspective:

Everybody in the organisation has been involved in mainstreaming, but it couldn't have happened without the resolve of the senior staff. For example, they allocated some extra funding so that I and a couple of others could take on mainstreaming roles by shedding some other duties. We wouldn't have achieved as much if the extra workload had just been dumped on us, on top of everything else. We also had a budget for training with our staff, and with our partners.

The bosses were realistic. They accepted that there would be mistakes and set-backs along the way. We were not under pressure to do everything in a really short time, which would have been impossible, but the process wasn't allowed to slip off the agenda either.

Another thing was that they used their influence to help us to involve people who were sceptical about mainstreaming – like the CBO director who ignored me at first, but attended the training sessions and really contributed to them, after meeting with my Director. So we've made steady progress, to the point where we've made changes in attitudes and to our systems, making sure, as best we can, that we and our partners take HIV and AIDS into account inside the organisation, and in fieldwork too.

His comments reveal the importance of a combination of the following elements:

- the commitment and involvement of senior staff;
- relieving key staff of some duties, in order to take on mainstreaming responsibilities;
- financial resources for training;
- seeing mainstreaming as a learning process;
- involving everyone, including partners;
- supporting staff to reduce their susceptibility to HIV, and to cope better with AIDS.

This element of internal mainstreaming relates to AIDS work with staff. It involves helping employees to reflect on their behaviour and attitudes through on-going experiential training, as well as providing HIV testing, counselling, and treatment, and assisting HIV-positive staff members to manage their condition. More generally, it aims to create a supportive culture within the organisation, by providing practical encouragement of positive living and measures to challenge discrimination. Here, an employee discusses his experience:

I joined this organisation after the mainstreaming process had begun. It was a big contrast to my old workplace. I'm not a health worker, but AIDS was in my job description, and I was soon invited to a session about AIDS. I expected to be bored by statistics and a lecture about morals, but it was more like a discussion group – it was 'men only', and we talked straight about all sorts of things, like what it means to be a man, and how 'manly' stereotypes can be dangerous for us. One month we discussed discrimination, and it really revealed some of my prejudices, and made me think a lot. Another time we had a joint meeting with the female staff, and all talked about how to discuss sex with our kids. We thought up some good ideas, and we all took comics home to share with our children.

Then one month a guy with HIV came in and talked about his situation, and about getting an HIV test. I had always thought it's better not to know – if you find you are infected, you'll just die more quickly – but he persuaded me otherwise. Our agency pays for staff to get counselling and testing from a local AIDS organisation, so I went, with one of my colleagues from the group. Thank God, I found that I am not infected. I'm trying to make sure I stay that way – a bit less booze, and some condoms in my pocket 'just in case'.

My friend said he was negative too, but later he was acting very strange, and when we sat and talked, he confided that his result was positive. We kept it secret for a while, but encouraged each other to live and love carefully, and to stay healthy. It was a long time before he fell ill for the first time, after a really heavy period of work. He decided to tell the personnel officer, so that he could get some support. I thought his secret would be out, but she kept it quiet. Later, he told some of his colleagues himself, and he mostly got support from them too – everyone here knows about AIDS, so there isn't the whispering and blaming that you get in other workplaces. And we're all willing to cover his work for him when he's away. He makes sure that his records are really clear, to make it easier for us.

He knows he will have to leave at some point, and has helped the personnel department to update his job description, ready for his successor. He has also used the organisation's offer of legal services to draw up a will, to make sure his wife and kids get what is theirs, when his time comes. He really is an inspiration. I admire his attitude, but the organisation must take credit too. It has helped us all to face up to AIDS – to handle it, rather than hide from it.

From this staff member's perspective, the NGO's efforts to support its employees have been effective for the following reasons:

- The sessions about AIDS are on-going, the groups are often single-sex, they cover a range of relevant topics, and draw on the skills and experiences of people living with HIV.
- The organisation pays for confidential voluntary counselling and testing from a specialist provider.
- Staff respect rules about confidentiality.

- The NGO provides support to help HIV-positive staff to cope with their condition, and to reduce the impacts of AIDS on their families.

- Both the employees and the organisation benefit from fostering a supportive culture.

Forecasting and planning for the costs of HIV and AIDS

Budgeting and financial planning are important concerns for internal mainstreaming. Ideally, an organisation can assess and manage the risks and costs posed by HIV and AIDS, through monitoring impacts, forecasting changes, and making adjustments as necessary. As such, the organisation can act to reduce its vulnerability to the impacts of AIDS.

In reflecting on her role, the Financial Controller describes her team's contribution to the mainstreaming process:

Five years ago we had not given AIDS any serious thought. I was jolted into action when a long-serving member of staff fell ill. She told me in confidence that it was AIDS. I felt so bad for her! I did everything I could to obtain treatment for her – there wasn't any policy for me to follow, and over time the costs far exceeded the normal amounts. She took loads of sick leave on full pay, and when she left she got a very good pay-out. I felt that the organisation owed it to her and her kids.

Later, I looked at the costs, and started calculating what would happen if more people fell sick. It was just guesswork, but the figures alarmed me. So with the personnel department we set up systems to gather the information that we needed – like how much sick leave and compassionate leave staff were taking, and trends in medical costs. I also got some advice from the National AIDS Control Programme about the likely HIV-infection rates among our staff. It's taken a long time, but after a lot of research, forecasting, and negotiations, we have been able to finalise a terminal-diseases policy which takes care of our staff while also protecting the organisation's financial viability.

Every year my department updates its five-year and ten-year forecasts for the cost implications of AIDS, so that everything is planned for. Recently we have improved our monitoring systems to include the costs of temporary cover when someone is ill, and recruitment costs when a staff member leaves or dies because of AIDS. We have shared the methods with our partners, and are helping several of them to begin to assess and budget for the costs of AIDS. I plan to use our evidence to influence our donors; they need to understand why, in this part of the world, personnel costs are rising. We need to be able to factor the costs of AIDS into project proposals.

Key factors from this narrative include:

- the advisability of being pro-active, by facing up to the possible costs of AIDS;

- the need for a policy on terminal diseases which is both affordable and fair to staff;

- the importance of monitoring systems to track the impacts of AIDS, and to use in advocacy;

- forecasting and planning for the costs of AIDS as an on-going process.

Modifying systems to reduce the internal impacts of AIDS

Organisations may be affected by AIDS not only because their staff are affected, but because they have systems which leave them vulnerable to the impacts of AIDS. Here, the Personnel Officer reflects on some of the ways that she has found to reduce that vulnerability by modifying how the organisation functions with regard to human resources:

The main strategy – what, for me, is at the heart of mainstreaming – is to become pro-active about AIDS. Rather than allowing AIDS to disrupt everything, I've tried to be one step ahead of it. This isn't simply in terms of making sure that we have suitable health policies, and counselling and awareness raising for staff. It's also about what's likely to change in the future. For instance, I can't assume that it will always be possible to recruit people with the right skills and experience; already the standard of applications is going down. So I'm trying to strengthen the training that employees get when they are in post. Sometimes short courses are appropriate, but also we encourage more experienced staff to work with the newer ones. We are developing a culture where people work together more, to share skills. This reduces the disruption when someone is away, perhaps because of AIDS, or if they are simply on holiday or maternity leave. There used to be a lot of disruption when someone was absent.

I've also worked to speed up our recruitment procedures. I don't tolerate the delays that used to happen. And I'm keen to make sure that we are a good employer. Our salaries are not the highest, but we have a reputation for being fair and supportive, and that is helping us to limit the turnover of staff, which is a good sign. My main challenge now is assisting our partner organisations to look at all these issues. Many of them don't have a personnel officer, nor formal policies and procedures, so it's difficult to know how best to help them to respond.

Her account demonstrates some key requirements for efforts to reduce the internal impacts of AIDS:

- being pro-active, by facing up to some of the inevitable or probable impacts of AIDS;

- looking for creative responses to likely problems, such as new ways of working and training, and ways of modifying those responses to fit partners' circumstances;

- eliminating features that compound the problems, such as slow recruitment procedures.

External mainstreaming

External mainstreaming of AIDS refers to adapting development and humanitarian programme work in order to take into account suscepti-bility to HIV transmission and vulnerability to the impacts of AIDS. The focus is on core programme work in the changing context created by AIDS. The process involves four main elements: building staff capacity; undertaking research which involves affected people; modifying the development or humanitarian work; and systematising attention to AIDS.

Building staff capacity to address AIDS indirectly

Much of the process of external mainstreaming is concerned with enabling development workers to understand the need for all programme work to be attuned to HIV and AIDS. Here, the imaginary NGO's Health Adviser describes how attitudes and skills have changed as a result of external mainstreaming:

It used to be that every document or piece of paper with the word 'AIDS' on it automatically ended up on my desk! I'm pleased to say that's changed: now information circulates to the other sectors too, and there is interest throughout the organisation. I think there has been a big change in attitudes among the staff in general, and among our partners. Part of the mainstreaming process was about understanding how AIDS links to everything else, and the workshops and discussions were – crucially, I think – supplemented by fieldwork. That's when the abstract connections became real: when you talk to people who are affected, you are reminded that their lives are not compartmentalised into sectors. So the idea that AIDS is only the business of the health sector quickly dissolved.

Staff did, however, resist the idea that we should concern ourselves with private matters – not only sex, but also things like domestic violence, and control over money within the family. I think a large part of it was due to shyness, and not knowing how to discuss such issues. Training and practice have helped, but the biggest encouragement is when the community members make the links, and verify the significance of such issues.

This narrative identifies several strategies for building staff capacity as part of the external mainstreaming of AIDS:

- getting all sectors and all staff involved;
- enabling staff to understand for themselves the links between AIDS and development and humanitarian issues;
- working with vulnerable people, and those affected by AIDS, so that the process is not theoretical, but applied to the situation in the field;
- and skills development to help employees to approach difficult issues.

Involving vulnerable people in needs appraisals and in development work

Involving vulnerable people in research and capacity building should have benefits for employees' understanding, but also for those vulnerable people themselves. As this imaginary woman recounts, the work becomes more attuned to the underlying needs of both AIDS-affected and vulnerable not-yet-affected households:

I used to attend our local women's group regularly, until about a year and a half ago, when my husband started falling sick. At about the same time, two women showed up at the group – from some organisation, they both wore trousers. Anyway, they asked the members to explain things about women's lives in our community, things such as women's work and men's work. Over several weeks they talked about all sort of problems – money, food, divorce, even things like women's diseases. Of course, I couldn't go. I was busy caring for my husband, and even when he got better I had to try and catch up with the jobs on the farm. But then one day the women in trousers made a special visit to meet us. My husband was asleep, exhausted. I sent the children outside and found myself telling them about my fears, about ending up like the woman in a film that was once shown in the village: her husband had AIDS, and she lost all her belongings to relatives. I explained how I need to raise money to meet our basic needs, because our savings were rapidly disappearing.

I didn't see the women again, but in time I heard that a new project was beginning, to help people to save money, and to get credit to do businesses. I think that some people were against me joining. They whisper that I am as good as dead, but a man from the project came and encouraged me to take part. I have managed to make some savings, and have benefited from a small loan which has enabled me to do some petty trading. With the next loan I plan to get a milk goat, and then breed more goats and sell the milk. My future is still uncertain, but at least now I have a bit more, which is mine whatever happens. And, in response to my questions, we are soon to be visited by someone from another organisation, who will tell us about inheritance matters.

Key points to note include the following:

- The community research with the women's group involved a range of relevant issues.

- The organisation also deliberately met with vulnerable people, to learn from them.

- The resulting project was designed in such as way as to include vulnerable individuals, and special efforts were made to counter stigma against them, and to encourage them to participate.

- The organisation has formed a complementary partnership with a specialist agency, which can respond to the need for legal advice.

Modifying development work

Community research as part of external mainstreaming should enable an organisation to understand how AIDS is affecting the people with whom it works, and their efforts to escape from poverty, and also how the organisation's work is helping or hindering them to avoid HIV infection and to cope with the impacts of AIDS. The outcome of such research should ideally be practical modifications to existing work, and attempts to tackle any negative consequences of the work, and to reduce susceptibility and vulnerability, particularly among those who are most susceptible to HIV infection and most vulnerable to the impacts of AIDS.

Here, a male farmer involved in one of the imaginary NGO's projects describes how the project has changed as a result of external mainstreaming.

I've been a member of this farmers' group for years now, and in general it's been good for me. I've got access to better seeds, and subsidised fertilisers and pesticides, plus I've learned some good tips. Over the years my harvest has increased, so I've had more money for my family and, well, some for a bit of fun elsewhere as well.

Now, you know how these projects like to have a lot of meetings, and people always filling in forms? Well, two years ago they held a special review. They asked us members about the project, and we told them what they should do, like getting us those good, big ploughs at subsidised prices. But then they also went and spoke to other people who aren't members, like men and women from the poorer households, even some of the youngsters, even my wife! I mean, yes my wife does the planting and the weeding, and the irrigation, and she also puts on the fertilisers and helps me with the harvest, but it's my farm, and it's my judgement which gets us the good results.

Anyway, after this review things began to change, like they encouraged women to join, and the young folk who are heading their families after their parents die of AIDS. And they began to offer different ways of doing things which don't involve so much cash or risk, like picking off pests by hand, instead of using pesticides. Really, I almost left, but somehow I stayed on. We never got those ploughs – too heavy, they said – but I have to admit that some of the new members, even the single women, are getting quite good crops, and they spend much less than me on their inputs. If we are ever short of cash, it's good to know that there are cheaper ways of doing things. And one of my friends who let his wife join says that they are getting on better, sharing the work and the profits, and having far fewer arguments over money! It's a strange thing to think that a farming project could help to grow better relations in the home!

This man's account alludes to several strategies for modifying work in the light of AIDS, including:

- consulting with people who are not participating in the project, and particularly vulnerable people;

- adapting what the project offers, to provide options that are more suitable for vulnerable people, rather than setting up a separate project;

- testing and promoting options which may be useful to not-yet-affected households, should they become affected;

- paying attention to issues of gender and age, with an eye to the positive effects of involving women and men, and people of different ages.

Modifying humanitarian work

External mainstreaming of AIDS should also make a difference to the lives of people, and particularly women and girls, caught up in humanitarian crises. Here a woman employee of the hypothetical NGO reflects on the impacts of mainstreaming AIDS in her experience of emergency work:

I've been involved in responding to two floods – the ones back in 1994, and the ones last year. It's funny, last year's were much worse, but our response was better. When I think of '94, I mostly remember feeling hopeless. There was so much that was wrong, and so little I could do. Like seeing some women leaving the chaos of the food distribution with practically nothing. Or when that woman insisted I went into a tent, to meet a young woman in a terrible state who had been raped. The only thing I could suggest was that they should report it, but I knew as well as they did that it would be pointless to do so.

But in the camps after last year's floods we paid much more attention to women from the start, and also got them involved in doing things where possible. So women distributed food rations to women, and some women whose husbands were selling their households' rations for alcohol were given their own ration cards. It was a lot fairer. Old people got their share of rations too, along with those who were bedridden. If we hadn't sought them out, I don't think we would have realised that there were so many people with AIDS and other chronic problems, hidden away. And all of the staff were much more aware of gender issues, and less tolerant of violence and rapes and stuff, which before were just seen as unfortunate but inevitable. Better systems from Day One meant that there were proper channels for complaints, and the necessary follow-up.

Of course, it made a big difference that there were more of us, and some specialist staff who did things like support women's groups to help victims of sexual violence. I think there was less violence though, because everything was much fairer and better thought out. For instance, the community groups took on the responsibility of providing protection for single women, and according to those women it mainly worked.

Her experiences show that successful external mainstreaming of AIDS in a displaced person's camp might entail the following elements:

- attention to gender issues from the outset;
- not only consulting women, but involving them in implementation;
- attending to other vulnerable groups, such as the elderly and sick;
- having systems for practical action, rather than mere policies;
- and having additional resources, including specialist staff, to achieve the above.

Systems to institutionalise AIDS as a mainstreamed issue

The final element of mainstreaming AIDS concerns the need to have mechanisms in place so that, once mainstreamed, attention to HIV and AIDS is institutionalised rather than forgotten. In the final voice from the imaginary NGO, the Director reflects on this necessity.

I've devoted my career to fighting the scourge of poverty. It used to mean I wore rubber boots and had dirt under my nails, but now it means spending too much time sitting in this office and in meetings! Still, development workers need to sit down regularly if they are to be organised, and I am a great believer in having good documentation and effective systems, and of enforcing that discipline on others.

When it came to mainstreaming AIDS, I was determined that we would not let it just slip by and be forgotten after a burst of enthusiasm and a few workshops. So I've required all of my managers not only to put checks for attention to AIDS in their systems, but also to test that the checks are working, and to adapt them as necessary. Some were better able to do this than others. It can be quite hard to think up reasonable indicators and methods for assessing whether what you want to happen is happening. We worked around this by getting the managers who understood how to do it to give some support to the others. So now, almost all of our planning, monitoring, and reporting systems have viable checks in them, to see if susceptibility to HIV transmission and the impacts of AIDS have been considered. And all job descriptions and annual reviews include a bit about attention to AIDS. So far, these mechanisms are keeping the organisation awake to the issue, while we go about implementing our core mandate.

Now we have all of that in place, I think it's time that we looked at doing, or supporting, some direct work on AIDS as well. There's a lot of need out there, and now my staff are far more aware of it and able to act on it.

The Director's narrative points to the significance of the following elements:

- leading by example;
- commitment to the process of institutionalising attention to HIV and AIDS;
- encouraging members of staff to share information and ideas;
- testing and modifying systems, rather than assuming that because they are in place, they work.

Supporting partners to mainstream

For organisations that work with partners, such as the hypothetical NGO in this chapter, mainstreaming AIDS will also involve advocacy and capacity building in order to encourage and support those partners to mainstream. The final imaginary voice in this chapter is that of the head of a community-based organisation which is a partner of the hypothetical NGO.

My organisation may only be small, but since our beginning we've had funding from thirteen different donors, each with its own priorities and favoured approaches and reporting formats! So when one of our donors, an NGO, came talking about mainstreaming AIDS, I really felt sorry – it seemed like another imposition on us, when we have so much to do. So I wasn't very enthusiastic to begin with. I just did enough to co-operate with them.

But later I went to one of their mainstreaming workshops, and was surprised to learn that they are taking it seriously themselves. It all began to make more sense when I heard about the effects that it is having on them and the work that they do. Now I've found that they are willing to offer us real support if we are interested, like advice based on what they've done, and training, and some extra money, which will be great, assuming that they are true to their word. I'm really impressed by what they've achieved among their staff – the openness and support – so I think that internal issues are going to be our priority to begin with. I'm not sure we'll be able to afford the luxury of their standards in things like medical treatment, but I know we can improve a lot, and plan ahead for the impacts of AIDS, so that the staff and the organisation will both benefit.

From the perspective of this CBO leader, the idea of mainstreaming seems attractive because its donor and partner, the NGO,

- seems to be genuinely committed to mainstreaming, as it is practising what it is preaching;
- is able to demonstrate positive outcomes from its mainstreaming, which the CBO would like to emulate;
- is offering practical and financial support to the CBO to help it to mainstream.

Summary

This chapter has conveyed some of the differences which mainstreaming might ideally make. Idealised accounts from fictional workers in an NGO, a CBO, and two community members illustrated key elements of internal mainstreaming, external mainstreaming, and the task of supporting partners to mainstream AIDS. The imaginary voices have explained how mainstreaming AIDS can improve things for community members, for employees of development and humanitarian organisations, and for the organisations themselves. The next three chapters move away from this chapter's idealism, to explore the actual experiences of NGOs and governments in responding to HIV and AIDS through mainstreaming.

Part II: Experiences of mainstreaming AIDS

7 Experiences of mainstreaming AIDS internally

Introduction

This and the following two chapters are concerned not with the arguments for mainstreaming or what it might look like, but with actual experiences on the ground. The case studies, specially commissioned for this book, provide much of the data, which are supplemented by information from published documents, from organisations' unpublished reports, and from informal feedback from individuals.

Chapter 5 argued that, in the context of an AIDS epidemic, 'business as usual' is a short-sighted and risky strategy. Indeed, the experience of organisations that have responded to AIDS suggests that the total cost can be significantly reduced if the decision to act is pre-emptive, rather than delayed until the emergence of serious problems (Barnett and Whiteside 2000:31).

The experience of organisations that have responded to AIDS suggests that the total cost can be significantly reduced if the decision to act is pre-emptive, rather than delayed until the emergence of serious problems.

Internal mainstreaming of HIV and AIDS is about changing organisational policy and practice, to reduce an organisation's susceptibility to HIV and its vulnerability to the impacts of AIDS. In other words, to reduce the likelihood of high levels of HIV infection among employees, and the chances of adverse consequences due to the impacts of AIDS. During the process of internal mainstreaming, the focus is on AIDS and the organisation, both now and in the future. Because an organisation's susceptibility and vulnerability are largely determined by those of its staff, AIDS work with staff is a key element. However, internal mainstreaming of AIDS also involves standing back, assessing the way in which an organisation functions in a time of AIDS, and making modifications to existing systems and policies in order to reduce its susceptibility to HIV and vulnerability to the impacts of AIDS. Some people see internal mainstreaming of AIDS as a prerequisite to external mainstreaming, following the rationale that an organisation needs to 'get its own house in order' before it can address the issues of mainstreaming AIDS at field level, or advise its partners to do likewise.

This chapter first considers experiences of AIDS work with staff, including awareness raising, counselling and HIV testing, and developing workplace policies. It then turns to efforts to modify the way in which organisations function, beginning with assessing and predicting the impacts of AIDS, and modelling the effects of various policies, in order to reduce the organisation's vulnerability. The chapter then reviews experiences of adapting existing internal systems, with the aim of reducing organisational susceptibility to HIV and improving the way in which organisations cope with the impacts of AIDS. It concludes with an overview of common problems.

Supporting staff to reduce their susceptibility to HIV, and to cope better with AIDS

This section focuses on the AIDS-work element of internal main-streaming of AIDS, with a focus on supporting employees, to reduce the likelihood of staff becoming infected with HIV, assisting those who are HIV-positive to cope with their condition, and helping them to reduce the impacts of AIDS when it does occur. Three main strategies are exemplified: awareness-raising and staff education; voluntary HIV counselling and testing; and development of workplace policies on HIV and AIDS. All these initiatives aim to help employees. However, the rationale for organisations investing in such strategies is not entirely altruistic: by helping staff members, an organisation aims also to reduce all the impacts of AIDS on itself (as illustrated in Table 5.2 on page 97).

Awareness raising

When we think of HIV/AIDS, we think of rural people and the poor. We forget that it is among ourselves, and that we need training and information. (Government employee, Oxfam Malawi Case Study 2001:14)

For almost all organisations, the first step taken in internal main-streaming is the most obvious one: HIV/AIDS-awareness training for staff, presenting basic facts about HIV transmission and usually going on to consider other issues such as voluntary counselling and testing, and positive living. SC UK reports that its training schemes

...usually consist of: health education and information, discussion of reproductive health issues, where to access specialist counselling and advice services, and writing a will. In some regions where the virus is particularly prevalent, staff training is now seen as an on-going activity, to ensure that personnel are aware of how to protect themselves and know of sources of support if affected by the virus, and also to facilitate an open supportive environment that will help in their work. (SC UK Case Study 2001:3)

Among the case studies for this book, two organisations submitted positive reports of involving people living with HIV and AIDS in their staff training. **ActionAid-Mozambique** is a partner to **Kindlimuka** – the first support group for HIV-positive people in Mozambique – whose members have contributed to awareness-raising work with ActionAid staff, and with many of ActionAid-Mozambique's partners. **Oxfam GB** has invited people living openly with HIV/AIDS to attend awareness-raising and training workshops in several countries, finding that a first-hand account generally makes the issues of HIV transmission, positive living, and illness real to the participants.

To be effective, awareness-raising sessions need to be repeated, both to allow new staff to take part, and to give existing staff the opportunity to attend refresher sessions, or more advanced sessions. Yet all too often an awareness-raising strategy comprises only one or two workshops, with no cycle of sessions being repeated or developed. **Oxfam Malawi** has found it difficult to bring new staff to the same level of understanding as that of existing staff; as a small organisation, it cannot keep re-running the course. It has tried to get around this problem by having some other on-going initiatives. Each office has a staff member who has volunteered to be the HIV/AIDS focal point, with duties that include managing the 'condom corner', where staff can get free supplies of condoms and the latest news and opinions on AIDS from a special notice board. Each office also organises a monthly session, lasting about 30 minutes, immediately following the regular monthly staff meeting, with a different person leading the discussion each time. Topics have included how to break the silence about HIV/AIDS within families, and what an infected person can do to support his or her survivors, such as making a will. As a result, many members of staff now report discussing HIV/AIDS with more people, both at home and at work:

> *In the Blantyre office, we've now got to the stage where we've had monthly meetings about issues as sensitive as promiscuity – about why men want to have so many partners. We couldn't have done that at first ... because, if you push issues from Day One, you won't get any dialogue. But now, we could put any issue on the table and talk openly about it.*
> (Oxfam employee, Oxfam Malawi Case Study 2001:10)

Oxfam Malawi has a small number of staff, a fact which may have made it easier to build trust, and to include all the staff in the awareness-raising activities, from the cleaner to the senior manager. (Larger organisations, however, have the option of running sessions tailored to meet the needs of various levels of staff, or single-sex sessions, which may facilitate communication and openness.) In Malawi, Oxfam's on-going activities

Too often an awareness-raising strategy comprises only one or two workshops, with no cycle of sessions being repeated or developed.

have given staff time to internalise the issues gradually. Occasionally, however, the monthly meetings have been cancelled, as staff struggle to balance their heavy workloads with on-going attention to AIDS.

ActionAid-Mozambique has also used staff meetings as a way of encouraging employees to accept the personal implications of HIV/AIDS. At one session, they used an adaptation of the *Stepping Stones* exercise 'What is Love?'. To begin with, everyone spoke convincingly about the importance of sexual fidelity in the fight against AIDS, but the conversation took a new turn when one person noted: '*Well, this is what we say, but I know for a fact that almost everyone here has had some extra-marital adventure*'. The HIV/AIDS Co-ordinator sees such public statements as a great step away from denial and towards frank discussion of the real obstacles to change.

ActionAid-Mozambique tried two other strategies to raise awareness and support staff. One initiative was a programme bulletin about AIDS and AIDS work. It was well received, but soon ceased publication, because the staff lacked the capacity to maintain it. The other strategy was to appoint 'peer educators': ActionAid teamed up with the SC UK programme in Mozambique to run a joint training course for staff who had volunteered to become peer educators and informal counsellors. Although the staff participated enthusiastically in the course, they subsequently found that they had too little time to organise information sessions or other activities, while the HIV/AIDS Co-ordinator had too little time to support them properly. Another difficulty was that, in general, staff members were reluctant to consult the peer educators, fearing that conversations would not be confidential. The strategy was further undermined by a high turnover of staff, linked to wider changes in the programme (ActionAid-Mozambique Case Study 2001:4).

The strategy of peer education has been more successfully used by the **NAMDEB diamond company** in Namibia, as part of a wider programme comprising STI treatment, voluntary counselling and testing, free condoms, and treatment for tuberculosis (TB) and other HIV-related opportunistic infections. However, the peer educators used centrally prepared resources to present information on HIV/AIDS to employees, and found that people soon became bored with the limited materials available. But because employees did show interest in other issues, the decision was taken to broaden the content of the peer educators' work, presenting a different topic each month, including malaria, TB, family planning, healthy lifestyles, child abuse, alcohol and drug abuse, stress, and child care, in addition to updates on HIV/AIDS and STIs. This appears to be a good example of a programme adapting and so sustaining interest by remaining relevant to the changing and broadening needs of employees (Rau 2002:87).

Although many organisations claim to do regular awareness raising, none of the case studies submitted to the author included details of their curriculum or training schedule, nor any assessment of impact. Only Oxfam Malawi mentioned needs assessment, getting the participants to complete an anonymous questionnaire before their workshop. This gave the facilitators an idea of the participants' existing knowledge, and enabled them to identify the topics that the participants most wanted to address. Unit 3, in the Resources section at the back of this book, is a simple questionnaire used by ActionAid-The Gambia to evaluate the effects of a basic AIDS-awareness workshop. In general, there seems to be a tendency for an awareness-raising session to be seen as a completed – and successful – activity, simply because it has happened. This is rather different from seeing on-going training, evaluated and tuned to staff needs, as part of a broader package of support for staff.

There seems to be a tendency for an awareness-raising session to be seen as a completed – and successful – activity, simply because it has happened.

Counselling and HIV testing

While awareness-raising sessions allow for education and group discussion about AIDS, they do not give individuals the privacy or time to reflect on their own situation. Many agencies, therefore, offer counselling services as an additional form of support for staff and, sometimes, for volunteers too. While ActionAid-Mozambique attempted to provide this kind of support informally via its peer educators, for more professional counselling most development organisations refer their staff to an ASO. This approach has the advantage of using counsellors from outside the staff members' own organisation, and the counselling can take place in another building: both important considerations if people do not want their colleagues to know that they are going for counselling.

A constraint on the use of counselling stems from the way in which it is perceived and used. In research with **ActionAid-Uganda**, undertaken in 1994, most staff saw counsellors as people to turn to when you fear, or know, that you have AIDS. As one employee said:

> *The way we are supposed to use the counsellor is not exactly what we have done. They said you don't necessarily have to be HIV-positive to come for this counselling, you can still be sensitised, to ask questions and all that. Instead, we are waiting for the signs of the rash...and then we go, looking for encouragement and support to dare to find out what status we are.*
> (Holden 1994:15)

When counselling is perceived as being indicative of HIV-positive status and the onset of AIDS, the act of seeking counselling may become stigmatised. As one ActionAid-Uganda officer put it, *'The moment they see me with the counsellor, they will suspect, and I will start being erased'* (Holden 1994:15).

For organisations, one motivation for offering counselling is to encourage staff to take an HIV test, which should support HIV prevention regardless of the result. It is hoped that those found to be HIV-negative will want to protect themselves and remain uninfected, while those who are HIV-positive are offered hope in the form of positive living, which includes avoiding re-exposure to HIV, and protecting others from transmission. However, a general reluctance to take an HIV test means that, as with counselling, it becomes a strategy for those who have reason to believe that they have begun to develop AIDS, so that some of the preventative potential of testing is lost. As two ActionAid-Uganda staff members, who were both in good health, commented:

> *So many of us have never had the courage to go and do a test...I can't go there now, because I don't know how I would deal with the problem...Should I lose heart? Should I commit suicide? Should I hunt for those who I suspect to have got me into this problem? So there is this fear, it is like going for an examination, whether you pass or fail...but with AIDS if you fail, there is no second chance.*

> *...staff do not go for blood testing. If you find out you are positive, you may die more quickly than one who did not know. Finding out could be worse than ignorance.*

(Holden 1994:14)

Individuals may be particularly doubtful about the wisdom of knowing their HIV status if they lack role models – people who are openly HIV-positive and reaping the benefits of positive living. ActionAid's Africa Region has an 'affirmative action' policy which stipulates that all programmes should employ an openly HIV-positive member of staff (Bataringaya 1999:1). **ActionAid-Burundi** is one of the programmes which has acted on the policy by getting a staff member through Greater Involvement of People Infected by HIV/AIDS (the GIPA initiative).

ActionAid-Burundi is fortunate in that their GIPA staff member (who is posted as a UN volunteer) is experienced in social work and trained as a counsellor. As a result of her skills and openness about her own HIV status, she is proving effective in sensitising and supporting ActionAid-Burundi staff, and others from partner organisations and the community.

'Many of us have never had the courage to go and do a test... it is like going for an examination, whether you pass or fail...but with AIDS if you fail, there is no second chance.'

Early in 2002, the programme reported that around thirty people – two thirds of them from ActionAid-Burundi – had met with her voluntarily, either in the office, or in a café, or at home. Almost half of those from ActionAid-Burundi had subsequently taken an HIV test. ActionAid-Burundi's case study says that *'Those who received positive results are accepting their conditions with a remarkable courage. One among them has created her own group for support to other people living with AIDS out of the ActionAid milieu and she is doing quite well.'* The case study attests to the significance of the GIPA volunteer as a role model, stating *'because of telling people her status, she helps others to demystify HIV/AIDS, and to no longer consider an infected person as candidate to death'*. In South Africa, a project which placed eleven GIPA fieldworkers in organisations' workplace programmes found that the fieldworkers were able to destigmatise AIDS and contribute significantly to the workplace programmes (Simon-Meyer and Odallo 2002:8).

ActionAid-Burundi's experience suggests a potentially useful strategy for others to follow as part of internal mainstreaming of AIDS. However, it is important to note that the success is due to a combination of the skills and openness of the volunteer, plus her focus on internal work. At least five other ActionAid programmes have appointed their GIPA volunteers to work on external matters, supporting AIDS projects, which has enabled them to make strong links with groups of HIV-positive people. There have been internal benefits too, in terms of demonstrating the worth of people who are HIV-positive, and making staff more alert to issues of discrimination and stigma. The **ActionAid Africa Regional Office** in Zimbabwe reports that while some staff initially discriminated against their first GIPA volunteer – for example, demonstrating anxieties over using the same cup and chair as her – employees handled a second GIPA volunteer in a much more relaxed and accepting way. Evidently, having an openly HIV-positive member of staff does influence other staff – embodying the principles of positive living, and demonstrating the organisation's policy on non-discrimination – but organisations have to decide whether to focus the individual's energies on internal or external work.

Workplace policies

Our department is losing a lot of manpower. We lost 20 per cent of our extension workers in one year.... the Department has no mechanism for HIV/AIDS – it has a procedure when someone dies, but nothing to protect them while they're alive.
(Government employee, Oxfam Malawi Case Study 2001:21)

Workplace policies formalise an organisation's position with regard to HIV and AIDS and its staff. Policies usually cover provision of awareness raising and counselling for staff, but should extend beyond those measures to a range of human-resource or personnel issues, such as staff health schemes, arrangements for sick leave and compassionate leave, and terms and conditions of employment with regard to HIV and AIDS.

Research by Oxfam Malawi in early 2001 with key respondents from seven organisations – including some NGOs/CBOs, a tea estate, and government departments – found that each one was affected by HIV/AIDS. The most common impacts were absenteeism, lower productivity, vacant posts, growing costs of health care and funerals, and overloading of employees. However, organisations' responses to these effects were limited. While most of the organisations were paying the costs of funerals for staff, and some were providing HIV education for employees, only one of the seven was developing comprehensive workplace policies (Oxfam 2001b). More extensive research by HEARD among South African NGOs and CBOs found as follows:

> Most of the sampled organisations were aware that they eventually would have to grapple with HIV/AIDS among their own staff and volunteers, and they knew this could have serious consequences for their organisations' effectiveness and sustainability. Many also knew they wanted to do something to prepare for this eventuality: to develop and implement policies that would help minimise the impact. However, many of them noted that there is a distinct lack of resources and guidance for organisations seeking to develop responses to HIV/AIDS, and argued that such resources were sorely needed.
> (Manning 2002:6)

We now consider the general experience of developing workplace policies within Oxfam GB and ActionAid, but we begin by outlining a small-scale initiative aimed at stimulating reflection and action on the need for workplace policies.

A workshop on workplace policies

In 2001, as part of its mainstreaming process, Oxfam Malawi held a two-day workshop for staff and partners, to consider AIDS and workplace policy and practice. After reviewing statistics on HIV and AIDS, the participants brainstormed about the effects of AIDS on their organisations. They then reviewed three documents: the Southern Africa Development Community Code of Conduct on HIV/AIDS and Employment; a draft national code on HIV in the workplace; and Oxfam GB's Policy

Management Guidelines for Critical/Terminal Illness. With these in mind, the participants divided into small groups to consider how they would handle several scenarios concerning AIDS and the workplace. This activity raised a lot of issues:

> *We looked at questions like: How do you support staff if they look like they are ill? How as a manager do you keep information confidential? How do you handle it if you know that someone is positive and their contract is up for renewal? What do you do if someone is showing signs of sickness – knowing that you shouldn't discriminate, but knowing that there is work that needs doing?*

(Oxfam employee, Oxfam Malawi Case Study 2001:12)

Feedback from the participants indicated that the workshop had given them a lot of food for thought. In particular, it helped them to appreciate the difficulty of achieving a proper balance between being a good employer – or getting a good deal as an employee – and protecting the organisation's self-interest. The workshop also revealed tensions between wanting to promote openness, so that staff members disclose their status and can be supported, and respecting each individual's right to privacy.

'What do you do if someone is showing signs of sickness – knowing that you shouldn't discriminate, but knowing that there is work that needs doing?'

When discussing the workplace scenarios, the participants found that the codes and draft policies helped to guide their decision making, but did not remove the element of subjective judgement, nor lead to automatic decisions. For example, one scenario read as follows:

> *An employee on a two-year contract falls ill for some time, and you know that it is HIV-related, because she told you. She recovers and works the final nine months with no problem. At the end of her contract, you need to get the same work done. She is competent, yet you fear future illness. What do you do?*

The small group working on this scenario decided that they would re-employ the individual on a one-year contract, subject to medical clearance. The other participants described this decision as discriminatory, because if her HIV status had not been known, she would have been given another two-year contract. As well as being unfair, they felt it would discourage other employees from disclosing their HIV status. The small group felt that the decision was fair, bearing in mind that the manager was aware of the likelihood of another bout of illness, and could not avoid considering the potential impact on the organisation.

However, although the workshop was a success, in terms of generating reflection and at times passionate debate on a subject that all participants agreed to be of great importance, some two years later the event does not seem to have resulted in improvements in policies or practices among the partners. In Malawi Oxfam did not have anyone with time or expertise to help the partners to follow through with development of their own workplace policies, nor did it identify anyone outside Oxfam to provide this service to them. Equally, the participants have not actively pushed Oxfam to provide such support.[1]

An agency-wide workplace policy

Oxfam GB decided to develop a single workplace policy for AIDS for all of its programmes, a process which has taken around two years. Key to stimulating and informing the process were pieces of work on predicting the impacts of AIDS in Southern Africa, and the likely costs of different scenarios in the Horn, East Africa, and Central Africa (discussed in detail later in this chapter). The process involved several drafts, discussion at many levels, and further development and consultation before final approval. It was found to be important that staff in highly affected countries should be involved throughout the process.

Oxfam's HIV/AIDS policy includes provision of ART to employees on contracts lasting one year or longer, or who have been in continuous employment for at least a year, and to one dependant per employee.

The first draft was a comprehensive 'Critical Illness Policy', which covered all chronic and critical health conditions, on the assumption that a separate HIV/AIDS policy might actually increase stigma by treating HIV separately. However, by the end of the process Oxfam had decided to adopt a specific and dedicated HIV/AIDS policy. There were several reasons for this, including the fact that HIV/AIDS has a greater impact on staff, gender equity, and programmes than other critical illnesses; that the associated stigma (especially against women) makes it essential to have a clear, proactive, and supportive statement of policy on HIV/AIDS; and that some of the policy commitments are specific to HIV.

From the work on various policy scenarios emerged a choice for Oxfam GB: whether or not to provide antiretroviral treatment as part of its policy. It was decided that investing in ART would make sense, as the costs would be offset by the benefits. In addition, as an advocate of access to antiretroviral treatment, Oxfam wanted to meet its ethical obligations to its own employees. As such, the HIV/AIDS policy includes provision of ART to employees on contracts lasting one year or longer, or who have been in continuous employment for at least a year, and to one dependant per employee. Once someone is on ART, he or she needs to stay on it for life, so Oxfam has undertaken to fund ART for staff for one year after they leave the organisation, for whatever reason. This allows departing employees time to secure alternative sources of treatment. It also means that a manager would not be prevented from dismissing a member of staff

– for example, for a disciplinary offence – because to do so would terminate that employee's treatment. In terms of funding, Oxfam intends to use commercial insurance to cover the costs of ART, but where this is not possible or cost-effective, Oxfam will fund the provision itself. In line with its own advocacy, the organisation's policy is to use high-quality generic ART, rather than the more expensive patented drugs.

However, because some field locations lack the clinics and professional staff to provide ART, Oxfam's policy is to provide treatment 'where adequate facilities are available locally'. Where the local infrastructure is inadequate, Oxfam will review the feasibility of linking internal needs with programme requirements to help to build medical infrastructure, either alone or with partners. This may prove to be problematic, in terms of deciding what constitutes 'adequate facilities', and the extent to which the agency is willing to invest in medical infrastructure.

While it has taken a lot of effort to get the policy finalised, Oxfam recognises that this is only the first step, and that the greater challenge lies in implementation. As a result, it is dedicating two Implementation Managers to roll out the workplace programme across the two most highly affected regions in Africa over 18 months. They will focus on the provision of treatment – such as identifying providers of ART, and setting up arrangements with them – but will also cover other elements of the policy, such as the provision of education and access to counselling and HIV testing.

In addition, Oxfam is providing an AIDS information pack to support each country programme's implementation of the HIV/AIDS workplace policy. This will comprise a leaflet for staff on the basic facts of HIV/AIDS and their employment rights, a staff handbook, a slide-presentation pack for induction of new employees, and a manager's guide. Programme managers will also receive a practical guide, outlining an approach to establishing a comprehensive education programme and to providing access to counselling and HIV testing for staff. The agency also intends to provide in-depth training for selected staff to help them to implement the policy, and plans to invest in improving financial and reporting systems to allow certain indicators for the policy – such as rates of absenteeism, medical expenses, and death-in-service benefits – to be monitored.

Locally developed workplace policies

ActionAid allows each of its country programmes to make its own policies, guided by a Global Organisational Development Framework, which sets out principles to which all programmes must adhere, and guidelines to inform local decisions about the details of policies and practices. With regard to AIDS, this decentralised approach has the advantage that policy decisions are made in context, to reflect local circumstances, which vary enormously, according to differences in national HIV rates and legal obligations. Moreover, if a policy needs to be adjusted, this can be done at the local level, with relatively little bureaucratic formality. However, ActionAid's approach means that employees in similar situations may be treated differently, according to which programme they work in. Moreover, every programme is faced with the difficult task of developing a workplace policy for HIV and AIDS, rather than benefiting from a single piece of work applicable to the whole agency.

ActionAid's main framework for organisational development refers in three places to HIV/AIDS (ActionAid 2001).

- First, it states the principle that, when recruiting, ActionAid does not discriminate on the basis of HIV status, among many other attributes, and it presents the following guideline: '*ActionAid encourages the proactive recruitment of people from the types of groups for which we work (e.g. women, specific castes, ethnic groups, disabled, people living with AIDS).*'

- Second, it requires all programmes to have, among other policies for staff welfare, a policy on HIV/AIDS and terminal illness, so that '*all ActionAid staff and their families are provided with sufficient updated information to protect them from and cope with HIV and other terminal illness infection*', and it states that there should be '*special financial assistance for people with HIV/AIDS and other terminal illness*'.

- Third, with regard to terminating employment, the document gives guidance that '*as far as possible ActionAid will provide an enabling work environment especially for staff suffering from terminal or seriously debilitating diseases, to continue working until such time as they are medically unable to do so*'.

In addition, in the context of disciplinary offences, there is a guideline stating that sexual harassment is among several behaviours which warrant immediate dismissal (although it is not clear if this extends to sexual harassment of community members).

The framework also includes a simple two-page appendix about human-resource issues and HIV/AIDS, which is included in Unit 4 in the Resources section at the back of this book. In addition to the above points, this appendix advises that HIV testing should not form part of the recruitment process, and that being HIV-positive should not prevent staff from taking advantage of training and career-development opportunities. It affirms the principle of the right to confidentiality, and suggests that staff declaring their HIV/AIDS status should have access to medical support, counselling, paid sick leave, voluntary termination of employment with benefits, and redeployment to lighter duties. Finally, the appendix gives guidance to the effect that refusal to work with someone who is HIV-positive should be a disciplinary offence.

On the ground, all ActionAid programmes in Africa have an HIV/AIDS and terminal-illness workplace policy which includes provision of information, HIV testing and counselling, and medical and terminal benefits. At the end of 2002, three programmes – Kenya, Malawi, and Uganda – were providing antiretroviral therapy. Recently, ActionAid's Africa Region has agreed that ART should be made available to staff across the continent, to ensure equity among the programmes. The precise mechanism to achieve this is still being developed; it will include a regional fund to assist country programmes which need help to pay for access to ART, due, for example, to high local costs for ART, or a lack of locally available insurance. The fund is likely to be established with about a half of one per cent of the region's annual budget; ActionAid's Global HIV/AIDS Co-ordinator recommends that keeping costs to less than one per cent should be acceptable, and has proposed the addition of a one per cent levy to project proposals. ActionAid's current commitment to providing ART to all staff who need it – first in Africa, but with plans to extend it world-wide – is based less on a cost–benefit assessment, and more on the principle that it should, and can, be done. ActionAid aims to collaborate with other agencies to share access to approved doctors and pharmacies, and hopes to develop 'treatment literacy' in its programmes, so that staff are more aware of nutritional issues, the principles of positive living, and preventative treatment, as well as the options and side-effects related to ART.

ActionAid's current commitment to providing ART to all staff who need it is based less on a cost–benefit assessment, and more on the principle that it should, and can, be done.

In addition to ensuring equitable treatment, another motive behind ActionAid's production of clear agency-wide guidelines about treatment is a desire to ensure that managers act consistently and wisely. Two experiences illustrate the dangers of leaving decisions in the hands of individuals. In one case a manager decided, without consultation, to pay for ART for a staff member. Because provision of ART was outside the programme's policy and budgets, the decision was subsequently reversed. In another programme, a manager approved a substantial sum for an HIV-infected staff member to undergo a treatment which would, supposedly, 'cure' AIDS. As outlined earlier, having clear policies can take pressure off managers, by removing the onus on them to make 'life and death' decisions.

ActionAid's experience of the response to workplace policies varies across country programmes, depending on the external environment, including levels of openness, availability of counselling, testing, and treatment, activism by HIV-positive people, and political commitment. The workplace policy in Uganda has had the greatest response, with several members of staff claiming access to ART, and a few openly admitting their HIV status. In contrast, the policies are underused in ActionAid programmes where stigma still prevails, and no one has yet taken up ART in Malawi or Kenya. As one project officer from ActionAid-Malawi commented:

Having clear policies can take pressure off managers, by removing the onus on them to make 'life and death' decisions.

> From my knowledge, there have been problems in making use of policies and support services. The fear of taking an HIV test and denial makes people who for instance know they have TB fail to access the right treatment which the organisation provides in its medical scheme...Generally, people are not open about their HIV status. Stigma and denial prevails. Some people who would otherwise have been treated end up dying because they were not open, and could not be referred to specialist clinics or even AIDS support groups.
> (ActionAid-Malawi Case Study 2001:1)

Even in ActionAid-Uganda, not all staff view the policy as a complete success. The case study from ActionAid-Uganda quotes positive views, such as *'I would actually say that our environment is very neutral, we have no stigma attached to HIV/AIDS, if anything there is a culture of openness, no denial at all, so the infected persons are just comfortable.'* However, in a personal communication, another employee reported: *'There is lack of openness amongst ourselves. The process is not very free. Someone can still not declare up to the last moment when all the signs and symptoms are there.'* [2]

ActionAid's experience shows that having workplace policies does not automatically lead to the eradication of stigma, to general willingness to take an HIV test, and to access to treatment of HIV-positive staff. This is even the case where life-extending ART is available, and echoes experience among businesses such as Barclays and Debswana, which offer ART but find that take-up is typically only one fifth of the numbers that would benefit from such treatment (Elwes 2002:22). As with AIDS work with community members, it can be very difficult to influence behaviours, even in the workplace situation where the numbers of people are relatively small and organisations have substantial influence over the immediate environment. Furthermore, as the participants at the workshop organised by Oxfam in Malawi found, although workplace policies may assist in decision making, they may not completely obviate the need for managers to make difficult subjective judgements concerning their staff and HIV and AIDS. However, workplace policies are important in setting out agencies' values and commitments with regard to AIDS, as part of their efforts to support their staff and to reduce institutional susceptibility to HIV and vulnerability to the impacts of AIDS.

Modifying the ways in which organisations function in the context of AIDS

This chapter has already described some direct ways in which organisations can try to reduce the impacts of AIDS on their functioning, by investing in AIDS work to support staff. For example, an HIV-positive employee who is assisted to live positively, and who has access to good-quality health care, is likely to contribute to the organisation more effectively, and for longer, than one who does not know his or her status, or feels a need to hide it, or is subject to prejudice in the workplace.

However, efforts to reduce the internal impacts of AIDS should entail more than supporting staff members to change their behaviour, whether with regard to safer sex, seeking counselling, or securing treatment. This is because the susceptibility and vulnerability of an organisation to HIV and AIDS are not determined purely by its employees' behaviour, but also by the ways in which the organisation functions. So this section concerns surveys by organisations to assess how their existing systems and policies might need to be modified, in the light of the current and future impacts of AIDS.

This section begins by discussing what should logically be the first step in facing up to AIDS: assessing and predicting its impacts, and analysing the costs and benefits of various policy responses, before proceeding to modify any policies. This process almost always involves research, partly because research findings are valuable for internal advocacy, to stimulate a further response. More fundamentally, however, managers need to undertake or commission research in order to gain a better sense of the effects that HIV and AIDS are already having on their organisation, and the impacts which they are likely to have in the future, if their decisions about how to respond are to be well informed.

Two types of research emerged from the case studies. The first is based on experiences and current impacts of AIDS, using *qualitative* feedback from staff members, while the second focuses on *quantitative* projections of the future impacts of AIDS on the organisation, and cost–benefit analysis of various responses.

Reviewing current impacts of AIDS

In 2001, Save the Children UK sent questionnaires to its programmes in Southern and Eastern Africa, in an effort to learn about the experiences of its staff. The responses – which were anonymous – suggest that approximately one third of staff members were caring for sick or disabled relatives, and a similar proportion had taken on responsibility for someone else's children. One third of respondents also reported taking unofficial leave in relation to HIV/AIDS; for example, in order to care for someone, collect medications, attend a funeral, or attend to orphans' needs.

Every employee is burdened by AIDS in some way, and this affects the organisation, because staff members spend time at work on AIDS-related personal business.

The review gave SC UK an opportunity to consult with staff members about their needs. The prime concern of respondents was the ability to afford treatment and get good-quality care. Respondents also requested more information about HIV and AIDS, and access to legal advice. They raised some controversial issues, including accusations of discrimination (in countries where staff health-care packages vary), of unfairness (where the number of dependants on a health scheme means that some children in larger families are excluded), and pleas for antiretroviral treatment to be made available.

The review process also involved consulting programme directors and human-resource managers, either through questionnaires or through interviews. These key informants raised a broad range of concerns, many of which focused on the welfare of staff, the inadequacies of health-care schemes, and the need to find better ways of providing comprehensive care for staff and their dependants. Two human-resource managers working in highly affected countries summarised the intangible and indirect impacts of AIDS on the organisation as follows.

- First, every employee is burdened by AIDS in some way, and this affects the organisation, because staff members spend time at work on AIDS-related personal business. Typical activities include organising visits and care of the sick; solving problems related to affected children and orphans; dealing with legal issues; arranging for funerals; and other issues connected with their extended families.

- Second, because co-workers in this organisation are emotionally involved in the lives of each other, one person's sickness or difficulties will affect the whole workplace.

- Third, the loss of someone in a key position has a particularly demoralising and disorganising effect on the whole workforce.

Three anecdotes from an agency which wishes to remain anonymous illustrate these intangible but nonetheless real impacts with some actual examples. One male staff member had several children, but the children had different mothers. When he died, two of the mothers claimed his terminal benefits, and several other women asked the organisation for support for their children. An office collection was taken for the burial, and the money was split between the two mothers who claimed the employee's terminal benefits. Resolving the issue consumed a lot of management time, and caused much stress.

Another employee had a sister who was HIV-positive, and the employee was absent from work a great deal in the two months before her sister died. Afterwards, she was preoccupied with settling her sister's affairs, including trying to secure her sister's pension for her children, and being embroiled in legal disputes regarding her sister's land. These bureaucratic struggles are very time-consuming: the organisation often allowed her to take a driver and a car to make visits to various officials, which had to be done during office hours. Sometimes the employee used her annual leave to do this, but at other times it was unofficial. The employee was also looking after her sister's children, the youngest of whom was HIV-positive and becoming ill. She was reported to lack concentration at work, which reduced her efficiency.

In another case, an employee fell sick while on leave. The organisation sent a driver, who took the employee to a nursing home, where he was treated and discharged. However, the clinic had tested the employee for HIV without his consent and revealed his positive result to the organisation's insurance company, which wrote to inform the organisation that the employee's insurance had been revoked, because AIDS was excluded under the terms of the insurance. The organisation explained the situation to the employee, who then attempted suicide by swallowing battery acid. He was admitted to hospital, where he received intensive care for several weeks. A decision was made to stop treatment and he was moved to a clinic, where he died a week later. His HIV diagnosis and attempted suicide disqualified him from receiving medical benefits, and the very high medical bill was technically the responsibility of his family. The situation was further complicated by two families claiming his terminal benefits, which, in the end, were partly used to pay the medical costs.

As these three cases illustrate, AIDS can have varied, and often unforeseen, effects on staff members, as well as serious repercussions for colleagues, and in particular, for the managers who have to make decisions about treatment and benefits. The SC UK review states:

> It is hard to quantify the toll it takes on Directors and other staff who have to make life-and-death judgement calls without clinical expertise, and live with them afterwards. The administrative time adds to costs, and the worries and stresses affect the health and quality of life of those involved. Many Programme Directors asked that decisions left to their discretion be taken out of their hands.
>
> (Save the Children UK 2001:34)

Another piece of research about the impacts of AIDS on Ministries of Agriculture in Eastern and Southern Africa found that issues of treatment and care are dealt with in an *ad hoc* manner (Topouzis 2001:14). And in South Africa, research among NGOs and CBOs suggests that the impacts of AIDS may commonly be heightened because decision makers tend towards generosity:

> ...levels of lost time may be exacerbated by organisations that attempt to be 'too kind' or 'too supportive' and fail to enforce personnel policies and reasonable expectations of sick and compassionate leave. Many organisations will find it difficult to terminate the employment of an ill employee, and will want to provide flexibility for those individuals even when they are ailing for many months or even years, missing vast amounts of work, and not fulfilling their duties. A large proportion of organisational personnel policies, for instance, allow for 'additional leave at management discretion', thereby laying difficult decisions about when to draw the line on leave and employment requirements on the shoulders of a few individuals. Although the desire to support employees in a time of need is certainly laudable, and in line with the philosophy and principles of the civil society sector, organisations must recognise that there is a significant cost to such flexibility, and that being too lenient may have serious implications for organisational sustainability.
>
> (Manning 2002:30)

Workplace policies are the most common way of giving managers guidance or rules to follow with regard to chronic illnesses. However, if such policies are to protect organisations from potentially excessive or unsustainable costs, then they need to be based on assessments of the future impacts and costs of AIDS.

Predicting impacts of AIDS, and analysing options for responding

Several large businesses have undertaken a thorough process known as an institutional audit to assess their AIDS-related risks. Barnett and Whiteside (2002:257) characterise these audits as having six components, including the following:

- personnel profiling (taking into account skills, replacement difficulties, and susceptibility to HIV infection among different groups of employees);

- 'key post' analysis (assessing if illness among particular staff positions would have a disproportionate impact on the organisation);

- the organisation's profile (in terms of resources and training and coping with staff absences);

- liabilities (staff benefits, and the degree to which particular staff are crucial to production);

- effects on, and options for, productivity;

- and the legal context in which decisions are being made.

In some cases, such as that of Debswana Diamond Company, the audit includes anonymous HIV testing, to obtain an accurate profile of HIV prevalence among employees (Barnett and Whiteside 2002:263). With the data available, the audits use models to quantify and predict the likely costs of AIDS. Some simple models are available on the Internet; users can enter data relevant to their company, and get a calculation of the likely costs of HIV and AIDS, mainly direct costs relating to health care, staff benefits, and recruitment (Rau 2002:28; see also the bibliography at the back of this book).

For NGOs and CBOs, however, a full institutional audit has a number of disadvantages. Fundamentally, it requires technical expertise which almost all organisations would need to buy in, but few could afford. For small organisations, modelling becomes statistically unreliable, because the small numbers involved make it impossible to predict impacts with any certainty. NGOs and CBOs also face the problem that it is hard for them to measure their 'output', unlike businesses, which can measure the quantities of what they produce, or monitor their profit margins.

An impact assessment for a hypothetical NGO

In an effort to explore the likely effects of AIDS on the 'not-for-profit' sector, the University of Natal's Health Economics and HIV/AIDS Research Division (HEARD) developed an impact assessment for a fictional organisation, 'NGO X' (for more information, see Manning 2002). The employee profile for NGO X reflects that of many NGOs in KwaZulu-Natal, with 30 staff members and 80 community volunteers. The volunteers are predominantly female, and tend to be older than the employees. The assumptions used in the HEARD model, concerning leave entitlements and health benefits, for example, are also based on those found in real organisations in South Africa. By building all of the assumptions and data into an impact-assessment model, HEARD is able to provide predictions for the impacts of AIDS on NGO X over the next 20 years.

The model's predictions raise three interesting points. First, it does not predict a sudden impact on NGO X, but a gradual build-up of effects year on year, mostly peaking after seven to ten years. Deaths due to AIDS, for example, are likely to peak after about nine years, at a level of one or two deaths each year among both employees and volunteers. Cumulatively, NGO X is expected to lose ten staff members and eleven volunteers over ten years. After 20 years, the model predicts that 19 members of staff members and 22 volunteers will have died from AIDS.

A second point of interest is the differing impacts of AIDS on the staff and volunteers of NGO X. While there are far fewer staff than volunteers, the numbers expected to die from AIDS are similar. This is because the volunteers are older, and so outside the age groups among which the majority of deaths from AIDS occur.

Thirdly, in terms of direct annual costs, the model predicts that these will peak at a level which is roughly equivalent to the average annual salary within NGO X. However, HEARD's model assumes levels of benefits which are very low, compared with those offered by many NGOs – for example, no medical or pension benefits, and a death benefit equal to just one tenth of the average monthly salary. Feedback from international NGOs shows that a death benefit equivalent to several months' salary – or one month for each year in service – is more common, as are comprehensive medical and pension schemes. The civil service also typically has low wages but relatively generous benefits, particularly with regard to pensions (Barnett and Whiteside 2002:304). The direct costs to government, therefore, will be much greater than those in the NGO X model.

It is important to note that the model has limitations. It does not, for example, include the less tangible impacts of AIDS on staff morale and stress levels, and the likely effects on the operations of the organisation.

Nor does it capture the differing impacts of illness in differing people, or types of worker. In the real world, the loss of employees in certain 'key posts' may have far-reaching consequences. And NGO X would have to change its whole way of working if, for example, it became unable to recruit and retain volunteers, owing to the demands that AIDS places on their lives.

Oxfam GB's impact assessments

In 2001 Oxfam GB decided to undertake an assessment of the likely internal impacts of AIDS on its programmes in Southern Africa. In this it was supported by Tony Barnett of the University of East Anglia, and Chris Desmond, who specialises in modelling the impacts of AIDS, from the University of Natal's Health Economics and HIV/AIDS Research Division (HEARD). Oxfam did not, however, hand over responsibility for the assessment to these specialists, but worked alongside them.

The first stage in the process entailed staff in the regional office gathering three sets of data: information on numbers of staff and dependants, their sex and age, and their geographical location; adult and youth HIV-prevalence rates for those locations; and a summary of staff health-care policies, identifying all the entitlements for employees in the various programmes, such as sick leave and holiday leave, and health and death benefits. When this had been done, Oxfam brought together a team of staff for four days, to review the data and do some basic calculations. This team contained a cross-section of people who knew Oxfam from various perspectives, and included people from the human resources and finance teams, AIDS specialists, and programme managers, with representatives from various countries within the region and from the head office.

In order to calculate the likely costs, the team had to make some assumptions. First, Oxfam GB provides health benefits to staff, their legally documented partners, and children up to the age of 18 for whom the employee has responsibility. However, the team did not have full information on the numbers involved, so they worked on the basis that each staff member has a partner plus two to three eligible dependants.

Second, the team worked with the assumption that Oxfam's staff and dependants are likely to have approximately the same HIV prevalence rate as the general population. (On the one hand, their risk may be higher, as Oxfam staff travel a lot, and have a regular income, while on the other hand their risk may be lower, because Oxfam staff are educated, and female employees have their own incomes.)

The team developed three scenarios: 'high prevalence' of 25 per cent; 'medium prevalence' of 15 per cent; and 'low prevalence' of 10 per cent. They decided to focus on the medium-prevalence scenario, as an average for the region. Taking 120 staff members and a hypothetical 120 spouses into account, this suggested that in Southern Africa Oxfam might have around 36 adults (15 per cent of 240) who are HIV-positive, and for whom it has some responsibilities.

However, many of these people would currently be asymptomatic, and would not begin to fall ill until some time in the future. Thus the team made a further assumption that five to ten per cent of those HIV-positive adults might be developing the opportunistic diseases which lead to AIDS. The calculations therefore suggested that, in any given year, between two and four members of staff, and a similar number of their spouses, might be incurring medical costs in relation to HIV and AIDS in the five countries. The team members reflected on their collective knowledge of sickness and death among Oxfam employees in the region, and found that the estimate of two to four members of staff living with AIDS seemed to be reasonable, a fact which gave them some confidence in their assumptions.

In Southern Africa Oxfam might have around 36 adults (15 per cent of 240) who are HIV-positive, and for whom it has some responsibilities.

The team's next task was to calculate the likely financial and non-financial costs of ill health and death, extrapolated over the next five years. They assumed that the number of cases of AIDS within Oxfam will increase, in line with the rising trend of HIV over the last ten years in the region, and as HIV-positive staff begin to suffer ill health. With the best available figures, they developed two scenarios for the costs of AIDS: one with antiretroviral therapy, and one without it. The financial costs included direct health-care costs and benefits such as death-in-service payments, plus some indirect costs such as paying for temporary cover for staff absent from work for more than one month. They also outlined the less tangible likely impacts of staff illness, staff staying at home to care for relatives, and other disruptions caused by absenteeism and funerals in Oxfam, its partner organisations, and the community. The team then made a number of recommendations, concerning health care for staff, their partners and dependants, and strengthening internal systems and practices.

This impact assessment for Oxfam GB in Southern Africa brought the issue of the likely impact of HIV and AIDS on to the agenda of the highest decision-making bodies within the organisation, particularly because the assessment pointed to substantial increases in costs, and raised concerns about how staff policies might need to be modified in order to protect the organisation from excessive costs, while also meeting its duty of care to its employees and their dependants.

To investigate further, and as part of developing an HIV/AIDS workplace policy, Oxfam secured the voluntary services of Tabitha Elwes (a senior professional, taking a year off from paid employment) to do further work on the same issue, but in the region of the Horn, East Africa, and Central Africa. She reviewed the HIV/AIDS policies and practices of a range of NGOs and businesses in the region, and assessed the various health-insurance options available. Some of the assumptions that she adopted were different from those used in Southern Africa. For example, she assumed that HIV prevalence among Oxfam staff is 10 per cent higher than national averages, because its staff are mobile, and a significant proportion are working in emergency situations, separated from their families. She assumed also that only 10 per cent of HIV-positive staff would have AIDS at any time, on the basis that employees are well nourished and have good health care, so are likely to be asymptomatic for longer than average. She then developed two quite detailed scenarios for future costs and benefits: one with provision of ART, and one without. The basic model is illustrated in Figure 7.1.

Overall, the model suggested that if Oxfam were to offer ART to employees and one dependant per employee, it would add about five per cent to the organisation's medical costs, rising to around 20 per cent in ten years' time. Significantly, however, her analysis suggested that these costs would be more than offset by savings arising from reductions in staff absences, recruitment costs, human-resources staffing, and death-in-service benefits, thus saving costs overall. Furthermore, less tangible benefits would result from providing ART as part of the overall workplace policy, through enhanced productivity, improved staff morale, retention of institutional knowledge, and the preservation of Oxfam's credibility. The economic case for providing ART was particularly compelling for employees, but less so for dependants, because Oxfam suffers fewer costs when it is a dependant, rather than a staff member, who is HIV-positive.

Three aspects of this second exercise are important to note. First, in the words of Tabitha Elwes, *'the analysis is as logical and as rooted in the available data as possible, but those data are very patchy... even basic data about HIV prevalence are questionable'.*[3] Second, the findings are specific to Oxfam, and are sensitive to the benefits offered and the assumptions made. For example, compared with organisations such as those represented by NGO X, Oxfam's calculations included relatively high costs for salaries,

Figure 7.1: Oxfam GB model for assessing the internal impacts of AIDS

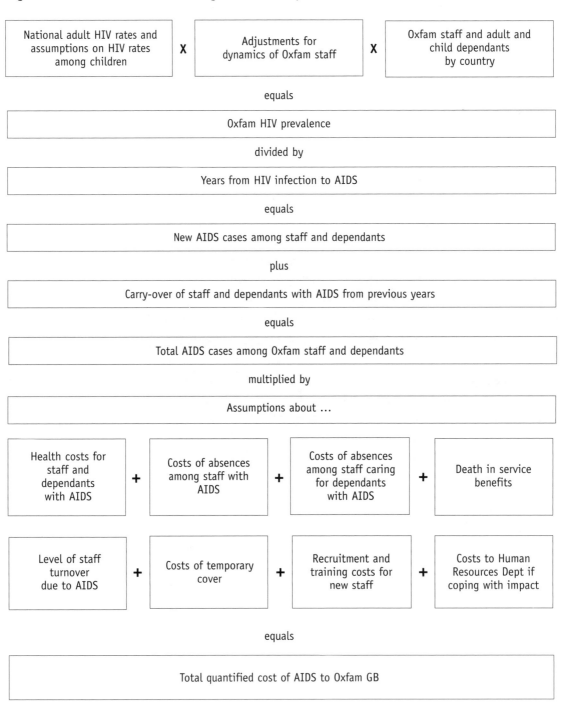

Source: Elwes (2002:5)

death-in-service benefits, and payments to temporary staff to cover staff absences. The model also assumed a high level of take-up of ART among HIV-positive staff (Elwes 2002). Third, although the analysis has enabled Oxfam to develop its HIV/AIDS workplace policy with some confidence, there are many variables and unknowns: the implementation and up-take will need to be monitored, with a view to modifying and improving them as necessary in the future.

Several lessons emerge from Oxfam's experience. One is that the process was limited by the availability of information from within the agency, and Oxfam needs to improve or set up relevant systems, if it is to project the impacts of AIDS with more accuracy in the future. (Moreover, such data are needed to monitor the effectiveness of workplace policies.) Another lesson from Southern Africa was that having staff engaging with the process of predicting impacts of AIDS was, in itself, a way of stimulating interest in, and a desire to respond to, HIV and AIDS within Oxfam. As such, the Regional HIV/AIDS Co-ordinator for Southern Africa sees the process of predicting the impacts of AIDS as a useful step to take at an early stage in the mainstreaming process.[4] Finally, Oxfam found that having a committed and competent person dedicated to the work in the Horn, East Africa, and Central Africa made a huge difference: the research and scenario-building were complex and time-consuming, and could not have been done so thoroughly if undertaken in addition to someone's ordinary workload.

Changing policy and practice

The outcome of efforts to review and predict impacts, and to analyse the costs and benefits of a range of varied responses, should be to change policy in ways that should reduce the organisation's susceptibility and vulnerability to HIV and AIDS. However, this aspect of internal mainstreaming of AIDS should not be limited to devising or modifying workplace policies. As with external mainstreaming of AIDS, where the repercussions of development work may inadvertently enhance susceptibility to HIV infection among community members, so the way in which an organisation operates may make its employees more susceptible. For example, if staff are posted far way from their families, they may be more likely to seek extra-marital sexual partners. Or female staff may be susceptible if they are not paid on time and have to seek financial support that entails some form of sexual exchange. Or if an organisation has a high turnover of staff, for whatever reason, then that would undermine its efforts to support staff through prevention, care, and treatment.

On the question of vulnerability to the impacts of AIDS, an organisation could be more vulnerable if, for example, it is slow to replace employees who have left, or lacks mechanisms to cover for unexpected staff absences. By making changes in its systems, an organisation might reduce its vulnerability, and so improve its ability to function, even though some of its staff are affected by AIDS.

However, this sub-section can present only hypothetical examples of possible links to organisational susceptibility and vulnerability, because the case studies did not provide any actual examples. (Chapter 12, however, provides some further ideas.) Oxfam GB recognises the need to reassess its long-term workforce planning, assuming that increasing numbers of staff will fall ill. To reduce the impact of staff absences, it might decide to concentrate on mitigating the consequences among staff, and/or focus on better succession planning, on increasing staffing levels to anticipate growing absenteeism, on improving induction processes, and on providing more rigorous in-service training. However, this process has not yet begun. Another intention is to review funding, budgeting, and monitoring procedures, in order to ensure that enough money is allocated to cope with the costs associated with AIDS. Within ActionAid, there is a suggestion of adding a percentage levy to funding proposals in order to cover such costs, but this has yet to be acted upon. The strategy would entail persuading donors to accept such a levy, an effort which may be facilitated by the fact that donors such as the British government's Department for International Development are increasingly adopting HIV/AIDS policies for the benefit of their employees, including the provision of ART.

Beyond Oxfam's work to develop a workplace policy based on predictions of the impacts of AIDS and the costs and benefits of responding, there is little evidence that organisations are modifying the way in which they function in the context of AIDS. This is not entirely surprising, however. The most common internal response to AIDS is that of supporting staff by doing direct AIDS work, the 'community' to benefit being that of employees and their dependants. In parallel with the situation in programme work, as described in Chapter 4, this direct response predominates because the most obvious and direct strategies are the bio-medical and behavioural ones of preventing HIV transmission among staff and supporting HIV-positive employees to cope better with AIDS.

In another respect, internal mainstreaming parallels external main-streaming, in that it involves agencies modifying their existing ways of working in the light of changes brought about by AIDS, in this case to address the causes of the organisation's susceptibility to HIV infection and the consequences of AIDS for the organisation. As a result it is, to date, less well developed. It is, however, important for a holistic internal response: regardless of their prevention work, all agencies in affected countries will have staff who are HIV-positive, and so will incur costs, particularly the indirect and (cumulatively) the systemic costs featured earlier in Table 5.2 on page 97. If left unchecked, these costs could affect the organisation's ability to implement high-quality programmes; by modifying systems and practices, organisations should be able to cope better with the impacts of AIDS.

Problems

The preceding sections have noted some problems faced by organisations which are internally mainstreaming AIDS. With regard to AIDS work, these include the likelihood that prevention efforts will be unplanned and sporadic, rather than on-going; that shortages of time and resources may limit efforts to support staff; and that employees may not take advantage of the counselling, testing, and treatment options offered to them. As for modifying how agencies function in a time of AIDS, organisations are often unsure how to assess and predict the impacts of AIDS, which can be a complex and costly process. The main limitation, however, is that the notion of modifying policies and systems in order to reduce organisational susceptibility and vulnerability is, as yet, under-developed, and there are few experiences from which agencies can learn. This section discusses some additional problems revealed by the case studies and by informal feedback.

A major problem is denial, both among employees, and within organisations. Following some work in Angola, one NGO manager reported:

> *...many of our staff simply still don't believe HIV/AIDS is an issue of relevance for them, or for Angola, so there's no way we could realistically expect them to do a good job of incorporating it. This goes beyond mere provision of information – we have to address people's attitudes and values along the way ... it's crucial that we give our staff a chance to work through some of the deeply personal issues involved.*[5]

An NGO employee in Yemen referred to '*a persisting culture of denial, manifesting as the tendency to deny the existence of culturally unacceptable risk behaviour such as multiple sex partners, extramarital sex, and homosexuality*', present not only among community members, but also among NGO and government staff.[6] Another NGO's HIV/AIDS Officer cited denial among members of middle management as a problem: for example, the

'We have to address people's attitudes and values ... it's crucial that we give our staff a chance to work through some of the deeply personal issues involved.'

organisation's internal awareness-raising efforts were being undermined by statements by managers that they would not use condoms.[7]

The HIV/AIDS Officer also noted that sexual relations among staff were common. This need not be problematic from the perspective of HIV transmission, if the activities are consensual and safe sex is practised, including correct use of condoms. However, it is often the case that organisations deny or ignore the occurrence of sexual relations among staff, so the issue is not discussed; or, where policies prohibit sexual relations among staff, they are rarely enacted. Moreover, sex in the workplace may not be motivated only by love or pleasure, but may be linked to bargaining or abuse. For example, an informant in Southern Africa was involved in HIV screening which revealed unexpectedly high HIV infection rates among a company's female employees. The cause was found to be that the women were being coerced into having (unprotected) sex with some of the managers, in order to keep their jobs. In NGOs, it is often denied that employees have sexual relations with community members, whether the activities are consensual or involve some element of exchange or pressure. Although many NGOs have codes of conduct for employees and condemn abuses of power, if organisations fail to confront these issues they may contribute to employees' denial about their own practices and risks, and be less likely to act on instances of abuse.

It is often the case that organisations deny or ignore the occurrence of sexual relations among staff, so the issue is not discussed.

Finally, with regard to AIDS work with staff, it is easy to assume that NGO employees understand the bio-medical or scientific aspects of the disease, but this may not always be the case. As one NGO officer stated, *'one constraint, particularly at local level, is the fact that staff are part of the community in which they work too – and those same beliefs that enable communities to deny the impact of HIV/AIDS also enable our staff to deny it'*.[8] On the one hand, because traditional beliefs regarding disease causation are seen to be 'uneducated', employees may not speak of them openly. Indeed, employees may deride the beliefs held by community members, and use them as examples of how 'we' need to educate 'them'. On the other hand, anecdotal evidence suggests that NGO employees at all levels may subscribe to ideas which do not fit with the dominant scientific explanation of HIV and AIDS. Staff members, for example, may consult traditional healers as well as medical doctors, in the desperate hope of finding a cure. (In the ActionAid example above, it was a senior member of management who approved expenditure for an AIDS 'cure'.) Or they may seek to understand HIV infection in non-medical ways. For example, in one NGO, an employee was dismissed, and the new person in the job fell sick shortly after beginning work; this sickness was interpreted by some colleagues as retribution from the sacked staff member.

With regard to impact assessments, aside from the technical challenges in undertaking the analysis, there is the potential problem that agencies may wish to suppress the results, particularly if they predict heavy impacts. This is rumoured to have happened in South Africa and Zimbabwe, where the findings of some government-sponsored studies have not been made public. For NGOs, the act of undertaking research into the effects of AIDS on staff and the organisation is likely to raise expectations among employees about improvements in health care and benefits which may not be easy to meet; in at least one case, managers have opted to not make the results widely available within the organisation. Such problems can be avoided if at the outset the parties plan how to disseminate and respond to the findings of the study. Experience suggests that where studies have been developed through a collaborative and consultative approach, with decision makers and staff involved throughout, there is a much greater chance that the findings will not hit a wall of denial, and will instead shape and encourage the response.[9]

Summary

This chapter has reviewed some experiences among NGOs of mainstreaming AIDS internally, mainly considering organisations' efforts to support their staff through AIDS work. The most common activity is awareness raising and education for employees, but this appears to be unplanned, and none of the organisations seemed to have assessed its effectiveness. The section on AIDS work for staff also discussed efforts to promote voluntary counselling and HIV testing. It identified impediments to employees' use of counselling and testing, and featured the case of ActionAid-Burundi, where an HIV-positive volunteer has successfully increased up-take among staff members. The section also described the differing approaches taken by Oxfam and ActionAid to workplace policies on critical illness. Experiences from ActionAid programmes illustrate that having workplace policies is not necessarily sufficient to create an open and supportive environment which helps both employees and the organisation to reduce susceptibility to HIV and vulnerability to the impacts of AIDS.

The chapter also presented less direct ways of responding to AIDS internally. It described how SC UK has assessed the current impacts of AIDS on its staff, and how Oxfam has undertaken work to predict the internal impacts of AIDS, using cost–benefit analysis of two scenarios to inform the development of its workplace policy. However, aside from workplace policies, the case studies did not provide any examples of agencies modifying their systems and practices in order to reduce their susceptibility and vulnerability to HIV and AIDS. The chapter proposed that the imbalance between the strategies of direct and indirect internal responses reflects the imbalance between the programmatic responses of AIDS work and modifications to existing work through external mainstreaming.

The final section of the chapter highlighted two aspects of personal belief and behaviour among employees which constrain efforts to mainstream AIDS internally: denial about the relevance of AIDS and about levels and types of sexual activity; and belief in non-biomedical explanations for HIV and AIDS. It also raised the problem of denial at organisational level, in terms of a lack of openness about sexual issues within the workplace, and unwillingness to accept unpalatable findings of studies of the internal impacts of AIDS.

Although this chapter demonstrates a gap between current experience of internal mainstreaming of AIDS and the idealised situation presented in Chapter 6, it has presented some useful experiences of AIDS work and predictions of the impacts of AIDS from which others may learn. Chapter 12 summarises the main ideas, which are accompanied by practical Units at the back of the book, to assist with the process of internal mainstreaming of AIDS.

8 Experiences of mainstreaming AIDS externally in development work

In general, development workers and government officials are as aware as anyone in Southern Africa of HIV/AIDS. However, few outside the health sector actively seek to minimise HIV transmission and impacts of the pandemic through their own work – they still consider this to be something that the health sector 'will take care of'. Despite much talk of 'multi-sectoral approaches' to HIV/AIDS, the reality is clearly one in which the majority of development activities simply continue to ignore the impacts of the pandemic.
(Oxfam 2001d)

Introduction

As Chapters 3 and 4 explained, external mainstreaming of AIDS is concerned with adapting existing core programmes to take account of the impacts of the pandemic, and thus maximising the positive effects of development work and minimising its unintended negative effects. This chapter first presents the experiences of some organisations which have tried to mainstream AIDS in development work, and then it reviews the main issues and problems illustrated by the case studies. Chapter 9 then considers mainstreaming AIDS externally in humanitarian work. Chapter 13 will consolidate ideas for both kinds of mainstreaming in programme work.

There are very few documented cases of external mainstreaming of AIDS, as the term is understood in this book. Many organisations use the term, but they mean different things; others may be attending to the causes and consequences of AIDS through good development practice, but without using the term 'mainstreaming'.

Different paths to different strategies

This section briefly considers how the main contributors to this book – ActionAid, Save the Children UK, and Oxfam GB – are going through processes of developing their responses to HIV and AIDS in their respective programmes and in their relations with their partners.

ActionAid's first initiative was taken in Uganda in 1987, supporting The AIDS Support Organisation, or TASO, the first support and service organisation for people living with AIDS in East Africa. That work partly stimulated the agency's Strategies for Hope project, which began documenting innovative community-based responses to AIDS in 1989. And that project led, in 1992, to a field-based programme, Strategies for Action, supporting and funding ASOs in Uganda and Malawi. Since then, ActionAid has focused its efforts on supporting NGOs and ASOs to do direct AIDS work. In 2001, it secured a major commission to channel funding from the British government to strengthen direct responses to HIV and AIDS at the national level in Africa, including improving the influence of community-based organisations on decision making.

ActionAid has also been an advocate for treating AIDS as a development issue. For example, in a publication entitled 'Don't Forget Poverty', the agency argues that *'work to tackle HIV/AIDS must deal with the context in which HIV is thriving'*, and that *'HIV/AIDS must be a central part of the development agenda...fighting poverty will not be possible without fighting HIV/AIDS'* (ActionAid Alliance 2002:1). The agency's primary focus, then, is on AIDS work with a development perspective, rather than development work which has mainstreamed AIDS. ActionAid's Global HIV/AIDS Co-ordinator reports that responses to HIV/AIDS tend to fall between locally identified thematic priorities such as gender-equity and education. Rather than being addressed as a cross-cutting issue, HIV and AIDS tend to be dealt with via support for ASOs – as she sees it, by *'putting AIDS back in its box'*.[1]

Like ActionAid, **Save the Children UK** has focused on responding to HIV and AIDS through supporting partners to implement AIDS work. The issue of AIDS has gradually gained prominence within the organisation, and it now forms one of four top priorities for the organisation's programme and advocacy work. The theme and the projects focus on prevention and care; but the agency has also been prominent in advocacy work concerning orphans, infant feeding, and children's rights in emergencies.

In contrast, despite funding some AIDS projects, **Oxfam GB**, with its focus on livelihoods support and humanitarian work, has not given priority to supporting partners to do direct AIDS work. For example, in 1995, leading programmes were devoting only about two per cent of their budgets to supporting projects concerned with HIV and sexual and reproductive health (Bailey 1995:8), although some staff were internally advocating the need to respond to AIDS. In 1999 the Health Policy Adviser brought together some employees who were interested in HIV/AIDS, to form an *ad hoc* group to discuss the issues and to consider possible responses. The formation of this group coincided with a major strategic review, in the course of which its members were able to get HIV recognised as a major component of Oxfam's strategic aim concerning the right to health care and education, and to raise the issue widely within the agency.

In Southern Africa, Oxfam's regional director gave one member of the group, then the Livelihoods Adviser for the region, the task of formulating a range of possible responses to AIDS. He linked with other organisations which had more experience in responding to AIDS, such as ActionAid, and attended a course about the future impacts of the pandemic. He became convinced of the need to act, and, in order to link closely with Oxfam's existing programmes, championed the idea of focusing on mainstreaming AIDS in development work. In 2000, a proposal to pilot mainstreaming in Malawi (both internally and in programmes) was approved by senior management, and the Livelihoods Adviser who had championed the idea became the region's HIV/AIDS Co-ordinator. The pilot project was later expanded to cover the whole Southern Africa region.

At Oxfam's annual Assembly in mid-2002, AIDS was generally recognised as a major threat to the agency's work.

The issue of AIDS has also gained wider prominence within Oxfam GB generally. In early 2001 the agency began its *Cut the Cost* campaign, which has challenged the way in which international trade rules are increasing the price of many basic drugs. At Oxfam's annual Assembly in mid-2002, HIV/AIDS was generally recognised as a major threat to the agency's work.

In comparison with ActionAid and SC UK, then, Oxfam GB's response in programmes and advocacy has concentrated on modifying existing work in key sectors, especially livelihoods and humanitarian response to crisis, so that these programmes better address the social and economic causes and consequences of HIV and AIDS. Oxfam is also campaigning for affordable access to basic drugs; but, compared with ActionAid and SC UK, it is doing less implementation and funding of direct AIDS work. One of the reasons behind investing in mainstreaming was that few NGOs are involved in that process, so the gap presented Oxfam GB with an opportunity to develop its 'comparative advantage' as an experienced development agency (Oxfam Malawi Case Study 2001:5). The decision was also linked to concerns within Oxfam about the costs, capacity, and sustainability of getting involved with delivering AIDS treatment and care, given that Oxfam GB is not a health-specific agency.[2] However, more recently, and perhaps connected to the agency's internal mainstreaming work, which has resulted in improved treatment for HIV-positive employees (see Chapter 7), Oxfam has decided to engage in AIDS work in certain circumstances: for example, when such work is needed in a programme area and no other agency is undertaking, or able to undertake, it.

This section has briefly described how ActionAid and Save the Children UK have developed their specialist responses of supporting AIDS work, rather than mainstreaming AIDS in other work, while Oxfam GB has so far focused mainly on mainstreaming. It is pertinent to note that ActionAid and SC UK could not have opted to begin with mainstreaming, because the idea had not been developed when their responses to AIDS began; in contrast, Oxfam GB addressed the question of how to respond at a time when the impacts of AIDS were becoming very evident, and the notion of mainstreaming was emerging.

The following sections consider in turn various aspects of the process of mainstreaming AIDS in development work; they draw mainly on Oxfam's experiences in Malawi, but also on elements of the less well documented work of other NGOs.

Mainstreaming activities

Training and capacity building

Awareness building among staff is a necessary first step toward understanding the cross-sectoral implications of HIV/AIDS and its relevance to project work.
(Hemrich and Topouzis 2000:97)

The case studies make it clear that employees and partners' employees need training and capacity building if mainstreaming is to have any chance of success. This is because the idea of mainstreaming AIDS externally is not widely understood, and because applying it requires staff to think about their work in new and different ways. More fundamentally, staff may need basic training about AIDS and how it affects them before they can consider its implications for their work. At a workshop run by **ActionAid-The Gambia** about AIDS and development, the facilitators, who worked in countries highly affected by AIDS, made the mistake of assuming that the participants from The Gambia already knew the basic facts about HIV and AIDS. When it became clear that this was not the case, the facilitators had to change the programme for the second day of the training in order to correct their omission.

In some cases, unfortunately, training in mainstreaming does not extend beyond this basic level. A review of mainstreaming projects with some African ministries of agriculture, for example, found that the training offered to staff tended to be health-specific, and focused on preventing HIV, rather than on modifying agricultural services in a time of AIDS (Topouzis 2001:22). On the ground, the outcome of these projects was mainly confined to AIDS education with farmers and fishermen.

In other instances, such as ActionAid's workshops about AIDS and development work, the training may not be part of an on-going mainstreaming process. At the aforementioned workshop in The Gambia, for example, the evaluation showed that participants had learned a lot. One commented, *'Before, I thought that AIDS was only something for prostitutes and young people, but now I realise it has no boundaries. I'll go back to my place and say that it's time to come together and discuss this, as everyone is vulnerable.'* Another said, *'I have learned that it affects everybody, so the idea of seeing it as a health problem should be scraped from our minds.'* However, despite such progress, the participants had not, by the end of the workshop, fully grasped how they might respond to AIDS through adapting their existing development work, rather than by initiating AIDS-specific work. They needed follow-up support, which they did not receive, to build on what they had learned, and so to change their development practice

'Before, I thought that AIDS was only something for prostitutes and young people, but now I realise it has no boundaries.'

John Snow International, an organisation which provides mainstreaming training, recommends that training sessions should be regular rather than isolated events, and must include people who have recently joined the organisation. Their experience suggests the following:

> *Training is an important first step in the process of mainstreaming HIV: it provides participants with the opportunity to think more creatively around the issue and to develop ideas which go beyond their traditional sectoral roles. Training alone, however, cannot achieve a mainstreamed response.*
> (Dey and Butcher 2002:14)

In South Africa, an NGO called **Project Empower** was funded by the Joint Oxfam HIV/AIDS Programme[3] to pilot an AIDS mainstreaming process with some partners of Oxfam Australia/Community Aid Abroad (a member of Oxfam International). A three-day workshop, attended by one or two people from each of the partner organisations, was key to their strategy. Participants applied themselves to questions such as 'What will be the impact of HIV/AIDS on your sector?', 'What is the impact of your sector on HIV/AIDS?', 'What are the gendered implications?', and 'What are the AIDS issues and challenges that can be addressed by your sector?' (Cabango 2000:22).

Project Empower considered the training to have been successful in some basic but significant ways. First, in a society where HIV and AIDS are not necessarily acknowledged, the organisers were pleased that all the participants ended up believing that HIV/AIDS exists. Second, participants all agreed that AIDS matters, and, despite their broad fields of work, agreed that their organisations should do something about it. Third, participants reported feeling more confident in talking about HIV/AIDS, and in exploring an appropriate response (Project Empower 2002a:6). Project Empower concluded that participants left the workshop with a generally high level of motivation, and found that two thirds of them took some action on returning to their organisations. A few took significant action, including developing an organisational policy; developing an organisational strategy and funding proposals; beginning internal and external awareness-raising campaigns; and linking with other organisations involved in HIV/AIDS work, in order to obtain support, materials, and technical assistance (Project Empower 2002a:5). Project Empower also identified a number of constraints faced by the partners, and problems with the pilot; these are referred to in the final part of this chapter. For now, suffice to note that the actions which participants took following the training, and with on-going mentoring from Project Empower, were to undertake AIDS work with staff, as part of internal mainstreaming, and to initiate AIDS-work projects, rather than initiating the external mainstreaming of AIDS.

In a society where HIV and AIDS are not necessarily acknowledged, the organisers were pleased that all the participants ended up believing that HIV/AIDS exists.

Oxfam's mainstreaming process in Malawi began with an awareness-raising workshop for all staff in 2000. It included basic facts, personal issues, and the fundamentals of external mainstreaming of AIDS. Several participants noted that one of the most important features of this workshop was the involvement of one of the few men in Malawi who are openly HIV-positive. For some Oxfam staff, this was the first time they had discussed HIV with someone living with the virus. The next stages were community research and then a programme review, as the next sections in this chapter explain. Following those activities, Oxfam in Malawi decided to dedicate the next Partners' Meeting (a regular one-and-a-half-day event) to skills building for external mainstreaming. The facilitators began by reviewing the situation in Mulanje District, and discussing AIDS as a development issue for Oxfam's existing livelihoods programme, with reference to the findings of the community research.

Oxfam and the partners then explored how attention to AIDS might be incorporated in the various stages of the project cycle. Staff from each partner organisation then developed initial ideas about how their work might be altered in response to AIDS. For example, two of the partners were supporting women to set up their own businesses, through dairy farming and mushroom cultivation. Both partners had noticed the impacts of AIDS, with women's income being reduced by the need to care for others, and businesses failing when the women themselves fell sick and died. One suggestion was for *'women to train their children and other family members – so that, if they become incapacitated or die, the work can continue'* (Oxfam Malawi Case Study 2001:38). Both the partners felt they should also undertake AIDS work by providing the women with information about HIV and AIDS. After considering possible modifications, participants discussed the likely constraints on mainstreaming, and possible ways around those problems. Finally, they returned to a discussion of the project cycle and agreed on some minimum standards, to allow them and Oxfam to monitor their progress in mainstreaming AIDS externally.

Learning from AIDS-affected and vulnerable households

Oxfam's community research in Malawi aimed to enable staff to find out about, and connect with, the ways in which AIDS is affecting people at village level: *'to go beyond statistics, and to better understand the reality of HIV/AIDS'* (Oxfam 2001c). The researchers included Oxfam staff and employees from Oxfam's CBO and government partners; the research teams consisted of members of various professions, and people working for various kinds of organisation. In March 2001 the researchers met together for three days of refresher training in HIV/AIDS and in participatory means of research, followed by five days of data collection in villages where one of the partners was already working. In all, the research involved four community meetings, 14 focus-group discussions (with same-sex participants in similar age-groups), and 19 in-depth interviews. As few HIV-positive people know their status, and few of those who do know that they are infected are open about it, it was not possible to focus directly on people affected by AIDS. Instead, several of the interviews involved people suffering from chronic illness, and households with a chronically sick member, or households which had experienced the death of a young adult due to a long illness.

One of Oxfam's staff summarised the main benefit for her as *'...linking a theory that I had learned earlier, to a practical situation in the village, and to discover that the practical situation is much more intense than the information that I had'*. Oxfam quickly compiled the findings of the research into a short report, which was circulated to key organisations and government departments. Among the findings were the clustering of the impacts of AIDS, with some families hit particularly hard. Also, it was noted that badly affected households become 'invisible' from the perspective of extension staff, because their members drop out of development activities, owing to ill health and lack of free time (Oxfam 2001b).

From April to June 2001, Oxfam and its partners held further consultations with affected families in nine villages, to identify ways in which current development approaches might unintentionally be neglecting their needs. As a Project Officer explained: *'We said, "this is what the research has shown us about the effects of HIV/AIDS, and we want to confirm if it's applicable to you". That was the departure point. We then went on to ask them what relevant approaches development agencies could use to make sure that affected people and households weren't left out in the future'* (Oxfam Malawi Case Study 2001:20). For Oxfam's Regional HIV/AIDS Co-ordinator, the community research was crucial to their mainstreaming efforts: as he asserts, *'the practical experience of talking with affected people about their issues, as opposed to talking about them, is the basis of real mainstreaming'.*[4]

> *'The practical experience of talking with affected people about their issues, as opposed to talking about them, is the basis of real mainstreaming.'*

The significance of learning from AIDS-affected households is illustrated in a review of natural-resource management projects supported by **COMPASS** (Community Partnerships for Sustainable Resource Management) in Malawi. One of the featured projects consisted of three income-generating activities which aim to alleviate poverty: rearing guinea fowl, keeping bees, and harvesting and juicing fruit from communally owned trees. Each initiative was said to be successful. However, while the project leaders assumed that all households were able to benefit equally from the income-generating activities, when the reviewers met with three AIDS-affected households, that found that this was not the case. Each had sold their guinea fowl before they had bred any offspring, in order to raise money for food or school fees; none had been included in the bee-keeping project; and all had been denied access to the fruit trees by more powerful people within the community (Page 2002:18).

Other strategies

This section looks briefly at three other strategies for mainstreaming AIDS in development work which emerged from the case studies: allocating responsibility for external mainstreaming; adapting systems; and networking.

Allocating responsibility for mainstreaming

Of all the agencies providing case studies, Oxfam is the only organisation to have allocated explicit responsibility for mainstreaming, by creating a new staff post at the beginning of the process. As the Regional HIV/AIDS Co-ordinator states:

> Without some dedicated time, people do try to engage, but responses are ad hoc, often not well thought through – and many simply don't try, because it seems a monumental task. If my post hadn't been funded, the situation in Oxfam, not only in Southern Africa but in terms of how the Senior Management Team in Oxford views the issue, would be different. This is not self-congratulation – it was only with some dedicated time of someone who understood how Oxfam works that we started to come up with specific proposals on what to do.[5]

As time has gone on, Oxfam's HIV/AIDS team for the Southern Africa region has gradually grown, as the scale of their mainstreaming and other AIDS work has expanded, while Oxfam Malawi has hired an officer dedicated to the issues of gender and HIV/AIDS. In each case there is tension over the extent to which each post-holder is able to achieve a balance between attention to external mainstreaming, internal main-streaming, and direct responses to AIDS.

There are also risks in having specialist staff. ActionAid-Mozambique reported that although the organisation needs AIDS-specialist staff, there is the danger that other staff expect them to handle all AIDS-related activities, which leads to the perception of AIDS as a distinct issue, separate from mainstream development work. An officer explained, 'The difficulty of a multi-sectoral programme like ours is that everyone is always very stretched in terms of space and time. When we know we have experts working in a particular field, such as HIV/AIDS, the tendency is to wait for those people to help out, rather than do the work ourselves' (ActionAid-Mozambique Case Study 2001:13). It seems reasonable to assume that this tendency is exacerbated when AIDS is being addressed directly as a special issue, rather than being mainstreamed as part and parcel of development work.

When responsibility for AIDS is decentralised, particularly in large organisations, individual members of staff in various departments are frequently designated as HIV/AIDS 'focal points'. This is an approach used by the NGO **ACORD** (Agency for Cooperation and Research in Development), which, although it has some staff dedicated to AIDS, also nominates focal points, who have other roles – they may be community development officers, agricultural extension staff, or gender officers.

The agency considers that this overlap helps to *'develop the collective understanding that HIV/AIDS is an issue that is relevant for other sectors'.* This appears to have happened most effectively in high-prevalence countries:

> *In countries where HIV/AIDS is not yet perceived as a major threat, it is true that such staff may be seen as solely responsible for HIV/AIDS and that others have no role to play. They may be labelled 'AIDS workers', and anything to do with HIV/AIDS is seen as being within the domain of the focal point people. But in other countries with mature epidemics, where there is openness and debate and political commitment to address HIV/AIDS, it is now widely recognised that all people have a personal and collective responsibility to deal with it.*
> (ACORD Case Study 2002)

In Malawi Oxfam has required all staff to revise their performance objectives to include action on HIV/AIDS.

However, research in Uganda with government ministries highlights the problem (already familiar from experiences of focal points for gender equity) that staff who are made 'focal points' are usually given this responsibility in addition to their existing workload. Moreover, they are often not well supported to act in their new role (Elsey 2002a:5). Also, they may come under pressure from colleagues if they are perceived to be distracted from departmental responsibilities, and are likely to view their additional responsibilities as a relatively low priority, because their jobs, and their pensions, relate to their core work, rather than their extra role with respect to AIDS.[6]

Modifying systems

Another mainstreaming strategy is that of adapting organisational systems, in an effort to institutionalise attention to HIV and AIDS in programme work. One method is to include AIDS in employees' formal responsibilities. In Malawi, for example, Oxfam has required all staff to revise their performance objectives to include action on HIV/AIDS. A new member of staff proposed the following objective: *'to provide support to the Gender/AIDS Officer on mainstreaming'.* His manager was unhappy with the implication that he was not actively involved in mainstreaming himself, so the objective was changed to *'ensure all my partners are mainstreaming HIV/AIDS, with support from the Gender/AIDS Officer'.*[7]

As already mentioned, in Malawi Oxfam and its partners set some minimum standards for mainstreaming AIDS. For example, at the problem-identification stage of the project cycle, partners should produce some data about the impact of HIV/AIDS on local people, and the relationship between AIDS and the problem that the project aims to address. For the project-design stage, the minimum standard is to demonstrate efforts to include AIDS-affected households in the target group, and to develop strategies that are accessible and relevant to those who are affected by AIDS (Oxfam Malawi Case Study 2001:36). Oxfam in Malawi has integrated AIDS into its systems for making grants to partners, so that HIV/AIDS is now included in the formats of its proposal guideline, recommendation report, grant agreements, and reporting guide (Oxfam Malawi 2002:12).

In addition to modifying its own systems, Oxfam Malawi has attempted to encourage its government partners to fit AIDS into their systems. Some of this advocacy has been undertaken by government staff, who, having taken part in the community research and programme review, saw the need for policy changes within their ministries. Oxfam is also taking an active role, through meeting with ministry staff, and linking with the Ministry of Agriculture and the National AIDS Commission as they develop ideas for mainstreaming AIDS, so that all the organisations can learn from one another's experiences (Oxfam Malawi 2002:15).

ACORD, ActionAid, and SC UK have all included HIV-related questions in planning frameworks, to try to ensure that the issue is not forgotten. An officer at ACORD explains: *'We are applying an HIV/AIDS-lens to programme identification, design and development...any new programme identification mission must include an analysis of the HIV/AIDS situation, its magnitude, current responses and gaps, and how HIV/AIDS may impact on the proposed programme in case no action is taken'* (ACORD Case Study 2002:1). ActionAid country programmes must consider AIDS in their country strategy papers and annual reports, and their plans are reviewed in the light of HIV prevalence, the extent to which AIDS is addressed within thematic priorities, and the amount of money allocated to responses to AIDS (Bataringaya 1999:2). For the purposes of mainstreaming, the limitation of these systems is that they are geared more towards direct AIDS work. For example, mainstreaming modifications to development work might involve additional costs, but would not necessarily show up in budgets as AIDS-related, because they would be unlikely to be directly concerned with AIDS. Expanding agricultural extension work to include vulnerable young people might involve training for staff and additional work at field level, but would not show up in budgets unless it were funded as a separate project for AIDS orphans, or if a special effort were made to expose the link between the expenditure and responding to AIDS through mainstreaming.

Complementary partnerships

Finally, the case studies provide a couple of examples of how networking with others may be useful if an organisation lacks capacity or experience to respond to AIDS. **ActionAid-Burundi** decided that promoting savings and credit schemes was an important strategy for its development work, but lacked the expertise to run a large-scale and sustainable programme. As a result, it is working in partnership with a co-operative bank, which trains the groups and handles the loan disbursements and recoveries, while ActionAid-Burundi takes care of the group-mobilisation and community-development aspects of the project. The scheme has 2,300 members and is benefiting poor people in the community, including those affected by HIV, because members do not need collateral in order to be eligible to join. The flexible loans may be used for a group project, or may be divided among the members for individual projects. The benefits to groups are varied. For example, one group has bought some land, which the members are farming together so that they no longer have to rent land in order to grow food. Having savings has helped the members to pay medical costs and school fees. The group is a source of mutual moral support among the members, who provide financial assistance and labour when one of them is ill.

As a second example, a review of how micro-finance institutions are responding to HIV and AIDS, found that the most common response was to add in AIDS work, in the form of awareness raising with savings and credit groups. Interestingly, the case study reports that *'those that did this through collaboration with health organisations, rather than doing the work on their own, initiated the work more quickly, more effectively, and at lower costs to themselves and their clients'* (Development Alternatives Incorporated 2000:28).

In Malawi, Oxfam's partner Wildlife and Environmental Society of Malawi (WESM) underwent initial HIV-awareness training for its staff. WESM then identified the local AIDS service organisation Banja La Mtsogolo to provide health-awareness services in communities where WESM operates.[8]

Adapting development work

This section focuses on Oxfam's experiences in Malawi, because this was the only case study provided by an organisation which systematically addressed itself to modifying development work as part of a wider mainstreaming process. It then briefly describes five other development projects which have not necessarily engaged in a formal process of mainstreaming, but have been sufficiently in touch with the issues of susceptibility to HIV and the impacts of AIDS to be influenced by them, for the good of the project participants.

Modifying an existing programme

This chapter has already explained how Oxfam Malawi and its partners undertook community-level research to learn about the impacts of AIDS and its implications for development work. Soon after that research, in June 2001, Oxfam and government staff met for a three-day workshop with the specific aim of reviewing and modifying the **Shire Highlands Sustainable Livelihoods Programme** (SHSLP), which supports the activities of the partners and communities that participated in the field research. Most of the workshop participants had taken part in the community research, so they were able to reflect directly on what they had learned.

The guiding principle for the review was that the programme should continue to focus on the core business of support for sustainable livelihoods; in other words, that the existing programme should be improved through small changes, rather than changing the whole direction of the work. The community research had shown how the most badly affected families were, unintentionally, being excluded from the development process. Thus, the guiding question of the review was *'How can development organisations better understand and address the particular needs of labour and time-constrained families, especially those affected by chronic illness and the death of young adults?'* (Oxfam Malawi Case Study 2001:24). In small groups, the workshop participants considered their work plans and performance indicators with attention to possible changes in four key respects:

- **Target groups:** Should we actively try to work more directly with young people, elderly people, single-parent households, people who are chronically ill, or other groups?

- **Activities:** Should we change the types of thing we are doing, so that we better address the needs of affected people?

- **Ways of working:** Should we modify or improve some of our methods, to reach badly affected people more effectively?

- **Partnerships:** Would working with others help us to be more effective?

Because the SHSLP programme is quite large and complex, reviewing it in this way was hard work. Some of the participants initially felt defensive about the process, because they felt that 'their' activities were being criticised, and were under threat. Some, who had a weaker grasp of the meaning of mainstreaming, suggested AIDS projects such as orphanages and home-based care. Other participants wanted to re-focus all activities to the point of exclusively serving AIDS-affected households. The facilitators kept reminding everyone of the aim of making small changes to improve existing work, rather than transforming the programme; as one participant commented, *'We felt like doing everything, but we had to think about what we could do best'*. The participants scrutinised all the proposed modifications to assess their viability, and the likelihood of their producing the desired result.

'We felt like doing everything, but we had to think about what we could do best.'

It was recognised that some activities might be necessary for general poverty alleviation, even if they were not accessible to everybody in the community. For example, raising goats for meat can take almost two years to show returns. AIDS-affected people need to achieve benefits more quickly than this, but other poor families can afford to engage in relatively long-term projects such as goat rearing, and working with them is still valid. In any case, affected households and not-yet-affected households are connected: the latter may be helping the former, and may become affected themselves in the future. General poverty reduction can improve their resource base, and so reduce their vulnerability to the impacts of AIDS.

However, recognising this, the participants proposed various possible changes, to be tried out in the programme, based on the four guiding questions outlined above.

- **Target groups:** First, participants discussed measures to modify their programme to include those living with HIV, those affected by AIDS or chronic illness, and those at high risk of HIV transmission. The participants agreed that, following the positive experience of the community research, affected families and those at risk should constitute categories to be included in future participatory appraisals. To try to ensure that this attention extends from the assessment stage to later steps in the project cycle, the participants resolved that one or two members of each Village Development Committee should represent households affected by AIDS or chronic illness. Forestry officers set themselves a target of ensuring that a third of their extension work in future would involve affected households. The participants also wanted to increase the proportion of resources allocated to affected families, so they set targets accordingly, to ensure, for example, that two out of five livestock loans, and three out of ten seed loans, should go to them. Initial feedback suggests that these modifications may be useful. The District Agricultural Officer reports that *'people appreciate the idea of* *having specific members of the VDC to represent affected families. They say "now, we can be sure of vulnerable people being heard and taken care of"* (Oxfam Malawi Case Study 2001:25). Anecdotal evidence suggests that the VDCs are paying more attention to vulnerable households, especially those headed by children and grandparents, and that more resources are being allocated to them.[9] However, at the time of writing, the food crisis and food-aid distributions in Malawi have thrown the agricultural loan programmes into turmoil, making it impossible to assess the impact of the modifications.

- **Ways of working:** The agriculture staff and water and sanitation officers agreed that more of their training activities should be held in the villages, instead of in venues outside the community. This was done to make it easier for all kinds of people, including those from AIDS-affected households, to attend. Agriculture staff planned to establish some demonstration plots in the fields of affected families, both to facilitate their participation, and to ensure that the work would be relevant to their needs and abilities.

- **Activities:** The participants recognised that some of the agricultural methods which they recommended are labour-intensive, and thus of little use to labour-constrained households, including those badly affected by AIDS. They therefore resolved to offer other options, which might be more realistic for vulnerable people, even if less effective and efficient. For example, whereas the extension agents used to promote a compost-making method which involves regular turning and watering, they plan now also to present a much less demanding alternative, which produces compost more slowly but does not require much management.[10] Similarly, they will promote a soil-conservation technique which entails planting vetiver grass along contour lines, rather than the heavy and labour-intensive work of creating contour bunds (Oxfam Malawi Case Study 2001:28). Forestry staff identified more easily manageable shrubs which they could offer to community members.

With regard to livestock, the participants felt that small livestock such as rabbits, chickens, and guinea fowl might be more suited than goats to the needs of poor and AIDS-affected households. Although goats are more prestigious, and their meat is preferred, they are more expensive and they reproduce more slowly. When a VDC lends someone a goat, it takes 11 months for the loan to be repaid, and a further 11 months before the recipient has offspring to keep. With rabbits, the loan can be repaid in only four months, and by then there should also be offspring to keep.

Small livestock such as rabbits, chickens, and guinea fowl might be more suited than goats to the needs of poor and AIDS-affected households.

In addition, rearing small stock is less labour-intensive; the animals can be raised in pens in the homestead by anyone, including children or people who are sick. Being smaller animals which reproduce well, they are also more easily divisible assets, allowing a family to eat or sell one or two on a regular basis, so obtaining protein or cash, while retaining breeding stock.

One of the more controversial of the proposed modifications was that AIDS-affected households should have access to loans at preferential interest rates. This is a practice which micro-finance experts discourage, because targeting certain types of people with lower interest rates can undermine the viability of a credit scheme, as well as creating stigma. However, there was no such expert at the workshop, and the modification was agreed. VDCs reported that they implemented this modification by using open village meetings to agree who should be eligible for the lower rates. In practice, their selection focused not on AIDS-affected households (which would stigmatise them, and might include relatively wealthy families) but on the most vulnerable households, including those headed by women, children, or elderly people, and the very poorest families. However, at the time of writing, the food crisis has led to soaring default rates, so the idea has not yet been put into practice.[11]

'A long-term change in attitudes and understanding is more important than any specific one-off changes in the logframe or plan.'

- **Partnerships:** Workshop participants noted that the Oxfam partners included organisations specialising in agriculture, community development, and youth, and that it would be important to develop stronger working relationships with other organisations which could complement the existing Oxfam programme by offering services directly related to HIV/AIDS. They identified such bodies as the District AIDS Co-ordinating Committee, the Mission Hospital, and the Government Hospital, various organisations providing home-based care, and the Ministry of Health.

In summary, it is clear that Oxfam's mainstreaming process succeeded in enabling staff to apply the ideas of mainstreaming to modifying their work. In the opinion of Oxfam's Regional HIV/AIDS Co-ordinator, *'Most are convinced that they must learn how to do their current jobs in different ways, in order to better address the ways in which the pandemic is changing the needs of communities. A long-term change in attitudes and understanding is more important than any specific one-off changes in the logframe or plan'* (Oxfam Malawi Case Study 2001:24).

However, it is notable that the initial discussions in Oxfam's process in Malawi were largely focused on the current impacts of AIDS on households, and possible future impacts; only later did the programme begin to address the issue of the project's relationship to susceptibility to HIV infection. For example, does the project somehow inadvertently increase susceptibility? If efforts to include and work with affected households are successful, then the project should have an indirect but positive effect on susceptibility, by supporting those households' efforts to cope with the impacts of AIDS. Two Oxfam partners, Malawi Centre for Advice, Research, and Education on Rights (CARER) and Women and Law in Southern Africa–Malawi Chapter, jointly realised that increasing numbers of widows and orphans were having property taken away by the relatives of deceased husbands. They began to educate men and women on the value of writing wills to help specific family members to retain property. They also started education work on Malawi's inheritance laws, to help widows and orphans to learn about their rights. The two partners have also raised awareness of inheritance issues among the District Assembly clerks responsible for administering the estates of deceased people, and among Ministry of Labour officers who counsel employees and their spouses about their entitlements under inheritance law.[12]

Some words of caution are appropriate. Most of the modifications mentioned above were proposed in a workshop for staff of Oxfam and its partners; they still had to seek the input of the participants' colleagues or community members. Subsequently some may have been found to be unacceptable, for cultural, operational, financial, or technical reasons. (For example, it is known that some people in Mulanje are not keen on raising rabbits, so the project will need to find alternatives, such as chickens or guinea fowl.) In subsequent work with community members, additional ideas were raised. The workshop helped to start the process, but it was clear that mainstreaming involves much more than a one-off design workshop. Mainstreaming of HIV/AIDS, as with any development work, should be based upon direct work with affected people; it should not be done on their behalf by programme staff.

The modifications also need to be tested and monitored to ascertain whether their outcomes are as desired: they might be less effective than hoped, or might have negative consequences for some people. For example, there are opportunity costs involved in each of the modifications: allocating more livestock and seed loans to affected households means fewer loans to other households, and if repayment rates were to fall, then the sustainability of the scheme could be threatened. Careful monitoring and evaluation are required if Oxfam and its partners are to learn about the impact of the modifications on AIDS-affected households and the wider community.

Reducing susceptibility to HIV infection

In its Oruchinga Valley Programme in Uganda's Mbarara District, the NGO **ACORD** has implemented a water project in response to needs identified by the community. Prior to the project, and particularly in the dry season, women and children were walking long distances to look for and collect water, and this problem placed a particular strain on households who were caring for sick people, such as those with AIDS. The journeying was also said to expose women and girls to the risk of sexual attack. ACORD's response included the construction of valley dams, paved catchments, spring protection, and household or institutional water-harvesting tanks. However, the agency was aware of rumours that the artisans who were recruited to train people in the construction and maintenance of the water containers sometimes abused their position to extract sexual favours from women and girls. As a result, ACORD established codes of conduct in collaboration with community leaders, and the Chair of the village water committee was charged with monitoring the conduct of artisans, who received training in HIV prevention.

A review of seven natural-resource management projects found that five inadvertently excluded households badly affected by HIV and AIDS, because the projects demanded extra labour and regular attendance at meetings.

The project has had a number of benefits, in terms of reducing the time spent by women and children in looking for and carrying water, so freeing up time for more productive activities, and for attending school. As such, the project has indirectly helped those women and children to reduce their susceptibility to HIV. It is also thought to have directly reduced their susceptibility, by reducing the need to walk before dawn to collect water, and so reducing the risk of attack. Moreover, by trying to prevent sexual abuse during the project, and giving women the skills and responsibility for maintaining the low-cost tanks, ACORD has tried to prevent the project inadvertently increasing their susceptibility. Furthermore, the women who were trained in constructing and maintaining the tanks now have a source of income, through building tanks for other community members.

Attracting the participation of people from poor and vulnerable households

In Malawi, a review of seven natural-resource management projects found that five inadvertently excluded households badly affected by HIV and AIDS, because the projects demanded extra labour and regular attendance at meetings. While one of the remaining projects was an AIDS project (growing herbs to treat people with AIDS), the other was a natural-resources management project which was managing to involve and benefit AIDS-affected households, along with other poor and vulnerable families. This was the **Bwanje Valley Environmental Rural Development Organisation** (or BERDO), which is being supported by COMPASS to provide equipment, materials, and training for re-afforestation, guinea-fowl rearing, bee keeping, wood conserving, and clay-stove production in 30 villages.

The reviewers noted that this was the only project that they visited where food aid was being linked to natural-resource management activities: maize obtained from the World Food Program was being distributed to community members in return for raising hundreds of tree seedlings. As a result, almost every household has its own wood-lot and collection of fruit trees, which will become assets providing firewood, timber, fruit, soil-improving leaf-litter, and nitrogen fixation. The team also observed a high take-up of other practices, such as guinea-fowl rearing and bee keeping, throughout the area. In essence, the reason seems to be that the project has adopted an incentive system whereby repayments are made not to the project, but to the community; for example, each household that receives a guinea fowl is obliged to give ten neighbours six eggs each, and is then allowed to keep the bird and all future eggs. The review team met with widows who were keen to take part, because the project has been designed so that participation leads to direct benefits. For example, a widow with five children was receiving seed from the project in return for making compost out of kitchen waste, leaf litter, chicken manure, and ash. Moreover, the compost was for her own use; by putting two handfuls of it into each planting hole, she can double her maize yield.

The review concluded that BERDO had managed to *'both involve and directly benefit large numbers of households severely impacted by HIV/AIDS. This NGO has proved that by linking natural resource management activities such as composting, tree planting and guinea fowl rearing with improvements in food security, even households that are severely impacted by HIV/AIDS can be motivated to participate'* (Page 2002:31). However, although the review lacks comparative information on the costs of the projects, it appears that part of BERDO's success is due to adopting a generous approach to incentives, which can motivate people to take part, while stopping short of giving 'hand-outs'. It may be that this kind of approach is needed in badly affected communities, if development agencies are to address related problems such as the unsustainable exploitation of natural resources.

Tailoring activities to the needs of vulnerable farmers

The NGO **African Farmers' Organic Research and Training** (AfFOResT) has pioneered specialist agricultural support for AIDS widows and other marginalised women farmers in Zimbabwe's Zambezi Valley. Its research with AIDS widows found that their main farming problems were shortages of money and labour, and a lack of farm-management skills. In contrast to standard agricultural extension, AfFOResT was able to tailor its approach to suit the widows' needs in two main ways. First, the widows were able to develop their skills and confidence by learning-by-doing together as a women's group in their 'farmer field school'. Second, building on the women's previous experience of growing cotton with their husbands, AfFOResT introduced them to growing cotton organically. This adaptation has the advantage that organic cotton production requires much less money, because there is no need to buy expensive pesticides. In addition, AfFOResT reports that growing organic cotton takes less time, because weeding is reduced by intercropping the cotton with cowpeas. Organic production offers other advantages to the widows, because scouting for pests and applying home-made herbal sprays is less physically demanding and time-consuming than travelling to market to buy pesticides, and carting water to dilute them for repeated applications (Topouzis and du Guerny 1999:49).

A safety net to catch excluded households

Chapter 4 included the experience of **Save the Children**'s **Kawempe Programme** in Uganda, which had added on an AIDS project to its existing work of improving child health by reducing common childhood diseases, increasing access to safe drinking water, and improving sanitation standards. In addition to its direct response to AIDS, the case study reports on a mainstreaming activity which began when the community management committee proposed a 'safety net', to allow the poorest people free access to tap-stands and improved latrines. The idea was discussed at community planning meetings, and it was agreed that the safety net should serve very old people with many dependants, and AIDS-affected families with no source of income. Beneficiaries are identified by members of the community and are then referred to the local council, before being approved by the community project-management committee for free access. The programme reports that the safety net is not impairing the sustainability of the facilities, because the numbers of people getting free access are not large; the committees are very mindful of the financial implications, and so they approve applications only from those who are very vulnerable. The programme also reports that the preferential treatment has not caused divisions, because the selection criteria and process are transparent. The safety net, then, is an example of a modification to a project to include vulnerable households which were otherwise being excluded.

Reducing vulnerability to the impacts of AIDS by addressing gender issues

ACORD's core focus in Mbarara District of Uganda is support for sustainable livelihoods, but the NGO also works on HIV/AIDS, and on gender equity as a cross-cutting issue. When women deprived of their legal rights raised concerns about outdated traditions, ACORD realised that the problem was undermining both the livelihoods programme and the HIV/AIDS work. On the one hand, where women were precluded from owning or inheriting land or property, this was affecting their ability to support themselves independently, and greatly worsening the effects of AIDS for widows whose resources were taken away from them. On the other hand, where women were still being treated as men's property according to traditional law, they lacked the power to negotiate sexual practice, and could even be subjected to a fine imposed by village elders if they dared to refuse to have sexual relations with their husbands.

Where women were still being treated as men's property according to traditional law, they lacked the power to negotiate sexual practice, and could even be subjected to a fine imposed by village elders if they dared to refuse to have sexual relations with their husbands.

In response, ACORD formed a partnership with the Ugandan branch of **FIDA**, the International Federation of Women Lawyers, to develop an awareness-raising project. ACORD took on responsibility for the awareness-raising and community-mobilisation aspects, while FIDA provided the technical input by conducting sessions with community members on topics such as will writing. After a strategic review, the project was adapted so that FIDA trained local people to act as paralegals, in order to increase the community ownership and the sustainability of the initiative. The paralegals have been trained to give advice on a range of issues, including separation and divorce, inheritance, will writing, children's rights and responsibilities, women's rights, and domestic violence. ACORD reports several positive outcomes in terms of women's livelihoods and their status, all of which have implications for susceptibility to HIV infection, or vulnerability to the impacts of AIDS, or both. These outcomes include the fact that more women and children are now able to stay on their farms and retain their property when they are widowed and orphaned; that local councils are increasingly able to protect their citizens' legal rights; and that the local police force is now proving to be a greater source of support to the community.

Issues raised by the case studies

Following the detailed case study from Oxfam in Malawi, and five brief examples of external mainstreaming from other agencies, this section considers three issues raised by the case studies in relation to mainstreaming AIDS in development work.

Direct and indirect responses to AIDS

The first issue relates to 'the imperative to do AIDS work', first discussed in Chapter 4. In Malawi, Oxfam's external mainstreaming process was founded on the principle of continuing but adapting core work, and then collaborating with AIDS specialists, rather than initiating AIDS work. As the proposal for the regional pilot project stated, *'Oxfam does not want to change its focus towards that of a specialist HIV/AIDS service organisation, but wants to address current strategic objectives differently'* (Mullins 2001:12).

For Oxfam programmes in sectors other than health, mainstreaming is a non-negotiable starting point; AIDS-focused work is an option.

There is clearly a need to build upon the complementary relationship between mainstreaming HIV/AIDS into specific sectors, and support for AIDS-focused prevention, care, and treatment. However, Oxfam wants to avoid the tendency common among development staff to switch their focus to AIDS-focused work, while completely overlooking the need to ensure that all other work – in sectors such as agriculture, off-farm income generation, education, and humanitarian response – actually meets the needs of those at risk of, affected by, or living with HIV/AIDS. The Regional HIV/AIDS Co-ordinator comments:

> *We have to get beyond the 'either/or' debate, and talk about how to support 'both/and' – and this involves careful analysis of which organisations are best placed to provide specific types of support. For Oxfam programmes in sectors other than health, mainstreaming is a non-negotiable starting point; AIDS-focused work is an option. We need to ensure that the well-intended desire to do AIDS work builds on efforts in other sectors, and doesn't unintentionally divert creativity from them, if we are to ensure that our long-standing programmes are more relevant to badly affected people, and to those at risk.*

The rationale behind this strategy was threefold. First and foremost, it was argued that Oxfam needs to mainstream HIV/AIDS internally and externally, but must increase its capacity if it is to do that effectively. As such, and as Chapter 5 argued, mainstreaming should be a high priority, which raises the question of whether it would be sensible also to embark on AIDS work. Second, even if Oxfam were to take on AIDS work, it would not discontinue its existing work in livelihoods support and humanitarian response. It is essential to make this on-going work more relevant to the changing needs of AIDS-affected societies. Third, there was the view that Oxfam should give mainstreaming a high priority in order to develop good practice, and to have solid grounds on which to promote the idea, given the dearth of external experience. That, it was argued, would be Oxfam's best possible contribution to the global response to AIDS.

However, these arguments have been challenged by individuals' desire to 'do something', and the feeling that it is not tenable for the agency to fail to respond to AIDS directly. For example, the Oxfam GB Health Policy Adviser believes that *'at the end of the day (having seen the latest CIA intelligence on HIV in Africa), mainstreaming in programmes may mean that we have to include prevention, treatment and care (via whatever means) in our programmes for livelihoods, education and so on'.*[13] Some also argue that it is hypocritical for an organisation to undertake AIDS work with its staff, as part of internal mainstreaming, and then decline to do AIDS work with communities. However, this argument ignores the fact that an organisation's relationship with, and dependence on, its relatively small number of employees is fundamentally different from its relationship with many thousands of community members. Organisations have specific obligations to their employees in return for their provision of labour, and, as Chapter 7 emphasised, AIDS work with them is motivated not by altruism but by a duty of care to employees, as part of the labour contract, and the need to protect the organisation from the impacts of AIDS. While development agencies exist to help community members to secure their rights, they do not (and cannot) take on responsibility for providing them all with, for example, education and health care to the standards enjoyed by their employees. In the opinion of the author, organisations which offer HIV-prevention and AIDS-care services to their staff but decide to confine their external response to mainstreaming, rather than risk also trying to do AIDS work, are not guilty of hypocrisy.

In Oxfam's mainstreaming process in Malawi, some participants felt strongly that Oxfam should do AIDS work, particularly after taking part in the community research, and learning at first hand about the challenges experienced by those affected by AIDS. Because there are few ASOs in the project area with whom Oxfam or its partners could form complementary partnerships, Oxfam decided that it would begin to fund existing and new partners to do AIDS work. However, the Regional AIDS team emphasised the importance of bringing in people with technical expertise to guide this process, because the Malawi programme lacks the technical expertise to assess applications and manage such grants.

In any case, Oxfam's process of mainstreaming AIDS in Malawi, which emphasised the need to adapt existing work rather than initiating AIDS work, has also (and perhaps mainly) resulted in focused AIDS work. For example, Oxfam's partners seem to be prioritising the initiation of new AIDS work, rather than modifying their existing programmes. Furthermore, the agency's annual report for 2001–2002, referring to the SHSLP, lists as 'mainstreaming' certain activities which include AIDS work, such as HIV/AIDS training for extension workers, VDCs, and local leaders, and promoting HIV/AIDS awareness and condom use through theatre (Oxfam Malawi 2002:20). This is not a problem if Oxfam and the partners are able to undertake both direct and indirect responses to AIDS effectively. However, and notwithstanding the effects of the food crisis, the limited feedback on the mainstreaming modifications to date suggests that there is outstanding and very important follow-up work to be done on the mainstreaming aspects of the response.

If 'being affected' is used as a criterion for allocating benefits, a relatively wealthy household which has experienced AIDS might be prioritised over a very poor but less directly affected household.

Focusing on specific target groups

Another issue suggested by Oxfam's work in Malawi is the potential for external mainstreaming to become understood simply as 'making sure that project benefits reach people with AIDS, or AIDS-affected households'. During their programme review, some participants wanted to re-orientate all activities exclusively to serving the AIDS-affected. Although this extreme view was tempered by the facilitators, this illustrates the danger that mainstreaming might become equated with thinking only of those people who are currently affected by AIDS. This is important for several reasons.

- First, the vague category of 'affected' covers a range of different experiences and impacts: not all people are equally vulnerable. If 'being affected' is used as a criterion for allocating benefits, it raises the possibility that, for example, a relatively wealthy household which has experienced AIDS might be prioritised over a very poor but less directly affected household. In practice, this did not happen: the VDCs and communities simply assessed which households were most vulnerable and needy. By doing so they provided a means for increasing the participation and resource base of some of the poorest community members, although, as has been stated, the consequences, direct and indirect, of channelling more resources to those households have not been explored.

- Second, by focusing too closely on households that are currently badly affected, development workers risk neglecting work with not-yet-affected, or not badly affected, individuals and households. Households experiencing few impacts of AIDS are likely to be better able to exploit the opportunities offered by development agencies, and so to protect themselves by reducing their susceptibility to HIV infection and their vulnerability to AIDS, should they become more badly affected. In contrast, badly affected and destitute households may be very poorly placed to participate in and benefit from development work, and may require quite different support through, for example, welfare-based community safety nets.

- Third, a focus on affected households and the impacts of AIDS means that issues of susceptibility to HIV infection, and in particular the risk that the project may inadvertently increase susceptibility, are forgotten. While many projects may be free of any such unwanted repercussions, examples such as that of ACORD's water project, described above, illustrate the need to consider the possibility.

- Fourth, the tendency to target 'affected households' may inadvertently divert attention from axes of difference within the household. For example, sex, age, social and economic position, and health status all influence susceptibility to HIV and vulnerability to the impacts of AIDS within a single household. A focus on 'affected households' may also lead agencies to ignore important interactions among households, such as the way in which members of extended families, neighbours, and friends do help one another in times of need. This 'traditional social safety net' is being threatened by the increasing burdens imposed by AIDS, but it should not be lost by focusing on individual households.

Supporting partners to mainstream

A recurring challenge for NGOs which fund other organisations, rather than implementing projects directly, is to decide how best to influence their partners' work. Many would agree with the view of Oxfam GB's Health Policy Adviser that it is necessary and right to promote attention to difficult issues: *'If we do not introduce the issues, then work on gender, violence against women, rights of HIV-positive women and men, and so on will never reach the agendas of big donors or partners.'*[14] However, the line between donor agencies encouraging partners and forcing them may be a thin one. In the words of the Programme Co-ordinator for Oxfam's support to partners in Malawi:

We're trying to avoid mainstreaming as being a case of 'Oxfam says so' –
as it needs to come from commitment and interest within the organisation.
Oxfam can have a role – in terms of encouragement and looking at
standards – but it's not a question of donor conditionality. We need to work

from the point of view of the 'added value' of mainstreaming to an
organisation and its work.
(Oxfam Malawi Case Study 2001:35)

While CBOs may (or may not) take a holistic approach to their work, the impetus for mainstreaming AIDS as a concept and process is most likely to come from outside, and in particular from donors. Although Oxfam employees in Malawi may not wish to force partners to adopt new ways of working, by setting minimum standards for mainstreaming AIDS throughout the project cycle, they have in fact imposed the issue on the partners' agenda.

The same dilemma applies to encouraging partners to undertake AIDS work. The Save the Children UK case study based on its Family Reproductive Health Programme in Ghana (featured in Chapter 4) notes that, with one exception, none of the participating CBOs was addressing HIV/AIDS, and that the agency had to *'place a major emphasis on HIV/AIDS issues to ensure that they would be adequately integrated into project activities'*. This initiative included a workshop at which SC UK explained the rationale for needing to address HIV/AIDS, and where the partners had to *'define specific action plans and strategies to fully integrate HIV/AIDS interventions into their current project activities'*.

Chapter 4 also described how one of ActionAid-Ethiopia's partners, Voluntary Council for the Handicapped, initiated and integrated AIDS work. This came about because the strategic direction of ActionAid-Ethiopia had changed, and while the agency wanted to continue the relationship with the partner, it did not want to provide repeat funding for the partner's community-based rehabilitation programme. Although the partner was initially reluctant to get involved with AIDS work, with support from ActionAid it was able to diversify its work to include responses to AIDS, and subsequently changed its name to Addis Development Vision. However, the process involved unequal power dynamics, as is clear from the Project Officer's reflections:

> *When I try to reflect over the whole thing now, I sometimes think, perhaps we*
> *have pushed them too much ... I ask myself, are we, as donors, driving their*
> *activities? Are we making it too difficult for them to say no? And then I say,*
> *as a donor-dependent organisation, they have somehow to be able to a certain*
> *degree accommodate the donor's interest.*
> (ActionAid-Ethiopia Case Study 2001:5)

Of course, the question of how best to support CBOs is one that funders face recurrently, and not only in relation to AIDS mainstreaming. But purely as a structural issue, the partnership approach involves an extra layer of capacity building and persuasion, and an extra layer of barriers to mainstreaming AIDS externally within grassroots organisations. With regard to government-directed development work, bilateral donors have been the main advocates for and funders of gender-mainstreaming projects, and more recently of AIDS mainstreaming. However, their line of influence has recently been cut in many countries, and particularly in Africa, by the strategic shift among governments to Sector Wide Approaches (SWAps). The idea of SWAps is that each government sector is in partnership with all its donors, and they jointly negotiate policy and expenditure. However, the recipient government acts as the final arbiter. Money from donors goes into a pool for the whole sector, and donors are no longer free to fund special units, training programmes, or separate budgets. (This is analogous to CBOs receiving money from their donors which is not tied to any particular activities.) While government ministries have the opportunity to include AIDS-mainstreaming activities in their sectoral work programmes, as yet there has been little effective action, because of a lack of understanding about mainstreaming AIDS, the lack of proof of its cost-effectiveness, and the general problem of shortage of finance within regular sectoral budgets (Elsey 2002a:2). In such a situation, the task of promoting mainstreaming within government ministries appears formidable.

Problems identified by the case studies

Limited understanding

A fundamental problem emerging from the case studies is confusion over the meaning of mainstreaming. For example, in research within the ministries of education and agriculture in Uganda, AIDS mainstreaming was commonly understood only as undertaking AIDS-awareness activities, with groups such as school-management committees and farmers (Elsey 2002a:4). Oxfam in Malawi cites lack of understanding as one reason why its partners are mainly initiating AIDS work, rather than starting with mainstreaming by adapting their existing work.[15] In ActionAid, the Global HIV/AIDS Co-ordinator also views a lack of understanding of mainstreaming gender and AIDS as a key impediment to the process within ActionAid (Bataringaya 1999:4). As ActionAid's Chief Executive explains, *'It is difficult to find enough good-quality people who really understand the issues and can connect HIV/AIDS with our core work with poor people. There are plenty of people out there coming at it from a medical or health-sector angle, but that's not what we need. It's a question of those who can really make the links with poverty and marginalisation.'*[16]

This confusion over terms and meanings is evident not only among field staff, but at the heart of the agencies, with the words 'mainstreaming' and 'integration' sometimes being used imprecisely and interchangeably. The confusion is compounded by the way in which the meaning of mainstreaming is still evolving. For example, at the beginning of its work to support Oxfam's partners in mainstreaming, Project Empower emphasised the principle of adapting core work. However, in its training materials, there was a movement towards encouraging partners to initiate AIDS work. By the end of the pilot project, they had developed a much broader understanding of HIV/AIDS mainstreaming as *a political process that seeks to shift power relations and promote, protect and advance the rights of women, men and children living with HIV/AIDS*' (Project Empower 2002b:4). Such changes are desirable in terms of agencies learning from experience, but until terms are agreed upon and used consistently within an agency – and more widely – confusion is likely to persist.

Donors can add to the confusion. One international NGO runs agricultural development programmes in Mozambique, and wants to mainstream HIV/AIDS in ways that will help HIV-affected families to benefit through agriculture. However, the main donor is requiring the organisation to include AIDS-specific activities, such as condom distribution and HIV-awareness lectures, while ignoring the fact that different approaches to agriculture could help vulnerable people to gain more secure access to food and income.[17]

The case studies do demonstrate progress in alerting staff to the dangers of AIDS and helping them to understand its impacts on development. For example, field staff from ActionAid-Mozambique report that several years ago they did not ask questions about how HIV/AIDS might have an impact on, or be affected by, the projects. The staff did not have enough knowledge, while the communities themselves prioritised projects such as constructing schools or health posts, without mentioning AIDS. But, as one officer stated, *'Now we realise that unless HIV/AIDS is taken seriously, those schools will be empty, hospitals will be full, and there will be no community participation in our programmes'* (ActionAid-Mozambique Case Study 2001:6). However, although ActionAid-Mozambique intended to address AIDS holistically, its response has mainly been to fund or initiate stand-alone or integrated AIDS work. 'Taking AIDS seriously' means trying to stop it by concentrating exclusively on education and awareness raising, rather than also mainstreaming attention to AIDS throughout all development work.

Another implication of the limited understanding is impatience: some people think mainstreaming of HIV is something that should be done quickly, so they can 'get back' to normal work. They need to understand that mainstreaming is a process; once started, it does not stop. It does not merely involve a technical quick-fix, and there is no overnight change from 'not mainstreamed' to 'mainstreamed'.

It is worth reiterating that development workers may be addressing AIDS indirectly through their normal work, without understanding, or even having heard of, the idea of mainstreaming AIDS. In the words of the HIV/AIDS Adviser for Save the Children UK:

> Much of the mainstreaming concept relates to realising, describing, and further developing the connections between development and AIDS that already 'exist' in development work. A project of ours in Cambodia involving market gardening in rural areas calmly informed me that for the 'first time this year no young people from the village left to work in Phnom Penh during the dry season'. They then asked me how they could get involved in HIV work, without realising how they were already, very effectively, contributing by reducing the increased risk of HIV infection which is associated with migration.[18]

Insufficient practical evidence of good practice

At the beginning of the AIDS pandemic, there was a lack of accessible guidance based on good practice to inform the response of community organisations to HIV and AIDS. Now there is a wealth of newsletters, best-practice briefings, guidelines, and other experience-based materials, which document and popularise key strategies such as peer-group education and home-based care. However, although some papers and reports exist, there is not much experience of mainstreaming – and even less good practice – for agencies to draw on. A trainer involved in mainstreaming AIDS within the British government's Department for International Development comments, 'As there are not many clear examples of mainstreaming, it is a challenge for DFID to be creative, pragmatic, and in the vanguard for developing mainstreaming strategies for HIV/AIDS.'[19] Although Uganda's government adopted a multi-sectoral approach as long ago as 1992, a recent review found 'very little real progress in mainstreaming HIV/AIDS within the core work of ministries. There has been much uncertainty of what HIV/AIDS mainstreaming means in practice and how to go about it. This seems hardly surprising, given the lack of international experience or clear definitions in this area' (Elsey 2002a:2).

Mainstreaming is a process; once started, it does not stop. It does not merely involve a technical quick-fix, and there is no overnight change from 'not mainstreamed' to 'mainstreamed'.

This lack of evidence of good practice means that organisations do not have examples of possible activities to inspire them, nor guidelines about the steps to take. As Barnett and Whiteside state, *'There is no prescription for dealing with impact. There has been no regional or national plan that addresses this in a holistic manner. Experience shows that there exists a sparse range of responses'* (Barnett and Whiteside 2002:343). And, at the field level, ActionAid-Mozambique's case study notes that *'country programme staff feel they need further guidelines on how to assess the possible, unintended effects on HIV/AIDS vulnerability of other programme interventions'*.

Because detailed guidelines do not exist, agencies need to experiment in order to generate experience-based lessons and recommendations, as Oxfam is doing in Southern Africa. A growing number of agencies, government ministries, and donors are coming together to identify and share such evidence. In May 2003, a number of organisations, including SC UK and Oxfam, came together to discuss lessons learned in mitigating the impacts of HIV/AIDS through agriculture and rural development. What was initially conceived as a small meeting for 10 or so individuals grew into a three-day workshop with 45 participants from 13 countries. One of the main issues, raised many times by agricultural and rural development specialists, was the growing need for agencies to focus on their own work, but to develop active partnerships with others who have complementary specialities. In particular, participants stressed the need for a permanent combination of development, humanitarian, and rehabilitation efforts, all in the same communities. Participants agreed on the need to run similar workshops in various countries, and to enable local CBOs, NGOs, government staff, and church groups to share the practical lessons that are seldom documented. Information is available at www.sarpn.org.za.

Insufficient technical assistance

Largely because mainstreaming HIV is a newly developing field, there are few people with experience to provide technical support. Although increasing numbers of organisations are interested in mainstreaming, they need technical assistance to understand what it can mean, and guidance on how to engage in the long-term process of trying to address both the causes and consequences of AIDS. Such support is not easily found, and the task is made more difficult by the lack of like-minded organisations to work with. For example, Oxfam's programme in Malawi has made some grants available to partners for training in mainstreaming AIDS. Staff found, however, that the training accessed by the partners was not really concerned with mainstreaming AIDS, but with AIDS work, and basic information on AIDS (Oxfam Malawi 2002:7). While larger agencies like Oxfam may, to some extent, be able to develop their own capacity to deliver mainstreaming training, the dearth of outside agencies to turn to for assistance is particularly problematic for smaller organisations. However, this situation should improve as organisations increasingly share their experiences of mainstreaming and develop practical guidelines, and as capacity-building agencies build their own ability to support mainstreaming.

There is therefore a great need to identify interested third-party service providers, such as organisational development specialists, agricultural training institutions, teacher-training colleges. and the like. Efforts to build the capacity of such institutions could be based on a principle similar to 'train the trainers' workshops, where the objective is to increase the numbers of people and organisations that could support mainstreaming efforts in a whole range of sectors in each country.

Lack of resources and commitment

Evidence from the case studies suggests that the mainstreaming process demands dedicated staff and funding until attention to HIV/AIDS is institutionalised, or at least until significant progress has been made. One of the major problems with Oxfam's pilot in Malawi is that most Oxfam staff and partner staff face multiple demands on their time, which has meant that efforts to mainstream AIDS have taken time to show results. The dedicated HIV/AIDS staff who were involved in setting up the process have a regional mandate, and an expanded mainstreaming pilot to work on, so they cannot be continuously involved with the process in the Malawi programme. The recent hiring of an experienced officer dedicated to work on gender and HIV/AIDS in Malawi should provide more sustained support.

ActionAid reports that although it has specialist AIDS staff, they are already overloaded by the demands of direct AIDS work, which impedes progress on the external mainstreaming of AIDS. The 'solution' of securing funding for new staff, and then recruiting and managing them, takes time. Oxfam's Southern Africa programme was able to find the resources from within Oxfam. ActionAid is seeking external funding for a mainstreaming pilot, as part of a broader project proposal. In either case, proponents of mainstreaming have to argue that mainstreaming is worth funding, despite the preference of most donors and agencies for funding more tangible and direct AIDS work. Furthermore, the funding period has to allow the mainstreaming process to develop. A mainstreaming project of Uganda's Ministry of Agriculture, externally initiated and funded, lasted only one year (Topouzis 2001:vi).

A lack of resources, and in particular staff time, also impedes efforts to support partners to mainstream AIDS. Project Empower found that it had too little time for mentoring and supporting the CBOs with which it was working, and that by focusing on achieving results in a short time, it sometimes moved too fast for the CBOs (Project Empower 2002a). For their part, the CBOs complained of a lack of funding for both internal and external mainstreaming, and commented that *'[with] the extreme pressure faced by many in terms of funding and staffing shortages... it is difficult and for some impossible to dedicate time and people to drive the HIV/AIDS mainstreaming process'* (Project Empower 2002a:5).

The funding period has to allow the mainstreaming process to develop. A mainstreaming project of Uganda's Ministry of Agriculture, externally initiated and funded, lasted only one year.

Resources depend on commitment. With external funding, as in the case of Uganda's Ministry of Agriculture, a mainstreaming project can come into being without significant internal commitment. This particular project was not located in a core part of the institution, and it did not win enough internal commitment to secure on-going funding when the pilot project finished. An evaluation reported that the project was perceived from within the ministry as an add-on which was 100 per cent funded by donors, and this eroded the ability of the ministry to sustain the initiative (Topouzis 2001:23). In Zambia's Ministry of Agriculture, weak commitment to mainstreaming AIDS meant that AIDS focal points and the HIV/AIDS committee lacked internal support, and hence influence, within the institution (Topouzis 2001:23).

The experience of Oxfam's Southern Africa AIDS team so far suggests that a lack of commitment slows down, or frustrates, the mainstreaming process. In their case, a core of well-placed people took on the issue of AIDS, and have been able to champion important changes across the organisation. Strong internal advocacy – and advocacy among partners – is needed if managers and other influential people are actively to support and sustain mainstreaming measures. ActionAid reports that a workshop on AIDS and development, involving its own directors and trustees, resulted in greater focus on HIV/AIDS across the agency, with correspondingly high levels of commitment and funding (Bataringaya 1999:4). Without this awareness and commitment at senior levels, field efforts can be frustrated, as stated forcefully by a programme-based AIDS specialist working for a large NGO:

One of the key constraints seems to be that the 'London office' in general, and areas of the world where HIV is not a visible problem, don't seem to be taking AIDS on as a serious issue. Until senior staff in London have had proper HIV sensitisation and awareness, and policy reflects the issues on the ground, the development work that we are doing won't be taken seriously.[20]

Summary

This chapter has reviewed initial experiences of mainstreaming AIDS in development work. It has described NGO and government-directed activities, including training, community research, allocating responsibility for mainstreaming, adapting systems, and forming complementary partnerships.

The chapter has also provided some examples of development work being adapted to suit the changing circumstances which AIDS has brought about. They included better targeting of people at risk or affected by AIDS; altering ways of working; modifying interventions; and forming new partnerships among organisations with complementary skills. When combined, these should help to make the development process more accessible and appropriate to households affected by AIDS. The chapter then briefly considered three issues: how the indirect response of mainstreaming is likely to be accompanied (or even eclipsed) by the direct response of AIDS work; the dangers in equating external mainstreaming of AIDS with reaching AIDS-affected households; and the question of how to influence partners to mainstream AIDS externally. Finally, the chapter reviewed the main constraints identified by the case studies, which were limited understanding of mainstreaming, the absence of good practice for external mainstreaming, and a lack of resources and commitment.

The chapter also outlined the different paths leading to the different responses to AIDS adopted by the three agencies sponsoring this book. ActionAid and Save the Children UK have long experience of AIDS work, and have focused their attention and resources on the strategy of responding directly, on integrating AIDS work, and on related advocacy initiatives. ActionAid intends to mainstream AIDS in its existing programmes. Save the Children has recently identified mainstreaming as a key priority for its HIV/AIDS work, and the agency is planning how to mainstream HIV across all its country programmes, especially those in sub-Saharan Africa and South-East Asia.

Oxfam's concerted response to AIDS began later, at a time when the impacts of AIDS were becoming evident in badly affected areas of sub-Saharan Africa, and the idea of mainstreaming was emerging. Oxfam took a strategic decision to invest in a comprehensive pilot project for mainstreaming, including providing the staffing and commitment which are required to begin and maintain the process. As a result, it has been able to make some useful progress in a short time. Moreover, the agency is getting 'added value' out of its pilot activities by devoting time to documenting experiences and using them to stimulate debate, for example, through newsletter articles, workshops, and its website.[21] Chapter 13 presents many of the lessons learned by Oxfam in Southern Africa. However, the pilot project is only one initiative; it may be interesting in terms of theory and ideas, but it has not yet proved itself in terms of sustaining its momentum or evaluating its impact. There is a long way to go before solid and replicable examples of good practice in mainstreaming can emerge.

9 Experiences of mainstreaming AIDS externally in humanitarian work

I would say that everyone is struggling with what to do about the HIV/AIDS crisis in the development context, and there are no easy answers or prescriptions; in the context of an emergency, the problem is even more challenging and acute.
(Oxfam GB Humanitarian Adviser[1])

Introduction

In humanitarian work, as with development work, external mainstreaming of AIDS is about modifying interventions, rather than necessarily initiating AIDS work. Chapter 5 described some of the ways in which humanitarian work may inadvertently heighten susceptibility to HIV infection, and exclude individuals and households affected by AIDS. Mainstreaming entails minimising those negative effects, while maximising the positive, though indirect, contribution of humanitarian work to reducing susceptibility and vulnerability.

In general, NGOs and the UN agencies are giving some attention to the issue of AIDS and emergencies, in the form of research, journal articles, workshops, and policy development. The 2002–2003 food crisis in Southern Africa, especially in Malawi and Zambia, has stimulated much new thinking on HIV/AIDS in humanitarian work. This chapter will identify some of the issues and possible future trends, but it should be noted that ideas in this field are probably developing more quickly than any other aspects of AIDS-related programme work. As was noted before the response to the food crisis began:

... action on the ground has been minimal to date. In many cases, humanitarian staff lack the capacity and confidence to implement the available guidelines on HIV/AIDS, and interventions are seen as a longer-term development or a clinical health question beyond their mandate. HIV/AIDS is rarely recognised as a possible symptom of the emergency itself. Generally, NGOs have approached HIV/AIDS as a health risk to staff, or purely as an operational challenge, to be seen in biomedical terms only.
(International Save the Children Alliance 2002:28)

For UNAIDS, the initial 'essential minimum package' for AIDS following a crisis comprises four bio-medical and behavioural interventions: adherence to universal precautions (minimising the risk of HIV transmission in medical settings); ensuring safe blood transfusions; provision of basic HIV/AIDS information; and supplies of condoms. Once essential services have been restored, attention should turn to providing other services, such as treatment of sexually transmitted infections (STIs), and treatment and care for people with HIV and AIDS (UNAIDS 1997:5-7). WHO and UNHCR take a wider perspective in their guidelines, recommending a 'minimum initial service package' which includes the above, plus measures such as preventing and managing the consequences of sexual violence (WHO 2000:27).

The case studies and literature review on which this book is based show that, as with mainstreaming AIDS in development work, few organisations make any distinction between undertaking stand-alone or integrated AIDS work and mainstreaming AIDS; and it is AIDS work which predominates. Reflecting the general situation, a survey of seven NGOs' HIV/AIDS programmes with refugees or displaced people found that the main focus of their work is on AIDS prevention. Of the thirteen programmes run by the NGOs – including SC UK, CAFOD, and ACORD – all of them promoted safer sex, the majority distributed condoms, and half were involved in supporting STI services. Three ran home-based care services, and one supported orphan-headed households with income-generating activities (Smith 2002:19).

However, in contrast to non-emergency AIDS work, responses to AIDS within humanitarian settings are few, and there is a great lack of documented experience of both integrating and mainstreaming AIDS in emergency work. Chapter 4 featured two examples of NGOs responding directly through AIDS work in camps for displaced people and refugees. This chapter describes three examples of work which attends to issues of gender and sexual violence, and two cases which are more explicitly concerned with the idea of mainstreaming AIDS in humanitarian work. First, however, there is a brief overview of the types of work that comprise the humanitarian response.

Varieties of humanitarian work

This book uses the phrase 'humanitarian work' to cover a range of responses to various kinds of crisis. One can crudely categorise these crises into two broad types. **Humanitarian disasters**, which are also commonly (and more accurately) referred to as 'natural disasters', are catastrophes caused directly by a natural phenomenon, such as a volcanic eruption, a hurricane, or flood. **Complex emergencies** are driven by conflict-related political crises, although a variety of other factors, which may include environmental influences such as drought, are often implicated. They are often protracted and they involve large-scale population displacement, non-natural deaths, and social disruption (Gundel 1999).

In the past, the appropriate humanitarian response to both kinds of crisis was judged to be the immediate provision of food and other commodities intended to save lives, and (in the case of complex emergencies) protection from danger. However, the concept of humanitarian assistance has recently become blurred, as humanitarian agencies link relief to development assistance, and as development agencies enter the domain of humanitarian assistance. The idea of a 'relief-to-development continuum' has emerged, based on the notion that relief assistance can sustain people through short-term periods of stress until the crisis is over, when rehabilitation begins, leading to a normal process of development (Gundel 1999).

One outcome is a trend towards attempting to incorporate best practice from development work into humanitarian work: for example, putting more emphasis on involving people from affected communities in the design and delivery of programmes, and conceptualising assistance in terms of support for sustainable livelihoods.[2] This is particularly the case where the crisis is slow to develop, and where agencies are able to work with people in their home communities. (For example, whereas famine is associated with large population movements, because people travel to receive food and medical relief aid from central locations, agencies in the 2002–2003 Southern African food crisis have generally worked with affected communities who have not, as yet, moved.) However, the literature on HIV and AIDS and humanitarian work mainly focuses on the 'relief' end of the spectrum, and the extreme case of large numbers of people living in camps, resulting from fast-onset and often complex crises.

Attending to issues of gender and sexual abuse

The layout of the camp did not take women's security into consideration when it was being set up. Often women's makeshift shelters were located at the edge of the camp, laying them open to theft, personal attacks and other atrocities. When food and clothing were being handed out, women were often elbowed out of the way by men and got very little or nothing at all. So they

*had to go to the men or soldiers afterwards to get some more or better stuff...
I am not saying that all the men or soldiers were brutes, but in conflict
situations, because people can be incredibly cruel, one has to guard against
such situations arising in the first place.*
(Liberian refugee, Kinnah 1997:9)

While humanitarian agencies may be mostly responding directly to AIDS
through AIDS work, they are giving increasing attention to issues of
gender, protection, and sexual abuse. Although the initiatives featured in
this section are not the products of 'AIDS mainstreaming', they are
certainly related to the process, and in particular to attempts to reduce the
ways in which humanitarian work may inadvertently heighten
susceptibility to HIV infection, such as those referred to by the Liberian
refugee quoted above. As we shall see, the two processes of gender
mainstreaming and AIDS mainstreaming are closely related.

*The two processes of
gender mainstreaming
and AIDS mainstreaming
are closely related.*

Gender and protection

One way for an agency to increase attention to issues of gender and
protection is to produce guidelines. For example, in 2001 **Oxfam GB**
drafted its mandate on gender and humanitarian aid, which sets out a
series of standards to inform and guide its humanitarian workers. They
relate to analysis (including assessment, planning, monitoring and
evaluation, and participation), staffing and personnel capacity, protection-
related issues, and technical indicators concerning water and sanitation,
food and nutrition, shelter, and health.

Another strategy is to appoint specialist staff with responsibility for
mainstreaming gender, or, in some cases, gender and HIV/AIDS. In an
effort to boost its gender mainstreaming, in 2000 **UNHCR** included a
Gender Adviser in one of its Emergency Response Teams for the first
time, working in Guinea and Sierra Leone. UNHCR reports that the
adviser was able to identify and follow up several gender-related issues
which would otherwise have been overlooked, such as getting locks put on
toilet doors, arranging assistance for single women who were struggling
to build their shelters, and raising awareness of the risks of sexual violence
(UNHCR 2001:21).

Oxfam GB's Humanitarian Department has a Protection Adviser, whose
role is to help Oxfam to understand and respond to crises in terms of the
threat posed to individuals and communities by violence, coercion, and
deprivation. In 2001 Oxfam hired two gender specialists, to help the
agency to improve the way in which gender is mainstreamed into its
humanitarian work. The gender specialists have joined assessment teams

in the field, helping to shape Oxfam's appraisals and plans. For example, in 2002 one of them worked on Oxfam's programme in Afghanistan for three months. Resulting initiatives for addressing gender equity as part of the humanitarian programme included the employment of women nationals; gender training for staff members; the creation of a gender and community development team; and the retraining of Afghan women engineers to participate in the reconstruction of the country. The country programme also decided to employ two gender advisers to give on-going support to gender mainstreaming. The UK-based gender specialists have been key to Oxfam's response to crises in Liberia and Sierra Leone, and in Southern Africa, as discussed below.

There are very few gender specialists, however, compared with the overall numbers of people working in a humanitarian programme. Training is a key way of increasing employees' understanding of issues related to gender, protection, and human rights. In the Resources section at the back of this book, Unit 9 includes the outline of a gender and protection workshop which Oxfam ran for its own staff and those of other agencies in Sierra Leone in 2002.

Another strategy to boost attention to gender and protection is to complement 'hardware' staff, who specialise in technical inputs such as water engineering, with 'software' staff, who concentrate on social aspects of humanitarian work, such as community consultation. Oxfam has been employing Public Health Promoters in its water and sanitation work in humanitarian programmes since the mid-1990s. They play a crucial role in ensuring the integration of social and technical aspects of programming, but increasingly programme mangers and engineers are themselves expected to take on such responsibilities. For example, both engineers and health promoters work directly with communities and authorities on the location and design of water and sanitation facilities, and they must ensure women's involvement in decision making.

Sexual exploitation and abuse in humanitarian aid programmes

Save the Children UK believes in listening to children, encouraging them to identify their problems and suggest solutions. In refugee camps in Liberia, for example, this process led the agency to act on a request from children and young people for their own clinic to deal with matters of sexual and reproductive health The outcome was a more accessible and less stigmatising service, which is helping to improve young people's sexual health, including reducing their susceptibility to HIV.[3]

A recurrent theme of the children's accounts in the camps of West Africa was the use of sexual transactions to obtain relief goods and access to services. In collaboration with UNHCR, Save the Children UK sent an assessment team to visit refugee camps in Liberia, Guinea, and Sierra Leone, and consulted various groups within refugee and returnee communities, as well as host communities. These groups included children, community leaders, government officials, and staff from international and national NGOs, UN agencies, and security forces.

The findings of the assessment were largely based on the testimonies of children. They indicated that sexual exploitation and abuse of children is 'extensive' in the communities that were visited. The report suggested that individuals from a range of groups were allegedly responsible for exploiting children, including adults charged with their protection, such as UN staff, staff of international and national NGOs, government officials, community leaders, and peacekeepers. It should be noted, however, that the assessment was not an in-depth piece of research or an investigation; as such, the allegations were communicated to all the relevant agencies, but were not investigated as part of the assessment mission. A subsequent UN investigation failed to substantiate the specific allegations against named individuals, although Save the Children UK still regards the general findings of the original study as valid.

'If you see a young girl walking away with tarpaulin on her head, you know how she got it.'

The children's accounts feature two broad types of exploitation and abuse. First, some male relief workers and peacekeepers buy sexual services from girls, mainly aged 13 to 18, paying in cash or in kind. The assessment summary report states that this practice *'appears to be widespread, and the majority of children consulted knew of at least one other child involved in such an exchange'*. The children involved felt that it was their only option in order to obtain food and other basic necessities, and to pay for their education. Second, some male relief workers, mainly national staff, trade humanitarian aid and services in exchange for sex. Children reported that NGO staff make excuses to withhold aid, such as *'Your name is not on the list'*, or *'The computer swallowed your card'*, until they get what they want. These allegations were corroborated by adults, such as the male refugee who claimed that *'if you do not have a wife or a sister or a daughter to offer the NGO workers, it is hard to have access to aid'*. In Guinea, a refugee leader summed up the situation as follows: *'If you see a young girl walking away with tarpaulin on her head, you know how she got it'*. Another allegation was that development workers demand sex in exchange for employment; as one female NGO employee put it, *'No girl will get a job in this camp without having sex with NGO workers'* (Save the Children UK 2002).

The main response to the report's allegations has been developed through the Inter-Agency Standing Committee, or IASC, whose members include UN agencies such as UNICEF, FAO, and UNHCR, as well as a wide range of international NGOs. The IASC set up a Task Force on Protection from Sexual Exploitation and Abuse in Humanitarian Crises, which produced a Plan of Action containing more than 40 recommendations, which have been endorsed by all the IASC members. The Plan of Action has several aims. First, to prevent humanitarian workers perpetrating exploitative and abusive behaviour – a task to be addressed mainly through the introduction of codes of conduct for staff, and appropriate disciplinary procedures. Second, to address the conditions that make women and children vulnerable to exploitation and abuse, by increasing their participation in planning, and minimising the ways in which distribution systems create opportunities for abuse. Third, to respond to the needs of people who are abused, through appropriate support and legal redress. Fourth, to manage and supervise all of the elements, and to monitor and evaluate their implementation. The objectives of the action plan, and its code of conduct for humanitarian workers, are featured in Unit 10 in the Resources section of this book.

In addition to collective action via the IASC process, the report prompted a range of responses within individual NGOs. For example, the Oxfam GB programmes in the region used the report's recommendations to audit their own work, and to identify the aspects needing most attention, including long-term goals such as the need to appoint more field staff, and particularly more women. One outcome is that in Liberia, Oxfam's water and sanitation programme has been ensuring that men, women, and children are aware that their rights to aid are not conditional on accepting sexual exploitation. The report also prompted Oxfam to circulate guidelines for sexual conduct among its humanitarian workers (McNairn 2002:8).

For Save the Children UK, the research into abuse is leading to a further study, aimed at understanding the key factors behind the abuse, in order to make the agency's response more effective. Insecure livelihoods are one factor which affects vulnerable people's susceptibility to exploitation and sexual abuse. Thus SC UK is taking forward the key recommendations of the report by addressing the question of the status of women and children in the camps, and their access to food and non-food items. In Sierra Leone, SC UK has trained community groups and humanitarian workers to respect the rights of children and has facilitated women's and children's representation in the camp-management structures. It has also strengthened recognition of the needs of single women, such that they are no longer registered as part of family groups, but now receive ration cards and access to shelter in their own right. SC UK is promoting the IASC code of conduct in training sessions for its own staff and other humanitarian workers.

Tackling sexual violence

A case from refugee camps in Tanzania illustrates how progress can be made on the issue of sexual violence, given the resources and will to do so. In 1998, following reports of increasing violence, the NGO Human Rights Watch investigated the work of **UNHCR** in Tanzania. It found that some staff '...*were defensive or dismissive about the problem of violence against women refugees. Some even tended to blame the victim, while others saw such violence as unfortunate, but "normal", or attributed sexual violence to Burundian culture. At that time, UNHCR lacked both community services staff with relevant training, and dedicated programs to assist refugee women'* (Human Rights Watch 2000:1).

Following publicity about violence in the camps, UNHCR was awarded a substantial grant to improve its programmes for refugee women in several countries, including Tanzania. Subsequent research by Human Rights Watch recorded that UNHCR had used the money to initiate *'more systematic, careful, and effective efforts to address the problem of sexual violence'* (Human Rights Watch 2000:2). Staffing was boosted by two new posts of Sexual and Gender Based Violence Assistant, two lawyers, and a security liaison officer working with the police deployed to work in refugee camps. Activities included raising community awareness of sexual violence and other gender-based forms of abuse; providing counselling for victims of sexual violence; following up rape cases with the police and courts; training police officers; and establishing distribution systems to ensure women's access to food, particularly in situations of domestic violence or divorce (Human Rights Watch 2000:2).

Efforts to mainstream AIDS: two case studies

This section presents two cases which relate explicitly to mainstreaming AIDS. First, ideas and strategies emerging from the unfolding response to Southern Africa's food crisis; and second, an initiative by one NGO to encourage its partners to mainstream AIDS in their humanitarian work.

Responding to the Southern Africa food crisis

The 2002–2003 food crisis in Southern Africa presents a particular opportunity for experimenting with mainstreaming AIDS. The food crisis is affecting countries which are all also severely affected by HIV and AIDS, and it has come at a time when more agencies are making the links between AIDS and wider development issues, including food security. In February 2003, for example, **UNAIDS** and the **World Food Programme** (WFP) made a formal agreement to work together, both in paying particular attention to vulnerable groups such as orphans in food programmes, and in advocating that food security becomes an integral part of responses to HIV/AIDS. UNAIDS proposes a response which prioritises food assistance, while giving more relief support, such as subsidies and quick-response distribution schemes, to save the most vulnerable households from destitution or disintegration. It also advocates expanded AIDS work in terms of prevention, treatment, and care, and long-term strategies to improve the lives and livelihoods of the rural poor (UNAIDS 2002b:29).

In general, it seems that organisations engaging in humanitarian programmes are paying more attention to HIV and AIDS, by working with HIV-aware partners or recruiting HIV specialists.[4] Some of the work may not be very different from what it might otherwise have been; for example, WFP and local NGOs are running school feeding programmes in some low-income neighbourhoods of Lusaka. Presumably this work aims to channel food to children, and thus encourage them to stay in school, but, with 85 per cent of households in the area caring for orphans, it will have positive effects on orphans and AIDS-affected households (UNAIDS 2002b:29).

For **Oxfam**, a community-based approach to the targeting and distribution of food aid aims to maximise equity and ensure community participation and representation, in order to minimise the problems that heighten susceptibility to HIV. Oxfam aims to meet vulnerable people's immediate needs and also protect their livelihoods from being lost or undermined. For example, in HIV/AIDS affected communities, programmes might include inputs of food or cash to meet immediate needs, together with longer-term agricultural activities such as encouraging short-cycle crop production, and the provision of labour-saving tools suitable for elderly people or adolescents.

A gender specialist was a member of Oxfam's assessment teams in Zambia, Zimbabwe, and Malawi, and the planning for Oxfam's response included analysis of HIV/AIDS and gender in an attempt to mainstream both of them, through programmes designed to promote food security, livelihoods, and public health. One outcome is that the country programmes have hired HIV/AIDS specialists for continuity, following the input of the gender specialist.

The main effect of efforts to mainstream AIDS and gender is that the programmes are aiming to focus on households that are thought to be vulnerable to the impacts of AIDS, including those already exposed to those impacts. These households may also be more susceptible to HIV infection. Hence the programmes are likely to focus on widows who are not supported by other households; vulnerable households which are female-headed; and households with orphans, or elderly, disabled, or chronically ill members. Oxfam also aims to channel support to vulnerable self-help community groups, and groups which are child-centred (especially orphan-centred). As with the WFP example, it is possible that the programme will not be very different from what it might otherwise have been, because even without an analysis of HIV/AIDS, Oxfam always aims to attend to the needs of vulnerable people within a community. However, by including, for example, chronic illness as a criterion of vulnerability, AIDS-related issues are made more explicit.

It is no longer possible for humanitarian workers to take a simplistic view of the world, in which a 'normal' development situation is occasionally punctuated by a short-term crisis, after which conditions return to 'normal'.

A more novel outcome in Oxfam's Zambia programme is that the analysis extended to the logistics of the programme, and considered potentially negative effects that might inadvertently arise. This revealed concerns about HIV transmission between truck drivers – often considered a high-risk group, because they travel widely and are away from their homes for long periods – and women and girls in the community, particularly given the latter's impoverished state, and their need for the food for which the truck drivers are responsible. Oxfam's response was to give the truck drivers training to increase their awareness of gender equity and HIV/AIDS, along with promotion of a code of conduct concerning sexual abuse and exploitation. Oxfam also distributed condoms to the drivers and to other agencies, and painted an AIDS logo on the trucks, alongside the Oxfam logo, to give the issue a higher profile.[5]

At the time of writing, the responses to the food crisis are still being analysed, and few of the interventions of Oxfam or other major agencies have been formally evaluated. However, Oxfam's Regional HIV/AIDS Co-ordinator has commented[6] that it is becoming obvious that AIDS increases vulnerability to the impacts of complex emergencies and disasters at all levels – from the infected individual to the affected household and community – because AIDS undermines the individual and collective ability to withstand external shocks. He observes that it is no longer possible for humanitarian workers to take a simplistic view of the world, in which a 'normal' development situation is occasionally punctuated by a short-term crisis, after which conditions return to 'normal': *'AIDS is changing this, and there can be no assumption that things will go back to what they were before.'* Agencies such as Oxfam need a better understanding of the way in which vulnerability is different in different locations. For example, much humanitarian work is focused on rural areas; but AIDS in Southern Africa is clearly affected by urban–rural relationships, and humanitarian responses are struggling to adapt. Many Zimbabwean families have some urban members and some rural members. Urban relatives often send money to the rural areas, while rural relatives reciprocate with food. AIDS is undermining these relationships: urban employees fall ill, stop sending money, and eventually return to their rural homes, where they themselves need financial support; rural areas can no longer produce sufficient food to send to towns. A series of vulnerability assessments in Southern Africa *'portrayed the complexity of the situation, demonstrating the increasingly uneven distribution of vulnerability within countries'.*[7]

Supporting partners to mainstream AIDS in humanitarian work

The NGO **CAFOD** has made a specific attempt to encourage its partners to mainstream AIDS in their humanitarian work, by developing an information leaflet about the issue. The leaflet, entitled *The Silent Emergency: HIV/AIDS in Conflicts and Disasters*, provides a brief but comprehensive summary of the issues, beginning with the consequences of emergencies and how they relate to HIV. Five sets of recommendations follow, under the headings of 'Disaster-preparedness Strategies', 'Initial Risk Assessment', 'Provision of Shelter, Water, and Food', 'Responding to Health Needs', and 'Children and Young People'. Power and powerlessness, including gender-related power issues, are presented as a cross-cutting consideration. Finally, the leaflet sums up the implications for humanitarian organisations.

In order to test the leaflet, CAFOD sent a draft of the text to nine of its partners, six of whom sent feedback, based on their use of the leaflet: they had circulated it to other organisations, published it in a humanitarian network's newsletter, and used it as a training resource and as a tool to review recent experience of humanitarian work. The partners also foresaw a variety of future uses, for example in developing disaster preparedness, formulating policy, planning programmes, training staff, and doing advocacy work. They also made comments on the content and layout of the draft leaflet.

CAFOD found that the impact of the leaflet was enhanced when followed up with face-to-face support. For example, one NGO employee told a visiting CAFOD officer that the leaflet said nothing new, and that the NGO was already doing everything that the leaflet recommended. However, further discussion led to a revelation: the NGO had provided food and blankets to women made homeless by a natural disaster – women whose partners had migrated for work, and who were now sleeping with their children in the city's main park. Apparently, however, the NGO had focused exclusively on its relief response and failed to consider that the women might be surviving by selling sexual services (CAFOD 2002:6). By ignoring issues of sexual health and livelihoods, they had overlooked a key threat to the women's long-term prospects of survival.

Information alone is not enough to ensure meaningful and sustained behaviour change.

CAFOD concluded that, as with a leaflet about safer sex, information alone is not enough to ensure meaningful and sustained behaviour change. Although their *Silent Emergencies* leaflet had proved useful (and has since been finalised and translated into other languages – see the bibliography for details), such a brief document needs to be augmented by more detailed guidance and tools to enable partners to mainstream AIDS in their humanitarian work.

Problems

A fundamental problem for attempts to mainstream AIDS in humanitarian work is the wide variety of crises, and the speed at which they often strike. To date, the literature on responses to AIDS concentrates on support for refugees or displaced people living in camps – but this is only one type of humanitarian work. As with mainstreaming AIDS in development programmes, there is a lack of experience for agencies to learn from, let alone good practice to emulate. In addition to this basic problem, this section reviews four further constraints on indirect responses to AIDS in humanitarian programmes.

Direct and indirect responses

As we have already noted, agencies generally prefer direct responses to AIDS, mainly through prevention initiatives, but also through treatment for sexually transmitted infections, and treatment and care for people with HIV and AIDS. However, in contrast to the response to AIDS in non-emergency situations, where direct AIDS work is far more common, the direct response is, as yet, fairly muted in humanitarian programmes; most relevant work is probably being done through broader projects to improve sexual and reproductive health, rather than through AIDS-focused projects. Furthermore, while efforts to mainstream AIDS are very few, humanitarian agencies are now paying more attention to the protection of women and girls, which means that susceptibility to HIV infection is increasingly being addressed.

The problem of denial

At the personal level, denial among humanitarian staff can block positive responses to AIDS, and related issues such as sexual and gender-based violence. This may be because staff assume that people do not engage in sexual relations in extreme circumstances, or because they deny that unacceptable or criminal behaviour may be occurring. For example, when asked about the relevance of reproductive health to his humanitarian programmes, a manager in southern Sudan responded: '...*reproductive health is not a priority...abortion is not a problem, they already have good child spacing ...violence is not occurring in Sudan, as the women are treasured*'. His assessment contradicted the findings of researchers in the area, however, to whom women described the problems of having too many children, the methods and consequences of attempting to abort a pregnancy, and the reasons for violence against them, which included refusal to have sex with their husbands, and mismanagement of household funds (Palmer 1998:27-28).

This type of denial is possible when humanitarian staff do not look for problems related to AIDS and sexual health, and so do not find them. It may also be connected to the predominance of male staff in emergency situations, and reluctance among women refugees to share personal information with them. As a female officer working for UNHCR recalls, '*I have walked around camps and seen doctors who have said "no problems" ...then I've gone into tents and found women who have been raped, who have severe gynaecological problems, who have all kinds of complaints*' (Marshall 1995:2). The basic but hidden problem of a lack of sanitary cloths can prevent women from queuing for rations, going to the clinic, or fetching firewood when they are menstruating. An assessment with refugees in Zimbabwe found that this was one reason why women and girls were not taking a full part in education and training activities (Marshall 1995:4). While a shortage of sanitary cloths may appear to be irrelevant or a low priority, it is one factor in the failure of girls and women to obtain the assistance that is their right, and which should, among other things, be helping to reduce their susceptibility to HIV infection.

At the institutional level there is a related block on responding to AIDS in emergencies, in the form of resistance to the idea that AIDS is relevant to, and hence a part of, the humanitarian response. CAFOD, following up the

NGOs that did not give feedback to its *Silent Emergencies* pilot, found as follows:

> *HIV was not considered an immediate priority in emergencies, when NGOs are confronted by seemingly more pressing needs for food, shelter, sanitation and medical care. That HIV-related considerations might influence how NGOs responded to these other needs is not commonly acknowledged. Emergency practitioners consider that HIV is a concern that will be taken up by those following on with (re)development programmes after the emergency has passed.*
> (CAFOD 2002:7)

'We have a beautiful policy on refugee women. We have guidelines. We have everything, but all this is only as good as the implementation.'

However, as WHO notes, if less visible issues such as STIs, HIV/AIDS, unsafe abortion, and sexual violence are neglected in the early stages of an emergency, because saving lives is the highest priority, they may continue to be neglected in the stabilisation phase, because they are not part of the repertoire of humanitarian responses (WHO 2000:24).

Limited capacity and resources

If agencies lack the capacity to respond to AIDS in emergencies – whether by integration or mainstreaming – it seems that lack of guidance is not the main reason. In the words of the deputy director of UNHCR's Protection Division, *'We have a beautiful policy on refugee women. We have guidelines. We have everything, but all this is only as good as the implementation'* (Marshall 1995:1). In the case of the refugee camps in Tanzania, cited above, the initial investigation by Human Rights Watch found as follows:

> *The guidelines often were not consistently implemented by UNHCR staff in the field. Some staff had not even been apprised of or trained in the content of UNHCR's policies on women. The guidelines often were not readily available, and in some cases UNHCR staff did not even know that they existed. Staff also did not understand that implementation of these guidelines on protection of refugee women was not a choice, but rather a routine and integral obligation on their part as UNHCR employees.*
> (Human Rights Watch 2000:4)

The WHO lists several factors which inhibit the implementation of guidelines on promoting reproductive health: attention to gender equity is not a priority at the institutional level; staff may be unaware of the problems, or not trained to respond to them; staff may also be reluctant to talk about sensitive issues such as sex and sexual violence (WHO 2000:13). CAFOD reports that organisations responding to emergencies rarely have any kind of disaster-preparedness strategy, and so do not think about how HIV-related issues might impact on their mode of operating when an emergency occurs (CAFOD 2002:7). If organisations do not give the issue any thought in advance, it seems very unlikely that they will pay attention to AIDS during an emergency, when there is little time for such considerations.

Of course, funding also influences the response on the ground. Limited funds oblige agencies to choose what posts and activities to prioritise, and what tasks to leave undone. As a senior physical planner from UNHCR notes, '...a camp that really considers women's issues, children's issues, and protection of the environment will cost far more money. And that is usually the problem. Many of these things just cannot be done for the same price' (Marshall 1995:3). And related to all of these issues is the element of commitment, or political will, to tackle AIDS and its related issues – by addressing the problem of denial, establishing a mandate, building capacity, developing preparedness, and securing funding.

'So many issues ... and so much chaos'

Finally, it is important to note that the problems which humanitarian agencies face are extremely complex. Emergencies can happen very quickly and affect large numbers of people. As one UNHCR operations team leader commented, 'There are so many issues in the camps, and so much chaos...and we are acutely under-staffed' (Marshall 1995:3). There are some key factors over which humanitarian agencies have little or no control, such as the location of camps, and matters of policing and law enforcement, which are the responsibility of the host government. In times of conflict, other issues which agencies do not control may become very significant, such as the presence in the camps of militia members among the refugees, and access to the camps. Governments may even be implicated in systematic violence against internally displaced people or refugees. And even in long-term refugee camps, humanitarian agencies may only be able to mitigate the effects of violence by reacting to its consequences, rather than addressing its causes (Crisp 1999:23).

The situation is better in more stable situations, where the people in need of assistance have not been displaced from their homes. However, agencies must still grapple with complex issues. For example, if the vulnerable households are to be identified by traditional and civil authorities, will stigmatised groups, such as single mothers or people with HIV/AIDS, be marginalised or excluded?

Summary

This chapter has reviewed some experiences and problems relating to the modification of humanitarian programmes in response to HIV and AIDS. There is very little relevant experience on which to draw, but the chapter has presented three cases concerning responses to sexual violence. There is a growing interest among humanitarian agencies in the broad themes of ensuring gender equity, the protection of vulnerable members of the community, and preventing sexual violence, which is evident in the existence of guidelines and policies.

The chapter has identified a series of problems which limit the impact of such guidelines and policies on the lives of people affected by natural disasters and complex emergencies. These include the strategy of responding to AIDS exclusively as a separate issue, rather than mainstreaming it also into core programmes; failure to challenge denial on the part of individual officials and members of staff; and a lack of capacity, funding, and the will to act. There is also the very real structural problem that, in a context where many factors are beyond their control, there are limits to what humanitarian agencies can do to reduce susceptibility to HIV infection and vulnerability to the impacts of AIDS.

Chapter 13 presents ideas for mainstreaming AIDS in humanitarian work, but first the next chapter considers lessons to be learned from experiences of mainstreaming gender in development and humanitarian programmes.

10 Learning from the mainstreaming of gender

The mainstreaming of gender in emergency responses is challenged by the complexity and variety of emergencies themselves … and by the range of actors involved…. This does not imply that the task is impossible, but it does require an enabling environment, a will to do, and an understanding that gender is not a means, but gender equality is the end. Gender mainstreaming is as much about doing the same things differently as it is about doing different things; it is as much about transforming organisational culture as it is about organising systems.
(McNairn 2002:5)

Introduction

The idea of mainstreaming HIV and AIDS is relatively recent, and, as the previous three chapters have shown, it has not been implemented widely enough for many lessons, let alone 'good practice', to have emerged. However, the idea of mainstreaming gender-related concerns has been applied to development and humanitarian programmes over a longer period of time. Although that process is still being developed, some significant lessons have already been learned, and they are reviewed briefly in this chapter.

General experience

As with the response to HIV and AIDS, it is possible to chart broad trends in the evolution of agencies' response to gender issues over time. Briefly, gender was largely ignored before the 1970s, with the assumption that development work benefited women and men, even if women mainly benefited indirectly, via men. In the 1970s, however, the fact that women were often excluded, and that development efforts could worsen gender inequality, led to attempts to 'integrate' women into the development process. Many institutions set up gender units, and the emphasis on 'Women In Development' resulted in a variety of women's projects and special measures for women. However, women remained marginalised from the development process, and improvements to women's status were slow to emerge. By the mid-1980s, and largely due to efforts of gender units to move the issue to the heart of the policy debate, the strategy was shifting towards the idea of bringing gender issues into mainstream development and humanitarian work. The notion of 'gender mainstreaming' was popularised when it became part of the Platform for Action, agreed at the Fourth UN Conference for Women in Beijing in 1995. Gender mainstreaming commonly applies to all sectors, with responsibility for addressing gender inequality diffused beyond specialised gender units, to make it a routine concern for all staff members.

Progress in advancing gender concerns tends to depend on the energy and tenacity of committed individuals, rather than institutional imperatives.

In general, there has been a broad shift among development agencies towards including gender concerns in policy documents as a matter of course, and trying to include attention to gender issues in processes such as the project cycle. However, evaluations of gender mainstreaming generally find that the impact on women's and men's lives is very limited, mainly due to the phenomenon of 'policy evaporation' (Derbyshire 2002:42). As recent research into gender mainstreaming in Uganda's Ministry of Health states, '...*while the commitment to a gender responsive health sector is clear on paper, these commitments appear to evaporate as policies are translated into concrete actions. This can be seen through the lack of gender analysis and responses within the various communicable disease strategies'* (Elsey 2002a:3). A review of gender-mainstreaming efforts by UNDP, the World Bank, and the International Labour Organization found some encouraging signs of change, with greater recognition among the agencies of women's productive roles and their relevance to a wider range of issues and policies than had previously been thought. However, it concluded that *'despite the attempts to integrate gender issues into their mainstream activities through a variety of procedural and institutional mechanisms, the challenge remains in ensuring that paper commitments are translated into concrete action'* (Miller and Razavi 1995:5).

More positively, a 2002 review of Oxfam GB's work with regard to gender mainstreaming found strong commitment to gender equality among individuals at all levels of the organisation. The review noted that, when leadership is exercised, Oxfam's work makes real progress towards advancing gender equality. Overall, however, implementation was found to be inconsistent, and progress in advancing gender concerns tends to depend on the energy and tenacity of committed individuals, rather than institutional imperatives. The review identified several key problems, which are included in the following analysis (Mohideen 2002).

Problems

The problem of 'policy evaporation' is caused by various interconnecting factors, with the most common described here. None of these problems appears to be insurmountable, but they do frustrate and limit the impact of efforts to mainstream gender in development and humanitarian work.

Understanding mainstreaming

General experience of gender mainstreaming is that expertise is typically limited to a few committed members of staff; the majority of employees do not understand the meaning of gender mainstreaming or, indeed, the meaning of gender itself. Oxfam's review of gender mainstreaming found that many staff are unsure how to translate Oxfam's gender-equality goals into practice, and that their limited understanding of the subject is a key reason why delivery on some programmes has not lived up to expectations. The review recommended that better staff induction, especially in emergency programmes, is needed in order to pass on Oxfam's institutional knowledge of gender to new employees (Mohideen 2002:22). However, whatever the quality of the induction, its impact is to some extent determined by the willingness of the employee to internalise gender issues and the idea of gender mainstreaming.[1]

In general, a lack of understanding of gender mainstreaming leads to inertia, or to faulty implementation; mainstreaming is confined to women's projects, and 'gender' is still viewed as a separate sector (Goetz 1995:4, Derbyshire 2002:42). Alternatively, gender mainstreaming may be reduced to the search for nothing more than a 'gender balance': for example, increasing the proportion of women working within organisations (Elsey 2002a:4). Oxfam's review found significant demand among its staff for practical, on-the-job training and support, but warned that a high staff-turnover rate has undermined capacity-building work concerning gender mainstreaming (Mohideen 2002:5).

Sharing responsibility

One of the key strategies for diffusing responsibility away from specialised gender units is to appoint some staff to act as 'focal persons'. As a manual for gender mainstreaming stresses,

> *Evaluations repeatedly and consistently conclude that effective gender mainstreaming in any context requires...gender focal persons...to take responsibility for spearheading, supporting and sustaining gender work. The role of these staff is not to take full personal responsibility for gender work, but to act as catalysts, supporting and promoting gender related skills*

and approaches amongst colleagues. The evidence is overwhelming that unless there are staff with designated responsibility, responsibility for gender equality all too easily becomes 'mainstreamed' out of existence.
(Derbyshire 2002:44)

Focal persons often prove to be less effective than hoped. Among the reasons for this are insufficient clarity about their roles; a lack of support and skills development; insufficient time and resources to do their work; and a lack of influence within the organisation. In addition, women are sometimes made focal points merely because they are women, rather than because they are interested or suitable. Overall, there is also the problem that the expectations of what can be achieved by focal persons may be unrealistic (Derbyshire 2002:44).

Management commitment and 'ownership'

Bringing about substantial change within any organisation requires the support of senior members of staff, because they have a great degree of influence over the allocation of resources, development of policy, and setting of priorities. Experience with mainstreaming gender in government ministries and agencies such as UNDP shows, however, that the initiative often comes from outside, from bilateral development agencies. When donors drive the gender-mainstreaming process, the organisations undergoing mainstreaming tend to lack commitment and ownership of the initiative. When the donors' grants dry up, so does the mainstreaming. The role of external agencies may also heighten cultural sensitivities, as found in a review of gender mainstreaming in the official development processes of six developing nations:

When donors drive the process, the organisations undergoing mainstreaming tend to lack commitment and ownership of the initiative. When the donors' grants dry up, so does the mainstreaming.

> *Where projects and institutions are set up primarily in response to an external initiative, there is little incentive to actively internalise and 'own' a policy initiative. Instead, its legitimacy is suspect and even though the funds are welcome, the imposition of 'alien' cultural notions regarding gender is deeply resented.*
> (Goetz 1995:5)

Where governments are adopting Sector Wide Approaches (SWAps), donors are no longer able to fund specific projects, although they may exert broader influence on government by affecting the total pattern of expenditure, through agreement on sectoral policies and priorities (Theobald et al. 2002:10). SWAps theoretically present opportunities for mainstreaming gender, but there is, as yet, insufficient experience to assess the degree to which these opportunities are being exploited – although the available reports for health-sector SWAps are not encouraging (Elsey 2002b:11). 'Gender mainstreaming' is sometimes equated with providing reproductive-health services, and there are some signs that SWAps may lead to greater emphasis on bio-medicine and curative urban facilities, at the expense of social understandings of disease and pro-poor primary health care (Elsey 2002b:16).

Oxfam GB has been able to make progress on gender mainstreaming partly because the initiative is its own, and senior staff are committed to the idea. However, its gender review revealed that commitment to, and leadership on, gender equality is uneven: political will at all levels of Oxfam's leadership is key to mainstreaming gender-equality issues in the agency's work (Mohideen 2002).

Finally, with regard to ownership there is a related issue of motivation. Two broad arguments are put forward to justify gender mainstreaming, and to motivate people to engage with it. The **ideological rationale** is based on a firm commitment to gender equality as a fundamental right in development, while the **pragmatic rationale** is based on the need to respond to gender issues in order to achieve development goals. The main danger of the pragmatic approach, which may be more likely to persuade decision-makers to adopt gender mainstreaming, is that women thus become a tool for furthering organisational objectives. For example, they may be targeted as recipients of micro-credit for the pragmatic reason that women generally have better repayment rates than men, so by focusing on them the project is more likely to be successful. In such instances, considerations such as the extra work burden for women are likely to be ignored, as are the training aspects and the empowerment potential of group solidarity, which would be emphasised by a women's micro-credit project driven more by ideology than by pragmatism.[2]

Other requirements

In addition to the three types of problem discussed above, the absence of some other requirements commonly contributes to 'policy evaporation'. At a general level, policy commitments to mainstream gender must be accompanied by budgeted resources, such as funds for gender units, research, and capacity building. These are generally insufficient. Oxfam's review of its gender mainstreaming found that its existing gender specialists were too thinly and inconsistently spread within the organisation to be able to advance gender-equality issues throughout the agency's work. The review recommended that specialists should be employed to work on each of the organisation's thematic priorities (Mohideen 2002:5).

It is also worth noting that gender mainstreaming may be 'going out of fashion': some practitioners believe that the relatively recent phase of enthusiasm for, and investment in, gender mainstreaming has been superseded by newer priorities, such as respect for diversity, the avoidance of exclusion, and responses to HIV/AIDS, with a resulting reduction in commitment to gender equality.[3]

The systems which are needed to embed gender-related concerns may also be lacking, or under-used, or inconsistently applied. They include checklists, guidelines, and measures such as the inclusion of gender concerns in job descriptions and terms of reference (Derbyshire 2002:42). The indicators that are used tend to be quantitative, with insufficient attention paid to qualitative changes. And, at a practical level, even if capacity-building efforts result in greater awareness and willingness to mainstream gender, a lack of tools can frustrate intentions to change policy and practice.

Fundamentally, the process of mainstreaming gender is not always reviewed or assessed, or if that does happen, organisations may fail to act on the issues identified. Oxfam's 2002 gender review surveyed earlier reviews and evaluations and found that *'many of the lessons... have not been learnt institutionally...the same issues are being identified over and over again...'* (Mohideen 2002:21).

Relevance to mainstreaming AIDS

This brief account suggests that the evolving approach to AIDS reflects what has already happened with gender. Just as it is often assumed that AIDS is the problem and AIDS work is the only appropriate response, so the cause of gender inequality was initially interpreted as being the exclusion of women, and women's projects were seen to be the appropriate response. This book's proposal to mainstream AIDS in addition to doing direct AIDS work parallels the shift from initiating women-specific projects to paying attention to gender issues throughout mainstream development and humanitarian work – in addition, where appropriate, to projects focused on either women or men.

The divide between ideological and pragmatic motivations for gender mainstreaming is similarly apparent with regard to AIDS. This book has emphasised pragmatic arguments, such as the fact that development agencies need to respond to AIDS internally in order to function in a time of AIDS, and externally in order to undertake effective development work in a context of AIDS. However, a more ideological perspective might emphasise not costs and efficiency, but the duty of organisations to support their employees and community members to secure their rights to health and dignity. While the advantages and disadvantages of each approach are debatable, it is worth noting that this contrast in motivations exists, and that it may have significant repercussions in terms not only of *why* but *how* AIDS is mainstreamed within an organisation.

Gender mainstreaming has made some real impact, but the experience has been far from straightforward, and could be interpreted as pointing to the futility of attempting to mainstream AIDS. A more optimistic interpretation is that gender mainstreaming has provided proponents of mainstreaming AIDS with some very important lessons and challenges in advance of beginning the process. It may be possible to avoid making the same mistakes. For example, it is now obvious that agencies need to secure both commitment and resources, to designate responsibility for promoting mainstreaming to skilled and properly supported employees, and to engage in on-going capacity building on the issue.

A second reason for optimism is that, despite the similarities between the themes of gender and AIDS, there are also some differences in how the two issues are experienced and perceived. The question of gender tends to provoke controversy and defensiveness. This is partly because it all too easily becomes a matter of men versus women; many a gender-awareness workshop has temporarily deteriorated into destructive conflicts of opinion. As such, gender-aware work becomes seen as something intended to benefit women at men's expense, rather than something to benefit everyone. Gender mainstreaming may be resisted also because the aspiration to achieve gender equity is seen as a Western imposition, at odds with local culture – and thus it all too often results in division or resentment, or is perceived to be irrelevant.

In contrast, in highly affected countries AIDS is increasingly recognised as a matter that affects everyone. Development workers are familiar with the impacts of AIDS at community level, if not from first-hand experience, at least through narratives of people falling ill and dying, and the consequences for orphans and disintegrating households. They are also likely to have been affected personally in some way; as Chapter 7 reported, research by SC UK among its staff in Southern and Eastern Africa found that one third of them were caring for sick or disabled relatives, and a similar proportion had taken on responsibility for someone else's children. It seems reasonable to expect that these experiences may make employees receptive to the idea of responding to AIDS, and perhaps more so than to gender inequality, because the impacts and outcomes are easier to see. Moreover, employees are likely to want internal mainstreaming of AIDS because all of them, potentially, stand to gain from better policies on terminal diseases, and protection against discrimination based on HIV status. Organisations may be more receptive to the idea, and hence to supporting mainstreaming processes, if they are experiencing financial costs and loss of capacity as a result of AIDS.

This is not to suggest that mainstreaming AIDS does not provoke controversy and resistance. For example, organisations may ignore the issue internally, for fear of the financial implications of paying for the medical treatment of HIV-positive employees. And AIDS is still an issue associated with stigma, denial, and marginalisation, a fact which may create resistance to mainstreaming on the basis that there is no point in wasting resources on people who are going to die anyway. Moreover, because AIDS and gender are closely linked, mainstreaming AIDS entails dealing with gender issues. However, the starting points for mainstreaming AIDS and mainstreaming gender are different and, arguably, the former proposal may be more favourably received than the latter, and so commitment and resources may be more easily mobilised for it. The next chapter concerns ideas for mainstreaming AIDS, both internally and in development and humanitarian work.

PART III: Ideas for mainstreaming AIDS

11 Strategy and guiding principles

Introduction

The preceding chapters have shown that agencies have not tried out the idea of mainstreaming AIDS sufficiently, or over a long enough period of time, to have developed a body of good practice. This points to a paradox: agencies need guidelines to help them to mainstream, but they need to mainstream in order to develop guidelines. The way out of this dilemma is for individuals and organisations to apply their good sense, their wider experience, and a willingness to learn, to their experiments with mainstreaming AIDS. Their initial mistakes and tentative successes will gradually form lessons which will, in turn, inform others.

Based on the wide range of experiences of internal and external mainstreaming of AIDS and gender, presented in Chapters 7 to 10, Part III aims to provide a set of practical ideas for mainstreaming AIDS. It is hoped that they will contribute to the on-going process of experimentation and development of the approach. To facilitate this, many of the ideas are presented in a series of ten user-friendly Units, to be found in the Resources section at the end of the book. Five relate to the key steps in the internal mainstreaming of AIDS, and the remaining five deal with aspects of mainstreaming in development and humanitarian programmes.

This chapter begins by outlining a broad strategy which agencies might follow in order to get started, and the main options available to them. It also introduces a set of guiding principles. The following three chapters present ideas for internal and external mainstreaming, followed by a consideration of some of the issues and challenges inherent in promoting and using the concept of mainstreaming.

Strategy

Mainstreaming, as proposed in this book, is about making development and humanitarian organisations and their work responsive and relevant to the changes brought about by HIV and AIDS. At its most simple, the crux of mainstreaming can be expressed in three questions, concerning the effects of AIDS on organisations and the people with whom they work, and the effects of the organisations' work on the people's susceptibility to HIV infection and vulnerability to the impacts of AIDS. These questions are summarised in Table 11.1.

Table 11.1: Mainstreaming AIDS – key questions

Internal mainstreaming	How do HIV and AIDS affect our organisation and its ability to work effectively against poverty, now and in the future?
External mainstreaming	How do HIV and AIDS affect the people we work with, in terms of their efforts to escape from poverty, now and in the future?
	How is our work helping or hindering them to be less susceptible to HIV infection and less vulnerable to the impacts of AIDS?

The questions are simple, but not so the process of getting them asked, answered, and responded to systematically as part of the on-going business of development and humanitarian organisations.

All change comes from somewhere. For any organisation, the initial impetus for mainstreaming AIDS could come from a variety of sources: first-hand experiences of managers or field staff; the conclusions of a programme review; a directive from head office; a funding opportunity; or the advocacy of another organisation. Whatever the source, experience suggests that if the mainstreaming process is to flourish, it needs at least one champion: someone who is interested in the idea, and who is able to learn about it, and to inspire others to become interested and involved. An initial strategy, therefore, is for a champion to recruit others to the cause of mainstreaming, establishing an informal group of like-minded people who choose to join together in order to assemble the basic ingredients for a more formal process of mainstreaming AIDS. Their internal advocacy might employ a variety of strategies, such as presenting the case for mainstreaming to senior management, or drawing on the experience and expertise of others to influence their organisation's decision makers, or focusing efforts on influential individuals who are likely to be receptive to the idea. Whatever tactics the champions use, they will need to be persistent, and to support their arguments with facts and proposals for action.

It may be useful to note three conditions which result from successful advocacy for change: *identification*, *ownership*, and *empowerment* (Barnett and Whiteside 2002:321). When applied to the promotion of mainstreaming within an organisation, the conditions that need to be fulfilled are as follows. First, key staff need to *identify with* the issue of AIDS, and to understand its connections to poverty and under-development. Second, they need to *own* the issue, in the sense of believing that AIDS is relevant to the work of their organisation. Third, key staff need to be *empowered* to act, through recognising mainstreaming as an effective way to respond, and one which they are motivated to try. If champions can fulfil those three conditions among key staff, then the most intangible, but potent, ingredient is in place: **commitment.**

Commitment, or 'political will', among senior and influential staff seems to be a critical factor, because it will help to secure the other basic requirement for mainstreaming: **resources**. This has two elements. One is the *capacity* to begin and sustain mainstreaming activities. This capacity may come from allocating or reallocating existing resources to main-streaming – by drawing on a training budget, for example, or using in-house trainers – or from securing new resources in the form of funding for mainstreaming.

Experience suggests that it is crucial to have some people with designated responsibility for mainstreaming.

The second element is *person power*, because experience suggests that it is crucial to have some people with designated responsibility for main-streaming (Derbyshire 2002:43). In larger organisations it may be possible to employ specialist staff; in all organisations, however, designated responsibility needs to be spread widely, and in this respect 'focal points' can be very useful. Staff members who are focal points do not take responsibility for mainstreaming; instead they act as catalysts for, and supporters of, the process. Their role is similar to that of the champions, but with the difference that they are formally recognised and strategically placed throughout the organisation. For focal points to be effective, they need to be clear about their role, and to be given enough time and resources to do the work, plus management support, and some level of influence within the organisation. They also need the personal motivation and skills required to understand and promote the mainstreaming agenda. At the senior level, it is helpful if a key decision maker takes the lead on mainstreaming.

There are two other strategies which can be used to encourage mainstreaming. They cannot, however, be used by individual champions: they are tools for institutions. First, agencies can encourage main-streaming by making funds available for the process. This is a strategy used by donors, particularly with regard to mainstreaming gender-related concerns, but it could also be used to facilitate mainstreaming responses to AIDS within an organisation. However, experience from gender mainstreaming shows that full external funding for the mainstreaming process may discourage a sense of ownership among staff. Second, donors and organisations can make mainstreaming, or aspects of it, mandatory, and they can attempt to enforce such a policy through programme review, budgeting, and funding processes.

Building consensus

Several of the case studies note the need for a process of exploring and agreeing upon an understanding of mainstreaming. ActionAid-Burundi identified the lack of an agreed definition, and the absence of a phase of explanation and training, as constraints which undermined ownership of the concept (ActionAid-Burundi Case Study 2002:26). Oxfam recorded that the mainstreaming process *'benefits from starting with agreed, clear outcomes and a vision of the desired situation in the future'* (Oxfam Malawi Case Study 2001:40). For gender mainstreaming, writing a mission statement or policy has proved to be a useful starting point. Such a document typically includes background information, policy commitments, and an outline action plan. However, as one manual emphasises,

> *The value of such a policy lies at least as much in its formulation as in its existence...it is a golden opportunity to involve as many staff and, where appropriate, external stakeholders, as possible. The process promotes widespread 'ownership' of the policy; enhances understanding and commitment to gender equality issues; ensures that the policy 'fits' with the organisational culture, structures and procedures; and substantially increases the chance that the policy will be implemented.*
> (Derbyshire 2002:47)

This suggests that adopting a participatory process for developing a mission statement may be a complex task. For AIDS, it is also unlikely to be a discrete activity: if staff need to know more about AIDS and mainstreaming in order to formulate a policy, then the process will merge with initial capacity-building activities. The process will necessarily be guided by specialists who, by virtue of their expertise, are likely to exert a disproportionate influence on the outcomes. Moreover, the content of the mission statement is likely to be predetermined to some extent, so the notion of its being developed in a fully participatory way seems improbable. It is perhaps, therefore, more realistic to conceive of a process of learning about and reflection on mainstreaming AIDS, beginning with a given definition, which contributes to the development of a policy or mission statement which is specific to the organisation.

Options

Whether or not an organisation decides to produce a mission statement or policy on mainstreaming responses to AIDS, there are choices to be made, particularly in terms of which aspects to adopt, and with what priority. The main components of the whole agenda are internal mainstreaming, mainstreaming in development work, and mainstreaming in humanitarian work. Organisations which work with partners have similar options with regard to supporting their partners. In addition, there are the options of implementing, or supporting partners to implement, direct AIDS work, and of aiming to integrate such work. And in situations of low HIV prevalence, organisations might opt for any of the elements already mentioned, or may choose to act on related issues, such as gender and sexual health. These options are summarised in Table 11.2 on page 222.

Oxfam's Southern Africa region made a strategic decision first to prioritise mainstreaming AIDS, rather than beginning with supporting direct AIDS work. Other agencies will face a similar choice in deciding which approaches to AIDS to emphasise, because few, except the larger and better-resourced agencies, have the capacity to take on several initiatives simultaneously. Moreover, for many organisations, responding to AIDS is likely to be one of several major changes taking place at any one time.

The sequence of events also offers scope for choice to organisations intent on mainstreaming AIDS. An organisation with sufficient capacity might opt to undertake different components of mainstreaming simultaneously. The processes might be separate, but they might also overlap. For example, an agency could combine aspects of external mainstreaming in its own programmes with support to its partners to do likewise. The alternative is to take a linear, or phased approach, dealing with each component in turn. Although slower, this would allow experience from each component to inform the following phases. For example, an agency could incorporate the lessons learned from its own external mainstreaming into its later efforts to support its partners to do likewise. One fact emerges very clearly, however, from the case studies and experience of gender mainstreaming: that awareness raising and basic training for staff is one of the first steps. It is essential to ensure a better understanding of AIDS and its personal and professional implications among a critical mass of staff before proceeding to other aspects of mainstreaming.

It is essential to ensure a better understanding of AIDS and its personal and professional implications among a critical mass of staff before proceeding to other aspects of mainstreaming.

Table 11.2: Responding to AIDS: options for development and humanitarian organisations

Internal mainstreaming of HIV and AIDS		
For all organisations, including those focused on AIDS work		
Supporting staff to reduce their susceptibility to HIV, **+** and to cope better with AIDS		Modifying how the organisation functions in the context of AIDS

External mainstreaming in development and/or humanitarian work			
For all development and humanitarian organisations			
Training and capacity building **+**	Community research **+**	Designing mainstreamed programmes **+**	Adapting systems

Options for AIDS work			
For all development and humanitarian organisations			
Form complementary partnerships with specialist AIDS organisations **or**	Fund or build capacity for other organisations to do AIDS work **or**	Engage in elements of AIDS work **or**	Engage fully in AIDS work

Supporting partners		
For all organisations working with partners		
Internal mainstreaming **+/or**	External mainstreaming **+/or**	AIDS work

In low-prevalence settings		
Scaled-down process of internal and external mainstreaming of AIDS **or**	Internal and external mainstreaming of related issues such as gender and sexual health **+/or**	The options relating to AIDS work, and to supporting partners

Guiding principles

The previous section listed some basic requirements for beginning and sustaining mainstreaming, in terms of commitment among key people, and allocation of human and financial resources. This section proposes seven principles which have emerged from the case studies.

First, mainstreaming is best approached as a **learning process**. It is not a one-off event, because, even if an organisation were successfully to institutionalise attention to AIDS, there would still be on-going activities such as training new staff. Moreover, the context is a dynamic one, so organisations need to be alert to changes in, for example, the availability and cost of antiretroviral treatments, patterns of HIV infection within the community, and trends in the impacts of AIDS on employees and community members. The process of mainstreaming entails agencies and individuals gradually learning to adapt their perspectives and to take account of AIDS in their work. This may take time; it requires realistic expectations and will involve mistakes, from which organisations need to learn if practice is to improve. It is only by agencies experimenting with mainstreaming, and documenting and sharing what they have learned, that progress will be made in developing the approach.

One cannot make mainstreaming happen by simply instructing staff to mainstream.

A second principle is that the process of mainstreaming should **involve employees as active participants**. This is very important for internal mainstreaming, because the initiatives which aim to support staff will be effective only if the staff, who are in effect 'project beneficiaries', have helped to shape their design and delivery. Consultation on controversial issues such as medical benefits, and sensitive issues such as confidentiality, is likely to be particularly important if workplace policies are to be accepted and used by employees. Staff also need to be actively engaged in activities relating to mainstreaming AIDS in programme work, because success requires changes in the hearts and minds of employees. One cannot make mainstreaming happen by simply instructing staff to mainstream.

Related to this is the third principle: mainstreaming must **involve people who are affected by HIV and AIDS**. Mainstreaming is not an academic exercise, but one which responds to the experiences of individuals, households, and communities affected by AIDS. If organisations are to understand the implications of HIV and AIDS for their work, then as part of the process their staff need to learn directly from women, men, and children affected by the pandemic. Moreover, if organisations are to make their programme work more relevant to the changes brought about by

HIV and AIDS, then they need to involve affected people in devising, implementing, and monitoring suitable adaptations to that work. Furthermore, involving people who are openly HIV-positive is a tried and tested strategy for challenging social stigma and may, among other benefits, help organisations to promote the idea of positive living to their staff.

The fourth principle proposed here is straightforward: people who are mainstreaming AIDS need to **attend to gender-related issues** throughout the process. Gender and AIDS are always connected, such that attention to gender issues is integral to all the elements of both internal and external mainstreaming of AIDS.

Involving people who are openly HIV-positive is a tried and tested strategy for challenging social stigma and may help organisations to promote the idea of positive living to their staff.

That organisations need to **learn from, and link with, others** is the fifth principle. It makes sense, for example, for organisations which are undertaking internal mainstreaming to share their training curricula, research on HIV statistics or employment law, and lessons learned, in order to reduce duplication of effort and so make the process more effective. Similarly, with regard to external mainstreaming, learning can be accelerated if agencies share their experiences of what seems to work and what does not. Connected to this is the possible need for specialist help: for example, assistance with training, professional advice about employment law, help in predicting future impacts, or advice about the feasibility of various modifications to programme work.

The sixth principle is that mainstreaming is aimed at **making changes as appropriate**, both internally and externally. In other words, unless the organisation and its work are already nearly ideal, the outcome of mainstreaming should be changes. However, these changes should be practical and plausible modifications to existing approaches, perhaps involving new initiatives within a programme, rather than a wholesale revolution in the way in which the agency operates. Furthermore, although the modifications are likely to aim to reduce the exclusion of AIDS-affected households from development projects, this does not mean that all activities must become totally accessible to AIDS-affected households.

Finally, it is critical to attend to practice and to **monitor progress actively**. Policies can set out excellent ideas, but they may then be ignored or misapplied. On-going monitoring of the application of the policies, and their effects, provides the opportunity to modify and improve both policies and practice. In the same way, planned activities and changes need to be monitored, assessed, and revised as necessary, as do methods to institutionalise attention to HIV and AIDS.

SUMMARY: principles for mainstreaming AIDS

- Approach mainstreaming as a learning process.

- Involve employees as active participants.

- Involve people who are affected by HIV and AIDS.

- Attend to gender issues throughout.

- Learn from, and link with, others.

- Make changes as appropriate.

- Monitor actively.

12 Ideas for internal mainstreaming

Internal mainstreaming is the process of changing organisational policy and practice in order to reduce the organisation's susceptibility to HIV infection and its vulnerability to the impacts of AIDS. It has two elements: doing AIDS work with staff, such as HIV prevention and treatment; and modifying the way in which the organisation functions, for example, in terms of workforce planning, budgeting, and ways of working.

Supporting staff to reduce their susceptibility to HIV, and to cope better with AIDS

The group of activities which belong under this heading should both directly benefit staff members and indirectly benefit the organisation. Together they aim to help staff as individuals to face up to AIDS, to avoid HIV transmission, and, if infected, to manage HIV and AIDS as best they can. And, because the functioning of any organisation, and especially perhaps a development organisation, is strongly influenced by its employees' performance, effective work to support them leads to indirect benefits for the organisation.

Helping staff to face up to AIDS

Many organisations begin with the most common activity – AIDS education for employees – without doing any research into how staff are experiencing AIDS, or assessing their needs for support. Questions about this could be built into research concerning the impacts of AIDS on staff members, which is discussed later in this chapter and is the focus of Unit 1, in the Resources section of this book. Alternatively, discussion of staff needs could form a later part of any initial AIDS education or awareness-raising workshop.

The impact of awareness-raising workshops can be strengthened – and measured – by first assessing the knowledge and attitudes of the prospective participants. A straightforward way to do this is to administer an anonymous questionnaire, part of which participants complete before the workshop, and part after it. The results enable trainers first to match the workshop to the participants' needs, and subsequently to measure changes in their knowledge and attitudes. A simple example, which covers understanding of HIV transmission, attitudes towards people with HIV and AIDS, personal risk assessment, and willingness to be open about HIV, is included as Unit 3.

The effectiveness of workshops can also be increased by ensuring that staff take an active role, discussing key issues together, rather than listening passively to lectures. It is sometimes beneficial for people to work in peer groups with people of the same sex or level of seniority. Inviting people who are openly HIV-positive to contribute to the workshop can make HIV and AIDS more real to participants, particularly in circumstances where few people are open about their HIV status. Hearing someone who is infected with HIV talk openly about his or her experiences and plans can also challenge stigma and provide a role model of positive living. In most cases, organisations will need to link with groups of HIV-positive people or local GIPA (Greater Involvement of People with AIDS) projects in order to find an infected person who is willing and able to fulfil such a role.

Inviting people who are openly HIV-positive to contribute to the workshop can make HIV and AIDS more real to participants.

The most basic awareness-raising workshops typically cover facts and myths about HIV transmission; the difference between HIV and AIDS; HIV/AIDS statistics; and the methods of preventing HIV infection. For individuals and organisations to benefit more fully, however, workshops need also to cover topics such as counselling, HIV testing, and positive living. Participants might also consider their own attitudes, in particular exploring and challenging issues of stigma and negative discrimination, as well as practical concerns such as care and support for people with AIDS. Ideally, workshops or discussion groups should not be one-off events, but part of an on-going process, with sessions focused on themes of particular importance to staff members. For example, the scope could be broadened to address factors which influence susceptibility to HIV infection, such as poor inter-personal communication skills and the abuse of alcohol and other drugs, or factors which mitigate vulnerability to the impacts of AIDS, including financial management and will writing.

In addition to equipping staff with information, and giving them a chance to consider the issues, AIDS workshops may act as an occasion for consultation and problem solving. For example, imagine that at the end of a basic AIDS workshop some participants identify access to good-quality condoms as a priority, and others express interest in using counselling and testing services. In a follow-up workshop, managers could present options to staff, in order to get their feedback; or staff could be given the task of proposing appropriate services themselves. As experience of good development practice suggests, involving the beneficiaries in the design of

---

SUMMARY: ideas for helping staff to face up to AIDS as a personal issue

- Learn about how staff are experiencing AIDS, and their needs for support.

- Use preliminary and follow-up questionnaires to match workshops to their needs, and to assess the impact of the sessions.

- Use active, participatory methods, rather than lecturing staff about AIDS.

- Feature openly HIV-positive resource people in the workshops.

- Organise on-going sessions, rather than one-off events.

- Arrange separate workshops or activities for employees in peer groups (same-sex groups, or people on similar levels of seniority).

- Go beyond the basics of HIV transmission to cover wider issues, according to participants' interests.

- Use workshops as an opportunity to develop other aspects of internal mainstreaming, by consulting with staff, or asking them to devise strategies.

---

a project increases its chances of success, because the project will match staff needs, and they will feel that they own it. (For advice about the procurement and storage of condoms, and for suggestions for good practice in the provision of voluntary counselling and testing, see the resources section of the bibliography.)

Creating a workplace policy

For most organisations, establishing a workplace policy, or revising an existing one, is a key part of the internal mainstreaming of AIDS. This policy may specifically concern HIV/AIDS, or more generally it may concern chronic and terminal diseases including HIV/AIDS, which may be a more holistic and less stigmatising approach. In either case, the workplace policy should be influenced by research (described in the next section) into how AIDS is already affecting the organisation, and how it is likely to affect it in the future. Such research is needed in order to determine if personnel policies need to be changed. The workplace policy also formalises the responsibilities of the organisation to its employees. Staff and managers then need only consult the workplace policy to be clear about their rights and responsibilities. Of particular importance is the need for clearly stated personnel policies on contractual terms and conditions for infected employees and those who need to take time off to attend funerals or care for others.

In devising a workplace policy, organisations seek to provide measures which benefit staff, and so benefit the organisation, while adhering to their legal obligations. This is likely to involve a time delay: organisations have to invest now in order to reap the benefits in the future. The appropriate level of benefits will depend on the organisation's staffing structure, and its employees' susceptibilities and vulnerabilities. If an organisation provides very generous benefits to employees, which are disproportionate to the benefits that the organisation will gain, it may risk undermining its functioning and finances, and so jeopardise its work. Alternatively, an organisation which provides very few benefits is likely to experience high costs in the long term, which may also jeopardise its work; they include absenteeism, poor retention of staff, and, perhaps, damage to its reputation.

Devising a policy may involve research into, for example, various methods of health insurance, with the idea of offering a more flexible package, so that employees can determine the balance of pension and health benefits that they opt to receive. It might involve deciding to establish central funds to cover treatment excluded from insurance cover, or to share costs and liabilities among programmes; it might also involve investigating the legal implications of changing employees' terms and conditions. This research may be complex and time-consuming, so organisations should ideally share their findings with other agencies in the area, to save duplication of effort. Organisations should also review their policies on recruitment and employment, to ensure that employees do not discriminate against people infected with HIV. (Some, such as ActionAid's Africa programmes, have adopted an 'affirmative action' policy to ensure that programmes *do* hire people who are openly HIV-positive.) The sources for some examples of good practice are included in the bibliography, while Unit 4 describes the key features of any workplace policy and presents the general text that ActionAid uses as guidance for its programmes around the world. In general, workplace policies on HIV/AIDS should include employment criteria; prevention activities in the workplace; and benefits and treatment for infected and affected employees (Rau 2002:38-40).

The process of devising or revising a workplace policy also requires consultation with employees. Unit 1 provides some ideas for getting feedback from employees on their experiences of HIV and AIDS, their perceptions of the main impacts that HIV/AIDS is having on the organisation, and their priorities for action. In areas with high HIV-prevalence rates, cost-cutting measures may be necessary, such as enforcing existing policies more strictly, reducing sick-leave allowances, or limiting the number of dependants who can be included in the

Organisations should ideally share their findings with other agencies in the area, to save duplication of effort.

organisation's health scheme. Understandably, staff are unlikely to welcome such measures. However, the changes are likely to cause less resentment if staff have been involved in the process and if they understand the constraints on the organisation, and the need to protect its sustainability. It therefore makes sense to avoid raising employees' expectations, and to be open about the findings of research into predicted impact, and the reasons behind the proposed changes to the policy. Moreover, revisions to workplace policies may also work in favour of employees. For example, the organisation may decide that it is unacceptable to stipulate HIV as a condition that is excluded from its health scheme, or – as Oxfam GB and ActionAid are doing – it may opt to provide antiretroviral treatment to staff who need it. Employees will benefit from having their entitlements formally recorded, rather than being subject to unpredictable decisions based on managers' discretion.

Employees will benefit from having their entitlements formally recorded, rather than being subject to unpredictable decisions based on managers' discretion.

Following consultation and revisions, organisations should issue the final policy and find ways of ensuring that staff and managers are aware of its contents; for example, giving all staff members a leaflet summarising the main points of the policy. When implementing the policy, managers may need other resources, such as guidance on non-discrimination or on practical issues such as procuring condoms. It is important to monitor the way in which the policy is used in practice. By assessing trends over time and investigating problems – for example, low take-up of counselling services, or medical costs that are higher than anticipated – it is more likely that the policy will support staff and protect the organisation's work from the impacts of AIDS. As Chapter 7 made clear, having a policy in place does not necessarily result in a supportive workplace where the impacts of HIV and AIDS are minimised. Careful follow-up is needed, to identify where problems exist and how they might be mitigated.

SUMMARY: suggestions to help organisations to develop workplace policies

- Base policies on research into the current and potential impacts of AIDS on the organisation.

- Make benefits available to employees which will also benefit the organisation.

- Attend to legal obligations to employees (which may vary from country to country).

- Involve and consult with staff, and explain to them the rationale behind policy decisions.

- Disseminate the content of the policy to managers and employees, and support its implementation.

- Monitor the policy's implementation, assess its effects, and modify the policy as necessary.

Modifying how organisations function in the context of AIDS

Internal mainstreaming entails more than supporting staff members to change their behaviour, whether with regard to safer sex, seeking counselling, or securing treatment. This is because the susceptibility and vulnerability of organisations to HIV and AIDS are not determined purely by their employees' behaviour, but also by the ways in which the organisations function. This section, therefore, concerns efforts by organisations to reflect on how their existing systems and policies may need to be modified. It begins by presenting ideas for assessing the current and future impacts of AIDS on the organisation.

Learning about the current impact of AIDS on the organisation

Guidance on internal responses to HIV/AIDS usually emphasises the need to predict future impacts, ignoring the complementary option of assessing the *current* internal impacts. This strategy, as used by SC UK and featured in Chapter 7, seems worth considering, however. It has the advantage of being a relatively straightforward process, providing an achievable and useful initial activity which may catalyse the process of internal mainstreaming. For example, the findings may be influential in securing the necessary commitment and resources – staff time or funding – to move on to the more complex business of predicting the impacts of HIV and AIDS, and analysing the various options for the organisation. The process also has the advantage that, as with good community work, it directly involves the staff – who will be the subjects and beneficiaries of any changes in policy and practice.

Some suggestions for research questions and themes are included as Unit 1, on pages 294–99. They include asking about employees' sense of organisational culture with regard to HIV and AIDS, and their perceptions of the impacts that HIV and AIDS are having on the organisation. They also include questions concerning the personal impacts that staff have experienced, the repercussions of those impacts for their work, and their perceptions of the main problems that they face in the workplace with regard to HIV/AIDS. The Unit also presents themes to discuss in more detail with key informants, and proposes questions for extending the scope of the research from assessing current impacts to asking employees for their ideas about what the organisation might do, and what their own priorities are.

In terms of methodology, face-to-face methods such as interviews or focus-group discussions enable researchers to interact with staff members, learn from them, and thus generate rich feedback. These methods may be particularly appropriate to use with key people, such as personnel officers. However, because qualitative methods such as these are time-consuming, they are likely to involve only small numbers of people. Furthermore, there is the disadvantage that, given the sensitivity of the subject, staff may be unwilling to disclose their experiences through face-to-face enquiry. Questionnaires reach larger numbers of staff more easily, and can be anonymous. They can also produce more standard data, allowing comparisons between, for example, male and female respondents, or staff in different regions. However, the results are dependent on the questions that are posed, and there is the danger that staff might misunderstand the questions. The ideal solution is, if possible, to undertake research which features both approaches. Some organisations may also be able to supplement data gained from staff by analysing existing data on topics such as sickness leave, medical costs, and staff turn-over. Overall, the results should provide an impression of how AIDS is already affecting staff, and hence the organisation itself. For the purposes of transparency and involving employees, the results should ideally be reported back to staff, along with information about the next steps which are proposed in the mainstreaming process.

SUMMARY: ideas for assessing the current impacts of AIDS on an organisation

- Use an anonymous questionnaire to obtain comparable quantitative data from a large number of staff members.

- Use face-to-face methods to get more detailed information from small numbers of staff, or from key staff.

- Ask staff about the impacts of AIDS on the organisation in general, and on themselves and their work in particular, and the problems that they face with regard to AIDS and the workplace.

- Extend the scope to ask for employees' ideas and priorities for action.

- Analyse existing personnel data.

- Report the findings back to employees, and tell them the next steps that the organisation is planning.

Predicting the impacts of AIDS on the organisation, and analysing the options for responding

A full institutional audit is a complex and time-consuming process which requires data and expertise that few NGOs or government departments possess (see Barnett and Whiteside 2002:253 for an outline). Moreover, much of the guidance available is aimed at large businesses, which can use computer modelling and HIV testing to undertake sophisticated predictions and analyses of the likely impacts of AIDS on their profits, and the cost-effectiveness of various ways of responding. However, there is little guidance that is specific to the needs of NGOs and other organisations which do not measure their success in terms of profit and loss; such organisations may require a more basic method.

The process presented here, and set out in Unit 2 on pages 300–302, is a more modest attempt to predict impact, which can be undertaken without the expense of hiring external experts. It aims to provide a method by which organisations can make rough predictions of the impacts of AIDS, bounded by 'worst case' and 'best case' scenarios. It must be stressed that all the figures in Unit 2 are fictional, and not derived from any real organisation; they are presented in order to demonstrate the logic of the calculations, but the numbers themselves are meaningless.

The model is presented with caution, however, because although it is based on the experiences of Oxfam GB, it has not been tried and tested over several years. It is certainly very crude when compared with the sophisticated models which do exist, so organisations might prefer to call on experts, or to explore some of the computer models available on the Internet (Rau 2002:28; see also the bibliography). And, as with all models, it may be of little use to small organisations, where the limited number of employees makes predicted impacts highly questionable. However, the ideas presented here may provide a useful starting point for larger organisations which need an accessible method for making rough predictions of the internal impacts of AIDS.

The spreadsheet chart in Unit 2 sets out calculations of the impact on a fictional organisation over five years. It begins by assessing the rate of HIV prevalence and cases of AIDS within the organisation. These calculations are based on the number of employees, and assumptions about the rate of HIV prevalence among them, and the proportion of HIV-positive staff who are in Stage 4 of infection (suffering from full-blown AIDS). They also make an assumption about how many of the employees with AIDS leave the organisation each year.

The next stage considers the direct financial costs to the organisation, in terms of health-care costs and terminal benefits (i.e. payments made when an employee retires due to ill health, or dies in service). The model makes assumptions about the average costs incurred for non-infected employees, and those incurred by staff with AIDS. It sets out what the costs would be without AIDS, and what they are predicted to be, given the earlier assumptions.

The final section concerns the impacts of AIDS on staff absences from work. Again, using assumptions about the amount of leave taken on average by non-infected staff, and the amount taken by staff with AIDS, the spreadsheet is able to present an estimate of the effect that AIDS might have on overall levels of absenteeism.

The model in Unit 2 is very simplified: it deals only with employees, two forms of benefits, and two forms of absenteeism. However, the unit describes the ways in which the model could be made more complex; for example, by including employees' dependants in the calculations, introducing different levels of HIV prevalence for different types of staff, and taking into account a wider range of costs, such as those of recruiting and training staff to replace those who leave due to AIDS. Once set up, the spreadsheet can also be used to show the effects of changing variables: for example, the number of eligible dependants per employee. Parallel spreadsheets can also be used to explore the costs and benefits of options such as providing treatment for opportunistic infections, or antiretroviral treatment for employees and/or their dependants.

The process of doing such calculations might be the responsibility of one or a few members of staff, but it is important that a wider range of staff should be consulted. The process may also involve seeking information from outside the organisation: for example, data about local HIV-prevalence rates, and the likely length of time that an employee with AIDS may continue to serve the organisation, according to the various treatment options.

The quantitative findings of such an impact assessment might also be combined with the aforementioned research into current impacts on staff experiences, to consider future impacts on unquantified factors such as quality of work, loss of experience, and staff morale. The findings of both forms of research – the impacts already experienced, and the impacts that are predicted – can then inform, and be used to support the case for, other aspects of internal mainstreaming of AIDS, in particular the formulation or revision of a workplace policy.

SUMMARY: ideas for predicting the internal impacts of AIDS

- Select a method which suits your organisation's needs, in terms of the cost of the exercise and the accuracy of the outcome.

- Allocate responsibility to one or a few members of staff, but involve others in the process.

- Adapt models to fit the organisation and its most relevant variables.

- Use the calculations to explore differing options which the organisation could adopt.

- Use the findings for internal consultation, and creating or modifying a workplace policy.

Changing policy and practice

The key outcome of the research described above should be a new or revised workplace policy which, if implemented effectively, will help to reduce the organisation's susceptibility to HIV infection and vulnerability to the impacts of AIDS. For example, outcomes might include the ability of HIV-positive staff to work and contribute to the organisation for longer, and adherence by all staff to rules about leave for funerals, to reduce absenteeism. Beyond the changes in workplace policies, however, organisations also need to examine how they function, with a particular emphasis on ways in which that functioning may be inadvertently making the organisation more susceptible and vulnerable.

Staff members may be more susceptible to HIV infection by virtue of their employment in the organisation. For example, health-sector staff may face the occupational hazard of infection through a needle-stick injury. This risk can be reduced by provision of correct equipment, and adherence to universal precautions. In the event of a needle-stick injury, or a rape, agencies can reduce the individual's risk of HIV infection by offering post-exposure prophylaxis (consisting of antiretroviral drugs).

Some of the employment-related factors which may enhance susceptibility to HIV may, however, be difficult to change. For example, some staff may need to travel regularly, and may have casual sexual relations when they are away from their families. It may be possible to reduce the number of trips by means of better planning, use of information technology, or decentralisation of responsibilities. However, in organisations whose offices are widely spread, the need to travel cannot be eliminated. (Nor, as the World Bank has suggested with regard to truck drivers (World Bank 1999:10), can employees' spouses travel everywhere with them!) An organisation can supply its staff with good-quality female and male condoms, but the onus is on individuals to use them consistently, or to refrain from sexual relations altogether.

Staff may also be more susceptible to HIV infection if they are posted away from home. For female staff who are posted away from their support networks, the simple measure of ensuring that they are paid regularly should reduce their need to seek financial support and engage in sexual bargaining. Another possibility is to allow staff regular 'long weekends' at home. This particularly applies to people working in intensive and traumatising emergencies, where measures such as respite breaks, counselling, and debriefing can help them to maintain mental health, and so be less likely to use unsafe sex as a coping mechanism. Such a measure might not involve extra expense, if employees are allowed to 'save up' hours of overtime work and then take off days in lieu. In stable settings, a more radical response would be to enable employees to have their families living with them at their posting: for example, suitable accommodation might be provided for teachers and their families. To conclude, it is important to assess, with staff members, if ways of working are making them more susceptible to HIV infection, and to take reasonable measures to minimise the risks.

In traumatising emergencies, measures such as respite breaks, counselling, and debriefing can help staff to maintain mental health, and so be less likely to use unsafe sex as a coping mechanism.

With regard to reducing the organisation's vulnerability to the impacts of AIDS, the earlier section on supporting staff has already covered efforts focused on employees. The idea of modifying the organisation's mode of functioning is concerned with changing policy and practice. After all, however good the organisation's HIV-prevention work, in highly affected countries all but the smallest organisations can be sure of having HIV-positive staff. However, as Chapter 7 showed, there are few experiences on which to draw. Instead, this section reviews some possible options, all related to human-resource and finance functions.

For **human-resource departments**, the main step is to consider future staffing needs in the light of the predicted impacts of AIDS on employees. If problems are expected, such as shortfalls in skilled staff (especially frontline professionals such as teachers, health workers, or agriculturalists), or higher levels of turn-over, the agency should make proactive attempts to reduce their impacts; for example, measures to retain existing staff (regardless of their HIV status), or to attract back professionals who have left or retired; offering on-the-job training if it is not possible to recruit qualified people; promoting career development within the organisation; and shifting from long and expensive training courses for a minority of staff to on-going capacity building for all staff, using short courses for rapid results. It may also be possible to improve the functioning of the department, by investing in it in order to speed up recruitment procedures and strengthen the provision of training.

To reduce the impact of absenteeism, the organisation could also consider team working, multi-tasking, and documentation of each post-holder's main work practices. Such measures are particularly important in the case of key posts, where the absence of the post-holder would have a disproportionate and serious impact on the organisation. In cases where there is forewarning of disruption, such as a staff member falling ill repeatedly, or declaring his or her HIV-positive status, additional efforts may further ease the impact. These might include arranging temporary cover, encouraging hand-over of information and skills, and reducing stress on the staff member by lightening his or her workload. All of these tasks become more feasible if the organisation fosters a culture in which HIV-positive employees are willing to declare their HIV status.

For **finance departments**, the task is to build HIV/AIDS into budgets, and to get those budgets funded. Having predicted future impacts, and agreed the workplace policy, it is necessary to fit all the expected costs into the organisation's budgeting. This will involve adjusting budgets related to staff salaries and benefits, and initiatives such as awareness-raising workshops, provision of condoms, counselling and testing, and health care. The budgets should also build in the expected costs of reducing susceptibility and vulnerability to HIV and AIDS, inasmuch as an organisation intends to make any of the changes outlined above. For example, there would certainly be budgetary implications if an agency were to begin to provide staff with accommodation for themselves and their families. If an organisation is also embarking on mainstreaming AIDS in external programmes, there will, of course, be additional budgetary provisions to make.

For both human resources and finances, organisations need to develop monitoring systems which will track and analyse costs and trends associated with AIDS and with internal mainstreaming of AIDS over time. This monitoring is likely to be particularly important for managers in large or decentralised agencies, where the impacts of AIDS and responses to it may not otherwise be apparent. Although monitoring systems need to fit each individual organisation, the suggested key indicators included in Unit 5 may be useful.

SUMMARY: ideas for changing policy and practice

- Investigate ways in which employees' susceptibility to HIV infection may be heightened because of their jobs and the way in which the organisation functions.
- Act within reason to reduce that susceptibility, by modifying policy and practice.
- Investigate ways in which the organisation's working makes it more vulnerable to the impacts of AIDS.
- Act to reduce that vulnerability, particularly within the spheres of human-resource policy and practice, and financial management systems.
- Identify key indicators, and actively monitor trends for both the impacts of AIDS and the impact of initiatives undertaken as part of internal mainstreaming of AIDS.

Figure 12.1: Summary of key steps in the internal mainstreaming of AIDS

Learning about the current impacts of AIDS on the organisation (see Unit 1)

Methodology
- Anonymous questionnaire to staff
- +/or face-to-face discussions with staff or groups of staff
- +/or interviews with key staff

Scope
- Focus only on staff experiences of AIDS and impacts on their work.
- Or extend questioning to include their ideas and priorities for action.

Undertake research, including analysis of any existing relevant personnel data.

Report on current impacts (and staff ideas and priorities)

Feedback to employees, with next steps in the process outlined.	Use in internal advocacy for next steps in internal mainstreaming.

Predicting the impacts of AIDS on the organisation

Methodology
- Full institutional audit, with expert help, and possibility of HIV-testing of employees.
- Or in-house process, using existing computer models, or devising one for the organisation (see Unit 2).

Scope
- Number of years to cover.
- Which variables to include (e.g. health costs, other benefits, leave taken).
- In the case of large organisations, which offices or regions to include.

Gather data, make assumptions, and do calculations.	Create a range of scenarios, e.g. 'best case' and 'worse case'.	Explore the costs and benefits of altering variables and of treatment options.

Report on predicted impacts and recommendations for action

Internal consultation and consideration

Figure 12.1: Summary of key steps in internal mainstreaming *continued*

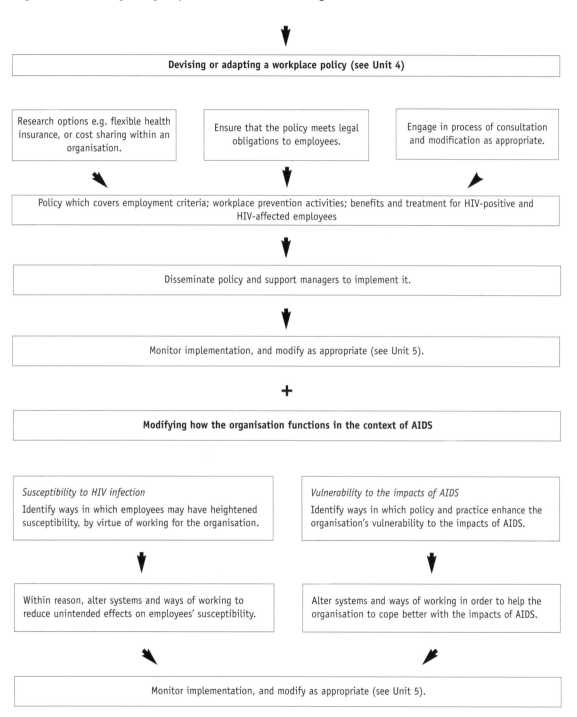

Summary

This chapter has presented ideas for internal mainstreaming under two headings: supporting staff, and modifying how the organisation functions. Figure 12.1 brings together all these ideas in the form of a flow chart. The chronology used, however, is different from that in the text: while many organisations begin with HIV-prevention work among staff, in Figure 12.1 AIDS work with staff comes after the business of assessing the current internal impacts of AIDS, and predicting future impacts. However, while this chronology makes theoretical sense, it is not to suggest that the steps presented in Figure 12.1 must be followed in that order.

13 Ideas for external mainstreaming

The aim of mainstreaming AIDS in development and humanitarian work is to adapt the work in order to take into account susceptibility to HIV transmission and vulnerability to the impacts of AIDS. The focus is on core programme work in the changing context wrought by AIDS, ensuring that new and existing projects are relevant to that context and contribute positively to the wider response to HIV and AIDS. This chapter looks first at development work and then at humanitarian work.

Ideas for mainstreaming AIDS in development work

This section considers ideas relating to four main steps for external mainstreaming in development work: training and capacity building; community research; designing development work which indirectly addresses HIV and AIDS; and adapting systems.

Training and capacity building

Training is the first activity in the process of external mainstreaming. It is needed because staff who are not AIDS workers – such as agriculturalists, educationalists, or community development workers – are very unlikely to feel able (or be able) to address AIDS through their work (Cohen 1999:2). If asked to consider the prospect, they are almost certain to think of AIDS education or other forms of AIDS work, or to resist the idea that they should address AIDS at all. Both reactions inhibit the mainstreaming of AIDS. Training aims to create the conditions that are needed for change:

- First, staff should *identify* with the issue of AIDS, and understand its connections with poverty and under-development.

- Second, they should *own* the issue, in the sense of believing that AIDS is relevant to their sector's work.

- Third, they should be *empowered* to act through recognising external mainstreaming as an effective way to respond, and one which they are motivated to try.

Some suggestions for the content of training courses aimed at achieving those three conditions are provided as Unit 6 on pages 316–22, including some ideas for measuring the impact of training for the external mainstreaming of AIDS. If participants have not attended basic AIDS-awareness workshops, they need to cover that ground before attending sessions concerned with external mainstreaming of AIDS.

Community research

Although the links between AIDS and development can be conveyed through training, this is no substitute for employees learning, at first hand, from people who are affected by AIDS, and learning about the various levels of vulnerability involved. The community-research element of external mainstreaming involves meeting with people of varying ages from the project area, including men, women, and older children who have been affected by HIV and AIDS. This section does not give comprehensive guidelines on undertaking research with community members, but provides some ideas concerning methods and contents of research in connection with mainstreaming. The ideas are presented more explicitly in Unit 7 on pages 323–8. The text assumes that the mainstreaming policy is being applied to an existing project, but the ideas could be adapted for use in preliminary planning for a new project, allowing AIDS to be mainstreamed within it from the outset.

Listening to peer groups is often more revealing than asking questions of a mixed group.

How to do the research, and with whom

In terms of methodology, discursive and exploratory qualitative methods are most appropriate. They could be simple discussions, guided by a series of open questions; or participatory methods which allow people jointly to analyse their problems and experiences. Some organisations might also want to undertake quantitative research, for example to ascertain the proportions of households affected by AIDS in various different ways, or to assess the proportions of various kinds of household (and so the levels of vulnerability) within a population.

In terms of axes of difference within a community, sex, age, and socio-economic situation are critical variables. To obtain general information, the researchers could work with peer groups, where the participants are of the same sex and at the same life stage (young men, for example). Listening to peer groups is often more revealing than asking questions of a mixed group: in full community meetings, age and status mean that some voices tend to predominate (older men, for example) at the expense of others (such as younger women). For more specific and sensitive topics, such as the experience of having someone with AIDS or chronic illness in the family, the discussions need to involve small numbers of affected people. Researchers need to meet with women and men, and to be alert to situations where individuals might prefer to talk privately. For these discussions, researchers could aim to meet with people affected in differing ways – such as care givers, grandparents looking after orphaned grandchildren, and widows – and should deliberately seek out those who are less able to participate in community meetings and group-based activities.

Topics to focus on

The research might begin by assessing perceptions of levels of illness and death, and the relative significance of various ailments. The focus could then move on to AIDS in particular or, if the topic seems too sensitive, to chronic illnesses in general. For peer groups, topics might include

- attitudes towards men and women who are thought to have AIDS;
- the number of households thought to have been affected;
- the effects on particular types of household, their individual members, and their livelihoods;
- trends in the impacts of AIDS on the household and community levels;
- and changes in attitudes towards AIDS and people with AIDS.

An alternative theme would be susceptibility to HIV, considering such aspects as beliefs about the causes of AIDS and means of protection from it, and general perceptions of sexual behaviour. Discussions with individuals or small groups of affected women and men should focus on their experiences of chronic illness, such as the different stages that they have been through, the impacts of illness on individual members of the household, and the ways in which they have responded. Researchers must tread carefully, referring to AIDS only if the respondents use the term, and respecting the fact that they may be willing to talk only in general terms. Unit 7 presents some ideas for working with groups and individuals on these themes.

Researchers must tread carefully, referring to AIDS only if the respondents use the term, and respecting the fact that they may be willing to talk only in general terms.

From these general themes, the research can then turn to the connections between the organisation's development work and AIDS. The aim is not a full evaluation of the development work by community members, but an exploration of possible interactions between the development project and both sides of the 'causes and consequences' equation: susceptibility to HIV infection, and vulnerability to the impacts of AIDS. The key question for researchers is whether the project is helping or hindering each of these. It is useful for researchers to give some thought in advance to what they are looking for; the points in the following four paragraphs are summarised in a table in Unit 7.

First, and on the positive side, researchers would be hoping for indications that the development work is helping to reduce susceptibility to HIV infection. For example, if the project is reducing levels of poverty, or empowering the poor, then it is addressing a root cause of susceptibility. Similarly, if it is connected to improvements in women's status or greater gender equality, it is also likely to be having an positive effect on susceptibility. Projects which lead to reductions in migration, and improvements in health, particularly sexual health, might also be reasonably assumed to be making a positive indirect contribution to the battle against AIDS.

Negative indicators include participants' increased spending on alcohol, other recreational drugs, or sex; and increased mobility or migration.

However, researchers also need to be alert to contrary feedback: indications that the project may inadvertently be increasing susceptibility to HIV infection. These negative indicators would, regardless of AIDS, suggest that there are problems with the development process, but they may be unlikely to emerge from ordinary appraisal and evaluation procedures, because development workers are not ordinarily looking for such issues and connections. Such indicators include, for example, participants' increased spending on alcohol, other recreational drugs, or sex; and increased mobility or migration. Other indicators are exclusion of poor or marginalised people, particularly young women; and greater gender inequality, for example, through shifts in power (for example, the power to make decisions and control resources) towards men. Unsafe sex between male development workers and girls or women, and sexual trading or sexual abuse in the context of access to project benefits, would also suggest that the project is increasing susceptibility to HIV infection.

There are three main indications which suggest that a project is helping to reduce vulnerability to the impacts of AIDS. First, the fact that poor and vulnerable households – including those headed by women, older people, and orphans, and those with a high dependency ratio – are participating and benefiting. Second, evidence that the project is reducing poverty and helping households, and particularly poor ones, to build up their assets, so that they will be more able to withstand the shock of AIDS should they be affected. Third, evidence that the project is leading to greater social cohesion, and building the capacity of community institutions to respond to development problems. This last point relates to reducing community vulnerability, in that a community which is fighting to attain its rights will be more robust when threatened by AIDS. It will also be more able to act to support hard-hit households, through 'community safety-nets', such as communal efforts to support households headed by orphans.

Other indications might suggest that the project is hindering efforts to cope with AIDS. For example, if a project promotes activities in which poor and vulnerable households fail to make progress because the activities are unsuited to them, then it may consume their time and savings while also undermining their confidence and social standing, all of which will increase their vulnerability. More generally, if a project promotes methods based on inputs of labour and capital which are unsustainable in the case of external shocks such as chronic illness, then it may make any participants who are hit by AIDS more vulnerable. Finally, if a project is excluding poor and vulnerable households, it may not be making them more vulnerable, but it is failing to help them to reduce their vulnerability.

With these indications in mind, the starting point for community research is to explore each peer group's experience of the project, and its impacts on various people's lives. This could be done through guided discussion, which might be more fruitful if combined with a visual participatory method to encourage the groups to debate and analyse their views and experiences. How to do this will depend on the project's aims and activities, and the length of time since it was established. The researchers would need to devise their method, or methods, in advance. Some suggestions are given in Unit 7. Possible topics include the following:

- Who is participating, how, and with what repercussions?

- Who is not participating, why, and with what repercussions?

- Who holds power and decision-making authority within the project, and with what repercussions?

Throughout the process, it is important for researchers to be alert to gender-related issues, and to AIDS-related questions, and to prompt interviewees accordingly if, for example, the repercussions for women or destitute or AIDS-affected households are not mentioned spontaneously. When working with peer groups of women and girls, researchers also need to be conscious of possible demands for sex in return for favours such as access to project benefits.

The scope of the community research could also be extended to include asking peer groups and affected individuals about different ways of doing things, in order to strengthen the positive aspects of the work and address its negative implications for susceptibility to HIV infection and vulnerability to AIDS. However, researchers would need to take care not to raise people's expectations of unrealistic benefits.

If the research shows that AIDS is having significant impacts, and that there are links between AIDS and the development project, then it should assist the external mainstreaming process in several ways. First, the staff who act as researchers should gain a better understanding of how AIDS is affecting the communities whom they serve, and how AIDS links to their work. Second, the staff should be more motivated to address AIDS indirectly through modifying their ways of working. Third, they will be better placed to negotiate and discuss possible project modifications with community members. Fourth, the findings of community research can be used to support advocacy for mainstreaming AIDS and for AIDS work, particularly if they are well documented.

SUMMARY: ideas for community research, as part of the external mainstreaming of AIDS

- Use discursive methods, with peer groups, and with individuals or small numbers of people affected by AIDS or chronic illness.

- First focus on themes related to susceptibility to HIV infection, and to the impacts of AIDS, paying attention to gender aspects, and to the implications for vulnerable people, throughout the process.

- Then move on to the development project, or the planned project, with a view to identifying ways in which it may help or hinder a range of community members' susceptibility to HIV and vulnerability to the impacts of AIDS.

- Consider extending the research to explore ways of designing or modifying the project to maximise the ways in which it indirectly addresses HIV and AIDS.

Designing development work which indirectly addresses HIV and AIDS

This sub-section concerns the crux of external mainstreaming: modifying existing development work, or designing new development work, so as to enhance the way in which it indirectly addresses HIV and AIDS. This part of the process is based on the findings of the community research, aiming to make practical changes to existing development approaches. Staff may have valid ideas and enthusiasm for AIDS-focused work, on which the agency may be able to act. However, these ideas should not divert all attention away from discussion of how to ensure that core business can be made more relevant to the challenges of HIV and AIDS, and so play a greater role in the overall response to them. For the external mainstreaming process to keep moving in the right direction, the task must be to continue with (but improve) core work.

The precise process for designing 'mainstreamed' work, or modifying existing work, will depend on circumstances. For example, for a small project it may be possible to bring together all staff and stakeholders, including community representatives, to discuss the research findings, and to agree on some strategies or modifications. For a larger and more complex project, it might be appropriate for a working group of staff, stakeholders, and community representatives to develop some proposals, which would then be sent out for wider consultation and revision at community level before they could be tried.

In all circumstances, however, the starting point is the findings of the community research, which should be able to answer the two questions at the heart of the external mainstreaming process. First, how do HIV and AIDS affect the people with whom we work, in terms of their efforts to escape from poverty, now and in the future? Second, how is our work helping or hindering them to avoid HIV infection and to cope with the impacts of AIDS? If the research findings do not address those questions, or if their validity is in doubt, it may be necessary to undertake more research with community members.

Modifications to the development approach are most likely to address the project's shortcomings by trying to reduce the ways in which it heightens vulnerability to the impacts of AIDS or susceptibility to HIV infection. However, they could also try to build on the positive findings of the research, by strengthening the ways in which the work helps to reduce susceptibility and vulnerability. Furthermore, ideas of what to do should stem from, and develop, useful responses among people who have been affected.

Although the modifications should be unique to each project, it may be helpful here to review some ideas for sectoral approaches to development. The majority of suggestions concern agriculture, because most examples in the literature are from NGOs working in that sector. However, this subsection also presents some ideas for economic development, microfinance, primary health care, water and sanitation, and education. It begins by framing a more general argument concerning overarching strategies to develop households' resilience and ability to withstand shocks such as HIV and AIDS, and the suitability of various approaches according to the degree of impact on the household.

Household coping strategies and their implications for development work

Studies of the dynamics of household livelihoods explain household coping behaviour in two stages: first, pre-emptive measures to reduce risk; and second, in the event of a shock of some kind, reactive measures to manage losses. Table 2.2 on page 29 outlined three phases of reaction, with examples of the strategies that households use when faced with the losses incurred through HIV and AIDS. In the first phase they use reversible strategies, by exploiting their protective assets, such as spending their savings. In the second phase they fall back on disposal of productive assets, such as selling land or tools. These strategies are difficult to reverse, and they affect the long-term capacity of the households to generate income and to grow food. The third phase is that of destitution, where households disintegrate, rely on charity, or migrate.

The ability of households to avoid Phases 2 and 3 depends on the resiliency of their Phase 1 strategies of loss management. And Phase 1, in turn, depends on the success or otherwise of the households' pre-emptive risk-reduction activities. These may include choosing low-risk income-generating activities which earn modest, but steady, returns, and diversifying agricultural and other income-earning activities. Other risk-reduction strategies are to build up savings and other assets which can be sold if the need arises (such as livestock, jewellery, and household goods); and, on the social side, preserving and investing in extended family and community ties (Donahue 2002:2).

These insights provide important pointers for interventions by development agencies, which are summarised in Table 13.1. They suggest that pre-emptive development work with AIDS-affected communities, or communities which are not yet badly affected, should focus on supporting households' risk-reduction strategies; for example, initiatives to help to improve and maintain income flows, and to plan for future shocks by building up assets. These can be characterised as methods to strengthen households' safety-nets, which reduce vulnerability to the impacts of AIDS; they also are likely to have the benefit of reducing susceptibility to HIV infection. In communities which are already hit by AIDS, work should also aim to support affected households to remain within Phase 1 of the reactive coping strategies, which are reversible, rather than moving on to Phase 2 and the disposal of productive assets.

However, by the time a household has reached the third phase – destitution – it has fallen through its own safety-net and is relying on whatever support is available from the community. In such circumstances, where the household has little scope for participation in general development work, it seems to be more appropriate for agencies to think in terms of supporting community safety-nets, in order to provide relief to destitute households (Baylies 2002:625, Donahue 2002:6); for example, AIDS projects supporting community efforts to give practical assistance to badly affected households. This kind of assistance may also help to prevent those households in the second phase from slipping into the destitution of Phase 3.

Clearly, the strategy for development agencies of strengthening household safety-nets falls within the remit of general development work, while that of strengthening community safety-nets is harder to categorise. It does involve community development work, in terms of supporting the capacity of the community to respond, but the mode is one of relief-based or welfare-based AIDS work. As such, it provides an example of how the overall response to HIV and AIDS requires both levels of work: development work with AIDS mainstreamed in it, and AIDS work. The following sections, discussing the mainstreaming of AIDS in development work, mainly correspond with efforts to strengthen household safety-nets.

Table 13.1: Summary of household coping strategies and their implications for development work

Household coping mechanisms	Development-agency interventions
Pre-emptive risk-reduction strategies	Strengthen households' safety-nets, e.g. • improving incomes and income flows • encouraging saving and accumulation of assets • avoiding use of productive assets
Reactive coping strategies: Phase 1 (reversible, using protective assets)	
Reactive coping strategies: Phase 2 (difficult to reverse, using productive assets)	Strengthen community safety-nets, e.g providing • help in caring for children • food, or help in growing food • goods such as clothes and soap
Reactive coping strategies: Phase 3 (destitution)	

(Source: adapted from Donahue 2002, and reproduced with the permission of the author)

Agriculture

Given that many rural people are highly dependent on agriculture for their livelihoods, this is a key sector for poverty alleviation. Ideas among NGOs for modifying agriculture programmes in order to take HIV and AIDS into account are mainly premised on the notion that there should be more work with, and greater efforts to assist, households whose food supplies are insecure, which may include those headed by elderly people, women, and children. From this stems the idea that programmes need to promote modified or new methods which are more suited to those households' needs and options. These methods are likely to be labour-saving, low-input, and low-risk strategies; they may arise from people's own risk-reduction strategies. Where possible, agencies should provide community members with a range of options, so that people can decide what best suits their situation. Also, note that these ideas are in addition to general ideas for programmes to improve food security, such as planting trees which yield fruit over a long period of the year, measures to improve the storage of food, and processing and marketing initiatives to increase the earning potential of crops.

More production might be located immediately outside the home, through establishing kitchen gardens, fruit trees, rabbits and poultry in hutches, and zero grazing for dairy cows.

The careful introduction of appropriate technologies, such as threshing machines, mills, wheelbarrows, and carts, may help to reduce demands on labour-constrained households. Some existing tools and techniques may be poorly suited to elderly, weak, or young people. For example, ploughing with oxen is very heavy work, whereas using a donkey and donkey plough is a more manageable, if lower-status, method. Appropriate technologies may also make food-processing viable, thus adding value to existing production.

Agricultural techniques can also be adapted to reduce labour demands. For example, time spent on weeding may be reduced through inter-cropping, and the task of ploughing can be reduced through mulching and minimum-tillage methods. More production might be located immediately outside the home, through establishing kitchen gardens, fruit trees, rabbits and poultry in hutches, and zero grazing for dairy cows. Being close to home makes these methods of production particularly suitable for farmers who are juggling domestic and agricultural tasks at the same time.

Other techniques could reduce the inputs required for farming. Composting, mulching, and application of manure or ashes resulting from burning crop residues can increase production without the expense of chemicals. Inter-cropping with nitrogen-fixing plants, bunding, and 'live fences' can limit erosion and help to maintain soil fertility. Water-conservation techniques may also increase production.

Certain livestock and crops may also be more appropriate to vulnerable households. For example, for milk production, goats are cheaper and easier to handle than cows. For meat or livestock to sell, rabbits, chickens, and guinea fowl are easier than larger livestock to raise, can reproduce more rapidly, and are a more divisible asset. While suitable crops vary according to location, it is possible in each setting to identify relatively low-risk crops, which require little labour but are reasonably nutritious (for example, Page 2002:33 for Malawi). These may be 'survival crops' which AIDS-affected households are already using, or tree crops yielding fruit and nuts within one or two years of planting.

Rabbits, chickens, and guinea fowl are easier than larger livestock to raise, can reproduce more rapidly, and are a more divisible asset.

The potential modifications and their suitability will clearly depend on the current activities of any programme, and on local farming systems. Note, however, that the general focus of the ideas suggested above is on sustainable livelihoods and improved nutrition for vulnerable people through modest but achievable forms of production, in tune with their own risk-reduction strategies. This is contrary to the predominant focus in agricultural policy on production rates and profit through 'high-tech' and high-status methods. This being so, organisations wishing to promote sustainable livelihoods must not only experiment with ideas such as those outlined here, but also prove their effectiveness in order to argue for policy change.

Micro-finance

Micro-finance projects, or savings and credit schemes, are another means of helping households to increase their incomes and to build up their assets, so reducing their vulnerability to the impacts of AIDS and, particularly for women, lowering their susceptibility to HIV infection by reducing the need to exchange sex for favours. Such projects are particularly appropriate for channelling support to vulnerable households, because the loans are very small and so encourage the participation of the poor, whose short-term trading activities easily benefit from injections of small amounts of money. The gains made are likely to be modest, but may be sufficient to make a difference in quality of life, and in resilience to survive crises. For example, one evaluation found that, compared with a control group of women, female clients of a village bank were spending more than twice as much on health care and their children's education, and had savings which were more than six times greater than those in the control group (Donahue 2002:3).

Mainstreaming modifications to such schemes aims to make them more responsive to members' needs in the context of AIDS. For example, if the rules result in the expulsion of someone who is sick or caring for someone else, it may be possible to make the rules more flexible. Members might be permitted to miss meetings, so long as payments are made, to take a rest between loan cycles but retain their membership, or to take out a smaller loan without being penalised by a reduction in the size of future loans. Rules may also be needed to protect the savings of married female members, which may otherwise be acquired by their husbands' relatives in the event of widowhood. For people who are excluded from micro-finance projects because they are too economically vulnerable, the provision of a simple community bank may enable them to save. If they are able to invest and build their savings, in time they may gain access to the credit facilities of the micro-finance service itself.

Rules may be needed to protect the savings of married female members, which may otherwise be acquired by their husbands' relatives in the event of widowhood.

Micro-finance does work in communities which are seriously affected by AIDS, but micro-finance projects are not recommended to give preferential treatment, such as lower interest rates, to members who are infected with HIV or affected by AIDS. If many members are AIDS-affected, preferential treatment may undermine the financial sustainability of the scheme. It also tends to create stigma and resentment among other members, undermining the cohesion that is needed for groups to flourish. (In any case, groups commonly devise their own ways of supporting members in times of crises, such as making grants or loans from an emergency fund.) Nor is it recommended to form special savings and credit groups for people who are HIV-positive, because the risk of default – which is ordinarily spread among members – is too high in a group consisting solely of particularly vulnerable members. This is partly why loan schemes run by Aids Support Oganisations (ASOs) tend to be unsustainable, with low repayment rates and irrevocable erosion of the loan capital (Donahue et al. 2001:28). In general, with regard to HIV/AIDS, micro-finance services are best positioned to serve those who are not yet badly affected (but who may well be supporting others affected by AIDS), and to help them to reduce their vulnerability to the impacts of AIDS, should it hit them. Micro-finance is not, however, an intervention that will pull destitute households out of poverty (Development Alternatives Incorporated 2000:12). As discussed earlier in this chapter, the phase of destitution seems to require welfare support through strengthening community safety-nets.

Allied to micro-finance is the idea of organisations supporting group-based micro-enterprises or income-generating activities. This strategy is used by NGOs and ASOs as a means for groups of HIV-positive people to raise money, and for community groups to raise money to fund safety-net projects for people affected by AIDS. However, group businesses are notoriously risky endeavours, which encounter enormous difficulties in generating significant profit; even among the successes, many organisations have had disappointing experiences in this respect (Donahue 2002:5; Mutangadura et al. 1999b:39; Page 2002). Sometimes the successes are measured more in terms of mutual support among members, rather than in increased income, and the cost-effectiveness of such projects is rarely considered. In general, loans targeted at individuals, and in particular at women, appear to more effective in terms of raising incomes and having positive outcomes for quality of life and household safety-nets, and so for reducing susceptibility and vulnerability.

Primary health care

Because primary health care is so closely connected to HIV/AIDS and AIDS work, it might seem to be a sector in which AIDS is already mainstreamed. In general, the sector is indirectly working to reduce susceptibility to HIV and vulnerability to the impacts of AIDS if it is improving the health status of community members. It does this by, for example, helping to maintain people's immune systems, treating STIs, and enabling people who are ill to recover and return to work, so protecting their livelihoods. However, there may be ways in which health-care services inadvertently contribute to susceptibility and vulnerability, which could be modified. For example, family-planning services should emphasise the option of condoms, and their protective function, among the choices presented to prevent conception. And primary health-care providers need to ensure that they do not deter people from seeking treatment through their attitudes and practice towards, for example, poor people in general or, more specifically, adolescents or unmarried women with STIs or unplanned pregnancies. Health services may also exclude poor people through the cost of treatment, a problem which might be dealt with informally by exempting particularly vulnerable patients from payment, or by establishing formal safety-nets.

HIV-positive people and their families are rendered more vulnerable when health staff conceal the diagnosis and prognosis of AIDS.

In terms of vulnerability to the impacts of AIDS, HIV-positive people and their families are rendered more vulnerable when health staff conceal the diagnosis and prognosis of AIDS. Good and well-given advice about positive living can help people with AIDS to prioritise appropriate treatment, rest, and foods, rather than exhausting their resources in the false expectation of a full recovery. Moreover, the practice of omitting AIDS as one of the causes of death on death certificates arguably contributes to denial about AIDS, and so heightens community susceptibility and vulnerability.[1]

Water and sanitation

In terms of HIV transmission, the main risk in water and sanitation projects seems to be the potential for sexual bargaining over access to the facilities. This could be reduced by having more women involved in their management, or as caretakers, with appropriate incentives to compensate for their time. An alternative or additional modification would be to raise awareness among all community members about the right of girls and women to access the facilities free of sexual bargaining, along with establishing a mechanism for reporting and dealing with complaints.

The possibility of exclusion from water and sanitation projects suggests two ideas for modification. First, where the poorest households cannot afford to pay for access to water and sanitation facilities, a safety-net of some kind could secure them that access, provided that it is designed and implemented in a way that does not threaten the sustainability of the project. Second, if stigmatisation were to prevent people from AIDS-affected households from using the facilities, action could be taken to counter the unfounded fears of contagion. The management committee could also act to secure access for excluded people.

Education

Education generally reduces both susceptibility to HIV and vulnerability to the impacts of AIDS. A girl who has received a basic education is, at least theoretically, more able to take charge of her life, earn a living, heed health-promotion messages, and plan for her future. She is also more able to claim her rights, for example, in terms of access to health care, or securing her inheritance rights. However, if while at school she is pressured or forced into unprotected sex by male teachers or pupils, her susceptibility to HIV infection is raised. One strategy to reduce this likelihood is to raise both teachers' and pupils' awareness of pupils' rights, and in particular the rights of girls and women, at the same time as establishing appropriate complaints procedures and disciplinary measures.

In general, the negative impact of education may be not so much to heighten pupils' susceptibility or vulnerability, but to fail to extend the benefits of education to children who are not in school, and to fail to equip those who are in school with appropriate life skills. With regard to exclusion, modifications might include offering bursaries, reducing school fees, or waiving fees for the poorest or most vulnerable children, and in particular girls, reducing the costs of attending school (school uniforms, books, and special project payments, for example). More flexible hours might also assist children who have other, competing responsibilities, to attend school. Curricula and teacher training could be adapted to make education more attractive and useful to pupils, by meeting needs for practical skills which are appropriate to their lives.

SUMMARY: ideas for devising development work which maximises the ways in which it indirectly responds to HIV and AIDS

- Modify work in all sectors to reduce the likelihood of unintended negative impacts on susceptibility and vulnerability, and to maximise the positive effects.

- Strengthen household safety-nets, through improving incomes and building up household assets by promoting low-risk agriculture and micro-finance initiatives suited to vulnerable households.

Adapting systems

The previous section proposed some practical ideas for modifying development work in various sectors, so as to make a greater contribution to the overall response to HIV and AIDS. If, however, mainstreaming is to become institutionalised, organisations need to alter the systems and procedures which guide and discipline both the staff and the organisation. More detailed suggestions about how to achieve this are to be found in Unit 8 on pages 329–31.

One set of systems which need attention are those concerned with employees' roles and responsibilities. For example, each staff member's responsibility for taking account of AIDS can be formalised by including it in all job descriptions, and in appraisal mechanisms. The same strategy can be used in terms of reference for consultants' work, and in induction procedures. Employees' terms and conditions should also include standards of behaviour – for example, regarding non-discrimination and honesty – and disciplinary procedures for offences such as corruption and sexual harassment or abuse. For the organisation as a whole, the commitment to responding to AIDS as a mainstream issue (and perhaps also as an issue requiring specialised AIDS work) can be enshrined in key documents, such as a mission statement.

The other systems which need to be adapted in order to institutionalise AIDS as a mainstream issue are those relating to the project cycle: all the tools and steps from start to finish need to attend to AIDS and gender, regardless of the sector.

At the **needs-assessment stage**, staff need should consider the current and likely future impacts of HIV and AIDS, and related issues such as gender inequality, sexual and reproductive health, sexual norms, violence, abuse of alcohol and other drugs, and migration. These can be explored through participatory appraisal methods, such as those described in the earlier sub-section about undertaking community research, and in Unit 7.

At the **project-planning stage**, staff need to consider those issues, and their links to the project, as described in the preceding section on designing development work which indirectly affects HIV and AIDS. Within the broader project objectives, employees need to strengthen the ways in which the project can help to fight AIDS indirectly, by reducing both susceptibility to HIV infection and vulnerability to the impacts of AIDS. Conversely, they must try, as far as is practicable, to avoid repercussions which are likely to worsen the situation indirectly, by increasing susceptibility or vulnerability.

These twin concerns also need to be borne in mind during implementation, and to be included explicitly in monitoring and evaluation measures and in reporting. Moreover, for AIDS to be successfully mainstreamed in an organisation's systems, monitoring and revision of the adaptations themselves are needed. This would involve checking that users understand the references to AIDS, and are able to use them in meaningful ways. Some suggestions for each stage of the project cycle are included in Unit 8.

SUMMARY: ideas for adapting systems in order to institutionalise the mainstreaming of AIDS within development organisations

- Include attention to mainstreaming AIDS in job descriptions, appraisal mechanisms, and documents concerning the organisation's purpose and approach.
- Deal with issues relating to HIV susceptibility in employees' terms and conditions of employment.
- Incorporate the actions needed to mainstream AIDS in all stages of the project cycle.

External mainstreaming in development work: a summary

This section has presented four steps in external mainstreaming by development agencies: training and capacity building; community research; designing development work which indirectly addresses HIV and AIDS; and adapting systems. With regard to the third step, the section has explained how development programmes which build on households' own risk-reduction strategies, such as trying to increase income and build up assets, are likely to be valuable in reducing both susceptibility to HIV and vulnerability to the impacts of AIDS. This section has also presented some ideas for mainstreaming AIDS within the sectors of agriculture, micro-finance, primary health care, water and sanitation, and education. All four steps are summarised in Figure 13.1.

Figure 13.1: Summary of key steps in the external mainstreaming of AIDS in development work

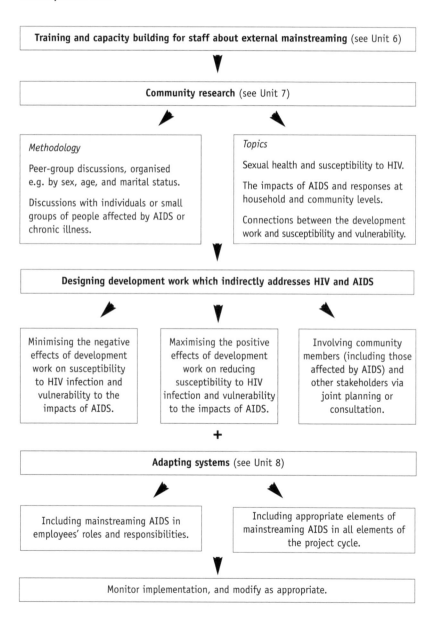

| Training and capacity building for staff about external mainstreaming (see Unit 6) |

| Community research (see Unit 7) |

Methodology

Peer-group discussions, organised e.g. by sex, age, and marital status.

Discussions with individuals or small groups of people affected by AIDS or chronic illness.

Topics

Sexual health and susceptibility to HIV.

The impacts of AIDS and responses at household and community levels.

Connections between the development work and susceptibility and vulnerability.

| Designing development work which indirectly addresses HIV and AIDS |

Minimising the negative effects of development work on susceptibility to HIV infection and vulnerability to the impacts of AIDS.

Maximising the positive effects of development work on reducing susceptibility to HIV infection and vulnerability to the impacts of AIDS.

Involving community members (including those affected by AIDS) and other stakeholders via joint planning or consultation.

+

| Adapting systems (see Unit 8) |

Including mainstreaming AIDS in employees' roles and responsibilities.

Including appropriate elements of mainstreaming AIDS in all elements of the project cycle.

| Monitor implementation, and modify as appropriate. |

Ideas for mainstreaming AIDS in humanitarian work

This section is closely linked to the previous one on mainstreaming AIDS in development work. Clearly, the two types of work have much in common, and there is, therefore, a great deal of overlap between the two types of response. This is particularly the case where the humanitarian work is in response to a slow-onset crisis, and when people are not displaced from their homes. In such cases, the response may involve building on, scaling up, and adapting existing development work, as much as launching new programmes. To avoid duplication, this section aims to outline ideas for mainstreaming which are specific to humanitarian work. It will focus on the aspect of the humanitarian response that most strongly contrasts with development work: support for displaced people or refugees living in camps.

Changes in sexual behaviour and rising rates of STIs are common repercussions when livelihoods are under acute pressure and populations are displaced.

As Chapter 9 made clear, there are very few documented experiences of mainstreaming AIDS in humanitarian work, and a large gap between policy and practice. The literature concerning AIDS and emergencies tends to centre on theoretical absolutes – all the things which ought to happen, all the things which agencies must do – and to recommend comprehensive programmes, the likes of which are uncommon in non-emergency development work. 'Best practice' exists on paper, and in policies, but there is little discussion of what is realistic, or what to try first. With this in mind, this section offers ideas (many of which are theoretical) rather than absolute truths. If more agencies can reach the point of piloting such ideas, then more progress could be made in formulating viable protocols on the basis of experience.

Many of the papers and policies about AIDS and emergencies concern direct responses to HIV/AIDS, usually integrated within sexual-health services or wider primary health care. As with AIDS work in non-crisis contexts, this is crucial work, particularly as changes in sexual behaviour and rising rates of STIs are common repercussions when livelihoods are under acute pressure and populations are displaced. Some key documents on tackling AIDS directly in emergency situations are included in the bibliography. However, the focus here is in on mainstreaming AIDS in core humanitarian programmes that provide shelter, food, water, and basic health services.

A 'do no harm' approach to mainstreaming

There seem to be two main differences between mainstreaming AIDS in development work and in humanitarian work in fast-onset crises involving population movements. First, in development work, most factors affecting people's lives are beyond the control of development agencies. In contrast, in humanitarian settings the quality of life is influenced by outside agencies in fundamental ways. This is not to say that individuals do not still influence their own lives, but to indicate the expanded sphere of influence that NGOs and others may have. For example, in refugee camps, agencies will play a part in deciding where people live; the types of food and non-food items that are mainly available, and who gets what; where people get water from; and the health services on offer. They also influence who gets the limited amount of formal employment available, and who benefits from training and education. This also applies, to a lesser extent, in situations where a population has been displaced but has integrated with the host community.

The decisions that agencies make – or which the community groups to whom they devolve responsibility make – have an impact on all the different kinds of people whom they are aiming to serve. Many of the known negative effects are increased gender inequality, sexual and gender-based violence, sexual abuse, and sexual trading. This fact justifies the principle that, given agencies' wide field of influence in such contexts, their frame of reference must extend to include these difficult but important issues. The special circumstances tend to shift the mainstreaming agenda away from AIDS to broader factors such as sexual violence, which demand attention in their own right, in addition to their connection with HIV transmission.

The second difference relates to phases within the humanitarian response. In the later stages, when a situation has stabilised, agencies should be undertaking development work, such as supporting households to develop their livelihoods, to build their assets, and to improve their skills and capacity. An agency which is doing development work in a humanitarian setting can meaningfully mainstream AIDS, as already discussed. For example, it can consider how to ensure that its programmes include and serve the development needs of AIDS-affected and other vulnerable households; how to reduce susceptibility to HIV infection through reducing poverty and empowering women; and how to help households to become less vulnerable to the impacts of AIDS. This also applies in slow-onset disasters, when the community has not been displaced.

However, in the early stages of a fast-onset emergency with population displacement, there is the short-term imperative of trying to meet basic needs and to help people to stay alive. While this relief phase lasts, it is probably not meaningful to think of fully mainstreaming AIDS. Quite aside from the logistical pressures that agencies face at such times, there is also a theoretical reason for this. The idea of mainstreaming AIDS depends on development work being able to address the root causes and consequences of the AIDS pandemic; but relief-based humanitarian work which only helps people to survive cannot address the deep development issues that drive HIV and AIDS. It is proposed, then, that in instances where agencies are necessarily focused on helping people to survive rather than to develop, it is more realistic and relevant to focus on a 'do no harm' form of mainstreaming, in terms of minimising the way in which humanitarian work may indirectly increase susceptibility to HIV infection. The rationale for prioritising this aspect of mainstreaming is that the work of humanitarian agencies seems to have the greatest influence on susceptibility to HIV infection, particularly in the early stages of the emergency response, and particularly when working in camp situations.

SUMMARY: general ideas for mainstreaming in humanitarian work

- Use the same principles and approach employed when mainstreaming in development work.

- Adopt a limited 'do no harm' form of mainstreaming, centred on minimising unintended negative effects on susceptibility to HIV infection, when humanitarian work is in a relief-focused stage.

- Adopt the full mainstreaming agenda in stable situations in which humanitarian work is moving towards development work.

Training and capacity building

Unlike mainstreaming AIDS in development work, many of the ideas for mainstreaming in humanitarian work are already present in policies and guidelines, via attention to gender-related concerns and issues of sexual and gender-based violence. Advocacy and training, then, may need to focus less on getting the issue recognised, and more on building commitment and capacity to close the gap between policy and practice. If senior staff are convinced of the need to do this, then training for other staff can begin. Such training might cover the links between emergencies, gender, and AIDS; the arguments for mainstreaming; and steps in the mainstreaming process. It could also include refugees' rights and the content of key policies, to ensure that staff understand their duties. This could then lead to considering the practical implications for the humanitarian response, allowing staff to define the next steps in mainstreaming for themselves.

Training and capacity building for field workers will depend on their relationship with the organisation. In some cases, and particularly where the crisis halts development work, or builds on existing development work, then it is the same employees and partners working in development who are staffing the humanitarian response. An organisation could, then, give these staff basic training in advance, through training on gender and emergencies, perhaps associated with courses concerning the external mainstreaming of AIDS in development work. The conceptual approach to addressing AIDS indirectly, and the skills to do so and to carry out community research, apply equally to both situations. In other cases, organisations have to recruit new employees (and/or work with new partners). Rapid induction training is then required. This might be facilitated by having simple, pre-prepared training resources. Some ideas for training – in advance or in the field – are included as Unit 9 on pages 332–7.

Ideally every employee in humanitarian work should have a thorough understanding of gender issues, and their relationship to AIDS, and be skilled in researching and devising appropriate responses. However, when under pressure, it may be more realistic to adopt a 'division of labour' strategy, whereby the emphasis of all but basic training is on capacity building for a cadre of staff. These can be characterised as 'software' staff, who concentrate on social aspects of humanitarian work such as community consultation or public-health promotion, working alongside 'hardware' employees who specialise in the technical inputs such as water engineering.

SUMMARY: ideas for training and capacity building for mainstreaming AIDS in humanitarian work

- Use existing policies and guidelines within training, to close the gap between policy and practice.

- Expose development staff to ideas about gender, emergencies, and mainstreaming in humanitarian work, perhaps at the same time as training them to mainstream AIDS in development work.

- Undertake rapid training for any new staff recruited for humanitarian work.

- Train all staff in gender issues, but focus further training efforts on certain cadres of staff, rather than trying to train everyone equally.

Emergency preparedness

Emergency preparedness is an important means of improving the overall quality of an emergency response, and good practice in this regard has already been documented. Within that wider task, preparedness for mainstreaming is likely to be critical to attempts to address AIDS indirectly: an organisation which does not consider mainstreaming issues in advance is highly unlikely to consider them when a crisis strikes.

Training in advance, and having training resources to hand, is part of being prepared for mainstreaming AIDS. It may also be worthwhile to identify potential employees in advance, particularly with regard to posts which may be difficult to fill, or goals such as 'employing more women'. Planning is another element: developing ideas and strategies for how to mainstream AIDS within the humanitarian response, and how to monitor its effects. This is likely to involve reviewing existing guidelines, making any changes that may be required, and thinking about how to proceed: for example, obtaining additional resources, or prioritising certain aspects, such as phasing from a 'do no harm' approach to full mainstreaming as the response shifts from a relief focus to a development mode. Organisations should also consider in advance the circumstances under which they would or would not become involved in direct AIDS work.

An organisation which does not consider mainstreaming issues in advance is highly unlikely to consider them when a crisis strikes.

Research is another element of preparedness for mainstreaming AIDS. Among all the other information which helps to inform the initial humanitarian response there should, as a minimum, be data on the HIV-prevalence rates in the region, differentiated by sex, age, and location. This information is available from UNAIDS, though it is very incomplete for areas where there is on-going conflict and disruption. For mainstreaming AIDS, however, other information is likely to be more useful, such as attitudes and practices concerning gender roles, sexuality, relationships, gender-based violence, and significant cultural differences between ethnic groups. Some of this information might be available internally, in the form of findings from community research as part of development work, while other data might be gathered from local CBOs and NGOs, government ministries, research institutes, and development literature.

Community research

Methods of needs assessment and other forms of research are already set out in agency manuals. The Sphere Project's *Humanitarian Charter and Minimum Standards in Disaster Response* (see the bibliography), for example, does pay attention to questions of gender and sexual and gender-based violence. Those questions correlate with the 'do no harm' form of mainstreaming, where an agency concentrates on reducing the likelihood that its work is inadvertently increasing susceptibility to HIV infection. The Sphere Project also promotes standards of good practice for involving women in decision making, and for considering equity and safety.

Research and consultation are key to good practice in humanitarian work, but may often be neglected, particularly in the early stages of the response when the need to act quickly to save lives takes precedence. However, if consultation can begin at the beginning, rather than some way into the response, then the work is likely to be more effective, particularly with regard to gender equality. Some of the researchers should ideally be women, because women and girls in the community are less likely to discuss sensitive problems with male researchers. If interpreters are required, some of these should also ideally be women. When the emergency has stabilised, it may be possible to train and involve community members in on-going research and consultation. This may be particularly effective if linked to action: for example, women's groups setting up support services for survivors of sexual violence, or, with regard to AIDS work, community-led home-based care programmes.

As with community research as part of development work, all kinds of people need to be involved, including marginalised and particularly vulnerable groups whose ideas and needs are otherwise ignored. It is almost always useful to discuss issues in peer groups, which might be formed on the basis of sex, age, current status (for example, unaccompanied child, or female household-head), clan or ethnic group, or any other significant axis of difference within the population. As a minimum, researchers need to listen to men and women separately. In addition they should ideally consult with members of the host community, who are also hugely affected by the crisis and entitled to benefit from the humanitarian response. If researchers are to use community representatives as key informants, women and younger people should be among them.

When an emergency stabilises and the work begins to shift towards a development approach, it is more plausible for agencies to think about the full mainstreaming agenda for AIDS. This may not require additional research if the relevant people and the relevant questions are included in needs assessment and consultation about developmental initiatives within the humanitarian programme. Adopting the whole mainstreaming agenda would involve attending not only to issues of gender, safety, and sexual and gender-based violence, but also to alcohol abuse, sexual behaviour, control of resources, and access to services. It is not practicable for all of these topics to be included in every piece of research or consultation, but including some discussion topics with each peer group should result overall in a better understanding of needs and dynamics, and better-designed responses. Unit 10 (pages 338–41) provides some ideas for doing this.

Designing humanitarian work which indirectly addresses HIV and AIDS

This section considers ways in which four standard aspects of a humanitarian response can take AIDS and related issues into account. They are not new; they are already formally enshrined in the Sphere Project's minimum standards and in some organisations' own codes. They mainly focus on the 'do no harm' approach of minimising increases in susceptibility to HIV infection, and reducing sexual and gender-based violence. As already stated, however, the ideas focus on the extreme situation of refugee camps; it is assumed that in humanitarian work with settled communities, the response is more likely to be more closely allied to that already outlined for mainstreaming in development work.

The type and layout of accommodation will affect refugees' susceptibility to HIV infection.

First, the type and layout of accommodation will affect refugees' susceptibility to HIV infection. Ideally, unrelated families should not have to share the same accommodation; if this is necessary, they need as much privacy as possible. Regarding settlement layout, one way to reduce the potential for tension and violence, including sexual violence, is to try to replicate the community's ordinary physical and social accommodation norms, rather than imposing new systems. Related to this is the idea of grouping households from the same village or location together. In any case, clustering shelters together increases social surveillance and self-policing. Unaccompanied women may be more vulnerable to the risk of rape and may need secure accommodation; the means of achieving this might be based on the community's pre-existing ways of protecting single women such as widows, or on new methods proposed by the women and the wider community: neighbourhood watch groups, for example. Certainly, single women must be consulted, and should not be housed in isolated areas, nor grouped together in ghettos.

Second, tap-stands, latrines, and washing facilities should ideally be decentralised, so that each is shared by a nearby group of households, rather than centrally located. This means that girls and women do not have to go long distances to reach them, which may be particularly dangerous at night. When this is not possible, for instance during the early stage of the response, organisations should consult women about how to allocate the available latrines; assigning them to a number of families, or designating them as separate facilities for men and women. Where latrines are sited in large groups, for example in public spaces such as market places, those for men and women should be separate, because communal arrangements provide more cover for potential attackers, and heighten women's fears. Providing lighting also reduces the risk of attack and lessens fears among users.

Third, one of the functions of nutritional assessments is to identify people who are malnourished and therefore eligible for supplementary food rations, in addition to the general ration. People who are malnourished by AIDS should be among them, but could be excluded by field workers who discriminate against them. It is known that in situations of limited resources (and particularly in the health-care sector) subjective judgement is used to prioritise some cases over others. However, such practices are against principles of equity. They may be mitigated by emphasising the duty of all employees to respect human rights, including those of people with HIV/AIDS. With regard to micronutrients, agencies could consider providing key supplements to boost the immune systems of people who are infected with HIV, or for the entire population.

Fourth, in camps and settled communities, there is the issue of distribution systems for food, shelter materials, basic items such as clothing, soap, and cooking utensils, and – depending on circumstances – water and firewood. The goal is for the systems to be fair, so that each individual gets the due ration. Some organisations are already giving all women the right to be registered independently and so receive their allocation in their own right, rather than through their partners. When food is desperately awaited, crowds and violence can stop women and other vulnerable people from getting their rations, or lead to the rations being taken from them. Organisations can reduce the risk of this through advance planning, security measures, and clear information about entitlements. Another strategy is to involve women in the actual distribution, so as to reduce unfair practices which discriminate against women. This idea should also reduce the incidence of sexual abuse or bartering in connection with distribution. However, this can be counterproductive, as in some cases women appointed to distribute items have become subject to intimidation and attack (WHO 2000:39).

Connected to distribution is the issue of collecting firewood, which may expose girls and women to sexual violence outside camps. Supervised wood-gathering may reduce the risks of attack. Agencies can also influence the amount of fuel required by each household by providing access to mills, or milled cereals, which cook more quickly than whole grain. Fuel-efficient stoves and cooking pots with well-fitting lids can also reduce the number of trips taken to gather fuel.

Fifth, the ideas that this chapter has already set out for mainstreaming AIDS in primary health care can be transferred to the emergency setting. They mainly concern preventing exclusion and discrimination on the basis of HIV/AIDS. Policies and ideas about the direct response, integrating AIDS work in primary health care and reproductive-health services, are included in the resources section of the bibliography.

For each of these five basic components of humanitarian work, organisations need to follow up their consultation with monitoring as the work is implemented. This monitoring could focus specifically on the groups of people known to be vulnerable, and most likely to be experiencing problems that might otherwise remain hidden. They may include unaccompanied women and girls, women and children who are heading households, the chronically ill and their carers, and – less clearly associated with AIDS but vulnerable nonetheless – elderly and disabled people. Monitoring needs to include not only the basic function of the service (for example, the quality of the drinking water) but also users' experience, in a wide sense, of the service. This includes being alert to repercussions which heighten susceptibility to HIV infection or vulnerability to the impacts of AIDS. Where appropriate, organisations then need to use monitoring data to stimulate action: for example, by disciplining agency staff or other personnel such as peacekeeping forces who are abusing their position of power, increasing security patrols in certain places, or tackling the exclusion of AIDS-affected people from project benefits.

Once an emergency has stabilised, and particularly if refugees or displaced people are unlikely to return for some time, humanitarian agencies may begin to shift to doing development work, such as investing in education, skills training, and income-generation activities. At this point, the approach to mainstreaming merges with that outlined for mainstreaming in development work in the previous section.

SUMMARY: ideas for designing humanitarian work which indirectly addresses HIV and AIDS

- Use existing codes and standards which concur with a 'do no harm' approach.
- Mainstream in all sectors, always with attention to gender issues and a special focus on vulnerable individuals and households.
- Monitor work and adapt it as necessary.
- Move to a full agenda for mainstreaming as soon as is practicable.

Adapting systems

As with external mainstreaming in development work, the task is one of institutionalising attention to AIDS. The same personnel measures apply – adding responsibilities related to AIDS to job descriptions and terms of reference, and including them in induction and training – along with enforcing appropriate terms and conditions. Unit 10 features some core principles for codes of conduct for humanitarian workers, which need also to be accompanied by means of accountability to beneficiaries, and methods of disciplining individuals who violate the standards. Finally, organisations need to adapt their own systems with regard to the project cycle; existing policies and guidelines provide a good starting place for this.

External mainstreaming in humanitarian work: a summary

This section has outlined the main ideas for mainstreaming AIDS in humanitarian programmes, insofar as they deviate from the ideas for development work. It has proposed that in stable situations, and where agencies are working in a developmental way with settled communities, they may adapt and use the ideas for mainstreaming AIDS in development work. However, in emergencies, such as those arising from fast-onset disasters with mass population movements, it may not be practicable to think of fully mainstreaming AIDS. Instead, during the relief phase, agencies might focus on a 'do no harm' approach to mainstreaming, which emphasises limiting the negative repercussions of the humanitarian response in terms of susceptibility to HIV, and gender-based and sexual violence. In this regard, the chapter outlined ideas concerning provision of accommodation, water and sanitation facilities, nutritional assessments, distribution systems, and health care. Figure 13.2 summarises the main components in the form of a flow chart.

Figure 13.2: Summary of key steps in the external mainstreaming of AIDS in humanitarian work

Training and capacity building for staff about external mainstreaming (see Unit 9)

+

Emergency preparedness

▼

Community research for a 'do no harm' approach to mainstreaming (Unit 10)

➤   ➤

Methodology	*Topics*
Peer-group discussions, organised for example according to sex, age, and current status (e.g. female heads of household).	Sexual health, sexual violence, gender inequality, and susceptibility to HIV.
Discussions with vulnerable individuals, e.g. unaccompanied girls and women.	Consultation about project design in order to minimise those factors.
Ideally, discussions with members of the host community also.	

+

Adapting systems (see Unit 8)

➤   ➤

Including mainstreaming AIDS in employees' roles and responsibilities.	Including appropriate elements of mainstreaming AIDS in all elements of the project cycle.

▼

Monitor implementation, and modify as appropriate.

▼

Move to full agenda for mainstreaming AIDS as the situation stabilises and relief work turns towards development work.

14 Issues and challenges

This chapter brings together some of the main challenges to the prospects for mainstreaming AIDS, both internally and externally. First, however, it focuses on two generic issues: supporting partners to mainstream, and the options facing organisations in countries with relatively low rates of HIV prevalence.

Supporting partners to mainstream AIDS

The principles and ideas already outlined in this book are generic, and so they apply equally to large development organisations and to small community-based organisations. For many larger agencies, however, the task may be not only to mainstream AIDS in their own organisations, and externally if they do such work, but to encourage their partners also to address AIDS indirectly through their core work. As we saw in Chapter 8, the balance between encouragement and coercion poses problems which funding NGOs must resolve whenever they opt to influence their partners' work. With regard to mainstreaming AIDS, the strategy is likely to be determined by existing dynamics and ways of working in partnership, and by the significance that the donor agency attaches to mainstreaming AIDS. Some might decide to enable partners to adopt new approaches through training, technical support, links to specialists, and funding, but to leave the final decision up to them. Others may attempt to enforce the mainstreaming agenda by imposing funding conditions. In either case, it is clear that the donor agency needs to be firmly committed to mainstreaming AIDS, if it is to be effective in supporting its partners to do the same. Where donor agencies have only a superficial interest in doing mainstreaming – because, for example, it is something which they need to be seen to be doing – then any lasting impact is very unlikely.

Strategically, if donors are concerned that partners should preserve their effectiveness, and are concerned with the more general health of the CBO sector as a part of civil society, they may want to emphasise the internal mainstreaming of AIDS. In doing so, they need to recognise, and be willing to pay, the internal costs which arise from mainstreaming AIDS, such as health care for staff and dependants (perhaps extending to antiretroviral treatment) and temporary cover for absences.

However, it is very difficult for small organisations to predict and budget for these costs, and particularly the direct costs incurred when a member of staff develops AIDS. An organisation employing 1,000 people, with an assumed rate of AIDS cases of two per cent, can budget for the costs of twenty people, and cope with variations around this figure. However, for a CBO with only ten staff and a similar rate of AIDS, one fifth of a person may be expected to have AIDS. Obviously, when a member of staff does fall ill, it will be a whole person rather than a fraction. The CBO could budget on the basis of one fifth each year. However, this would be insufficient if someone did develop AIDS; and, if there was no case of AIDS, many donors would not allow the money to be carried over to the next year. One way to get around this problem is for donor agencies to encourage their partners to have proper workplace policies and to budget accordingly, but to hold a central fund on which any partner can draw.[1] By budgeting centrally for the total number of people employed by all the partners, the donor agency ought to be able to make appropriate provisions. However, the situation is complicated by the fact that many CBOs receive support from several donors simultaneously.

Clear record keeping and budgeted contingency plans can help to reduce the problems created by the absence of key post-holders.

The other implication for small organisations is that it is all the more important to share knowledge and practices, so as to minimise disruptions when an employee is absent. Although small organisations may have more fluid work practices and a less rigid division of labour than large agencies, they may be more vulnerable with regard to sickness among people in key posts. For example, computing or accounting skills may be confined to one person. Clear record keeping and budgeted contingency plans can help to reduce the problems created by the absence of key post-holders.

Experience so far suggests that partners may need more support in external mainstreaming than in internal mainstreaming, particularly in terms of understanding the indirect links between their work and AIDS, and devising appropriate modifications. Donor organisations could provide additional support beyond workshops, such as assisting partners in their community research, and in their process of defining and trying out adaptations.

SUMMARY: ideas for agencies which are supporting partners to mainstream AIDS

- Ensure that your agency is committed to mainstreaming, and understands it, before attempting to influence partners.

- Devise and fund an appropriate mix of support and persuasion.

- Help partners to budget for the internal costs of treatment for HIV and AIDS.

- Remember that internal mainstreaming of AIDS requires partners to modify the work of their organisations in the context of AIDS, and not only to address the health implications for their own members of staff.

- Accept that internal and external mainstreaming may mean higher costs, both financial and non-financial.

Mainstreaming AIDS where HIV-prevalence rates are low

Much of this book has referred to experiences from countries in southern and eastern Africa, where the rates of HIV prevalence are high, and the impacts of generalised HIV epidemics are already very evident. However, beyond those regions are nations where HIV prevalence is much lower, with epidemics characterised as being either nascent or concentrated among certain risk groups. The following ideas for mainstreaming AIDS in such settings are theoretical, and fall into three categories. One option is to do nothing, which has the merit of being cost-free, and gives organisations the opportunity to wait for mainstreaming lessons to emerge as other agencies experiment. However, in the mean time, the agency gains nothing and loses the opportunity to pre-empt HIV and AIDS through either of the other options. In addition, it may incur higher costs in the long term.

A second option is to engage in the same mainstreaming processes as described in this section of the book, but at a lower level of intensity. This approach is akin to disaster preparedness, in the sense of preparing both employees and the organisation for the possibility of rising HIV prevalence and its associated risks and repercussions. In large organisations with programmes around the world, the strategy also means that all programmes are on an equal footing, and are all poised and able to respond. AIDS can strike in nations that are not highly affected; for example, one of Oxfam GB's first known instances of an HIV-positive employee was in a country with low HIV-prevalence. The disadvantage of this approach is that it is likely to be very difficult to motivate people to invest in mainstreaming AIDS where HIV rates are low. This is true for internal mainstreaming, but even more so for external mainstreaming, where none of the impacts of AIDS will be evident. Both employees and community members are likely to struggle to appreciate the probable consequences of AIDS and their implications for development or humanitarian work.

A third option is to focus less on mainstreaming AIDS, but instead to apply mainstreaming processes to other related issues, such as gender equality, sexual and reproductive health, and creating household safety-nets. This has the advantage that, rather than attempting to impose an agenda of AIDS on employees and community members who have few concerns about AIDS, organisations can respond to issues which give rise to current concern, and which require attention regardless of whether or not HIV rates rise. It has the disadvantage that additional work specific to AIDS would be necessary if HIV rates were to rise.

As the first option requires no further explanation, and the second is based on all that has come before – i.e. mainstreaming AIDS – this section outlines some ideas for the third option.

Internal mainstreaming in low-prevalence settings

With regard to internal mainstreaming, measures to support staff could simply focus on wider health issues, including STIs (which include HIV), because it is beneficial for employees and the organisation alike if staff are motivated to look after their physical and mental health. Staff could jointly examine organisational culture to see if some elements – such as alcohol use and abuse at workshops, or outside working hours – might usefully be changed. Non-health topics which might be of interest to staff include financial management, communication skills, and conflict resolution. All of these might have current appeal and relevance, but also indirect benefits in terms of reducing susceptibility to STIs, including HIV infection, and vulnerability to external shocks, including AIDS.

With regard to workplace policies, gender is probably the most likely topic to seem relevant to staff and to fit the organisation's needs. A similar mainstreaming process, based on the same broad principles, could then be applied: facing up to the issue through research, then learning through workshops before devising a policy. Ideally the non-discrimination section of any policy could also cover HIV/AIDS (along with other factors such as age, ethnicity, and disability). The process and outcome would be useful to the organisation in terms of formulating its values with regard to gender, and agreeing on measures to promote equality and to act against discrimination.

In terms of modifying how the organisation functions, several of the measures outlined for mainstreaming AIDS internally would be beneficial to organisations unaffected by AIDS. For example, many organisations do not have effective systems for coping with expected absences of staff (such as maternity leave), let alone unexpected staff shortages caused by illness, or sudden departures when an employee leaves without giving notice. Even when a member of staff gives notice, there is commonly a period when other employees have to cover the post while the recruitment process goes on, sometimes slowly and ineffectually. Moreover, where people tend to work independently and not share work tasks, organisational culture may be unsupportive and isolating. A lack of information about staff leave and the implementation of personnel policies may also add to inefficiency, or unfair treatment of staff. Setting up systems to gather such data would, in time, allow management to analyse staff costs and options with greater accuracy. Overall, addressing any or all of these issues would help an organisation to function, and reduce its vulnerability to impact as and when AIDS strikes its employees and their families.

Many organisations do not have effective systems for coping with expected absences of staff (such as maternity leave), let alone unexpected staff shortages caused by illness.

External mainstreaming in low-prevalence settings

The concept of mainstreaming AIDS is based on the notion that development and humanitarian work well done is, indirectly, acting against HIV and AIDS. In that sense, all that the agencies need to do is to keep doing their work. However, the rationale for mainstreaming AIDS is that development and humanitarian work may inadvertently be working to exacerbate susceptibility and vulnerability, and that mainstreaming can reduce that tendency, while also strengthening the ways in which the work acts to reduce susceptibility and vulnerability. This argument is valid even if HIV is not present, because the underlying causes, such as gender inequality and poverty, remain. In other words, work which does not take the factors of gender inequality and poverty into account may be working with, rather than against, them. While poverty reduction is assumed to be to be at the heart of development and humanitarian work, this does not mean that the work is always pro-poor, and the way in which gender issues can be ignored and gender inequality exacerbated is well documented. In situations where HIV prevalence is low, or where AIDS is not recognised as an issue, organisations could opt to review their work in order to make it more poverty-focused and pro-poor. This might result, for example, in refocusing agricultural extension work towards supporting subsistence farmers with few resources.

Alternatively, or in tandem, organisations could adopt a process of gender mainstreaming. This might result, for example, in agricultural extension work being reorientated to include women farmers, and to respond to their needs more effectively. The bibliography includes sources of information on gender mainstreaming.

It is important to note, however, that neither of these processes is the same as mainstreaming AIDS. While attending to AIDS requires knowledge of, and attention to, issues of gender and poverty, there are core aspects of mainstreaming AIDS which would not be dealt with through becoming more poverty-focused or through mainstreaming gender. These aspects are concerned with the impacts of AIDS, now and in the future, and both within organisations and among community members. Hence, an organisation which attends to poverty or gender in a low-HIV setting would still need to attend to mainstreaming AIDS if a generalised HIV epidemic emerged. However, the organisation's work in the low-prevalence phase would have begun to fight HIV and AIDS before they became significant, so laying important foundations for the subsequent process of mainstreaming AIDS.

Work which helps to build civil society through empowering community organisations seems to result in more robust communities which are better able to meet their needs and respond to new challenges.

Within development and humanitarian work, certain types of programme may be particularly relevant to acting against AIDS in advance of rising HIV-prevalence. At the general level, this includes all efforts to empower women, to address sexual and gender-based violence, and to improve the status of women and girls. A more specific route is sexual- and reproductive-health programmes, and in particular efforts to reduce unwanted pregnancies, and to promote biomedical treatment of STIs. It also includes all poverty-focused efforts to support livelihood security, and in particular to assist poor households to raise their incomes and to build up their assets, so becoming less poor and less vulnerable to the impacts of external shocks. Organisations could also aim to help people to build up their productive assets, for instance by planting fruit trees or cash crops which take time to establish but then provide a reliable harvest, with relatively low labour requirements. A less obvious route involves improving the productive use of income, aimed at enabling men and women to analyse their expenditure and to realise more of the poverty-alleviating potential of their income.

In terms of strategy, and regardless of sector, work which helps to build civil society through empowering community organisations seems to result in more robust communities which are better able to meet their needs and respond to new challenges (Barnett and Whiteside 2002:88). Any inclusive development and humanitarian work which helps to build social capital and cohesion is a force against poverty and gender inequality, and hence, indirectly, it works against HIV and AIDS.

Finally, although this section concerns options for responding to the agenda for mainstreaming AIDS in low HIV-prevalence settings, it is important to remember the option of AIDS work. While HIV-prevention programmes are needed in highly affected nations, where HIV is concentrated among population sub-groups there is the opportunity to try to reduce the rate of new infections among those groups, and to prevent HIV from crossing over to the broader population. It is a more plausible proposition, for example, to reap significant gains by investing in needle-exchange programmes for injecting drug users, and in comprehensive programmes for concentrated groups of commercial sex workers, than to undertake HIV prevention for a whole population. Moreover, the strategy of STI treatment as a means of reducing the rate of new HIV infections is more effective when focused on members of high-risk groups, before HIV infection becomes generalised, because they are likely to transmit HIV to greater numbers of people (Barnett and Whiteside 2002:329).

Challenges to mainstreaming

This section reviews the main challenges that confront advocates of AIDS mainstreaming; but it deals only with those problems that are specific to mainstreaming AIDS, rather than ones which pervade wider development and humanitarian work. It begins by identifying the main brakes on starting the mainstreaming process, and then discusses some of the challenges within the process.

Brakes on getting started

Advocates of mainstreaming AIDS face many problems in their efforts to persuade organisations to accept the argument for mainstreaming, and to commit themselves to action.

Lack of clarity over the meaning of mainstreaming

The term 'mainstreaming AIDS' is used to mean different things, and often to mean nothing very specific, which makes it difficult for everyone from donors and governments to NGOs and CBOs to talk to each other about the issue. It also makes the whole topic confusing and contradictory, which may deter some people from exploring the notion of mainstreaming AIDS. Moreover, the confusion over terminology may undermine implementation, if organisations embark on their mainstreaming process without a common sense among employees of what they are trying to achieve. All of this may add up to situation in which the term 'mainstreaming' becomes degraded or discarded, along with the concepts and aims behind it.

Alternatively, however, growing interest in mainstreaming, and more debate around the concept, may lead to greater clarity over time. Although there will never be a single definition or understanding on which everybody agrees, if key agencies such as UNAIDS and FAO were to adopt a precise shared meaning, some of the confusion would be dissipated.

Mainstreaming is complex to explain and difficult to promote

Mainstreaming is not an obvious strategy. It requires people to think 'out of the box', in a holistic way.

Mainstreaming AIDS is a difficult concept to promote, particularly in comparison with the task of advocating for direct AIDS work. To begin with, mainstreaming is not an obvious strategy. It requires people to think 'out of the box', in a holistic way; and the arguments behind it are a little complex. This means that advocacy for mainstreaming AIDS involves explaining mainstreaming; and even if advocates' explanations are straightforward but thorough, their audiences may not understand mainstreaming very rapidly, or may misunderstand the concept. A further problem is that the outcomes of mainstreaming AIDS are not, by its nature, very visible, so may not be easily captured and conveyed, as part of advocacy for mainstreaming, in words or pictures. Of course, advocacy is further challenged by the current lack of experience in mainstreaming, and the shortage of hard evidence that proponents of mainstreaming can present in support of their arguments.

To meet this challenge, advocates of mainstreaming need to find ways of presenting the logic of the concept, and illustrating the process and its outcomes, in more easily digestible ways. The concept is always going to be more complex than, say, the straightforward case that HIV-positive people have a right to treatment; but it should be possible to improve the way in which the case for mainstreaming is phrased and presented. A lengthy book such as this, for example, is quite unsuitable for many constituents within development work, but could be repackaged in a workbook format, or as a set of short booklets. The case for mainstreaming could also be simplified by compromising on the detail; for example, presenting mainstreaming as being mainly about reducing vulnerability, so setting aside the whole aspect of susceptibility, and of inadvertent negative effects of development work on both aspects.

In addition to finding better ways to communicate about mainstreaming, advocates need more experience to which to refer, in order to demonstrate that mainstreaming can enhance the contribution made by development and humanitarian work to the overall response to AIDS. This requires agencies not only to experiment with implementing mainstreaming, but to monitor and evaluate their work, to document it thoroughly, and to share their experiences. These requirements present further challenges, which are considered later in this chapter.

Mainstreaming lacks a constituency of advocates

Another brake on mainstreaming AIDS is that it lacks a natural constituency of advocates. Experience from gender mainstreaming is that advocacy by women's pressure groups has been a significant factor contributing to change (Derbyshire 2002:30). AIDS advocacy is mainly done by groups of people who are HIV-positive and are fighting for their rights to be protected, and in particular for access to treatment. For AIDS activists, these immediate and important issues understandably predominate. Advocacy for mainstreaming AIDS requires a longer and broader perspective, and a more complex analysis; it seems more likely to emerge from development agencies and other institutions than from the grassroots. Indeed, as the impacts of AIDS on organisations, communities, and development work are becoming more obvious in highly affected regions, interest in mainstreaming AIDS is also growing. Although the distinctive strategies of mainstreaming AIDS and integrating AIDS work are usually mixed up, growing interest among donors, planners, and development agencies presents an opportunity for advocates of mainstreaming AIDS to exploit.

Organisations lack the resources to undertake mainstreaming

While large development organisations which are determined to mainstream should be able to find the funds to do so from within, small organisations are more likely to depend on funds from outside. However, the problems outlined above mean that mainstreaming is not a high priority for donors. They are usually much more willing to provide funds for HIV-prevention programmes, or for programmes supporting orphans or providing care (although they may sometimes refer to these activities as 'mainstreaming'). Even donors that seek to fund 'impact mitigation' projects generally prefer such work to be clearly designed to deliver benefits to people directly affected by AIDS, rather than taking the broader approach of adapting existing development work.

Even where donors do not fund mainstreaming itself, organisations' costs, which are passed on to donors in project budgets, may rise as a result of mainstreaming. For example, where CBOs lack health policies and measures to support staff, their budgets and costs may rise following internal mainstreaming. (Equally, where CBOs lack policies and spend large amounts at 'management discretion', their costs may fall and budgets may become more accurate.) And where organisations decide to upgrade the treatments available to employees who are HIV-positive, financial costs may rise, while the benefits – in terms of continuity, staff morale, and the reputation of the organisation – remain absent from the accounts. Furthermore, an organisation which has mainstreamed AIDS externally may incur costs in terms of modifying its programme work, and with regard to what it can realistically achieve if its development work takes account of AIDS and includes AIDS-affected households. Poorly informed donors may simply ascribe new budget lines and higher core costs to bad management, and opt to invest in organisations which appear to offer 'better value'. Proponents of mainstreaming can lead by example, in their roles as donors to partners, and by demonstrating commitment to their own processes for mainstreaming AIDS. They can then use their experiences to promote mainstreaming to their own donors, and within the wider development community.

It might be argued, however, that undertaking mainstreaming can be a relatively low-cost activity, in terms of the money needed. If an organisation can find the staff time for the process, it may be able to conduct training and community research with little financial outlay. After all, although the process involves time and commitment, it is about adapting existing work and systems, rather than initiating new projects. Even internal mainstreaming need not be very costly if it does not adopt the highest standards of comprehensive health care and antiretroviral treatment. For example, a CBO which provides no health-care benefits to staff might undertake to pay for condoms and treatment for STIs, but might stop short of any further benefits. While this would not be ideal for the employees or for the organisation, it would be a pragmatic improvement which the CBO could afford to undertake.

However, even where an organisation does not need substantial funds to mainstream, it may need technical support. As the idea of mainstreaming gains more prominence, and as people become more aware of the challenges that AIDS is presenting to their work and their organisations, there is more interest in the concept. However, along with confusion over what mainstreaming means, there is uncertainty about what it is supposed to achieve, and how to go about it. The proactive manager who seeks support will find a limited range of publications, and, with the exception of institutional audits, almost no organisations able to offer practical and experience-based technical support. This is not to say that such support cannot emerge – there are organisations with the relevant skills to apply themselves to mainstreaming – but simply that, as yet, they are not numerous.

Short-term survival vs. long-term strategy

One of the constraints on HIV-prevention and behaviour-change programmes is that for poor people the everyday problems of surviving today displace any consideration of possible problems in the future. Women and men who live 'hand to mouth' do not typically invest much time in constructing long-term plans. When seeking to mainstream AIDS, one problem frequently encountered is that donor-dependent NGOs and CBOs may similarly prioritise immediate issues – their own survival, in the sense of getting another grant – at the expense of long-term planning. Many 'partnerships' have a lifespan of only a few years, linked to a project grant, and few donor agencies are willing to commit their resources to long-term partnerships.

However, while mainstreaming may not be immediately attractive to organisations unable to afford the luxury of long-term planning, it might become more appealing with sufficient support. NGOs and CBOs may be particularly open to the idea of mainstreaming AIDS internally if they are already feeling the impacts of AIDS, and their sense of 'needing to do something' is growing. Managers may be attracted to the idea that mainstreaming AIDS can help their organisations to survive AIDS by pre-empting financial and operational crises. Another possible appeal of mainstreaming is that it may, in time, improve organisations' ability to secure funds from donors, if they can demonstrate that they are prepared for AIDS, and that their work will respond to the challenges that it presents.

Challenges within mainstreaming

Organisations attempting to mainstream AIDS are likely to face many challenges. This section features three particular issues: the lack of complementary partners with whom to make links; the problem of developing effective monitoring and evaluation for mainstreaming; and the need to develop modes for shared learning and networking.

Lack of complementary partners

External mainstreaming means that development and humanitarian organisations should first adapt their core work, rather than beginning with AIDS projects, and then form complementary partnerships with specialist organisations which are dealing with AIDS directly. However, in practice those specialist organisations may not exist, or may not cover all aspects of AIDS work, or may be unable to extend themselves to form meaningful partnerships. In such a situation, a small organisation which had intended to mainstream AIDS might, realistically, face two options: continue with mainstreaming and ignore the need for AIDS work, or abandon mainstreaming and embark on AIDS work. If it had sufficient capacity, it could attempt to undertake both strategies, but at some risk to the quality of both initiatives. A larger organisation with more capacity might well be more able to adopt both strategies, and have the additional option of funding and supporting one or more other organisations to begin AIDS work. Each would have to make its own decision, according to its circumstances. This is to acknowledge, however, that the theoretical ideal of focusing on mainstreaming AIDS and then forming complementary partnerships may not be practical in many situations, and that, given the imperative to do AIDS work, many organisations may still prioritise their direct response to AIDS over the strategy of mainstreaming.

Monitoring and evaluation

Monitoring and evaluation are notoriously weak components of much development work, and mainstreaming AIDS is, so far, no exception. However, monitoring and evaluation are critical for learning about what is effective, for ensuring that modifications resulting from mainstreaming do not do more harm than good, and for assessing the impact of mainstreaming AIDS. Advocacy for mainstreaming AIDS also needs documented examples of its positive effects; the theoretical arguments in this book need to be supported by data from actual experience.

Suitable means of measuring progress in terms of process, outcomes, and impact need to be generated by practitioners, to fit the work that they are doing and the things that they are trying to achieve. However, it is possible to outline some general ideas here. For example, all levels of main-streaming involve training and capacity building, and a clear indicator of progress is the fact that a workshop has happened. But organising a workshop is not the same as building capacity, nor is receiving feedback from participants that they enjoyed the workshop the same as demons-trating benefit in terms of improved knowledge, skills, confidence, or motivation. Workshops which fail to achieve these outcomes waste precious resources and will undermine the mainstreaming process. Preliminary and follow-up workshop questionnaires, such as that presented in Unit 3, are a quick and low-cost way of approximately assessing outcomes. They also help to focus managers' and trainers' minds on defining the aims of the workshop. Crucially, the results of workshop evaluations can help to improve future workshops on the same topic, and reveal outstanding issues in need of attention. Trainers' observations from a workshop should also be instructive, but it should be remembered that they are probably subjective, in the sense that trainers may have a vested interest in portraying the process as successful.

Monitoring and evaluation needs not only to seek and record process and outcome indicators, but also to assess impact. For example, a workshop about modifying an agricultural project has outcomes in terms of agreed modifications, including ensuring that vulnerable adolescents are included in agricultural training and use inputs offered by extension workers. The workshop participants agree on a single indicator to capture the outcomes of the modifications: the proportion of heads of household (or acting heads of household, caring for bedridden elders) aged under 25 in receipt of loans of rabbits. They also agree that extension agents should record who gets livestock loans, noting the age and sex of the head of household, or acting head. The workshop participants set the target that the vulnerable adolescents should form 20 per cent of the total recipients within two years, and that at least 50 per cent of those receiving livestock loans should be female. Over time, the indicator will allow project staff to track whether the modification is implemented, and to what extent against the target.

Monitoring and evaluation of mainstreaming AIDS needs to build on existing systems of data collection and analysis.

However, staff will also need to track the impact and sustainability of the measure. They could use quantitative methods, such as tracking changes in the adolescents' asset levels, but that would be very time-consuming. Qualitative measures in the form of adolescents' personal accounts may be more feasible and sufficient. Another measure would be to track the rate of loan default among different groups within the project. This would reveal if the modification had altered the cost-effectiveness of the project, and provide warning of any threat to sustainability, or need to change procedures. For example, if the adolescents had a very high default rate, staff might need to reconsider whether or not the modification of targeting adolescents with livestock loans is sustainable. Alternatively, if the adolescents' rate of loan default is lower than average, this might suggest that they could form a greater proportion of the overall total.

It is important to note that monitoring and evaluation of mainstreaming AIDS needs to build on existing systems of data collection and analysis. Special measures are required only for the mainstreaming pilot process, until it ceases to be a special project and has become institutionalised. For example, one planned outcome of internal mainstreaming might be to ensure that attention to AIDS is included in induction programmes, job descriptions, and employee appraisals within 12 months. The personnel department sets the process in motion, and assesses progress at the end of the year. It also tries to assess the impact by checking appraisal records, and by talking with staff members, to learn about their attitudes to AIDS as part of their work, and any action they may have taken. If the measures do not seem to be working – for example, many staff are unaware that AIDS features in their job descriptions – then managers and personnel staff would need to consider how to improve them, or to try other measures. However, if the measures seemed to be helping to spread responsibility for AIDS widely within the organisation, they would then become part of standard procedures.

One critical aspect of assessing internal mainstreaming is the need to maintain confidentiality.

One critical aspect of assessing internal mainstreaming is the need to maintain confidentiality. It would not be appropriate, for example, to release data on the number of staff claiming certain benefits because they are HIV-positive. Clinics can use codes rather than names to protect the identity of those who are claiming HIV-related treatment, but in small organisations using the number of claimants as an indicator of the success of a workplace policy would be intrusive. There are, however, other measures which can track the impacts of AIDS on staff and the effects of workplace policies on staff and the organisation without compromising confidentiality. Unit 5 (pages 311–15) presents some ideas, and a few are mentioned here.

Staff attitudes and practices – for example, concerning condoms, counselling, alcohol use, and sexual relationships with community members – could be tracked by means of an anonymous questionnaire, administered once a year. Numbers of days' absence could be recorded by category, such as sickness, sickness of a dependant, compassionate leave, funeral, or holiday. This information could be presented in the form of averages, or in large organisations as averages for different types of worker, categorised for instance by sex or by grade; recording and comparing it year by year would help to update predictions of the impacts of AIDS on the organisation. Financial impacts could be monitored not only in terms of the average medical cost per person, but also as the percentage of staff reaching the maximum allowable expenditure, or other measures appropriate to the workplace policy. For monitoring the cost of treatment, and to allow more accurate budgeting, medical or insurance costs could be calculated and tracked as a percentage of the overall expenditure on salaries. If an organisation does incur AIDS-specific costs, such as the cost of antiretroviral treatment, then these could be analysed as distinct costs, provided that confidentiality is protected.

Finally, an organisation's monitoring and evaluation measures need to be realistic, in two senses. First, the expectations of mainstreaming (or, indeed, direct AIDS work) must be achievable and measurable. The familiar project goal of 'minimising HIV transmission' fulfils neither of those criteria. Expecting a partner agency to mainstream AIDS, and requiring the process to have an impact on its work within the final year of funding is similarly unrealistic. Second, very complex methods of monitoring progress and measuring impact may be too expensive and time-consuming to be justifiable. Reasonable methods do require time and commitment, but it may be necessary to rely on proxies and compromises to prevent excessive demands.

Shared learning and networking

Once organisations can, by virtue of their monitoring and evaluation, confidently identify their successes and failures, in order to learn from each other they need to share their experiences. At present organisations lack specific means for exchanging lessons from mainstreaming AIDS. To date, efforts to share ideas about mainstreaming AIDS have mainly been appended to modes of sharing which are focused on AIDS work, such as a satellite session at the 2002 World HIV/AIDS Conference, and short articles in newsletters about HIV/AIDS. However, these modes of information exchange, focused on AIDS work, are unlikely to nurture or accommodate increasing levels of dialogue about mainstreaming AIDS, given the continued need for communication on the many aspects of direct responses to AIDS. Moreover, the mainstreaming agenda needs to draw in people from outside the community of AIDS experts and AIDS activists. While those people may be involved in mainstreaming AIDS, the learning process will be based on the experiences of professionals and practitioners from ordinary development and humanitarian work.

For proponents of AIDS mainstreaming, there appear to be three reinforcing strategies to follow. First, to continue to broaden the AIDS agenda to include mainstreaming AIDS, using existing AIDS publications and forums. Second, to promote the idea through existing modes of information exchange for wider development work, such as generic or sector-specific conferences, workshops, journals, and newsletters. This might be done most effectively by development professionals, rather than by AIDS specialists. Third, to develop new streams of learning and sharing about mainstreaming AIDS: for example, local workshops or networks. The gradual spread of access to the Internet among development organisations provides new low-cost opportunities for debate and exchange on the issue, for example, through web pages and virtual networks.

Summary

This chapter has presented some of the issues and challenges inherent in the concept of mainstreaming AIDS. It concludes Part III of the book, which has aimed to synthesise all the experiences and ideas from the case studies and the literature that were reviewed for this book, in order to present ideas for mainstreaming AIDS internally and externally. The third part of the book has put forward some common-sense principles which have a good deal in common with general good practice in development:

- Involve staff and beneficiaries.

- Listen to the most vulnerable people.

- Learn from the process, including the mistakes.

- Pay attention to policy and practice.

- Monitor and evaluate.

At the heart of all this is the idea that mainstreaming AIDS can result in practical changes which make genuine differences, and that those differences can help organisations to function effectively, and to work indirectly against AIDS, despite the impacts of AIDS on their staff and on community members.

The ideas proposed here have covered a full mainstreaming process, which might be replicated among many field offices, or among organisations and their partners. Mainstreaming AIDS does not, however, appear to be an 'all or nothing' process. Mainstreaming internally but not externally is better than not mainstreaming at all. Providing staff with condoms but not voluntary counselling and HIV testing is better than nothing. The comprehensive approach described here – predicting impact, building capacity, fully supporting staff, establishing a workplace policy, changing personnel and financial procedures, conducting community research, modifying programmes, developing preparedness, and adapting systems – may be desirable but difficult. Every organisation considering mainstreaming AIDS needs to determine its own priorities, and the extent to which it can commit itself to the whole process, as illustrated in Table 11.2 (page 222). Similarly, every organisation needs to make strategic decisions about the relative emphases to place on mainstreaming AIDS in its ordinary work and on doing direct AIDS work.

15 Conclusion

Good development work is, indirectly, AIDS work

In June 2001 the United Nations held a General Assembly Special Session devoted to HIV/AIDS, with the aim of intensifying international action and mobilising resources to fight the pandemic. The Special Session resulted in a Declaration of Commitment, which was signed by 180 countries. Among many other commitments, the signatory nations agreed by 2003 to

> ...have in place strategies, policies and programmes that identify and begin to address those factors that make individuals particularly vulnerable to HIV infection, including underdevelopment, economic insecurity, poverty, lack of empowerment of women, lack of education, social exclusion, illiteracy, discrimination, lack of information and/or commodities for self-protection, all types of sexual exploitation of women, girls and boys, including for commercial reasons.
> (UNAIDS 2002d:22)

This book, in essence, has argued not that those factors should be addressed in order to respond to AIDS, but that development work to address those factors is vital in its own right, and needs to be relevant to the context of AIDS. In countries which are highly affected by AIDS, development and humanitarian organisations are engaged in tackling inequality and poverty in a situation where AIDS relentlessly compounds and deepens those problems. This book has proposed that those organisations can use internal mainstreaming of AIDS to reduce and cope with the impacts of AIDS, and so continue with their work to tackle inequality and poverty, despite the effects of AIDS on their employees and on their functioning. The book has further argued that development and humanitarian organisations need to mainstream AIDS externally in order to ensure that their programme work is responsive to the changes in societies and families brought about by AIDS. Fundamentally, the book has presented an additional strategy to that of responding to AIDS directly through AIDS work: it has defined and proposed ideas for the option of mainstreaming AIDS, in the interests of ensuring that existing development and humanitarian work is indirectly working to address, and not exacerbate, the AIDS pandemic.

Chapter 2 presented a model which illustrated how the causes of susceptibility to HIV infection and the consequences of vulnerability to the impacts of AIDS reinforce each other, and showed that both are intimately connected to key issues of under-development, poverty, and gender inequality. While HIV-prevention work is important, it is not sufficient – because it cannot address the underlying causes of susceptibility to HIV infection. Equally, while work involving care and treatment of people living with AIDS is essential, it may not tackle vulnerability to the consequences of AIDS, particularly among the not-yet-affected. A second model in Chapter 2 illustrated how AIDS work and development work interact and reinforce each other, to form an alliance which addresses HIV and AIDS more holistically.

Chapter 5 argued that, despite advances in treatment for HIV-positive people and evidence from a few countries that behaviour change can affect local AIDS epidemics, the problem of AIDS is endemic and has no obvious solution. Organisations concerned to respond to AIDS therefore require a long-term perspective, because they are not dealing with an epidemic which is expected to peak and then recede. The menu of possible responses to AIDS is, at present, limited to direct measures: education, condom promotion, voluntary counselling and HIV testing, promotion of 'positive living', care, support, treatment of opportunistic infections, antiretroviral therapy, support for orphans. To that menu, this book has argued, should be added development and humanitarian work with AIDS mainstreamed in it. Development and humanitarian work, when well done, is indirect AIDS work. Consider the comments of this man in northern Ghana:

> The seed banks have helped me and my family a lot. I remember some years ago... a lot of our young men and women left the village during the hungry period to seek greener pastures in the big cities... a lot of them went and did not return to their spouses again, thus causing a lot of marriages to break. But today things are different. The grain banks have made it possible for me and everybody in this village to have access to grains at any time of the year, and very cheap too. As I am talking there is a lot of millet stocked in the bank, so my wife doesn't need to travel any long distance to buy it. There is always enough to eat, and you can see the children looking happy and healthy and playing.
> (ActionAid 2002b:12)

The ActionAid project to which he refers aimed to improve food security. There is no mention of AIDS in the project proposal, nor in the achievements of the project. And yet the project has indirectly reduced young people's susceptibility to HIV infection, and (in addition to its other benefits) may help households to cope with the impacts of illness. This book proposes that if the project staff were to learn about and act on the idea of mainstreaming AIDS, their food-security work might make an even more positive response to the problems posed by the pandemic. They might, for example, decide to investigate and deal with unseen ways in which the project could be inadvertently increasing susceptibility to HIV transmission and vulnerability to the impacts of AIDS.

Furthermore, not only is development work, when well done, indirect AIDS work, but development work with AIDS mainstreamed in it may sometimes be more appropriate than specialised AIDS work targeted at AIDS-affected households. For example, in countries such as Tanzania where there are low levels of school enrolment, it may be more cost-effective, and more equitable, to invest in improving the education system itself, for the benefit of all children, including those who are vulnerable, rather than focusing resources on getting orphans enrolled (Ainsworth and Filmer 2002:32). And savings and credit schemes designed to help poor households to improve their livelihood security may be more sustainable, and yield greater benefits, than schemes which exclusively serve people who know that they are HIV-positive. In an ideal world, the population as a whole would have access to good-quality basic services of education and health care, which would include special measures for people affected by AIDS. In the real world, politicians, planners, and development professionals are faced with difficult choices. This book has argued that continuing with development work, but with AIDS mainstreamed in it, is the most effective course of action for mainstream development organisations which cannot realistically both mainstream AIDS and do AIDS work.

Development work with AIDS mainstreamed in it may sometimes be more appropriate than specialised AIDS work targeted at AIDS-affected households.

It is interesting to note that where organisations propose special measures to meet the needs of AIDS-affected households, in practice the criterion for accessing the special measures tends to become not AIDS itself, but the vulnerability and impoverishment of the households. While 'AIDS-affected' is a useful phrase, many organisations realise that targeting on the basis of AIDS may increase stigma, and may also be unfair. For example, a household with some assets and good support systems whose head had died of AIDS would be eligible for assistance, while a landless and isolated household whose head had died from alcoholism would not. Moreover, the notion of 'AIDS-affected' becomes meaningless in communities with a long-established HIV epidemic, where every household is affected by AIDS in some way. Organisations which seek to mainstream AIDS need to understand and respond to the particular consequences of AIDS, by learning from AIDS-affected households. However, development organisations do not necessarily have to reorientate their work to focus on serving AIDS-affected households.

The need to keep focused on core development work which tackles the causes of susceptibility to HIV infection and reduces vulnerability to the consequences of AIDS is very evident at the level of government policy and public services. In highly affected countries, alongside AIDS work, it is crucial for governments to invest in poverty-reduction efforts, including preventing public services from collapsing, and promoting gender equality. As Loewenson and Whiteside (2001:16) have stated,

> Poverty reduction strategies need to be backed by pro-poor policies to secure the educational needs of youth and orphans, ensure access to shelter and social services, enhance food security, ensure access to safe water, and provide an adequate income security to deal with the consumption needs generated by AIDS.

Although this book has focused on the idea of mainstreaming AIDS at the local level, through the work of NGOs, CBOs, and local government, the concept of mainstreaming AIDS applies equally to national and international policies. Collins and Rau (2000:56) argue that every level of development work has a role to play:

> ...mainstreaming implies training extension workers to recognise signs of agricultural stress due to labour shortages or asset constraints. Mainstreaming stimulates agricultural planners to promote labour-saving crops or labour-sharing systems. It should encourage agricultural and finance ministers and banks to loosen credit, increase farm prices, and reintroduce subsidies on basic foodstuffs. Mainstreaming involves doing—or doing better—what one is supposed to be doing anyway.

Integrating AIDS work or mainstreaming AIDS?

This book has distinguished between the strategies of AIDS work and mainstreaming AIDS. It has also described the 'imperative of AIDS work' which partly explains why direct responses predominate in development and humanitarian work to date. The book has proposed that internal and external mainstreaming of AIDS is an essential, and often more appropriate, initial response to AIDS for development and humanitarian organisations, rather than doing AIDS work alone or – the other option – doing nothing. However, the book has not suggested that the strategy of mainstreaming AIDS should replace that of responding directly to AIDS through AIDS work; both strategies are needed, and they complement each other. Some organisations, in particular the larger and relatively well-resourced ones, may have the capacity to undertake both strategies.

For example, in northern Tanzania the NGO ACORD runs a Low External Inputs for Sustainable Agriculture (LEISA) programme, which promotes inexpensive and modest techniques and technologies, such as applying manure and ashes as fertilisers, using ashes and herbs for pest control, using inter-cropping to suppress weeds, making micro water-catchment areas in fields, applying ethno-veterinary practices to improve the quality of livestock, and using locally made wheelbarrows to ease agricultural work. ACORD reports that between 1995 and 2000 the LEISA project led to an average increase in crop production of 51 per cent, and an increase in livestock production of around 100 per cent. Food security among participating farmers greatly improved, while the cost of inputs declined, because farmers had substantially reduced their dependence on industrial inputs. Moreover, sales of market-garden produce had boosted the incomes of participating households. ACORD believes that the LEISA programme has not only made a significant impact on resource-poor farmers, who have been able to increase their crop and livestock productivity while investing less labour and less money, but has also been particularly suited to households affected by AIDS.

This outcome, in a region with a generalised HIV epidemic, was not an accident, but the result of listening to farmers and responding to their needs. (At the outset, the agency had proposed a different strategy of helping farmers to increase productivity by increasing the use of industrial inputs, which the farmers felt was expensive and unsustainable.) Although ACORD does not describe a process of mainstreaming AIDS as such, the project was relevant to the problem because community members were concerned about AIDS and its impacts, and the project was adjusted accordingly. ACORD decided also to respond to AIDS directly, by raising awareness and setting up informal methods of counselling and home-based care. The NGO also established an AIDS Support Fund to uphold the legal and inheritance rights of orphans and widows, and it offers credit for income-generating activities through the government's Village Widow and Orphans Committees. The project was able to initiate, and to some extent to integrate, AIDS work because ACORD already had technical expertise in implementing AIDS projects, on which the LEISA project was able to draw (White 2002:45-50).

However, although the LEISA project appears to have been able to respond to AIDS indirectly through external mainstreaming and directly through AIDS work, other organisations may not manage to adopt both strategies without compromising the quality of their work. As such, many organisations wishing to respond to AIDS will have to make a strategic choice: whether to focus on AIDS work or on external mainstreaming of AIDS. While this book argues that all organisations should consider undertaking internal mainstreaming, it is hoped that by presenting the case for external mainstreaming organisations will, at least, have a sense that AIDS work is not the only option for responding to AIDS through programme work. The limited experience to date suggests that organisations are unlikely to undertake 'pure' mainstreaming, because of the strength of the imperative to do at least some AIDS work.

Two of the case studies commissioned for this book raised the question of whether integrating AIDS work might be a first step towards mainstreaming AIDS. The evidence from the three sponsoring agencies perhaps suggests otherwise. On the one hand, ActionAid and Save the Children UK have focused their commitment and resources on responding to AIDS through supporting AIDS work, with the result that mainstreaming AIDS has received comparatively little attention. On the other hand, in Southern Africa Oxfam has made rapid progress in piloting mainstreaming of AIDS, partly because it has committed resources to that strategy, which it selected in preference (initially) to expanding its support for AIDS work. It is possible that having integrated AIDS work might help the process of mainstreaming AIDS, if it means that the organisation and its staff gain a thorough understanding of the related issues. However, if the organisation and staff see AIDS as a special issue, and tend to focus on AIDS-specific problems and responses, then having integrated AIDS work might inhibit the mainstreaming of AIDS.

Prospects for mainstreaming AIDS

This book has described many barriers to mainstreaming AIDS, along with a range of problems which have arisen from gender mainstreaming. One interpretation, therefore, is that the prospects for mainstreaming AIDS are rather bleak. However, there are a number of reasons for a more optimistic prognosis.

First, some organisations are aware that direct AIDS work is a worthwhile but inadequate response. Their behaviour-change programmes are not potent enough to stop girls and women from trading sex for favours, or to empower them to insist on safer sex, nor to persuade poor men that they should compromise their present pleasures in order to prioritise the need to protect their future health. And organisations that support people living with AIDS find that they can help individuals to accept and manage their HIV status, but cannot undertake the development programmes which might lift their households from poverty, and break the reinforcing cycle of the causes and consequences of AIDS. Although AIDS work is seen to be the default response to AIDS, there is a growing realisation among organisations of all sizes that the complexity of the problem demands a wider range of responses. Along with 'impact mitigation', the idea of mainstreaming AIDS is now attracting attention and interest.

A second factor which may advance mainstreaming is that in highly affected countries the impacts of AIDS on organisations and communities are becoming obvious and hard to ignore. Sick employees, vacant posts, low morale, and rising health-care costs all illustrate the need for internal mainstreaming of AIDS. The business sector has more experience in internal mainstreaming than the not-for-profit sector, partly because it is motivated more by self-interest and the need to protect profit margins. However, NGOs, like commercial companies, wish to survive, and are beginning to recognise the need to protect themselves from AIDS, and to take action to preserve their ability to function effectively despite AIDS. Similarly, external mainstreaming is also likely to be stimulated when organisations experience the impacts of AIDS on their work, such as low levels of participation, and failing development projects. The way in which organisations, employees, and community members are experiencing the impacts of AIDS also suggests that mainstreaming AIDS may be more attuned to their priorities, and less controversial, than the idea of mainstreaming gender.

Mainstreaming does not ask all organisations and ministries and employees to step out of their sector and become AIDS workers, or AIDS educators, or AIDS activists.

Third, there are some aspects of mainstreaming which may make it a more attractive and viable prospect than the proposition that all sectors should engage in AIDS work. Fundamentally, mainstreaming does not ask all organisations and ministries and employees to step out of their sector and to become AIDS workers, or AIDS educators, or AIDS activists. Instead it proposes that they augment their existing professional expertise by learning ways to take account of gender, AIDS, and sexual health. In addition, the mainstreaming process does not require community members to prioritise AIDS as a problem, and it does not require organisations to impose an agenda of AIDS work. Both parties can still focus on community priorities, but with concerns about susceptibility to HIV infection and vulnerability to the impacts of AIDS built into the project as appropriate.

A fourth reason for optimism with regard to the prospects for mainstreaming is that it is beginning to happen; books such as this are part of a growing movement concerned with learning about mainstreaming AIDS and developing good practice. And success breeds success. Within the Oxfam Southern Africa region, the number of people involved in mainstreaming AIDS has grown as the pilot project in Malawi has developed and is generating interest in other countries. It is hoped that gradually the regional programme will build up a critical mass of employees and partners who understand and are practising mainstreaming. Furthermore, with Oxfam's commitment to sharing lessons, networking, and promoting mainstreaming, other organisations should also become involved, and specialist support organisations may emerge.

In conclusion, this book argues that mainstreaming AIDS internally and externally is both necessary and possible. Readers may contest the argument for mainstreaming, but perhaps this book will further stimulate and contribute to the debate about expanding the response to AIDS. However, the only way to test the book's assertion that mainstreaming can maximise the way in which development and humanitarian programmes work indirectly against HIV and AIDS is through experiment and practice. HIV and AIDS have radically changed the context of development and humanitarian work, and now development and humanitarian work needs to change accordingly.

Resources

Part III of the book presented some general ideas for mainstreaming AIDS. This section offers some practical suggestions to help readers to consider how they might apply the ideas in their own organisations.

Some of the suggestions are based on the actual work of agencies featured in the case studies, but others are suggestions which have not (yet) been applied in real-life conditions. All of them are intended as food for thought, rather than tried and tested tools which are ready to use without any adaptation.

Internal mainstreaming

Unit 1   Researching the current internal impacts of AIDS

Unit 2   Predicting the internal impacts of AIDS

Unit 3   Assessing the impacts of AIDS education

Unit 4   Devising or adapting a workplace policy

Unit 5   Monitoring the internal impacts of AIDS and the effects of internal mainstreaming

Mainstreaming in development work

Unit 6   Training for mainstreaming AIDS in development work

Unit 7   Undertaking community research for mainstreaming AIDS in development work

Unit 8   Adapting organisational systems

Mainstreaming in humanitarian work

Unit 9   Training for mainstreaming AIDS in humanitarian work

Unit 10   Undertaking community research for mainstreaming AIDS in humanitarian work

Unit 1: Researching the current internal impacts of AIDS

This unit addresses the task of investigating the current impacts of AIDS within an organisation. It sets out the types of question that your organisation might want to ask its employees or volunteers, in order to learn from them. For example, the findings should show whether AIDS is seen as an issue affecting the organisation as a whole, or only parts of it. They should also provide important information on the extent to which the organisation is seen to be a supportive environment in which infected and/or affected people can work without fear of stigma or discrimination. The unit also includes some ideas for needs assessment, which should inform your organisation's next steps in internal mainstreaming of AIDS.

Staff questionnaire

A questionnaire is a useful means of gathering comparable quantitative data and some qualitative feedback from large numbers of people. A self-administered questionnaire also has the advantage that respondents can reply anonymously (and therefore frankly).

- Your organisation could send its questionnaire to all employees, or to a representative sample of staff.

- If referring directly to AIDS seems too blunt, you could instead refer to chronic or terminal illnesses, giving some examples of what you mean.

- The questionnaire should clearly state that it is confidential and anonymous. Employees could post their completed copies in a box, so that they do not have to hand them to anyone in person.

- Ask respondents to say if they are male or female, and to give other information which is useful for effective internal mainstreaming, but which will not compromise confidentiality. For example, it may be interesting to know if there are differences in the opinions and experiences of staff in different salary bands or types of job, or among people based in different places.

- If your organisation has good records of sick leave and related matters, some of the questions may be unnecessary.

- Questions from this questionnaire could be incorporated in an annual survey of employees' knowledge, attitudes, and practice concerning

AIDS, as part of the process of monitoring the impacts of internal mainstreaming (see Unit 5 on pages 311–5).

Experiences

The following questions concern employees' opinions about AIDS and your organisation (which is referred to here as 'XYZ'). Here are some suggested themes (presented in italics and not intended to be reproduced in the actual questionnaire) and some possible questions.

A question about employees' sense of AIDS in XYZ

- In your view, are HIV and AIDS present among your XYZ colleagues?
  1 Not at all
  2 Hardly at all
  3 Maybe
  4 Probably
  5 Definitely

Questions about employees' attitudes and organisational culture

- With regard to general conversations about HIV/AIDS among XYZ staff, we
  1 Never talk about it
  2 Rarely talk about it
  3   Sometimes talk about it
  4 Often talk about it
  5 Talk about it all the time

- With regard to talking about personal issues related to HIV and AIDS, we are generally
  1 Very secretive
  2 Secretive
  3 Inclined to confide in one or two people
  4 Inclined to confide in several people
  5 Completely open

- In terms of reacting to colleagues who have HIV/AIDS, or whose partners have HIV/AIDS, we are generally
  1 Very unsupportive
  2 Unsupportive
  3 Neutral
  4 Supportive
  5 Very supportive

- Please add anything else that you would like to say about attitudes towards HIV/AIDS among your colleagues.

Questions about employees' observations of the impacts of AIDS on XYZ

- To what extent do you think that AIDS has affected morale among staff at XYZ?
  1 Very badly affected
  2 Badly affected
  3 Some effects
  4 A little affected
  5 Not affected at all

- To what extent do you think that HIV and AIDS have increased the amount of time that employees at XYZ are absent from work?
  1 Increased enormously
  2 Increased a lot
  3 Increased
  4 Increased a little
  5 No increase at all

- Please add anything else that you want to say about the impacts of AIDS within your workplace.

Questions about personal impacts of AIDS on employees

- Have you or a close relative suffered from sickness due to HIV/AIDS?

- How many dependent children do you have in total?

- How many of them have become dependent on you as a result of HIV/AIDS?

- To what extent has HIV/AIDS affected the amount of time that you are absent from work?
  1 Increased enormously
  2 Increased a lot
  3 Increased
  4 Increased a little
  5 No increase at all

- Please rank the types of leave that you use for reasons associated with HIV/AIDS, marking the type of leave that you use most frequently as 1, through to 5 for the type that you use least frequently:

  __ Sick leave

  __ Compassionate leave

  __ Time off to attend funerals

  __ Annual holiday leave

  __ Unofficial leave

- Please add anything else that you would like to say about the impacts of AIDS on you and your work.

Needs

These questions aim to gain an understanding of the AIDS-related problems that employees face in the workplace, and the priorities that they accord to various courses of action that XYZ might take.

The questions here are only suggestions; they would need to be adapted to suit your organisation, according to the policies, benefits, and staff-support services already in place. When asking staff about their needs, you should try to avoid raising their expectations. For example, you could state that the questionnaire is part of a process of assessing costs and deciding what the organisation can and cannot afford to do.

- What are the main problems that you experience with regard to HIV/AIDS and its impacts on your workplace?
- How do you rate the current XYZ health scheme?
  1 Very poor
  2 Poor
  3 OK
  4 Good
  5 Very good

- Here is a list of things that XYZ might be able to do to support you and your colleagues. Please rank them from 1 to 10, with **1** being the measure that you consider most important, and **10** being your lowest priority.

  __ Provide education about HIV and AIDS and free condoms to all staff.

  __ Get HIV/AIDS covered by the health scheme.

  __ Give staff access to confidential counselling and HIV testing.

  __ Increase the maximum level of benefits that each employee can claim from the health scheme.

  __ Give staff access to legal advice.

  __ Increase the number of dependants that each employee can include in the health scheme.

  __ Tackle stigma and discrimination with regard to HIV and AIDS within XYZ.

  __ Make special benefits available to staff members with AIDS.

  __ Set up a savings and credit scheme for staff.

  __ Allow staff to record hours worked overtime, and to take that time off at a later date.

- Can you suggest other ways in which XYZ might support its staff with regard to AIDS?

- Please add anything else that you would like to say about the problems and needs of staff in relation to AIDS.

Interviews with key respondents

The staff questionnaire should result in some comparable information. For example, the findings might show that a quarter of all staff have taken on extra responsibilities for children as a result of AIDS, and that female staff are absent from work more often as a result. Or that the respondents accorded top priority to improving the health scheme among the things that they would like the organisation to do. The open questions might also result in some unexpected findings: for example, accusations from respondents in one programme that some staff are getting higher benefits than other employees.

To gain a more detailed understanding of the impacts of AIDS, your organisation might also consider conducting interviews with key members of staff, such as personnel officers or managers. If the interviews take place after the analysis of the questionnaires, the key informants may be asked to respond to the findings and to add information. For example, they might be asked to give their impressions of how AIDS is affecting male and female members of staff differently, or their experience of administering the health scheme and its limitations, or responding to accusations of unfair treatment of employees.

Topics to discuss with key respondents might include the following.

- Organisational culture and staff attitudes towards AIDS.

- Existence of any data which might show the impacts of AIDS, such as rates of sick leave.

- Impressions of impacts of AIDS on XYZ, such as low staff morale, and reduced productivity.

- Reasons for staff absenteeism, trends, types of leave taken.

- How cases of AIDS among employees have been handled, and with what outcomes for the organisation and the employees.

- Rate of staff turnover and ease with which XYZ can recruit qualified replacements.

- Prospects and means for improving XYZ's internal response to AIDS.

Unit 2: Predicting the internal impacts of AIDS

This unit is concerned with trying to predict the possible future impacts of AIDS on an organisation. By undertaking such predictions, organisations can anticipate and address likely problems, such as high medical costs or damaging levels of absenteeism. The process can also help to assess the costs and benefits of various ways of responding to AIDS within the workplace.

The spreadsheet chart gives a fictional example of calculations to assess the impacts of AIDS over five years on a medium-sized organisation. It should be noted that all the figures in the chart are invented, and not derived from any real organisation. They are presented in order to demonstrate the ideas, but the numbers themselves are meaningless; for example, the costs given do not relate to any real currency. Any organisation making its own predictions would need to produce all its own figures, including HIV-prevalence rates, and the likely proportion of HIV-positive employees with AIDS.

The basic model

The model presented here is a simple and crude one. It is offered because very little guidance is available to NGOs and other organisations which cannot afford to undertake a full institutional audit. It is based on work done by Oxfam GB, but it has not been tried and tested, in the sense of monitoring the outputs against several years' experience.

- As with any attempt to predict impact, the results depend on a series of assumptions.

- The results will be more accurate if the organisation already collects data on variables such as the costs of staff benefits, and levels of absenteeism, with which to inform the assumptions. Alternatively, the assumptions might be based on the results of research into the current impacts of AIDS on the organisation (see Unit 1), or on data from comparable organisations.

- Data on HIV prevalence among particular groups of people, the proportion of HIV-positive people who have AIDS, and predicted trends in HIV prevalence are all needed for the calculations. The nation's AIDS Commission is one place to start this research; NGOs or

ASOs may also be able to help. UNAIDS Fact Sheets summarise the available national-level data, including the results from surveillance sites, for almost every country in the world. (See the bibliography at the end of this book.)

Building on the basic model

- If an organisation had different types of employees or volunteers who were thought to have different rates of HIV infection, it could do a separate chart for each group. This would make the overall analysis more accurate. However, there would be a danger of discrimination if, for example, the results were used to argue against employing certain kinds of people.

- An organisation would also need to construct separate charts if different types of people within the organisation were entitled to different benefits.

- The analysis could be extended to cover ten or more years.

- The analysis could be made more comprehensive by including more variables. For example, if the organisation pays for the medical costs of employees' dependants, then that should be included. The analysis could also take into account the effect of employee absences caused by caring for sick relatives, and attending funerals, plus the costs of recruitment and training for new staff.

- For a 'worst case' scenario, the organisation would need to modify all the assumptions pessimistically: for example, to allow for a higher rate of HIV infection, and higher levels of leave taking. Similarly, by making more optimistic assumptions it could derive a 'best case' assessment.

- The spreadsheet can also be used to assess the costs of possible changes to policies by changing any of the variables. For example, it is easy to see the effect of altering the level of the terminal benefit, or of changing the maximum allowable health-care costs per person.

- The analysis could also be extended to explore the effects of paying for antiretroviral treatment, by estimating the costs of such treatment, and modifying assumptions concerning the proportion of staff developing AIDS, the proportion leaving, and absenteeism among staff with AIDS.

Predicting the internal impacts of AIDS: a fictional example

	Year 1	Year 2	Year 3	Year 4	Year 5	Notes and assumptions
Predicting the prevalence of HIV and AIDS within the organisation						
A: number of employees	100	100	100	100	100	Assume staff levels are static
B: assumed proportion of employees who are HIV+	20%	22%	24%	27%	29%	HIV trends suggest 10% growth per annum
A x B = **C:** estimated number of HIV+ employees	20	22	24	27	29	
D: assumed proportion of HIV+ employees with AIDS	15%	15%	15%	15%	15%	Use national average of 15% of HIV+ people at stage 4 of HIV infection
C x D = **E:** estimated number of employees developing AIDS each year	3.0	3.3	3.6	4.0	4.4	
F: estimated number of employees leaving due to AIDS, by the end of each year	1.5	2.4	3.4	3.7	4.1	Assume 50% leave at end of year, 25% at end of next year, remaining 25% at end of third year
Predicting direct financial costs						
G: maximum allowable health costs per employee	1,000	1,050	1,103	1,158	1,216	Assume 5% inflation
A x (30% of G) = **H:** likely health costs, without AIDS	30,000	31,500	33,075	34,729	36,465	Assume average employee uses 30% of maximum
(A - E) x (30% of G) = **I:** likely health costs for employees without AIDS	29,100	30,461	31,874	33,342	34,864	
E x G = **J:** likely health costs for employees with AIDS	3,000	3,465	4,002	4,622	5,339	Assume staff with AIDS will use maximum of allowable health costs
(I + J - H)/H = **estimated percentage increase in health costs as a result of AIDS**	7%	8%	8%	9%	10%	
K: average terminal benefit entitlement	1,500	1,575	1,654	1,736	1,823	Average payout, assume 5% inflation
F x K = **cost of terminal benefits paid due to AIDS**	**2,250**	**3,780**	**5,606**	**6,475**	**7,479**	
Predicting absenteeism						
L: maximum allowable days of sick leave per employee	50	50	50	50	50	Per year; average employee uses 50% of this
M: maximum allowable days of unpaid leave per employee	60	60	60	60	60	Per year; average employee uses none of this
A x (50% of L) = **N:** likely absenteeism, without AIDS	2,500	2,500	2,500	2,500	2,500	
(A - E) x (50% of L) = **O:** likely absenteeism among employees without AIDS	2,425	2,418	2,409	2,400	2,390	
(E x L) + (E x M) = **P:** likely absenteeism among employees with AIDS	330	363	399	439	483	Assume staff with AIDS will take maximum sick leave and maximum unpaid leave
(O + P - N)/N = **estimated percentage increase in absenteeism as a result of AIDS**	**10%**	**11%**	**12%**	**14%**	**15%**	

For a worst-case scenario, modify all assumptions pessimistically, e.g. higher rate of HIV infection, and higher levels of leave taking. Similarly, adapt with more optimistic assumptions for a best-case assessment.

Unit 3: Assessing the impacts of AIDS education

It is common for organisations to consider AIDS-education sessions to have been successful simply because they have happened, and staff or volunteers have attended. But it is easy to assess the impact of a workshop on participants' knowledge and attitudes by giving them a questionnaire to fill in before the training, and the same questionnaire to complete after the training. If they fill in the questionnaire prior to the training, you can also use it as a form of needs assessment, to gauge, for example, how much participants know about HIV and AIDS, their attitudes towards people who are HIV-positive, and their perceptions of their own risk of becoming infected.

The questions should cover the topics that are being included in the training.

- They might include factual questions which test participants' knowledge, along with subjective questions about how they view or feel about various aspects of AIDS.

- In order to use the questionnaire as part of a needs assessment, you should ensure that the returned forms can be analysed in time to influence the content and emphasis of the workshop. This means either asking participants to fill in the questionnaire in advance (for example, on arrival at the workshop), or ensuring that someone will analyse the results during the workshop's introductory session.

- Ask participants to fill in and return the questionnaire immediately and alone; the results will be invalid if they go away and discuss with others what the 'right' answers might be.

The following questionnaire was used by ActionAid-The Gambia at a basic AIDS-awareness workshop and was supplemented, at the end of the workshop, with a qualitative evaluation in which the participants gave feedback on what they felt they had learned, and their opinions of the workshop process.

Anonymous questionnaire

Please fill in this form and put it in the box in the meeting room.

There is no need to give your name.

1 **Are you**
   ❑   a man or   ❑   a woman?

2 **In general, how can HIV be transmitted?**
   (Tick as many boxes as you like.)

   ❑   Toilets   ❑   Kissing

   ❑   Penetrative sex   ❑   Mosquitoes

   ❑   Shaking hands   ❑   Blood transfusions

   ❑   In the womb   ❑   Breast feeding

3 **If someone is infected with HIV, which of these statements is
   true?** *(Tick as many boxes as you like.)*

   ❑   He or she has AIDS.
   ❑   He or she may not have AIDS yet, but will almost certainly
       develop AIDS.
   ❑   He or she could stay healthy for a long time.
   ❑   He or she can pass HIV to other people only when he or
       she is sick.
   ❑   He or she could pass HIV to other people.

4 **In general, do you think that people who have sexually transmitted
   infections have been promiscuous?**
   1   Definitely
   2   Very likely
   3   Likely
   4   Perhaps
   5   Not likely

5   If you knew that one of your colleagues was infected with HIV,
    would you feel happy to continue working with him or her?

    1   Definitely
    2   Very likely
    3   Likely
    4   Perhaps
    5   Not likely

6   If you knew you had HIV but were in good health, would you tell
    someone at your workplace in confidence?

    1   Definitely
    2   Very likely
    3   Likely
    4   Perhaps
    5   Not likely

7   In general, do you think that male staff at your workplace are
    vulnerable to sexually transmitted infections and HIV?

    1   Definitely
    2   Very likely
    3   Likely
    4   Perhaps
    5   Not likely

8   In general, do you think that female staff at your workplace are
    vulnerable to sexually transmitted infections and HIV?

    1   Definitely
    2   Very likely
    3   Likely
    4   Perhaps
    5   Not likely

9   Do you think that you are vulnerable to STIs and HIV?

    1   Definitely
    2   Very likely
    3   Likely
    4   Perhaps
    5   Not likely

Note, the correct answers to the only two factual questions are as follows:

2   HIV can be transmitted through penetrative sex, in the womb, via blood transfusions, and via breast feeding.

3   If someone is infected with HIV, he or she may not have AIDS yet, but will almost certainly develop AIDS; could stay healthy for a long time; and could pass HIV to other people.

Unit 4: Devising or adapting a workplace policy

For any organisation, the process of drawing up and finalising a workplace policy which addresses HIV and AIDS can be quite lengthy. It is often HIV specialists who see the need for a policy, and who must then convince management and the personnel department. The people who are drafting the policy need to draw on special research into the current and predicted impacts of AIDS on the organisation (see Units 1 and 2), in addition to research into the organisation's options for providing health care and other benefits to its employees. They also need to take account of legal parameters such as the requirements of national law about employment terms and conditions. Organisations should consult staff about the draft policy, and may then need to revise it before the policy can be finalised.

The final content of each organisation's workplace policy depends on its own circumstances, its values, and the outcomes of the process of consultation. There are, however, a number of general principles of good practice in workplace policies concerning HIV/AIDS. For example, the Code of Good Practice on Key Aspects of HIV/AIDS and Employment from South Africa's Department of Labour Employment Equity Act (reproduced in Stein 2001:31) states that workplace policies should include the following features:

- the organisation's position on HIV/AIDS;

- an outline of the organisation's HIV/AIDS programme for staff;

- details of employment policies (for example, on HIV testing, employee benefits, performance management, and procedures to be followed to determine medical incapacity and dismissal);

- standards of behaviour expected of employers and employees and appropriate measures to deal with deviations from these standards;

- grievance procedures;

- the means of communication within the organisation on HIV/AIDS issues;

- details of employee assistance available to persons affected by HIV/AIDS;

- details of implementation and co-ordination responsibilities; and

- monitoring and evaluation mechanisms.

Family Health International has published a guide for managers about HIV/AIDS workplace programmes. With regard to workplace policies, it provides a comprehensive checklist of points to include, plus examples of the workplace policies adopted by two organisations, and case studies of implementation by eight businesses (Rau 2002: 38-40, 79-84, 85-101; see the bibliography for advice on how to obtain a copy).

The following example is from ActionAid's Global Organisation Development Framework (ActionAid 2001:22-24), which summarises the agency's core principles with regard to human-resources issues and gives guidance for policy development by all its programmes around the world. This ActionAid example does not present best practice as such – for example, it makes no mention of giving employees access to post-exposure prophylaxis following rape or occupational exposure to possible HIV infection. However, ActionAid's statement does set out the main issues in a clear and succinct way, to be used and adapted by its programmes according to their context.

ActionAid Global Organisation Development Framework: Appendix concerning Human Resources and HIV/AIDS and Terminal Illness, February 2001

Recruitment

Principles
During recruitment, ActionAid does not discriminate against people with HIV/AIDS and other terminal illness.

ActionAid encourages the recruitment of people with HIV/AIDS and other terminal illness.

Guidelines
HIV testing is not a requirement at any stage of the recruitment process.

There is no reference to HIV testing in recruitment material or advertising.

Staff development and training

Guidelines
HIV status or other terminal-illness status does not preclude staff from accessing training and career-development opportunities.

Staff training, induction, and orientation specifically address HIV/AIDS and other terminal illnesses, and include in-depth discussion of people's concerns and attitudes towards those living with HIV/AIDS and other terminal illness.

Staff welfare and benefits

Principles

ActionAid promotes, supports, and protects the well-being of its staff in the context of HIV/AIDS and other terminal illness.

People with HIV/AIDS or other terminal illness have the right to confidentiality about their health status.

Guidelines
Declaration

Any member of staff wishing to declare his/her HIV/AIDS status or other terminal-illness status can do so either through a counsellor or through a member of staff with line-management responsibility in ActionAid.

If a member of staff informs another of his/her HIV status or other terminal-illness status, this information is not disclosed to any other member of staff, including HR managers and medical personnel, without consent.

Prevention

Information and education on HIV/AIDS and other terminal illness is made available at all times.

In working areas where there is any possibility of accident, first-aid instructions are prominently displayed, explaining the universal precautions that need to be followed when dealing with blood.

There is first-aid training for staff in order to minimise hazards. Safe working conditions are ensured, and latex gloves are included in all first-aid kits. Where appropriate, condoms are provided on all work sites.

Staff are trained to take the strictest precautions regarding all contact with blood and body fluids as potential risk.

Support

ActionAid provides psycho-social support in the form of counselling to those who are traumatised as a result of getting infected by HIV/AIDS or other terminal illness.

Medical support is provided if a staff member declares his/her HIV/AIDS status or terminal-illness status.

Staff members with declared AIDS or any other terminal illness are entitled to a period of sick leave with pay.

Voluntary termination of employment

Staff members with AIDS or any other terminal illness will be advised to continue to work as long as they can and to take advantage of medical benefits. However, if a staff member requests that his or her services be terminated, he/she shall be granted gratuity and terminal benefits.

Redeployment and transfer

Guidelines

Any staff member who has declared his or her HIV/AIDS status or other terminal-illness status and becomes unable to work consistently in that position is re-deployed to a position and location more suitable to his or her condition.

Such re-deployment carries the existing salary, terms, and conditions.

Re-deployment or transfer is supported by counselling.

Grievance and discipline

Guideline

Refusal to work with or other discrimination against a staff member with HIV/AIDS or other terminal illness is unacceptable. In such situations, disciplinary action is taken.

Unit 5: Monitoring the internal impacts of AIDS and the effects of internal mainstreaming

This unit concerns monitoring results of the internal mainstreaming of AIDS; ideas for external mainstreaming are integrated within Units 6 to 10.

Organisations which have good internal monitoring systems are better able to assess the impacts that AIDS is having on them, and so are also able to make more accurate predictions about the likely future impacts of AIDS. Effective monitoring can also help organisations to gauge the effects of their efforts to mainstream AIDS internally.

Each organisation should select its own monitoring indicators according to its situation and capacity, and the internal mainstreaming activities that it is undertaking. This unit suggests some possible indicators, to stimulate thinking about what might be appropriate in your organisation.

- Organisations need to select a sufficient number and range of key indicators in order to monitor whether changes are occurring, while bearing in mind the costs of gathering and analysing the data.

- When organisations select indicators, they also need to consider the means of collecting the data (who and how) and the means of analysing it (again, who and how). This should ensure that the indicators are appropriate to the organisation's capacity, and that not only the indicators but also the method of monitoring are established.

- Indicators for the impacts of internal mainstreaming of AIDS must arise from each organisation's particular aims, priorities, and planned activities with regard to internal mainstreaming.

Human resources: basic management-information indicators

This is information which any agency might gather regardless of AIDS, but which becomes particularly pertinent for organisations in AIDS-affected countries. This type of monitoring would therefore be the priority for organisations in less-affected countries if they wanted to prepare for the possibility of an AIDS epidemic while also generating useful management information. Possible indicators include the following:

- *Number of employees*: preferably differentiated by sex and age group and, if the organisation has staff spread across areas with differing rates of HIV, by location too.

- *Number of dependants (spouse plus children) per employee*: your organisation does not need these data unless it extends benefits to employees' dependants.

- *Days absent per employee*: this figure could be split according to the types of leave that your organisation allows, such as sick leave, holiday leave, compassionate leave, absences relating to dependants, absences to attend funerals, unpaid leave. You might also want a category for all 'other' forms of absences. This measure would not be specific to AIDS, but would enable your organisation to track broad trends in absenteeism.

- *Numbers of employees ending employment due to ill-health*: to track trends in the impacts of AIDS and other illnesses on staff turnover, express this number as a percentage of total staff.

- *Numbers of employees dying in service*: again, this number would need to be expressed as a percentage of total staff, and would apply to the impact of both AIDS and other illnesses.

Personnel costs: basic financial indicators

Again, this is information which any agency might gather regardless of AIDS, but which becomes particularly pertinent for organisations in AIDS-affected countries. Possible indicators include the following:

- *Medical costs*: these could be monitored in various ways, depending on the benefits offered to employees and their dependants. For example: average medical costs per employee or per person; proportion of employees or people incurring the maximum allowable medical costs, or costs exceeding a certain level; or total medical costs, expressed as a percentage of all salaries. If it is possible without compromising confidentiality to gather data on the medical costs incurred by members of staff who have declared themselves to be HIV-positive, such information would help to increase the accuracy of planning and predictions of the financial impacts of AIDS on the organisation.

- *Recruitment and training costs*: it may be possible to develop some measures to track recruitment and training costs for new members of staff, again to enable better planning and predictions of future impact.

Preventing infection and reducing vulnerability: indicators of the success of efforts to support staff

These types of indicator will help to monitor the impact of those internal mainstreaming initiatives that are designed to help staff to reduce their susceptibility to HIV infection and their vulnerability to the impacts of AIDS. As confidentiality is crucial, it is very important to consider how it can be protected. Personnel staff, for example, must be obliged to respect employees' right to privacy on this subject.

- *Employees' knowledge, attitudes, and practice*: these could be measured through an annual anonymous survey of all employees, or of a representative sample. Although a single survey would provide managers with some information, repeating the survey regularly would ensure that the organisation had a current assessment, despite staff turnover. KAP surveys are a common tool for assessing communities' knowledge, attitudes, and practice with regard to AIDS, so your organisation could adapt an existing survey to make a self-administered questionnaire for use by employees. The survey could cover all aspects of your organisation's measures to support staff, such as attitudes and practice with regard to safer sex, voluntary counselling and testing, feelings towards HIV-positive colleagues, perceptions of the impacts of AIDS within the workplace, and personal impacts of AIDS (see also Units 1 and 3).

- *Condom distribution*: if your organisation is supplying condoms to employees, it should record deliveries and dispatches as part of stock control, to ensure that the oldest in-date stock is distributed first, and that all locations always have sufficient stocks of condoms. The data can also be used as a proxy indicator for condom use by employees, by dividing the number of condoms distributed by the number of employees per location. If condoms are distributed by making them available in gender-segregated toilets, it would also be possible to monitor the uptake among male and female staff. If your organisation were to supply both male and female condoms, then distribution of each type should be monitored.

- *Voluntary counselling and HIV testing*: while the identity of staff taking up counselling and testing services must be kept confidential, your organisation could establish a system to monitor the number of staff accessing the service, and whether they are male or female. It might also be relevant to know how many sessions each employee attends, as an indicator of how useful (or otherwise) they find the service.

- *Special measures for HIV-positive members of staff*: if your organisation makes special benefits available to HIV-positive members of staff, such as antiretroviral treatment, it may be possible to monitor uptake of those benefits. However, if there is a risk that such an indicator might compromise confidentiality, then it should not be used. Organisations might also learn from each such claimant about his or her experience of the workplace policy by means of a confidential evaluation, perhaps conducted by a member of staff selected by the HIV-positive employee. This should provide important feedback on what aspects of the policy are and are not working, from the perspective of the affected employee.

If an organisation has made other changes to employees' benefits – such as access to savings and loans schemes, or the right to accrue overtime and spend it as time off in lieu – then it would also need to monitor the uptake and outcomes of those measures.

Indicators for initiatives to modify the functioning of the organisation

As before, appropriate indicators should arise from what an organisation aims to achieve in terms of modifying systems and practices, in order to reduce its susceptibility to HIV and vulnerability to the impacts of AIDS. They might include some of the following.

- *Proportion of employees receiving their salaries on time* if delayed payments were thought to be contributing to susceptibility to HIV infection.

- *Qualitative feedback from staff concerning measures to reduce work-related susceptibility*: for example, from health staff regarding whether they are able to apply universal precautions, to protect themselves from workplace exposure to HIV; or from distantly posted staff, regarding their uptake of measures to enable them to see their families more often.

- *Proportion of job applicants meeting essential requirements*: this indicator might be particularly pertinent to certain types of job for which the organisation is experiencing or expecting difficulties recruiting suitably skilled people.

- *Average number of days from vacancy to filled post:* this could serve to measure improvements in the efficiency of recruitment procedures.

- *Rate of staff turnover*: an important indicator if retaining existing staff becomes a priority for an organisation.

- *Proportion of posts judged to be vulnerable to the post-holder's absence*: this indicator would entail identifying the key characteristics of vulnerability, such as whether other members of staff between them know how to do all the tasks for each post, and whether each post-holder has accessible systems and has removed barriers (such as passwords or keys) which would prevent other employees from covering their workload.

- *Funding for, and expenditure of, budgets associated with internal mainstreaming of AIDS*: these indicators would involve checking that all planned activities are included in budgets, and then monitoring expenditure against budgets as a proxy for the level of activity, and a means of improving the accuracy of budgeting in the future.

Unit 6: Training for mainstreaming AIDS in development work

Chapter 13 proposed that training for external mainstreaming of AIDS has three objectives:

1 Participants should *identify with* the issue of AIDS, and understand its connections to poverty and underdevelopment.

2 They should *own* the issue, in the sense of believing that AIDS is relevant to their sector's work.

3 Participants in the training should be *empowered* to act through recognising external mainstreaming as an effective way to respond, and one which they are motivated to try.

This unit suggests ways in which organisations might train their staff or partners to achieve those objectives. Such training should ideally be linked to field research, so that staff learn at first hand from communities and individuals affected by AIDS (see Unit 7).

- First make sure that participants understand the basic facts about HIV transmission and AIDS.

- Although training for mainstreaming AIDS necessarily requires facilitators to impart categories, ideas, and definitions, they can still use participatory methods, to ensure that participants engage with the topic and learn for themselves.

Understanding the links between development and AIDS

This theme concerns the first two objectives, which require not only that participants intellectually understand that development and AIDS are linked, but also that they should believe that the link is relevant to them and their work. In a sense, the challenge is to win their hearts and their minds. Below we present some ideas about how to achieve this.

Analysing the complexity of AIDS

Development workers sometimes have limited perceptions of the problem of AIDS: for example, if ignorance about AIDS among community members is the problem, then AIDS education must be the solution; if promiscuity is the problem, then encouraging faithfulness must be the solution. To understand AIDS as a development issue, participants need a more complex appreciation of the many factors that cause susceptibility to HIV infection. One way to do this is to use case studies of people affected by AIDS to stimulate discussion in small groups. The examples should preferably represent various kinds of people and a range of reasons for being infected or affected. Local case studies would be best, but you could use or adapt the testimonies 'voiced' in Chapter 2 of this book (pages 27–31). Ask the groups to analyse the case studies, using spider diagrams to illustrate the sequence of events and the relevant development issues.

Explaining the cycle of causes and consequences

The model of causes and consequences (page 26) is one way to explain the idea that HIV flourishes because of problems of underdevelopment, and in turn AIDS makes those problems worse. You could get participants to identify the causes of susceptibility to HIV infection and the consequences of vulnerability to the impacts of AIDS within their case-study analyses (for definitions for those two terms, see the Glossary). You might also use or adapt Figure 2.1 to illustrate the idea of the cycle of causes and consequences. Participants should see that HIV prevention is not a simple matter of education or better behaviour, but that susceptibility to HIV infection is linked to core problems of poverty and gender inequality. They should also appreciate that the many impacts of AIDS undermine development work and can heighten susceptibility to HIV infection.

Explaining the gender dimension of HIV and AIDS

Chapter 2 introduced a fictional twin brother and sister (pages 32–4) to illustrate how women tend to be more susceptible to HIV infection, and to suffer more of the impacts of AIDS. You could ask small groups of participants to consider the ways in which twins might experience AIDS differently. You could leave the process open, or give them some guidance: for example, to consider biological differences between the twins, differences in sexual behaviour, and differences in degrees of control over their lives. Or you could ask them to construct a timeline of adolescence, marriage, and so on.

Understanding the meaning of external mainstreaming of AIDS

This theme is concerned to help participants to proceed from seeing AIDS as a development issue to understanding how development organisations can respond to AIDS as a development issue. Possible activities include the following:

Exploring the difference between AIDS work and mainstreaming AIDS

If you ask participants what can be done about AIDS, they will probably list AIDS-work activities of HIV prevention and AIDS care and treatment. If you refer them back to the case studies that they have already used, and the development problems which they identified, the participants should find that AIDS work addresses some of the problems, such as lack of knowledge about HIV, but not the deeper problems, such as poverty and gender inequality. You could compare the strategies of doing AIDS work and mainstreaming AIDS, using the definitions and examples in Chapter 3 of this book.

Thinking about comparative advantage

It may be helpful to ask participants to consider where their organisation's comparative advantage lies with regard to responding to AIDS, perhaps using Table 5.3 on page 107. Unless the participants are already experienced in health-promotion work, they should see that their expertise lies at the third level of the micro-environment. It depends on your organisation's position how you handle participants' desires to respond directly to AIDS by initiating AIDS work rather than mainstreaming AIDS: for example, it depends whether your organisation is able to do both, is already doing AIDS work, or is limiting itself to mainstreaming AIDS in existing work.

Learning how to do external mainstreaming of AIDS

This theme concerns helping participants to take the vital step from understanding the meaning of external mainstreaming to applying it to their own day-to-day work.

Core questions for external mainstreaming of AIDS

Chapter 13 distilled the essence of external mainstreaming in two questions:

1. How do HIV and AIDS affect the people with whom we work, in terms of their efforts to escape from poverty, now and in the future?

2. How is our work helping or hindering them to be less susceptible to HIV infection, and to be less vulnerable to the impacts of AIDS?

You could rephrase these two questions to fit your organisation's vocabulary. For example, in Southern Africa Oxfam uses a rights-based approach in all its programming, and so refers to 'enabling people to achieve their rights and to live with dignity', rather than 'escaping from poverty'. Participants could explore possible answers to the questions. The first question should not pose a major intellectual challenge if participants have understood the model of causes and consequences, and can use that framework to consider the effects that AIDS is having, or may have, on the people with whom they work. They could then think about how those effects relate to their development work. The participants may find the second question more difficult, particularly with regard to the idea that their work might be inadvertently increasing susceptibility to HIV infection or vulnerability to the impacts of AIDS. You could use the examples from Chapter 5 to illustrate how development work can do those things, and exclude AIDS-affected households, and so unintentionally work with AIDS rather than against it. The participants could then consider how they might deal with any ways in which their work may be hindering rather than helping, and how they might strengthen the positive aspects of their work as an indirect response to AIDS.

Next steps: undertaking community research, and modifying development programmes

Much as the participants can explore the two questions for external mainstreaming in a workshop, this is not the same as discussing them with the people with whom they work. Moreover, the mainstreaming process aims to modify existing development programmes in the light of community research, in order to ensure that the development work is indirectly working against, rather than with, AIDS. Participants need a sense of these two next steps, and how they are to take them, so that they understand what is to follow the training workshop.

Measuring the impact of training for external mainstreaming of AIDS

This unit began by proposing three objectives for training for external mainstreaming of AIDS, and now suggests some ways of evaluating the impact of such training. The facilitators should have a good sense of the success or otherwise of the workshop through the ideas emerging from the small groups of participants, and from individuals' comments. For example, it would be a good sign if a group of agricultural advisers were to think about how they exclude orphan-headed households, and to discuss ways of making the techniques that they promote more suitable to those households. Alternatively, if the agricultural field workers were to miss the connections between their work and AIDS, and to concentrate on talking about AIDS prevention or care, that would indicate that the training had not been successful for that group of participants.

- In addition to facilitators' observations, you could consider using a preliminary and follow-up questionnaire, to measure the impact of the training on all participants as individuals. Although it is difficult through a questionnaire to capture individuals' sense of mainstreaming and their perceptions of AIDS, it might give the facilitators an idea of participants' feelings about AIDS and their work, both before and after the training.

- If you are unsure of the participants' knowledge and attitudes with regard to AIDS, begin the questionnaire with questions about HIV transmission and their perceptions and feelings (see Unit 3).

- Make the questionnaire anonymous, and encourage participants to fill it in quickly and without consulting each other. Stress that it is a simple and rough measure of how participants feel about AIDS, and that there are no right answers.

- An alternative way of asking the same questions, but with instant visual feedback (rather than having to analyse questionnaires) is to write each question on a large sheet of paper, and to put the sheets on tables around the room. Ask participants to mark their answer to each question with a pen or sticker. If you don't want them to be influenced by others' opinions, you will need little covered boxes, into which participants could drop stones or slips of paper in order to 'vote' for their answer. For the final, open-ended, question, participants would need to write down their answers on small pieces of paper, and pin them up or put them in a box.

- **Which one of the following statements is closest to how you feel?**

  -- AIDS is mainly about morals. Religious leaders and organisations must convince people of the need to protect themselves from AIDS.

  __ All development workers are responsible for working together to prevent HIV infection and to stop AIDS.

  __ AIDS is mainly a health issue, so workers in the health sector are mainly responsible for responding to AIDS.

  -- AIDS is a special issue which requires special responses, such as the work of AIDS organisations, and of groups of people living with AIDS.

  __ All development workers are responsible for fighting AIDS indirectly through their development work.

  __ AIDS is mainly an issue of education. Workers in the education sector have to protect the next generation from HIV infection.

- **How relevant do you feel that AIDS is to your work?**

  1   Not at all relevant

  2   Only a little bit relevant

  3   Fairly relevant

  4   It is relevant

  5   Very relevant

- **Have you done anything in your work in the last 12 months which is relevant to AIDS?**

  1   Nothing at all

  2   One or two things

  3   Some things

  4   Lots of things

  5   All of my work is relevant to AIDS

- **What does the phrase 'mainstreaming AIDS' mean to you, if anything?**

Unit 7: Undertaking community research for mainstreaming AIDS in development work

The aim of this unit is to encourage research with community members, in order to learn more about the connections between AIDS and development work. The research may have several objectives, including the following.

1 Development workers will build on theoretical knowledge gained from training for external mainstreaming of AIDS. By doing practical research into the connections between AIDS and their development work, they will become more skilled in mainstreaming and more motivated to do it.

2 AIDS-affected community members will be able to voice their experiences and so to influence development practice as appropriate.

3 The organisation will learn about the connections between susceptibility to HIV infection, vulnerability to the impacts of AIDS, and its development work, and so will be better able to mainstream AIDS effectively in its development work.

Before beginning the research, the participating development workers would need to discuss and prioritise the types of information that they are seeking, and from whom, and how they intend to get it. They may also need some training or refresher sessions in research methods, particularly if they are using participatory approaches, and especially if they lack confidence in, or experience of, doing research on personal issues and taboo topics such as sex and death. The following general principles should be borne in mind.

- The research should be conducted in a place where the organisation is already working, or, for a new project, where it intends to work.

- It should involve people of varying ages, including men, women, and older children who have been affected by HIV and AIDS; some agencies may wish to use formal sampling techniques to ensure that they also listen to a representative segment of the population.

- Research with peer groups is likely to be more revealing than asking questions of a mixed group, or a larger community meeting.

- Researchers must be alert to the danger of stigmatising individuals through questioning them about this sensitive subject. In some instances it may be more appropriate to speak of 'chronic illnesses among adults', rather than to talk about AIDS.

- Researchers should also be aware that community members' responses will be influenced by factors such as culture, ethnicity, gender, age, and status, and so they are perceptions rather than fact. For example, it is relevant if relatively powerful men view poor female-headed households as being beyond help and therefore not a priority for development assistance, but it does not mean that it is true.

Contextual information about HIV and AIDS and related topics

This kind of research does not relate directly to the project's activities, but to the context of the project, in terms of community members' beliefs and attitudes towards AIDS, and their experiences of AIDS and its repercussions. Here are some suggested themes, together with some general methods for exploring those themes, which might be adapted to suit the context in which your agency is working.

Learning about perceptions of AIDS in comparison with other health issues

Ask peer groups to discuss and draw symbols for the illnesses among adults which they consider to be most serious in their community, in terms of their effects on individuals and their households. Ask the participants to rank the illnesses, either as a group, or individually (in which case, give them all equal numbers of stones with which to indicate their views of the relative gravity of the illnesses).

Exploring susceptibility to HIV infection

Ask peer-group members to list the ways in which men and women can be exposed to a sexually transmitted infection. Be prepared for non-scientific theories about causation, such as witchcraft, or activities unconnected with sex. Ask the participants to focus on the medically recognised methods of STI transmission which they have identified. Referring only to those means, ask them to think about various kinds of sexual behaviour in the community, and to place them on a spectrum from 'not at all likely to result in an STI' to 'very or most likely to result in an STI'. Then explore the factors that lie behind the different types of behaviour. For example, if it is said that some people have several different sexual partners, ask why: the behaviour might be explained in terms of seeking pleasure, or needing support, or the influence of alcohol, or other reasons. Explain that you are interested in the types of behaviour, rather than actual individuals. The discussion should reveal information about the various peer groups' perceptions of sexual behaviour, and why different groups may be susceptible to HIV infection for different reasons.

Exploring perceptions of, and community responses to, people affected by AIDS

Ask the participants to consider the general case of a household in their community directly affected by AIDS. In what ways might other men and women support that household? And in what ways might other people make life more difficult for the people affected? Explore which kind of reaction is more common, and ask if the responses of the community might differ according to the circumstances of the AIDS-affected household. For example, what are the typical responses to the poorest households, or to households headed by women or girls, by orphans, and by elderly people? What is the status of those households within the community: are they still included and considered part of the community, or are they seen as 'hopeless cases'?

You could explore some of the same issues with AIDS-affected households, to understand how other households and the wider community have responded in positive and negative ways towards their situation.

Exploring the impacts of AIDS

Ask the participants to categorise the various ways in which households are affected by AIDS. Ask them then to rank the categories, from the most common to the least common effects. For example, the most common effect may be the obligation to attend funerals, followed by taking responsibility for orphans, followed by having a relative sick with AIDS. If possible, get some sense of what proportion of all the households fall into each category. Then, for each category, explore the repercussions for the households, and for their different members (men, women, boys, girls), particularly in terms of workloads and livelihoods. If necessary, prompt the participants to discuss the effects on the poorer and poorest households, and ask which households are able to withstand the effects of AIDS without sliding into poverty. You could also ask the participants about the wider effects on the whole community, and trends that they have noticed in terms of the impacts of AIDS.

When discussing the actual impacts of AIDS with AIDS-affected households, you could draw a timeline, or simply discuss the chronology of impacts. For each effect, encourage the respondents to explore the repercussions on various members of the household and on their livelihoods. For example, if a woman begins her story with the day when her eldest child returned from the city because he was very sick, then you might ask what difference that made to her life, what did she stop doing in order to care for him, what effects did it have on her spouse, or on her daughters living in the village? When the story reaches the present day, you may be able to ask respondents to talk about how they perceive their future prospects, and what factors may be key to the difference between recovering from the impacts of AIDS and being permanently impoverished.

Connections between the organisation's development work and AIDS

This part of the research concerns exploring the possible interactions between the development project and the 'causes and consequences' of HIV/AIDS. Researchers need to be alert to indications that the project may be reducing or increasing susceptibility to HIV infection, and reducing or increasing vulnerability to the impacts of AIDS. The chart on page 326 suggests some indications that the project is working either against or with HIV and AIDS.

Researchers need to bear in mind these positive and negative indications during the research, and ask questions accordingly.

Signs that the project is indirectly working against HIV and AIDS

Indications that it helps to reduce susceptibility to HIV infection:

- empowerment of the poor;
- improvements in women's status;
- reductions in poverty levels;
- greater gender equality;
- reductions in migration;
- and improvements in health, particularly sexual health.

Indications that it helps to reduce vulnerability to the impacts of AIDS:

- Poor and vulnerable households – including those headed by women, older people, and orphans, and those with a high dependency ratio – are participating and benefiting.
- The project is reducing poverty and helping households, and particularly poor ones, to build up their assets.
- The project is leading to greater social cohesion, and building the capacity of community institutions to respond to development problems.

Signs that the project is inadvertently working with HIV and AIDS

Indications that it inadvertently increases susceptibility to HIV infection:

- greater gender inequality;
- shifts in power (e.g. decision-making and control of resources) towards men;
- exclusion of poor or marginalised people, particularly women;
- increased spending on alcohol, other recreational drugs, or sex;
- increased mobility or migration;
- unsafe sex between community members and development workers;
- and sexual trading or sexual abuse in return for access to project benefits.

Indications that it inadvertently increases vulnerability to the impacts of AIDS:

- exclusion (and stigmatisation) of poor and vulnerable households – including those headed by women, older people, and orphans, and those with a high dependency ratio – at any stage of the project cycle;
- activities from which such households fail to benefit, because the activities are unsuited to them;
- and methods based on inputs of labour and capital which are unsustainable in the case of external shocks such as chronic illness.

Exploring the project's repercussions with project participants

Ask a group of project participants about the types of people who are participating in the project. Generate a 'spider diagram', with the project participants at the centre, and legs representing the impacts of the project. (If a wide range of people are taking part in the project, you may need to do a separate spider diagram for each.) For example, for an agriculture project, one leg of the spider might represent the fact that project participants have to attend training sessions, which take them away from their farms, which means having to hire labour, or having to work harder to make up for lost time. Another leg might represent the fact that the training has led to increased use of fertilisers, and so more debt among the participants, but also that productivity has increased, so that overall participants' incomes have also risen, and many have improved their houses and bought clothes and other goods. Be sure to ask about any differences in the involvement, repercussions, and outcomes for men and women.

You could then discuss which types of people are not participating in the project. Pay attention to the reasons why vulnerable households may not be taking part. Discuss the participants' ideas about how the project might change in order to encourage excluded households to take part, and pay attention to the participants' attitudes towards the excluded households.

Exploring reasons for exclusion

This is a follow-up activity with groups of people who are excluded from the project (as opposed to households which could participate but choose not to, for example, because the levels of credit available are too low to attract them). Ask them to categorise the various reasons why they are not taking part in the project. For each reason, explore ways in which the project might be changed in order for them to be motivated and enabled to participate. Avoid raising their expectations that the changes they suggest will automatically be made.

Exploring power dynamics within the project

Ask peer groups of project participants to draw a 'chapati diagram' of the project, focusing on who makes decisions and the relative influence of different groups within and related to the project. For example, a group of women may place the Village Development Committee at the centre of their diagram, because the committee decides who gets livestock loans. They put the project's NGO near the centre, because the NGO provides the livestock and exerts a lot of control on the committee. They put their husbands at some distance from the committee, because they can sometimes influence committee members, and place themselves at the edge of the diagram, because they feel they have little influence over the project. When the diagram is complete, ask who belongs to the most influential groups, and how they make their decisions. Explore biases in decision making, probing if necessary about treatment of vulnerable households and gender biases. Be alert to the possibility that access to project benefits might depend on, or involve, sexual exchange. Where the power dynamics of the project are excluding groups of people, such as women or vulnerable households, explore ways in which decision making could be modified to make it fairer.

Measuring the impact of community research

This unit suggested three possible objectives for community research as part of the process of mainstreaming AIDS externally. The most readily available measure of success would be the extent to which the participants' report of their research findings demonstrates that the objectives have been met. Does the report illustrate that the participating development workers understand mainstreaming? Does it show connections between AIDS and the development project, and are the views of people affected by AIDS evident in the report? The degree to which the objectives have been met could also be explored at a post-research workshop, where the participants share and discuss their findings, and their experiences of undertaking the research.

Unit 8: Adapting organisational systems

This unit suggests some ways in which an organisation might seek to institutionalise attention to AIDS by adapting its own systems.

Employees' roles and responsibilities

Job descriptions, terms of reference, and appraisal mechanisms

Incorporate attention to AIDS in documents which define the responsibilities of employees and consultants, and ensure that it is an integral aspect of performance assessment. Use vocabulary which is familiar to staff and which the organisation has adopted for its own discourse. Beware vague and general references to 'attention to AIDS'. Expand them in more explicit terms; for example: 'being alert to, and acting upon, the ways in which development work can increase or decrease both susceptibility to HIV infection, and vulnerability to the impacts of AIDS'.

Terms and conditions of employment

With regard to reducing HIV transmission, employees' terms and conditions could specify expected standards of behaviour, and refer explicitly to behaviour officially deemed unacceptable, including sexual abuse, sexual harassment, and sexual trading, both within the workplace and with community members. (Unit 10 includes the core principles of a Code of Conduct for humanitarian workers.) Employees' terms of employment might also include codes of non-discrimination, taking account of gender, sexual orientation, and HIV status, to be applied both within the workplace and in local communities. Employees' terms and conditions should also specify reporting methods and disciplinary procedures in cases where any employee's behaviour contravenes the stated standards and codes.

Overarching values

Any organisation which has a mission statement or other document setting out its values and priorities should incorporate AIDS in that document. Again, each organisation needs to use its own wording to express its commitment, but here is a possible model, to be adapted according to the particular context:

We believe that AIDS is a key development issue, because HIV transmission is driven by factors of under-development, and because AIDS is negatively affecting the development process. We are committed to ensuring that our development work makes an effective contribution to the fight against AIDS. We achieve this by ensuring that our development work is reducing susceptibility to HIV infection and vulnerability to the impacts of AIDS. While our work focuses on tackling poverty and gender inequality, we will also work in collaboration with specialist AIDS organisations, as appropriate.

The project cycle

The task of institutionalising attention to AIDS within the project cycle will vary according to the organisation's current practices and work focus. This section makes some general suggestions.

Needs assessment

Given that most HIV transmission is connected to sexual activity, and sex is a personal subject, needs assessment which takes AIDS into account will almost always involve work with same-sex peer groups, their membership differentiated further, if possible, by age or life-cycle status. The process should incorporate learning about sexual behaviour and sexual health, and the impacts of AIDS, and should include listening to the experiences of households directly affected by AIDS (see the first part of Unit 7). This should supplement more standard needs-assessment information about gender-related divisions of labour, power dynamics, axes of difference within the community, and the assets and different needs of different groups. If an agency beginning work in a new community felt that direct references to sexual health and behaviour would be too direct, it could use a much broader approach, such as asking about livelihoods and the choices that confront vulnerable households.

Planning

Project planning needs to take into account the current and likely future impacts of AIDS, and their implications for defining the project's target groups, methods, interventions, and means of sustainability. While planning should in any case pay attention to the particular needs and resources of various groups within the community, in AIDS-affected communities it is particularly important to attend to, and consult with, poor households headed by women, orphans, and elderly people, and those with high dependency ratios. If the project intends to serve those and other vulnerable households, it must be planned in such a way that the methodologies and types of intervention suit them. Although one cannot predict the repercussions of implementation, it is possible to explore hypothetical effects and outcomes with potential participants, in advance of implementation. This should allow the organisation to anticipate some of the likely problems, including ones which might heighten susceptibility to HIV infection or vulnerability to the impacts of AIDS. In terms of project aims and objectives, it makes sense to make explicit references to features of the design which are intended, among other things, to enhance the way in which the project works against AIDS, and to include specific means of monitoring those features.

Monitoring

On-going monitoring needs to include measures for project features which should be reducing susceptibility to HIV or vulnerability to the impacts of AIDS. For example, a project plans that men and women will be equally represented on the project committee, in order to guard against discrimination against female-headed households and the likelihood of women having to engage in sexual trading in order to gain access to project benefits. Calculating the proportion of men and women on the committee, as a single measure, does not tell the organisation anything about discrimination or sexual trading. A simple additional measure would be the proportion of project participants that are female-headed households, in comparison with their representation in the community. The existence or not of sexual trading could be explored with women in the project review, or through on-going discussion with vulnerable female participants. Given the gendered nature of AIDS, and the significance of gender issues to all development work, methods of monitoring should record males and females separately, so that they can also be analysed separately.

Review

While reviewing the project's aims and objectives, the organisation needs to keep an eye on unforeseen indirect links between the project, HIV, and AIDS. The basic questions are whether the project is working against AIDS, by reducing susceptibility to HIV infection and vulnerability to the impacts of AIDS, or inadvertently working with AIDS by increasing susceptibility and vulnerability. The second part of Unit 7 offers ideas for how to do this, including exploring the repercussions of the project and its differing effects on men and women, reasons for exclusion from participation in the project, and power dynamics within the project.

Unit 9: Training for mainstreaming AIDS in humanitarian work

This unit has much in common with ideas in Unit 6 for training staff to mainstream AIDS in development work. Training for mainstreaming AIDS in humanitarian work could have similar objectives, but adapted to suit emergency conditions:

1 Participants will *identify with* the issue of AIDS, and understand its links to poverty, gender, and life-threatening crisis.

2 They will *own* the issue, in the sense of believing that AIDS is relevant to their sector's work, and to the humanitarian response to crises.

3 Participants will be *empowered* to act as a result of recognising external mainstreaming as an effective way to respond, and one which they are motivated to try.

This unit offers some ideas for training to meet those objectives. It also presents the outline of an actual workshop – focused on gender and protection – run by Oxfam GB in Sierra Leone in 2002. Clearly, however, the appropriate training package for any agency will depend on circumstances, such as whether it is possible to train staff thoroughly in advance of an emergency, or if the training must necessarily be rapid, after the sudden onset of a crisis. Many humanitarian organisations already have codes of conduct and ways of working which they might adapt to include the idea of mainstreaming AIDS. Moreover, the content of training will depend on the strategy that the organisation adopts.

Full mainstreaming of AIDS requires staff to consider the ways in which their work may increase or reduce susceptibility to HIV infection and vulnerability to the impacts of AIDS. Chapter 13 suggested that in the unstable phase of an emergency, agencies might choose to focus on a limited approach described as 'do no harm': trying to minimise the way in which their work may make people more susceptible to HIV infection. This would fit in with the increasing attention given by humanitarian agencies to the reduction of sexual and gender-based violence, and attention to gender issues. Opting for that focus, rather than adopting the whole agenda for mainstreaming AIDS, is not ideal, however, because it leaves undone the aspects of actively reducing susceptibility to HIV infection, and of attending to the issue of vulnerability to the impacts of AIDS. Organisations should therefore aim to take on the full mainstreaming agenda during the stabilisation phase of an emergency.

- Make sure that participants understand the basics of HIV transmission and AIDS.

- Although training for mainstreaming AIDS necessarily requires facilitators to explain categories, ideas, and definitions, they can still use participatory methods so that participants engage with the topic and learn for themselves. This may be difficult in situations where there is pressure to conduct training as quickly as possible, but it is nonetheless important.

Understanding the links between humanitarian work and AIDS

This theme concerns the first two objectives, which require participants not only to understand intellectually that humanitarian work and AIDS are linked, but also to believe that the link is relevant to them and their work. Here are some ideas for how to achieve this.

Analysing the links between crisis conditions, humanitarian work, and AIDS

Give small groups of participants case studies of individual experiences of large-scale, life-threatening emergencies. These cases should illustrate the ways in which such crises directly increase susceptibility to HIV infection: via rape, sexual violence, commercial sex work, sexual trading, and changes in sexual behaviour resulting from displacement and social dislocation. They should also illustrate how decisions made by humanitarian agencies can make the situation worse. Get them to listen to the voices on page 28 and pages 121–2 and to consider examples on pages 79–81 of ways in which humanitarian work can increase susceptibility to HIV infection. Ask the groups to analyse the case studies, using spider diagrams to illustrate the sequence of events and the relevant issues for their work.

Explaining the gender dimension of humanitarian crises and HIV/AIDS

Chapter 2 presented a fictional twin brother and sister (pages 32–4) to illustrate how women tend to be more susceptible to HIV infection and to bear more of the impacts of AIDS. You could ask small groups of participants to use the same approach to consider how the twins might experience a large-scale crisis differently, and how they differ in terms of susceptibility to HIV infection and vulnerability to the impacts of AIDS. Alternatively, if you are very short of time, you could prepare a presentation about this in advance, perhaps with male and female facilitators or participants role-playing the twins.

Understanding the meaning of external mainstreaming of AIDS

This theme is concerned with helping participants to move from seeing AIDS as an issue which is relevant to humanitarian work, to developing a sense of how agencies can respond to AIDS through their humanitarian work. Possible activities include the following.

Exploring the difference between AIDS work and mainstreaming AIDS

If you ask participants what can be done about AIDS, they will probably list AIDS-work activities of HIV prevention and AIDS care and treatment. If you refer them back to the case studies, they should see that raising awareness of HIV would probably do little to reduce susceptibility to HIV infection, because that is caused by a range of deeper problems, including poverty, gender inequality, and disempowerment. You could compare and contrast the strategies of doing AIDS work and mainstreaming AIDS, using the definitions and examples in Chapter 3 of this book, particularly the one on pages 46–7 concerning water and sanitation, which refers to humanitarian work.

Thinking about comparative advantage

It may be helpful to get participants to consider where their organisation's comparative advantage lies in terms of responding to AIDS, perhaps using Table 5.3 on page 107. Unless the participants are already experienced in health-promotion work, they should see that their expertise lies at the third level of the micro-environment: meeting basic needs, and then working towards development work within an emergency setting as soon as it is practicable. How you handle participants' desires to respond directly to AIDS through initiating AIDS work, rather than main-streaming AIDS, depends on your organisation's particular position: for example, whether your organisation is able to do both, and whether any other agency is already responsible for doing AIDS work within the wider humanitarian response.

Learning how to do external mainstreaming of AIDS

This theme concerns helping participants to move from understanding what external mainstreaming means to thinking in practical terms how they might go about it.

'Do no harm'

If, in the early stages of its response, an organisation opts for this limited approach, then the key question for staff is 'How can we minimise the ways in which our work may heighten susceptibility to HIV infection?'

Employees need to consult, plan, design, and act in such a way that they avoid the following outcomes, which are likely to increase susceptibility to HIV infection:

- giving exclusive power to take decisions and control resources to men;
- excluding vulnerable or marginalised people, particularly women;
- not giving priority to the safety of women and girls when establishing physical facilities such as accommodation, and water and sanitation infrastructure;
- failing to ensure that men and women receive equal rations, and that women can receive theirs in their own right;
- ignoring the prevalence of sexual trading or the sexual abuse of women or children in return for access to project benefits;
- failing to consult and do on-going monitoring with vulnerable groups such as female-headed households and adolescents;
- failing to provide effective channels for complaints.

In addition, managers would need to try to minimise the likelihood of humanitarian workers engaging in unsafe sex with community members; they can do this by ensuring that workers are informed about HIV transmission and are supplied with good-quality condoms. Workers should also be well aware of the codes of conduct that are expected of them, and the disciplinary measures which apply if they transgress those codes by, for example, trading access to project benefits for sex.

Full mainstreaming of AIDS

Chapter 13 suggested that the essence of external mainstreaming could be expressed in the form of two questions, which are adapted here to fit humanitarian work:

1 How does AIDS affect the people with whom we work, in terms of their efforts to survive and rebuild their lives, now and in the future?

2 How is our work helping or hindering them to avoid HIV infection and to be less vulnerable to the impacts of AIDS?

Both questions are relevant for agencies aiming to adopt the full agenda for mainstreaming AIDS in humanitarian work. Participants could explore both questions theoretically, drawing on the model of causes and consequences on page 26, and the examples in Chapter 5. However, the lack of documented experience with regard to AIDS and the humanitarian response to crisis means that this book lacks detail about how such work may increase or reduce vulnerability to the impacts of AIDS. This information gap makes community research to learn about the links between humanitarian work and AIDS all the more necessary. For ideas on undertaking community research for mainstreaming AIDS in humanitarian work, see Unit 10.

Outline of a gender and protection workshop

This workshop was run twice by Oxfam GB in Sierra Leone in 2002, for a total of 64 participants from 26 agencies. This outline presents the main content of the workshop, omitting feedback sessions, energisers, tea breaks, and so on.

The objectives of the workshops were that at the end of the programme participants would be able to do the following:

- Explain the meaning of 'humanitarian protection'.

- Describe the human rights of women, men, and children.

- Identify abuses of these rights and recognise how they can occur.

- Describe specific actions that NGOs can take to improve protection of vulnerable people.

- Explain why and how 'gender' is important in planning for protection.

Day 1

- Introductions, outline, and objectives.

- Definition of humanitarian protection. Key words: *human rights, respect, human dignity.*

- The need to consider both men and women:

  Exercise: biological versus socially constructed differences; gender roles as learned behaviour.

  Group work: men's work and women's work; perceptions of the opposite sex.

  Small-group discussion: good and bad aspects of gender roles.

  Exercise: identifying women's and men's activities.

  Plenary discussion: gender-balanced participation.

- Correlation between gender equality and development. Criteria for a gender-aware NGO.

- Human rights:

  Discussion: defining human dignity. Introduction to Universal Declaration of Human Rights.

  Key concepts: *inalienable* rights; human rights of women and girl children.

  Brainstorm: requirements for life with dignity.

  Group work: The Declaration of Human Rights; human rights and the situation of refugees, returnees, displaced people.

- How human rights are violated in conflict:

  Role plays, preparation and performance: identifying protection issues.

Day 2

- The purpose of rules, laws and conventions: protection and fairness:

  Discussion: the needs and rights of boys and girls, Declaration of the Rights of the Child, and challenges in protecting the rights of children.

  Group work: selected Articles from Rights of the Child.

- Child abuse and exploitation: brief introduction and overview:

  Exercise: Defining exploitative work.

  Case studies: Determining whether children are being exploited.

- Sexual exploitation: who, why, and its effects:

  Recognising risk factors in our fields of work.

  Preventing sexual violence: camp mapping to minimise opportunities.

  Case study: analysing and responding to sexual exploitation.

Day 3

- Red Cross Code of Conduct and Standards of Accountability: raising the awareness of NGOs and communities.

- Current protection concerns: the UN/SCF Report on Exploitation of Refugees in West Africa:

  Exercise: rating agency performance on protection.

  Plenary: consensus on priority concerns.

  Guidelines for reporting protection concerns; Agency Response Checklist; appropriate responses.

  Strategies for involving communities in protection campaigns.

- Children and gender roles: stereotypes and how we learn them:

  Group work: effect of gender stereotypes on children.

Unit 10: Undertaking community research for mainstreaming AIDS in humanitarian work

This unit suggests additional themes which humanitarian agencies need to include in their needs assessments and consultations, if they are to mainstream AIDS in their work.

Limited mainstreaming: 'Do no harm'

If, in the early stages of its response, an organisation opts for this limited approach, then the key question for employees is 'How can we minimise the ways in which our work may heighten susceptibility to HIV infection?'

Unit 9 listed things that agencies must avoid if their work is not to increase susceptibility to HIV infection. The main implication for community research is that agencies need to consult with and listen to vulnerable and marginalised people, particularly women, and to explore with them and other community members how to deliver services in ways that avoid the common pitfalls which increase susceptibility to HIV infection. For example, as it is well known that camp layout can make women and girls more vulnerable to attack, agencies should design services and infrastructure with safety and community cohesion in mind, and they should consult with community leaders and women, including unaccompanied women. For every intervention, agencies should consider questions of gender, equity of access, and safety. Such questions should also be included in on-going monitoring: by asking vulnerable groups, for instance, if they are getting their fair share of rations, and asking about sexual and gender-based violence.

Measures to reduce harm

As Chapter 9 showed, the UN's Inter-Agency Standing Committee responded to reports of widespread abuse by employees of humanitarian agencies with several measures intended to reduce the level of harm. The three goals and associated objectives in its Plan of Action (Inter-Agency Standing Committee 2002) are reproduced (with permission) below.

Prevention

To create an environment free of sexual exploitation and abuse in humanitarian crises, through integrating the prevention of and response to sexual exploitation and abuse into the protection and assistance functions of all humanitarian workers:

- to adopt and incorporate into codes of conduct, specific responsibilities of humanitarian aid workers to prevent and respond appropriately to sexual exploitation and abuse and to adopt appropriate disciplinary procedures for when violations occur;

- to ensure that agency situation analyses and needs assessments identify vulnerabilities to sexual exploitation and abuse and provide a basis for improved programme planning that minimises risks and opportunities for sexual exploitation and abuse;

- to ensure that camp governance is conducted in an equitable manner that empowers women and children, and reduces the risk of sexual exploitation and abuse, and to ensure that distribution processes, including the quantity of assistance and distribution methods, are designed and implemented in a manner that reduces opportunity for sexual exploitation and abuse;

- to develop mechanisms to ensure that agencies providing humanitarian relief are accountable to the communities they serve, with respect to both prevention efforts and response mechanisms.

Response

To provide basic health and psycho-social care to survivors of sexual exploitation and abuse and ensure they have access to appropriate avenues for recourse and redress:

- to develop mechanisms that allow survivors of sexual exploitation and abuse to report incidents of sexual exploitation and abuse; access legal, judicial or community-based recourse systems; and seek redress, including disciplinary action against perpetrators;

- to provide survivors of sexual exploitation with appropriate support.

Monitoring and supervision

To ensure regular monitoring and supervision of the provision of protection and assistance in humanitarian operations, with awareness of risks and opportunities for sexual exploitation and abuse:

- to develop mechanisms to ensure accountability of humanitarian agencies to governments and donors in the implementation of actions to prevent sexual exploitation and abuse;

- to ensure monitoring and supervision of programming for protection from sexual exploitation and abuse and to support staff at a field level to implement the Plan of Action.

The Plan of Action also proposes some core principles for a Code of Conduct for humanitarian workers, which specifically addresses issues related to sexual abuse, and, therefore, to susceptibility to HIV infection. This may be useful for individual agencies to adapt and incorporate in their workers' terms of employment.

Core Principles of a Code of Conduct

Humanitarian agencies have a duty of care to beneficiaries and a responsibility to ensure that beneficiaries are treated with dignity and respect and that certain minimum standards of behaviour are observed. In order to prevent sexual exploitation and abuse, the following core principles must be incorporated into agency codes of conduct:

- Sexual exploitation and abuse by humanitarian workers constitute acts of gross misconduct and are therefore grounds for termination of employment.

- Sexual activity with children (persons under the age of 18) is prohibited regardless of the age of majority or age of consent locally. Mistaken belief in the age of a child is not a defence.

- Exchange of money, employment, goods, or services for sex, including sexual favours or other forms of humiliating, degrading or exploitative behaviour, is prohibited. This includes exchange of assistance that is due to beneficiaries.

- Sexual relationships between humanitarian workers and beneficiaries are strongly discouraged, since they are based on inherently unequal power dynamics. Such relationships undermine the credibility and integrity of humanitarian aid work.

- Where a humanitarian worker develops concerns or suspicions regarding sexual abuse or exploitation by a fellow worker, whether in the same agency or not, s/he must report such concerns via established agency reporting mechanisms.

- Humanitarian workers are obliged to create and maintain an environment which prevents sexual exploitation and abuse and promotes the implementation of their code of conduct. Managers at all levels have particular responsibilities to support and develop systems which maintain this environment.

(Inter-Agency Standing Committee 2002:1)

Full mainstreaming of AIDS

When an agency undertakes development work in a humanitarian setting, it may adopt the full agenda for mainstreaming AIDS, by considering these two key questions:

1 How does AIDS affect the people with whom we work, in terms of their efforts to survive and rebuild their lives, now and in the future?

2 How is our work helping or hindering them to avoid HIV infection and to be less vulnerable to the impacts of AIDS?

Unit 7 presented some ideas for conducting research which addresses these questions by exploring both contextual information about AIDS and related topics, and possible connections between AIDS and the project. Those ideas are broadly transferable to a humanitarian setting, where particular attention needs to be paid to listening to the concerns and experiences of vulnerable groups.

In humanitarian programmes involving several agencies, it should be possible to avoid duplication if one agency undertakes contextual research and shares the data with the other organisations. For example, research into sexual behaviour and perceptions of AIDS could most easily be integrated into needs assessment for sexual-health and reproductive-health programmes. Research into community reactions to AIDS-affected households, and those households' experiences and responses, could fall under the remit of primary health-care outreach, or could be undertaken by any agency which should be considering the particular needs of AIDS-affected households among other vulnerable groups.

Notes

Preface

1 The Consortium is now known as the UK Consortium on AIDS and International Development: www.aidsconsortium.org.uk.

Chapter 1

1 For the accurate medical terms, see Grant and de Cock (2001).

Chapter 2

1 See www.who.int/bct

2 Dr Henry Phiri, District Health Officer, Kasungu Hospital, Malawi, cited in a report entitled 'Saving Grace', The Guardian Unlimited, 8 February 2002, www.guardian.co.uk

3 Elizabeth Reid, speaking at the VIIIth International Conference on AIDS in Africa in December 1993.

Chapter 3

1 Mainstreaming workshop held at Liverpool School of Tropical Medicine, 10-12 December 2002, attended by participants from Uganda, Ghana, and South Africa, and facilitated by Helen Elsey and Sue Holden.

Chapter 4

1 www.vso.org.uk/raisa

2 Personal communication, Janet Duffield, former HIV/AIDS Co-ordinator for ActionAid-Mozambique.

3 Ibid.

4 For example, Webb (2001:2) notes that most of the projects endorsed in the UNAIDS 'Best Practice' documents have not been evaluated.

5 www.stopaidscampaign.org.uk/index.asp?30435275

6 Personal communication, Grace Malindi, Assistant Director of Agricultural Extension, Ministry of Agriculture and Irrigation, Malawi.

7 Personal communication, Rick James, Senior Trainer and Consultant, INTRAC (International NGO Training and Research Centre).

Chapter 5

1 Personal communication, Dan Mullins, Oxfam GB Southern Africa Regional HIV/AIDS Co-ordinator.

2   Personal communication, Chandra Mouli, WHO.

3   www.developmentgoals.org

4   Ibid.

5   Personal communication from Akua Ofori-Asumadu, HIV/AIDS focal point
    in Ghana's Ministry of Education, and Rachel MacCarthy, HIV/AIDS focal
    point in the Ministry of Local Government, at Mainstreaming Workshop held
    at Liverpool School of Tropical Medicine, 10-12 December 2002.

Chapter 7

1   Personal communication, Dan Mullins, Oxfam GB Southern Africa Regional
    HIV/AIDS Co-ordinator.

2   Personal communication from an ActionAid-Uganda employee.

3   Personal communication with Tabitha Elwes, who took a year off from
    working for Spectrum Strategy to volunteer for Oxfam GB.

4   Personal communication, Dan Mullins, Oxfam GB Southern Africa Regional
    HIV/AIDS Co-ordinator.

5   Personal communication, programme officer in an international NGO
    working in Southern Africa.

6   Personal communication, Rogers Bulsuwa, ICD Yemen.

7   Personal communication, HIV/AIDS officer in an international NGO,
    working in Southern Africa.

8   Personal communication, programme officer in a national NGO, working in
    West Africa.

9   AIDS Analysis Africa, September 2001, and personal communication from
    Rose Smart, HIV/AIDS consultant and HEARD Research Fellow, who cites
    The Five Cities Study in Namibia (www.siapac.com.na) as an example of a
    study carried out in this participatory way.

Chapter 8

1   Personal communication, Jacqueline Bataringaya, Global HIV/AIDS
    Co-ordinator, ActionAid.

2   Personal communication, Mohga Kamal-Smith, Oxfam GB Health Policy
    Adviser.

3   The Joint Oxfam HIV/AIDS Programme, or JOHAP, is managed by Oxfam
    Australia/Community Aid Abroad on behalf of Oxfam Canada, Oxfam
    Ireland, and Novib. At the time of funding, Project Empower was known as
    the Cabango Collective.

4   Personal communication, Dan Mullins, Oxfam GB Southern Africa Regional
    HIV/AIDS Co-ordinator.

5   Personal communication, Dan Mullins, Oxfam GB Southern Africa Regional
    HIV/AIDS Co-ordinator.

6   Personal communication, Dinah Kasangaki, HIV/AIDS Focal point for
    Ministry of Agriculture, Animal Industries and Fisheries, Uganda, at
    mainstreaming workshop held at Liverpool School of Tropical Medicine,
    10-12 December 2002.

7   Personal communication, Nellie Nyang'wa, Programme Co-ordinator, Oxfam Malawi.

8   Personal communication with Kondwani Mwangulube, Oxfam GB Regional Development and HIV/AIDS Adviser, 2003.

9   Personal communication, Nellie Nyang'wa, Programme Co-ordinator, Oxfam Malawi.

10 Personal communication, Nellie Nyang'wa, Programme Co-ordinator, Oxfam Malawi.

11 Personal communication, Nellie Nyang'wa, Programme Co-ordinator, Oxfam Malawi.

12 Personal communication with Lugede Chiumia, Oxfam Malawi's Project Officer for Rights, Shire Highlands Sustainable Livelihoods Programme.

13 Personal communication, Mohga Kamal-Smith, Oxfam GB Health Policy Adviser.

14 Personal communication, Mohga Kamal-Smith, Oxfam GB Health Policy Adviser.

15 Personal communication, Nellie Nyang'wa, Programme Co-ordinator, Oxfam Malawi.

16 Personal communication, Salil Shetty, Chief Executive, ActionAid.

17 Personal communication, Dan Mullins.

18 Personal communication, Douglas Webb, HIV/AIDS Adviser, Save the Children UK.

19 Personal communication, Kate Butcher, John Snow International.

20 Personal communication, HIV/AIDS Officer in an international NGO, Southern Africa.

21 www.oxfam.org.uk/hivaids

Chapter 9

1   Personal communication, Rosemarie McNairn, Oxfam GB's Gender & Representation Adviser.

2   Personal communication from Marion O'Reilly, Senior Health Adviser, Oxfam GB Humanitarian Department.

3   Personal communication, Liz Hughes, SC UK Programme Officer for West Africa.

4   Personal communication, Rosemarie McNairn, Oxfam GB's Gender & Representation Adviser.

5   Personal communication, Rosemarie McNairn, Oxfam GB's Gender & Representation Adviser.

6   Personal communication, Dan Mullins, August 2003.

7   'Maintaining the Momentum', Summary Note of the Regional Consultation on Humanitarian Assistance Needs in Southern Africa', 11-12 June 2003, Johannesburg.

Chapter 10

1   Personal communication, Rosemarie McNairn, Oxfam GB's Gender & Representation Adviser.

2   Thanks to Angela Hadjipateras, Research & Policy Officer (HIV/AIDS) at ACORD, for this point.

3   Personal communication, Angela Hadjipateras, Research & Policy Officer (HIV/AIDS), ACORD.

Chapter 13

1   For example, in one community in Malawi, people complained that the hospital authorities deliberately conceal AIDS as a cause of death from relatives; because widows and widowers are not alerted to the possibility that they are HIV-positive, they go on to re-marry, and do not engage in safe sex (Page 2002:24).

Chapter 14

1   Personal communication, Dan Mullins, Oxfam GB Southern Africa Regional HIV/AIDS Co-ordinator.

Bibliography

This bibliography is divided into three sections: (1) the case studies on which the main text is based; (2) details of the secondary sources cited in the text; and (3) practical resources such as fact sheets, guidelines, checklists, and training packages, most of them available free of charge via the Internet.

The case studies

In addition to the following case studies, many individuals supplied informal evidence and commentary; such data are acknowledged in the endnotes as 'personal communications', without the person's name if he or she preferred to remain anonymous.

ACORD Case Study (2002), written by Dennis Nduhura, Susan Amoaten, Ellen Bajenja, and Angela Hadjipateras

ActionAid-Burundi Case Study (2002), written by Dr Juma Mohamed Kariburyo, with the assistance of Josephine Niyonkuru

ActionAid-Ethiopia Case Study (2001), focusing on Voluntary Council for the Handicapped, written by Abeba Bekele

ActionAid-Malawi Case Study (2001), written by Lawrence Khonyongwa

ActionAid-Mozambique Case Study (2001) 'HIV/AIDS Integration: ActionAid Experience in Mozambique', written by Rachel Waterhouse

ActionAid-Uganda Case Study (2001) 'Integrating AIDS in Development and Emergencies Work in Uganda: A Research Report', written by Dr Stella Neema, assisted by Phoebe Kajubi, Grace Odolot, and Joseph Okello

Joint Oxfam HIV/AIDS Programme in Southern Africa Project Empower (formerly Cabango Collective) Case Studies (2002 and 2001), written by Dawn Cavanagh and Lyn Elliott respectively

Oxfam Malawi Case Study (2001) 'Kulimbana Ndi Edzi: Taking Action on AIDS', written by Sarah Lee

Save the Children UK Case Study (2001), written by Susan Amoaten and Douglas Webb

Save the Children UK Ghana Case Study (2001), written by Akua Kwateng-Addo, edited by Susan Amoaten

Save the Children UK Peru Case Study (2001), written by Carmen Murguia and Susan Amoaten

Save the Children UK Uganda Case Study (2001), written by Dr Hussein Mursal, edited by Susan Amoaten

Literature

Wherever a web address is given, the document was available free of charge at that website at the time of writing – June 2003. However, the address given is not for the precise location of the document, because these tend to change, but for the website itself. Many sites have a search function which will help you to locate particular documents.

ActionAid (2001) 'Global Organisational Development Framework', version 1.0, internal document

ActionAid (2002a) 'AIDS orphans and education in Kenya', unpublished interview data from a research project

ActionAid (2002b) 'Emergencies Impact Review', London: ActionAid, www.actionaid.org

ActionAid Alliance (2002) 'Don't Forget Poverty: International AIDS Conference, Barcelona, July 2002', London: ActionAid, www.actionaid.org

ActionAid-Uganda (1998) 'The Integration of HIV/AIDS in ActionAid-Uganda', unpublished workshop report

Ainsworth, M. and D. Filmer (2002) 'Poverty, AIDS and Children's Schooling: A Targeting Dilemma', Policy Research Working Paper no. WPS 2885, www.worldbank.org

Ainsworth, M., K. Beegle, and G. Koda (2002) 'The Impact of Adult Mortality on Primary School Enrolment in North Western Tanzania', Departmental Working Paper, www.worldbank.org

Akukwe, C. (2002) 'Africa and NEPAD: what about HIV/AIDS?', *The Perspective*, 23 April 2002

AmfAR (2002) 'Facts for Life: What You and the People You Care About Need to Know About HIV/AIDS', American Foundation for AIDS Research, www.amfar.org

Ayieko, M. A. (1997) 'From Single Parents to Child-Headed Households: the Case of Children Orphaned by AIDS in Kisumu and Siaya Districts', research project report, University of Illinois and UNDP, www.undp.org

Baier, E. G. (1997) 'The Impact of HIV/AIDS on Rural Households/ Communities and the Need for Multisectoral Prevention and Mitigation Strategies to Combat the Epidemic in Rural Areas', Rome: FAO, www.fao.org

Bailey, M. (1995) 'Review of HIV and Sexual Health Work Supported by Oxfam', unpublished report , Oxfam GB

Badcock-Walters, P. and A. Whiteside (2000) 'HIV/AIDS and Development in the Education Sector', University of Natal, Durban, www.und.ac.za/und/heard

Barnett, T. and A. Whiteside (2000) 'Guidelines for Studies of the Social and Economic Impact of AIDS', UNAIDS Best Practice Collection, UNAIDS/00.32E, Geneva: UNAIDS, www.unaids.org

Barnett, T. and A. Whiteside (2002) *AIDS in the 21st Century: Disease and Globalization*, Basingstoke, UK: Palgrave Macmillan

Bataringaya, J. (1999) 'Integrating HIV/AIDS into Development: Lessons from ActionAid', unpublished presentation to SAfAIDS

Bataringaya, J. (2000a) 'Integrating HIV/AIDS into the work of development organisations: the experience of ActionAid', *Sexual Health Exchange*, October 2000

Bataringaya, J. (2000b) 'Looking Deeper at Integration of HIV/AIDS in Development Organisations and Programmes', internal ActionAid document

Baylies, C. (2002) 'The impact of AIDS on rural households in Africa: a shock like any other?', *Development and Change* 33(4), 611-32

Blinkhoff, P., E. Bukanga, B. Syamalevwe, and G. Williams (1999) *Under the Mupundu Tree: Volunteers in Home Care for People with HIV/AIDS and TB in Zambia's Copperbelt*, Strategies for Hope Series No 14, Oxford: ActionAid

Boseley, S. (2002) 'AIDS cuts life expectancy to 27', *Guardian*, 8 July 2002, London: Guardian Newspapers, www.guardian.co.uk

Cabango (2000) 'Mainstreaming HIV/AIDS', training manual and trainers' notes, internal document

CAFOD (2002) 'Report of the Findings of the Work to Pilot the "Silent Emergency" leaflet', working draft

Campbell, C. (1997) 'Migrancy, masculine identities and AIDS: the psychosocial context of HIV transmission in the South African gold mines', *Social Science and Medicine* 45(2): 273-81

CARE Vietnam (2001) 'Mainstreaming AIDS in Quang Ngai: Final Report', internal document

Christian Aid (2002) 'Listen to Africa – a G8 Summit Briefing', London: Christian Aid

CIA (Central Intelligence Agency) (2000) 'The Global Infectious Disease Threat and Its Implications for the United States', www.cia.gov

Cohen, D. (1999) 'Mainstreaming the Policy and Programming Response to the HIV Epidemic', Issues Paper No 33, New York: UNDP, www.undp.org

Collins, J. and B. Rau (2000) 'AIDS in the Context of Development', UNRISD Programme on Social Policy and Development paper number 4, Geneva: UNRISD and UNAIDS, www.unrisd.org

Crisp, J. (1999) 'A State of Insecurity: the Political Economy of Violence in Refugee-populated Areas of Kenya', UNHCR New Issues in Refugee Research Working Paper No 16, Geneva: UNHCR, www.unhcr.ch

Derbyshire, H. (2002) 'Gender Manual: A Practical Guide For Development Policy Makers and Practitioners', Social Development Division, DFID, www.genie.ids.ac.uk/gem

Development Alternatives Incorporated (2000) 'The MBP Reader on Microfinance and HIV/AIDS: First Steps in Speaking Out', unpublished resource document prepared for the Africa Regional Microcredit Summit, Harare, Zimbabwe, October 2000

Dey, R. and Butcher, K. (2002) 'Mainstreaming HIV as a Development Issue', abstract from the XIV International Conference on AIDS, Barcelona, 7-12 July 2002

Donahue, J. (1998) 'Community-Based Economic Support for Households Affected by HIV/AIDS', Health Technical Services Project Report of TvT Associates, The Pragma Corporation, USAID HIV/AIDS Division

Donahue, J. (2002) 'Children, HIV/AIDS and Poverty In Southern Africa', unpublished paper presented to the Southern Africa Regional Poverty Network, 9–10 April 2002

Donahue, J., K. Kabbucho, and S. Osinde (2001) 'HIV/AIDS – Responding to a Silent Economic Crisis Among MFI Clients in Kenya and Uganda', unpublished action research study for MicroSave-Africa, AFCAP, and SUFFICE/Uganda

Elsey, H. (2002a) 'Opportunities and Challenges for Mainstreaming HIV/AIDS and Gender in SWAPs: Preliminary Findings from Research in Uganda, April–July 2002', unpublished paper, DFID/Liverpool School of Tropical Medicine

Elsey, H. (2002b) 'Sector Wide Approaches: Opportunities and Challenges to Mainstreaming Gender and HIV/AIDS', unpublished paper, DFID/Liverpool School of Tropical Medicine

Elwes, T. (2002) 'Overview of Risk Analysis Model', internal Oxfam GB document

Engh, I., L. Stloukal, and J. du Guerny (2000) 'HIV/AIDS in Namibia: The Impact on the Livestock Sector', Rome: FAO, www.fao.org

FAO (2001) 'The Impact of HIV/AIDS on Food Security', Meeting of Committee on World Food Security, Rome: FAO, www.fao.org

Ghana Ministry of Education (2002) 'Work Place Manual', HIV/AIDS Secretariat, Ministry of Education, Accra

Gillan, A. (2002) 'Sex abuse scandals tarnish work of aid agencies in Africa', *Guardian*, 20 April 2002, London: Guardian Newspapers, www.guardian.co.uk.

Gisselquist, D., R. Rothenberg, J. Potterat, and E. Drucker (2002) 'HIV infections in sub-Saharan Africa not explained by sexual or vertical transmission', *International Journal of STD and AIDS* 13(10) 357-666

Goetz, A. M. (1995) 'The Politics of Integrating Gender to State Development Processes: Trends, Opportunities and Constraints in Bangladesh, Chile, Jamaica, Mali, Morocco and Uganda', Occasional Paper No 2, Geneva: UNRISD, www.unrisd.org

Government of Malawi and The World Bank (1998) 'Malawi AIDS Assessment Study', www.worldbank.org

Grant, A. D. and K. M. de Cock (2001) 'ABC of AIDS: HIV infection and AIDS in the developing world', *British Medical Journal* 322:1475-78, www.bmj.com

Gundel, J. (1999) 'Humanitarian Assistance: Breaking the Waves of Complex Political Emergences', Centre for Development Research Working Paper 99.5, August 1999, www.cdr.dk

Hemrich, G. and D. Topouzis (2000) 'Multi-sectoral responses to HIV/AIDS: constraints and opportunities for technical co-operation', *Journal of International Development* 12:85-99

Holden, S. (1994) 'Looking at AIDS as a Development Issue: an Exploration with ActionAid-Uganda', internal ActionAid document

Holden, S. (1995) 'Beyond Control: An Alternative Perspective of AIDS of Sub-Saharan Africa', MA thesis, Flinders University of South Australia

Huber, U. and B. Gould (2002) 'Primary School Attendance in Tanzania – How Far is it Affected by Orphanhood?', unpublished paper, University of Liverpool

Human Rights Watch (2000) *Seeking Protection: Addressing Sexual and Domestic Violence in Tanzania's Refugee Camps*, New York: HRW, www.hrw.org

Inter-Agency Standing Committee (2002) 'Plan of Action', unpublished paper from the Task Force on Protection from Sexual Exploitation and Abuse in Humanitarian Crises, www.humanitarianinfo.org/iasc

International Save the Children Alliance (2002) 'HIV and Conflict: A Double Emergency', London: Save the Children UK

IRIN News (2003) 'Uganda: Leading User of Antiretrovirals', 13 February 2003, www.irinnews.org

Jackson, H., R. Kerkhoven, D. Lindsey, G. Mutangadura, and F. Nhara (1999) *HIV/AIDS in Southern Africa: The Threat to Development*, London: CIIR

Jacobson, J. (1992) 'Women's health: the price of poverty', in M. Koblinsky, J. Timyan, and J. Gay (eds.), *The Health of Women: A Global Perspective*, Boulder: Westview Press

James, R. and D. Mullins (2002) 'Supporting Partners Who Are HIV+: Giving Aspirins or Antiretroviral Drugs?', unpublished paper

Jordan-Harder, B., Y. A. Koshuma, C. Pervilhac, and U. Vogel (2000) 'Hope for Tanzania: Lessons Learned from a Decade of Comprehensive AIDS Control in Mbeya Region', GTZ, www.gtz.de/aids/english or (in summary) from www.unaids.org

JTK Associates (1999) 'Study for the Government of Swaziland About the Impacts of AIDS on the Education Sector', unpublished report

Kaleeba, N., J. N. Kadowe, D. Kalinaki, and G. Williams (2000) *Open Secret: People Facing up to HIV and AIDS in Uganda*, Strategies for Hope Series No 15, Oxford: ActionAid

Kelly, M. J. (1999) 'The Impact of HIV/AIDS on Schooling in Zambia', paper presented at the XIth International Conference on AIDS and STDs in Africa, Lusaka, 1999

Kinnah, G. (1997) 'An account of a personal experience', in 'Refugees, Displaced People and their Vulnerability to HIV/AIDS: Report on the Seminar on NGO Action, 28-29 October 1996', London: UK NGO AIDS Consortium

Klouda, T. (1995) 'Responding to AIDS: are there any appropriate development and health policies?', *Journal of International Development* 7:467-87

Lifeworks (2002) www.lifeworks.co.za

Loewenson, R. and A. Whiteside (2001) 'HIV/AIDS Implications for Poverty Reduction', New York: UNDP, www.undp.org

LoveLife (2000) 'The Impending Catastrophe – A Resource Book on the Emerging HIV/AIDS Epidemic in South Africa', South Africa: LoveLife, www.kff.org

MAAIF and FAO (2002) 'The Impact of HIV/AIDS on Agricultural Production and Mainstreaming HIV/AIDS Messages into Agricultural Extension in Uganda', Ministry of Agriculture, Animal Industry and Fisheries and FAO, www.fao.org

Manning, R. (2001) 'AIDS and Democracy, What Do We Know? A Literature Review', unpublished paper, University of Natal, Durban, www.und.ac.za/und/heard

Manning, R. (2002) 'The Impact of HIV/AIDS on Civil Society: Assessing and Mitigating Impacts: Tools and Models for NGOs and CBOs', University of Natal, Durban, www.und.ac.za/und/heard

Marshall, R. (1995) 'Refugees, feminine plural', *Refugees* 2, www.unhcr.ch

McNairn, R. (2002) 'Gender in Humanitarian Response: Department and Programme', internal Oxfam GB document

Miller, C. and S. Razavi (1995) 'Gender Mainstreaming: A Study of Efforts by the UNDP, the World Bank and the ILO to Institutionalise Gender Issues', Geneva: UNRISD, www.unrisd.org

Mohideen, R. (2002) 'Gender Review Synthesis', May to June 2002, internal Oxfam GB document

Monitoring the AIDS Pandemic (2000) 'The Status and Trends of the HIV/AIDS Epidemic in the World', report from the MAP network symposium, 5-7 July, Durban, www.unaids.org

Monitoring the AIDS Pandemic (2001) 'The Status and Trends of HIV/AIDS/STI Epidemics in Asia and the Pacific', provisional report, Melbourne, Australia, 4 October 2001, www.unaids.org

Mullins, D. (2000) 'Briefing Paper on Impacts of HIV/AIDS', internal Oxfam GB document

Mullins, D. (2001) 'Proposal: Regional HIV/AIDS Mainstreaming Programming, September 2001 – April 2003', Oxfam GB in Southern Africa, internal Oxfam GB document

Munyombwe, T., D. M. Pfukenyi, and U. Ushewokunze-Obatolu (1999) 'HIV/AIDS in livestock production in the smallholder sector of Zimbabwe', pp 25-35 in Mutangadura *et al.* (eds.) (1999a)

Mutangadura, G., H. Jackson, and D. Mukurazita (eds.) (1999a) *AIDS and African Smallholder Agriculture*, Harare: SAfAIDS

Mutangadura, G., M. Mukurazita, and H. Jackson (1999b) 'A Review of Household and Community Responses to the HIV/AIDS Epidemic in the Rural Areas of Sub-Saharan Africa', UNAIDS Best Practice Collection Key Material, UNAIDS/99.39E, www.unaids.org

Ncube, N. M. (1999) 'The impact of HIV/AIDS on smallholder agricultural production in Gweru, Zimbabwe, and coping strategies', pp 14-24 in Mutangadura *et al.* (eds.) (1999a)

NEPAD (2001) 'The New Partnership for Africa's Development', NEPAD Document, signed in Abuja, Nigeria, October 2001

NIAID (2000) 'HIV Infection and AIDS, An Overview', National Institute for Allergy and Infectious Disease, www.aegis.com

Oxfam GB (2001a) 'Flyer 4: Workplace Policy on HIV/AIDS', Lessons learned in mainstreaming AIDS, Oxfam GB, www.oxfam.org.uk

Oxfam GB (2001b) 'Flyer 6: Findings of Local Research on HIV/AIDS', Lessons learned in mainstreaming AIDS, Oxfam GB, www.oxfam.org.uk

Oxfam GB (2001c) 'Flyer 5: Researching HIV/AIDS at the Local Level', Lessons learned in mainstreaming AIDS, Oxfam GB, www.oxfam.org.uk

Oxfam GB (2001d) 'Mid-Term Report: Learning Project on Mainstreaming HIV/AIDS as a Development Issue', internal document

Oxfam GB in Malawi (2002) 'Joint Oxfam Programme in Malawi Annual Report May 2001–April 2002', internal document

Page, S. L. J. (2002) 'The Impact of the HIV/AIDS Epidemic on the Ability of Malawian Communities to Manage their Natural Resources', COMPASS and Development Alternatives International, COMPASS Draft Document 55, December 2002

Palmer, C. (1998), *'Reproductive Health for Displaced Populations*, ODI Relief and Rehabilitation Network Paper No 24, London: Overseas Development Institute

Panos (1998), 'AIDS and Men: Old Problem, New Angle', Media AIDS Information Sheet, London: Panos

Piot, P. (2001) 'Facing the Challenge of AIDS', Address by UNAIDS Executive Director to a UN Symposium on Nutrition and HIV/AIDS, Nairobi, 3 April 2001, www.unaids.org

Project Empower (2002a) 'Rights Based Approaches to HIV/AIDS Mainstreaming: Implications for Future Planning', draft 1, June 2002

Project Empower (2002b) 'Constructing A Rights Based HIV/AIDS Mainstreaming Approach: Lessons from South Africa', draft 1, March 2002

Rau, B. (2002) *Workplace HIV/AIDS Programs: An Action Guide for Managers*, USA: Family Health International, www.fhi.org

Richards, P. (1999) 'HIV/AIDS and African agriculture: does technology have to change?', pp 102-12 in Mutangadura *et al.* (eds.) (1999a)

Rugalema, G. (1999) 'It is not only the loss of labour: HIV/AIDS, loss of household assets and household livelihood in Bukoba District, Tanzania', pp 41-52 in Mutangadura *et al.* (eds.) (1999a)

Save the Children UK (2001) 'Review of Terms and Conditions Regarding Chronic Illness', internal document, November 2001

Shah, M.K., N.Osborne, T. Mbilizi, and G. Vilili (2002) 'The Impact Of HIV/AIDS On Agricultural Production Systems And Rural Livelihoods In The Central Region Of Malawi', unpublished paper, CARE International in Malawi

Shaw, M. and M. Jawo (2000) 'Gambian experiences with Stepping Stones: 1996-99', *PLA Notes* 37: 73-8

Simon-Meyer, J. and D. Odallo (2002) *The Faces, Voices and Skills behind the GIPA Workplace Model in South Africa*, UNAIDS/02.36E, Geneva: UNAIDS, www.unaids.org

Smith, A. (2002) *HIV/AIDS and Emergencies: Analysis and Recommendations for Practice*, ODI Relief and Rehabilitation Network Paper No 38, London: ODI

Smith, A. and J. Howson (2000) 'Safely through the night: a review of behaviour change in the context of HIV/AIDS', *PLA Notes* 37:92-9

Sphere Project (2000) *Humanitarian Charter and Minimum Standards in Disaster Response*, Oxford: Oxfam Publishing, www.sphereproject.org

Stein, J. (2001) 'HIV/AIDS and the South African Media: Workplace policies and programmes', The Centre for AIDS Development, Research and Evaluation (Cadre), www.cadre.org.za

Stillwaggon, E. (2000) 'HIV transmission in Latin America: comparison with Africa and policy implications', *The South African Journal of Economics* 68(5) 985-1011

Stillwaggon, E. (2002) 'HIV/AIDS in Africa: fertile ground', *The Journal of Development Studies* 38(6) 1-22

Theobald, S., H. Elsey, and R. Tolhurst (2002) 'Gender mainstreaming and sector wide approaches in health: key areas for debate', *Journal of Health Management* 4(2) 119-33

Thompson, B. and A. Whiteside (1999) 'Transport and HIV/AIDS: movement, risk and response', *HIV/AIDS Action in Developing Countries* 5:8

Topouzis, D. (1998) 'The Implications of HIV/AIDS for Rural Development Policy and Programming: Focus on Sub-Saharan Africa', Rome: FAO and UNDP, www.fao.org

Topouzis, D. (2001) 'Addressing the Impact of HIV/AIDS on Ministries of Agriculture: Focus on Eastern and Southern Africa', Best Practice Digest, Geneva: FAO and UNAIDS, www.unaids.org

Topouzis, D. and J. du Guerny (1999) 'Sustainable Agricultural/Rural Development and Vulnerability to the AIDS Epidemic', Geneva: FAO and UNAIDS

UK NGO AIDS Consortium (1996), 'Effective HIV/AIDS Activities: NGO Work in Developing Countries – Report of the Collaborative Study', London: UK NGO AIDS Consortium

UK NGO AIDS Consortium (1997), 'Refugees, Displaced People and Their Vulnerability to HIV/AIDS', Report on the Seminar on NGO Action, London: UK NGO AIDS Consortium

UN (2001) 'United Nations General Assembly Special Session on HIV/AIDS Fact Sheet', New York: UN, www.un.org/ga/aids

UNAIDS (1997) 'Blood Safety and AIDS', UNAIDS Point of View, Best Practice Collection, Geneva: UNAIDS, www.unaids.org

UNAIDS (1999) 'Questions and Answers: Mother-to-Child Transmission of HIV', Background Briefing, Geneva: UNAIDS, www.unaids.org

UNAIDS (2000a) AIDS *Epidemic Update, December 2000*, Geneva: UNAIDS, www.unaids.org

UNAIDS (2000b) 'Mother-to-child Transmission of HIV', Technical Update, September 2000, Geneva: UNAIDS, www.unaids.org

UNAIDS (2000c) *HIV/AIDS and Educational Planning in Africa*, Best Practice Digest, www.unaids.org

UNAIDS (2001) *AIDS Epidemic Update*, December 2001, Geneva: UNAIDS, www.unaids.org

UNAIDS (2002a) 'Epidemiological Fact Sheets on HIV/AIDS and Sexually Transmitted Infections: Sierra Leone 2002 Update', Geneva: UNAIDS, www.unaids.org

UNAIDS (2002b) 'AIDS Epidemic Update', December 2002, Geneva: UNAIDS, www.unaids.org

UNAIDS (2002c) 'AIDS as a Security Issue', Fact Sheet, Geneva: UNAIDS, www.unaids.org

UNAIDS (2002d) 'Report on the Global HIV/AIDS Epidemic', XIV International Conference on AIDS, Barcelona, 7-12 July 2002, Geneva: UNAIDS, www.unaids.org

UNAIDS/GTZ (2002) 'Mainstreaming HIV/AIDS: A Conceptual Framework and Implementing Principles', unpublished draft, Ghana: GTZ

UNDP (2000) 'Botswana Human Development Report 2000', Gabarone: UNDP, www.undp.org

UNHCR (2001) 'A Practical Guide to Empowerment', UNHCR Good Practices On Gender Equality Mainstreaming, Geneva: UNHCR, www.unhcr.ch

VSO (2002) 'Building on Strengths, RAISA Annual Review 2001–2002', South Africa: VSO, www.vso.org.uk

Wallace, T. (1996) 'Report on a Gender Training Workshop', internal ActionAid document

Webb, D. (1997) 'Adolescence, Sex and Fear: Reproductive Health Services and Young People in Urban Zambia', Central Board of Health/UNICEF, Lusaka

Webb, D. (2001) '"Best practice" in HIV/AIDS programme development', *SAfAIDS News* 9(2) 2-6

Welbourn, A. (1995) *Stepping Stones: A Training Package on HIV/AIDS, Gender Issues, Communication and Relationship Skills*, London: ActionAid

White, J. (2002) 'Facing the Challenge: Experiences of Mitigating the Impacts of HIV/AIDS in Sub-Saharan Africa', NRI, www.nri.org

WHO (2000) 'Reproductive Health During Conflict and Displacement: A Guide for Programme Managers', Geneva: WHO, www.who.ch

WHO (2002) 'The World Health Report 2002', WHO, www.who.ch

Wilkins, M. **and** D. **Vasani** (2002) 'Mainstreaming HIV/AIDS: Looking Beyond Awareness', VSO Experience in Focus, South Africa: VSO, www.vso.org.uk

World Bank (1999) *Intensifying Action Against HIV/AIDS in Africa: Responding to a Development Crisis*, Washington: The World Bank

World Bank (2002) 'HIV/AIDS Blunts Progress In Getting All Children Into School By 2015', news release no 2002/298/HD, 7 May 2002, www.worldbank.org

Resources

This section provides details of some key resources, with advice on how to obtain them. Note that all UNAIDS documents are available to download from www.unaids.org. Alternatively, hard copies of most of their documents may be obtained free of charge from local UNAIDS offices, or by written application to the Information Manager, UNAIDS, 20 Avenue Appia, CH-1211 Geneva 27, Switzerland, or by telephoning UNAIDS on +41 22 791 4651.

Mainstreaming AIDS

Internal mainstreaming

Workplace HIV/AIDS Programs: An Action Guide for Managers by Bill Rau (2002) outlines practical steps in developing a workplace programme of prevention and care, as part of an internal mainstreaming initiative. Can be downloaded from www.fhi.org, or ordered from the Publications Co-ordinator, Family Health International, PO Box 13950, Research Triangle Park, NC 27709 USA. Fax: (919) 544-7261. Free copies are available to organisations in the South: send a letter on headed paper, explaining the work that you do and the way in which you intend to use the publication.

The publication also gives information about four basic impact-assessment tools, which can be accessed via the Internet (Rau 2002:29). In June 2002, these two were accessible:

- A comprehensive impact-assessment tool, devised by Family Health International. It is most appropriate for larger businesses which seek in-depth analysis of the impact of HIV/AIDS on company costs and operations. Contact FHI at www.fhi.org

- A simplified on-line version of a model called AIM-B, produced by The Futures Group and the Global Business Council on HIV/AIDS, available at www.fgeurope.com. It estimates the main direct costs of HIV/AIDS in terms of health care, recruitment, and benefits. It does not estimate the epidemic's impact on productivity, labour relations, workforce morale, or absenteeism. The Futures Group can, however, give advice on how to conduct a more thorough analysis.

The International Labour Organisation's *Code of Practice on HIV/AIDS and the World of Work* (2001) can be downloaded from www.ilo.org – just click on the HIV/AIDS link. The site also has fact sheets and statistics relating to AIDS and work.

'Guidelines for Studies of the Social and Economic Impact of AIDS' (2000), written by Tony Barnett and Alan Whiteside, provide an overview of the issues, and practical guidance. Part of the UNAIDS Best Practice Collection, ref UNAIDS/00.32 E.

UNAIDS' 'HIV/AIDS and The Workplace' (1998) and 'Voluntary Counselling and Testing' (2000, ref WC 503.6) are technical texts with relevance to internal mainstreaming. 'The Male Latex Condom' (2001) consists of guidelines and fact sheets concerning the procuring and distribution of male condoms; several documents concerning the female condom are also available from UNAIDS.

Internal and external mainstreaming

Oxfam GB is developing part of its website for information exchange on the subject of mainstreaming AIDS: go to www.oxfam.org.uk/hivaids for key documents and updates, which, it is planned, will eventually include a toolkit for mainstreaming. If you do not have access to the Internet, write to Oxfam GB at Postnet Suite 183, Private Bag X15, Menlo Park 0102, Pretoria, Republic of South Africa.

Helen Elsey *et al.* at the Liverpool School of Tropical Medicine have produced a resource pack, entitled *HIV/AIDS Mainstreaming: A Definition, Some Experiences and Strategies* (2003), with support from DFID's HIV/AIDS Knowledge Programme and HEARD. It can be downloaded from www.und.ac.za/und/heard, and some hard copies may become available through DFID field offices.

Humanitarian work and AIDS-related issues

CAFOD's simple A3-size leaflet, *The Silent Emergency: HIV/AIDS in Conflicts and Disasters*, illustrates the AIDS-related consequences of emergencies, and features key recommendations for the modification of the work of humanitarian agencies. It is available to practitioners free of charge in small quantities from CAFOD, Romero Close, Stockwell Road, London, SW9 9TY, or by e-mail at hiv@cafod.org.uk; it can also be ordered on line at www.cafod.org.uk/hivaids/silentemergform.shtml

UNHCR has numerous guidelines and practical documents relating to the protection of women, and preventing and responding to sexual and gender-based violence. It can also supply training resource packs entitled 'Action for the Rights of Children' (produced by UNHCR and Save the Children), which are intended to improve the care and protection of boy and girl children in emergency situations. All these documents can be downloaded from www.unhcr.ch, or supplied as hard copies by UNHCR offices.

You can download or order the publication *The Sphere Project: Humanitarian Charter and Minimum Standards in Disaster Response* (2000) from www.sphereproject.org. This sets out common standards for humanitarian agencies and includes practical guidance on subjects such as needs assessment.

WHO's 'Reproductive Health During Conflict & Displacement: A Guide for Programme Managers' (2000) gives a thorough overview of the phases of humanitarian response with regard to reproductive health, including HIV and sexual violence, at www.who.ch.

A range of materials about reproductive health (RH) and refugees is available from the Reproductive Health for Refugees Consortium at www.rhrc.org. They include a five-day training manual about RH programming for refugees, an awareness-raising training module about RH issues for refugees, needs-assessment field tools, and an interagency field manual on RH in refugee settings.

UNAIDS' 'Refugees and AIDS' Technical Update (1997, ref WC 503.71) covers the basic responses to prevent HIV transmission in health settings, followed by guidance on more comprehensive AIDS-prevention and care work, to be undertaken when the situation stabilises.

Information about AIDS

www.census.gov/ipc/www has country profiles which include surveillance data from HIV sentinel testing in many countries. The site also has an HIV/AIDS surveillance data base.

UNAIDS provides an epidemiological fact sheet for each country in the world, along with its annual *AIDS Epidemic Update,* which summarises the global situation, and a wide range of other materials.

The AIDS Education Global Information System, at www.aegis.org, includes basic fact sheets, as well as more detailed information for people who are HIV-positive, access to news and publications about AIDS, and a glossary of AIDS terms.

There are also many websites providing information about AIDS and treatment, such as www.avert.org and www.thebody.com, which has an 'ask the expert' facility. The central website for GNP+, the Global Network of People Living with HIV/AIDS, is at www.gnp-plus.net. You can also find a range of electronic discussion groups, including groups concerned with antiretroviral treatment and nutrition and HIV/AIDS, at www.satellife.org

AIDS and development

The World Bank's website www.worldbank.org/aids-econ provides a great deal of information about responding to AIDS, and the impacts of AIDS, from an economic perspective.

HEARD at the University of Natal has produced a range of materials concerning responses to AIDS, which include elements of both AIDS work and mainstreaming AIDS. They have 36 'AIDS Briefs', serving a range of sectors and professions, 11 'Toolkits' written for government ministries and departments, and another toolkit for local government. They can all be downloaded from www.und.ac.za/und/heard. Alternatively, e-mail freeman@nu.ac.za, or write to HEARD, University of Natal, Durban, 4041, South Africa to obtain hard copies.

Gender mainstreaming

There is a database of good practice in gender mainstreaming among UN agencies at www.un.org/womenwatch/resources/goodpractices

'The Gender Information Exchange' (or 'Genie') site allows users to search donor agencies' gender resources, including policy documents, sectoral reports, guidelines, good-practice cases, bibliographies, background papers, research reports, and tools. The site also provides a searchable database of gender-related country profiles, and a database of consultants specialising in gender issues: www.genie.ids.ac.uk

The GEM part of the Genie site at www.genie.ids.ac.uk/gem concerns initiatives to implement the UK government's gender policy in development work. It contains key texts, case studies, checklists, tools and methods, facts and figures. It also has a range of thematic bibliographies on subjects such as gender mainstreaming, training, violence against women, and conflicts and emergencies.

www.siyanda.org provides a searchable database of materials to support practitioners' efforts to mainstream gender, along with forums where they can discuss their ideas, experiences, and resources.

Gender, AIDS, and sexual and reproductive Health

Unifem and UNAIDS have a site devoted to gender and AIDS at www.genderandaids.org

ActionAid, ACORD, and Save the Children UK have updated their publication *Gender and HIV/AIDS: Guidelines For Integrating a Gender Focus into NGO Work on HIV/AIDS* (2002). It may be ordered from www.savethechildren.org.uk

ActionAid's *Stepping Stones* training package by Alice Welbourn (1995) concerns gender, HIV, communication, and relationship skills. It is designed for use with whole communities to challenge gender-related and intergenerational inequalities. For more information about translations, how it has been used, and with what results, visit www.steppingstones feedback.org and www.actionaid.org. The training package is available from TALC, PO Box 49, St Albans, Herts, AL1 5TX, UK, or via www.talcuk.org/stratshope

Gender or Sex: Who Cares? Skills-building Resource Pack on Gender and Reproductive Health for Adolescents and Youth Workers is a training pack by Maria de Bruyn and Nadine France (2001). It offers a series of participatory workshop activities, and concentrates particularly on violence, STIs and HIV, unwanted pregnancy, and unsafe abortion. Download or order from www.ipas.org; available in English and Spanish.

Gender, HIV and Human Rights: A Training Manual, by Madhu B. Nath (2000), includes training modules intended to raise awareness of the gender-related dimensions of HIV/AIDS. Available from www.unifem.org in English, French, and Spanish.

Index

Figures and tables appear in *italic* type.

For acronyms and abbreviations, consult page xiv.

AIDS on the Agenda: readers' feedback

Please fill in and return this form, to help the publishers of this book to assess how it has been received by readers. If you have shared your copy of the book with other people, perhaps you could also share a copy of this questionnaire with them. All the feedback that we receive will be valuable in developing future initiatives, such as training materials about mainstreaming AIDS.

You may wish to photocopy this questionnaire and post it, when completed, to **Dr Mohga Kamal Smith, Oxfam, 274 Banbury Road, Oxford, OX2 7DZ, UK**. Alternatively, you can obtain an electronic copy by e-mail from aidsfeedback@oxfam.org.uk or download one at
www.oxfam.org.uk/what_we_do/issues/hivaids/index.htm

a. **How much of this book have you read? Please circle one answer.**

1	2	3	4	5
A few bits	Quite a bit	Most of it	Nearly all of it	All of it

b. **If you or your organisation have already used the Resource Units or other elements of the book, please explain how, and with what outcomes.**

c. **This book has tried to make a distinction between the strategy of mainstreaming AIDS and the strategy of doing direct AIDS work. How clear is the difference between the two strategies to you?**

1	2	3	4	5
Not clear at all	Not very clear	Not sure	Fairly clear	Very clear

d. **In your opinion, how useful is the distinction between the strategies of mainstreaming AIDS and of doing AIDS work?**

1	2	3	4	5
Not at all useful	Not very useful	Not sure	Fairly useful	Very useful

e. This book argues that external mainstreaming of AIDS is a basic initial strategy which all development and humanitarian agencies in affected countries should adopt. What do you think?

I	2	3	4	5
Disagree totally	Mainly disagree	Not sure	Mainly agree	Agree totally

f. This book also argues that if development and humanitarian agencies do not have the capacity to undertake both mainstreaming and AIDS work, their most appropriate contribution to the wider response to HIV/AIDS is to mainstream. What do you think?

I	2	3	4	5
Disagree totally	Mainly disagree	Not sure	Mainly agree	Agree totally

g. In your opinion, what were the best things about this book?

h. And the worst things about this book?

i. Is there anything else that you would like to say concerning the above questions or any other aspects of the book?

j. Your job title or professional affiliation:

k. Your sex:　　　　□ Male　　　　　　□ Female

l. Your type of organisation (please tick one box only)

　　□ Government organisation　　□ Religious organisation

　　□ Profit-making organisation　　□ None (independent consultant)

　　□ Non-government organisation　　□ Other (please state)

　　□ Community-based organisation

m. Are you or your organisation already involved in:

　　AIDS work?　　　　Internal mainstreaming?　　　External mainstreaming?

　　□ Yes　□ No　　　　□ Yes　□ No　　　　□ Yes　□ No